MW00806913

Sustainable School Architecture

DESIGN FOR PRIMARY AND SECONDARY SCHOOLS

by
Lisa Gelfand, AIA, LEED-AP
with Eric Corey Freed, LEED-AP

WILEY

John Wiley & Sons, Inc.

100%
TOTAL RECYCLED PAPER
100% POSTCONSUMER PAPER

This book is printed on acid-free paper. ∞

Copyright © 2010 by John Wiley & Sons, Inc.. All rights reserved

Published by John Wiley & Sons, Inc., Hoboken, New Jersey

Published simultaneously in Canada

No part of this publication may be reproduced, stored in a retrieval system, or transmitted in any form or by any means, electronic, mechanical, photocopying, recording, scanning, or otherwise, except as permitted under Section 107 or 108 of the 1976 United States Copyright Act, without either the prior written permission of the Publisher, or authorization through payment of the appropriate per-copy fee to the Copyright Clearance Center, 222 Rosewood Drive, Danvers, MA 01923, (978) 750-8400, fax (978) 646-8600, or on the web at www.copyright.com. Requests to the Publisher for permission should be addressed to the Permissions Department, John Wiley & Sons, Inc., 111 River Street, Hoboken, NJ 07030, (201) 748-6011, fax (201) 748-6008, or online at www.wiley.com/go/permissions.

Limit of Liability/Disclaimer of Warranty: While the publisher and the author have used their best efforts in preparing this book, they make no representations or warranties with respect to the accuracy or completeness of the contents of this book and specifically disclaim any implied warranties of merchantability or fitness for a particular purpose. No warranty may be created or extended by sales representatives or written sales materials. The advice and strategies contained herein may not be suitable for your situation. You should consult with a professional where appropriate. Neither the publisher nor the author shall be liable for any loss of profit or any other commercial damages, including but not limited to special, incidental, consequential, or other damages.

For general information about our other products and services, please contact our Customer Care Department within the United States at (800) 762-2974, outside the United States at (317) 572-3993 or fax (317) 572-4002.

Wiley also publishes its books in a variety of electronic formats. Some content that appears in print may not be available in electronic books. For more information about Wiley products, visit our web site at www.wiley.com.

Library of Congress Cataloging-in-Publication Data:

Gelfand, Lisa.
  Sustainable school architecture : design for primary and secondary schools / by Lisa Gelfand.
    p. cm.
  ISBN 978-0-470-44543-3 (cloth)
  1. School buildings–Design and construction. 2. Sustainable architecture. I. Title.
  LB3205.G45 2010
  371.6'2–dc22

                                                                    2009033998

Printed in the United States of America

10 9 8 7 6 5 4 3 2 1

To Arthur S. Harris
For insight and inspiration

CONTENTS

DEDICATION   iii

PREFACE   ix

ACKNOWLEDGMENTS   xi

CHAPTER 1
AN INTRODUCTION TO
SUSTAINABLE SCHOOLS _____ 1

Introduction   1

Need for Sustainable Buildings   2

Benefits of Sustainable Schools   3

  Higher Student Test Scores   3

  Lower Operating Costs   3

  Increased Student Attendance   4

  Enhanced Teacher Performance and
  Satisfaction   5

  Increased Building Life   6

  Lower Environmental Impact   6

  Changing Attitudes   6

Elements of Sustainable Schools   7

  Community-Based Planning   7

  LEED and CHPS   8

  Integrated Design   9

  School as Campus   10

  Environmental Curriculum   10

  Flexibility for Multiple Uses   11

  Water Efficiency   11

  Energy Efficiency   12

  Resource Efficiency   12

  High-Performance Learning Spaces   14

  Daylighting   14

  Improved Air Quality   16

  Thermal Comfort   16

  Improved Acoustics   16

  Commissioning   17

Putting It All Together   18

CHAPTER 2
PLANNING STRATEGIES _____ 19

Introduction   19

Selecting the Team   20

  Goal Setting   20

  Architectural Contract Considerations   24

  Roles of School Boards, Districts, and Individual
  Schools   26

  Working Group   27

Integrated Design   28

  Site Selection   28

  Social Forces   31

  School as Campus   33

  Climate Considerations   36

  Solar Orientation   36

  Small Schools   37

Funding the Sustainable School   39

  Capital Funding   39

  Life Cycle Costing   41

  Supplementary Funding for Sustainability   42

Case Studies   45

  Seabird Island School   45

  Druk White Lotus School   48

CHAPTER **3**

DESIGN STRATEGIES _____ 53

Introduction   53

Integrated Design   53

Formal Considerations   54

   Precedent   55

   Context and Function   56

   Building Type   58

   Visual Expression   58

Spatial Considerations   60

Unique K–12 Considerations   61

   Budget   61

   Robustness   61

   Hygiene   61

   Acoustics—Guest Essay, Ethan Salter   62

   Developmental Considerations   71

Conclusion   74

Case Studies   74

   Sidwell Friends School   74

   Chartwell School   77

   Woodward Academy Middle School   80

CHAPTER **4**

DAYLIGHTING _____ 83

Introduction   83

Benefits of Daylighting   83

Early Precedents   86

Site Design and Daylighting   87

Daylighting Light Requirements   91

Building Design for Daylighting   93

Specifics of Opening Design   96

Artificial Lighting   102

Case Studies   105

   Blach Intermediate School   105

   Bronx Charter School for the Arts   108

CHAPTER **5**

BUILDING STRUCTURE AND
ENVELOPE _____ 111

   by Eric Corey Freed, LEED-AP

Introduction   111

Initial Considerations in Wall Design   112

Alternative Wall Construction
Methods   114

   Design Strategies   116

   Sheathing   116

   Wall Finishes   117

Insulation   117

   Batt Insulation   118

   Loose-Fill Insulation   118

   Spray Foam Insulation   118

   Rigid Foam Insulation   119

Weatherizing   119

Water and Moisture Control   120

Openings   120

   Windows   120

   Shading Devices   122

   Doors   124

Acoustics   124

Roof Design   124

   Green Roof   **126**

Case Studies   129

   Whitman Hanson Regional High School   129

   Tarkington Elementary School   132

CHAPTER **6**

HEATING, VENTILATING, COOLING,
AND PLUMBING _____ 137

   by Ron Blue, PE, LEED-AP

Introduction   137

Comfort   137

System Types   138
    Central versus Individual System   139
    Radiant Systems   140
    Forced Air Systems   141

Design for Natural Ventilation   143

High-Performance Strategies   145
    High-Efficiency Equipment   145
    Chilled Beam Cooling   146
    Geoexchange Heat Pumps   146
    Solar Thermal Energy   149
    Cogeneration   150
    Controls   150

Water   151
    Use of Nonpotable Water   151
    Water-Saving Fixtures   152

Closing   153

Case Studies   155
    Centennial PK–12   155
    Loyola Elementary School   159

CHAPTER **7**
LANDSCAPING AND SITE DESIGN____163
The Third Teacher—Guest Essay, Susan Herrington   163

Introduction   166

Stormwater/Groundwater Management   168

Heat Islands   170

Paving   171

Fields   172

Water-Efficient Irrigation Systems   175

Miscellaneous Site Uses   178

Planting the Play Environment   180

Integrating Sustainable Practices   185

Case Studies   186
    Strawberry Vale School   186

    Pine Jog Elementary School and Florida Atlantic University Pine Jog Environmental Education Center   189
    Chum Creek Outdoor Education Centre   192

CHAPTER **8**
FINISHES, EQUIPMENT, AND FURNISHINGS____197

Introduction   197

Product Information   198

Flooring   200
    Carpet   200
    Resilient Flooring   201

Wall Finishes   202

Ceilings   204

Paints and Coatings   207

Casework and Furnishings   207

Computers and Office Equipment   208

Specialties   208
    Lockers   208
    Toilet Partitions   209

Case Studies   210
    Hazelwood School   210
    New Jersey City University Academy Charter High School   213

CHAPTER **9**
COST AND BIDDING PROCESS____217

Introduction   217

High Cost   219
    Higher Building Standards   219
    Durability   220
    Public Contracting   221

Alternative Project Delivery Methods   224
    Partnering in Public Contracting   224
    Innovative Project Delivery Methods   226

Contracts 227
Construction Contract Considerations 227
Bidding 227
Flexibility 228
Where to Draw the Line 229

CHAPTER **10**
CONSTRUCTION 231
Introduction 231
Sustainable Job-Site Operations 232
Construction and Demolition Waste Management 236
Indoor Air Quality Protection during Construction 237
Verification 238
Commissioning 239
Postoccupancy 240
Prefabrication 240
Deconstruction versus Demolition 242

CHAPTER **11**
OPERATIONS 245
Sustainable Schools—Guest Essay, Virginia Waik and Rosanna Lerma 245
School Culture 246
School Facilities as Vehicles for Learning 248
Foundations of Democracy 248
Tuning Sustainability for Teaching 248
Sustainability and Curriculum 253
Operations 254
Material Durability and Maintenance 254
Equipment Durability and Maintenance 256
Postoccupancy Evaluations 257
Staff Training 257

Monitoring 259
Supplies 260
Transportation 263
Food Service 263
Community Connections 264

CHAPTER **12**
MAINTENANCE 267
Preventive Maintenance 268
Mold and Microbial Control Techniques 269
Pest Control 271
Maintenance Techniques 273
Cleaning Products 275
Snow Removal 275
The Last Word 276
Case Studies 277
A.P. Tureaud Elementary School 277
Andrew H. Wilson Elementary School 279

CHAPTER **13**
A LOOK INTO A FUTURE FOR EDUCATION 281
Introduction 281
Information Technology 281
Adaptation 283
Trailblazing Projects 285
School and Community Interface 285
New Models of Sustainability 288

APPENDIX 289
LEED Scorecard 289
CHPS Scorecard 290
Section 01350 293

INDEX 314

PREFACE

[Jaime Lerner, former mayor of the renowned Brazilian city of Curitiba, has said that there are] a lot of people who are specialists in proving change is not possible. What I try to explain to them when I go to visit is that it takes the same energy to say why something can't be done as to figure out how to do it.

—Bill McKibben, *Hope, Human and Wild: True Stories of Living Lightly on the Earth*

THE GOAL OF THIS BOOK is to help you figure out how to plan, design, build, and run a sustainable school. It can be done. It has been done in some very unlikely places. It needs to be done in many more places.

Another goal of the book is to show you why. With the massive demands our current way of life is making on the resources and fellow creatures of the planet, we need to rethink the way we are doing things and educate our children to rethink our activities some more. Schools are a major activity on their own. Reductions in their energy use and environmental impact would be a good thing to achieve even if they did nothing else. But schools are also where our children first see their society at work, where they watch us act as much as they hear us speak. The example we provide through the design of our schools will grow exponentially.

The book is organized to track sustainable school architecture through all its phases. First we look at the urgency of the need and the benefits that accrue to the sustainable school. Next we look at steps in bringing the community and its team of designers and educators and contractors together to embark on creating the school. The design chapters of the book examine the ideas that give form to schools, the systems that make them run, and the materials that make them real.

The bidding and construction chapters examine how to put the construction team together and then how to manage the significant energy used and site impacts accrued during construction. A large part of sustainable school architecture is sustainable school construction.

This is the point where many architects stop. But sustainability is not about a snapshot or a ribbon cutting at the start of the life of a school. It is about creating a facility that will continue serving kids and communities over many years of change. We look at the roles of maintenance and operations staff in creating the culture of the school and in creating a way of life in the school that is sustainable. We look at how their activities should inform design. And then we look at how schools might be made and run differently in the future.

We hope that the readers of the book include not only other designers but also the educators, maintenance people, businesspeople, contractors, parents, and neighbors who have formed such a vital part of the teams we have been privileged to know while creating sustainable schools. Inevitably there may be too much of one kind of information and not enough of another for each reader. Each chapter offers links to references that take you deeper into each topic. We include 20 case study schools. The accomplishments of school communities from around the world show that sustainable schools have been built and maintained and can be built on as models for sustainable schools for the future.

Green building organizations, such as the United States Green Building Council (USGBC) and the Collaborative for High Performance Schools (CHPS), have created rating systems aimed specifically at schools. CHPS has a wonderful collection of best practice manuals to assist design teams. LEED and CHPS rating systems can help benchmark a community's accomplishments and ambitions in relation to our current understanding of sustainability. Each chapter lists the relevant credits for the phase in LEED for Schools. CHPS credits are similar.

For us, the benchmark for a sustainable school is the quality of the learning environment. A sustainable school is bright, full of fresh air, comfort, and a happy quiet. Its campus has room for nature, just as nature has the space for us. It is a center for the lives of the children's families as well as a privileged and peaceful place for children to grow and develop. Where design teams have accomplished this in public schools, in old buildings, in cities, and high in the mountains, we salute them and offer their examples in the hope that one day soon all schools will be built sustainably.

ACKNOWLEDGMENTS

MY THANKS to all the educators, school communities, and fellow professionals who have talked about sustainable school ideas, and tried them out in projects, and taught me about the things they do, and helped me see the things I do through their eyes. I bring the experience of architectural practice to the book, so I have needed everybody's help to write this book. I want to thank my friends and contributors who have read and written and sketched and taken pictures of crossing guards and cats and children at play.

Particular thanks to Ken Rackow, for roping in the pictures and the paperwork; to Chris Duncan, for reading and clear thinking and for years of support for sustainable design; to Susan Herrington and Rosanna Lerma and Doree Friedman and Ron Blue, for bringing invaluable insights from their allied fields and for years of fruitful collaboration; to Aaron and Ashley and Ariane and Dan and Nicole for their support of the project even when it interfered with their real work; and to Sandy and Deven and Steve, for helping research and track down photos. I also want to thank the rest of my office for their patience in putting up with the demands on my time as we busily try to keep improving our design.

I have dedicated the book to Arthur Harris, the marvelous principal of Blach School, from whom we really learned about education, and I would like to thank all the rest of the educators we have worked with and their strong grasp of what sustainability could mean in a school environment. In particular, I would like to thank Margaret Gratiot, the former superintendent of the Los Altos School District, for embracing sustainability not as a pilot but as an approach for the entire district, and Randy Kenyon, the business officer, for making it happen. At that time it was an idea but newly reborn, and they were pioneers. I want to thank all the clients and school communities that are helping us make school environments better and more sustainable.

I have had the pleasure to serve on the technical committee of Collaborative for High Performance Schools, as has my partner Chris, and I want to thank the CHPS staff, the PG+E staff, and the Green Advisory Committee to the California Division of the State Architect, for helping to push sustainability ever forward and for talking through many of the ideas in this book.

Thanks to the team at Wiley for their support. And finally, I would like to thank my friends and family and my own sons, who have made me look at education with new eyes. My sons bring a bracingly critical intelligence to schools and architecture and sustainability—after all, for the sake of their generation, we had better start now, and start doing it right.

chapter 1

AN INTRODUCTION TO SUSTAINABLE SCHOOLS

Sustainable Development is development that meets the needs of the present without compromising the ability of future generations to meet their own needs.

—1987 UN Brundtland Commission Report

INTRODUCTION

SUSTAINABILITY IS ABOUT TIME, the invisible dimension. Although the only sure thing about the future is that it will come, concern for the future is at the basis of concern for sustainability. The world could be in very big trouble right now—facing inundation of coastlines housing tens of millions of people, a die-off of species as large as the mass extinction that made way for mammals. Or maybe not.

But data unarguably show that humanity's activities as builders and farmers and producers and consumers have changed the world, and are changing the world at this moment. Climates are changing. Glaciers are melting. The oceans uptake one-third of the carbon dioxide produced by human activities. Their waters have become measurably more acidic. Due to the relatively small change in ocean chemistry so far,

shelled creatures already produce thinner shells. The impact of their demise on the food chain is too complex to predict.

At the time of the Brundtland Commission report, world population was about 5 billion. Almost 25 years later, it is almost 7 billion. If all 7 billion live the lifestyle of Americans, the increased impact of human activities would be exponential. With 5% of the world's population, the United States already produces 25% of the world's greenhouse gas emissions.

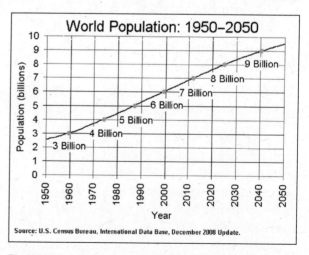

The 2008 U.S. government world population projection shows a population of 7 billion by 2011. *Source: U.S. Census Bureau*

It is about time for sustainability. In the Brundt-land Commission definition, the first requirement is meeting the needs of the present. The needs of nations to feed, house, educate, and support fulfilling lives for their growing populations are needs of the present. How can this happen without compromising the future? *Developed, technological nations must reduce, not just hold steady, their impacts on the biosphere.* While it is important to prevent irreversible harm to remaining wild and biologically rich areas such as tropical rain forests, sustainability must start in the over-consuming homes, cities, farms, and forests of temperate zone nations. This book examines how and why schools can lead the way toward sustainability in general.

NEED FOR SUSTAINABLE BUILDINGS

Constructing and operating buildings generate tremendous environmental impacts. In the United States alone, buildings account for:

- 72% of electricity consumption
- 39% of energy use
- 38% of all carbon dioxide (CO2) emissions
- 40% of raw materials use
- 30% of waste output (136 million tons annually)
- 14% of potable water consumption[1]

It is possible to reduce the impacts of buildings drastically with technology, materials, and methods available without any further research. One challenge is that this large reward can be gained only on an incremental, home-by-home, office-by-office basis. Unlike reining in big point source air and water polluters such as factories or power plants, any approach to reducing the impact from the building sector as a whole must include each individual building.

Leaking windows, lack of insulation, and obsolete systems make this building an energy hog. *Source: Gelfand Partners Architects*

New buildings comprise only a small percentage of the building stock in any given year. To substantially reduce the impact of the building sector as a whole, the efficiency of existing buildings needs to be improved. The $5 billion weatherization program adopted as part of the 2009 U.S. stimulus package is an example of the kind of program that can improve energy efficiency on a broad scale by operating at an individual building scale. New buildings with beautiful solar panels may be the face of sustainability in 2010, but the lowly caulk gun is likely to produce more gains in real energy use reduction.

BENEFITS OF SUSTAINABLE SCHOOLS

A compelling moral and educational case exists for demonstrating environmental stewardship in schools where children first learn what it is to be in the world in the society of other people. And as in any other project breaking ground today there is reason to fear that time has run out simply to do less harm. Even doing no harm is not enough. And if neither fear nor virtue motivates, there is also the business case that shows that energy efficiency and healthy environments rapidly pay back their investors.

School construction is a large market on its own, comprising approximately 5% of all construction in the United States in 2007. Sustainable practices in schools would have a measurable impact on energy and resource consumption for society as a whole.

But the benefits of sustainability are not all, or even primarily, to the outside world. A brief look at the advantages to the core mission of the school supports the value of sustainability in design, construction, and operation. Sustainable schools are better environments for learning.

Higher Student Test Scores

An analysis of over 21,000 students in Colorado, California, and Washington by the Heschong Mahone Group showed that the controlled admission of natural light through skylights and windows, "daylighting," in classrooms was strongly associated with higher student performance in reading and standardized testing. Students in the California classrooms with the best daylighting progressed 19% to 20% faster than students in the classrooms with the least.[3] Students in Colorado and Washington similarly showed 7% to 18% higher test scores at the end of the year in daylit classrooms than students in classrooms with the least daylighting.

Studies of classroom acoustics have also supported the connection between better student hearing and better student learning. Global Green, in "Healthier, Wealthier, Wiser: A National Report on Green Schools," cited a study showing students in quiet third-grade classrooms to be 0.4 years ahead of their peers in noisy classrooms in reading, and 0.2 years ahead in math.[4]

Lower Operating Costs

Energy costs schools money. It comes out of their general fund and thus directly competes with the costs

School and education construction is a major economic activity.
Education construction: The past 10 years

($ Billions)	1998	1999	2000	2001	2002	2003	2004	2005	2006	2007
School Districts	$17.095	$16.039	$21.567	$26.777	$24.343	$28.638	$29.088	$22.962	$25.325	$20.283
Colleges	$7.330	$13.964	$14.703	$14.732	$16.205	$19.469	$12.186	$14.561	$11.306	$12.656
All Education	$24.425	$30.003	$36.270	$41.509	$40.548	$48.107	$41.274	$37.523	$36.631	$32.939
New Construction	$12.097	$14.431	$19.139	$20.112	$22.505	$31.596	$20.656	$21.220	$19.031	$21.942
Adds/Mods	$12.328	$15.572	$17.131	$21.397	$18.043	$16.511	$20.618	$16.303	$17.600	$10.997

Source: Courtesy *American School & University magazine*[2]

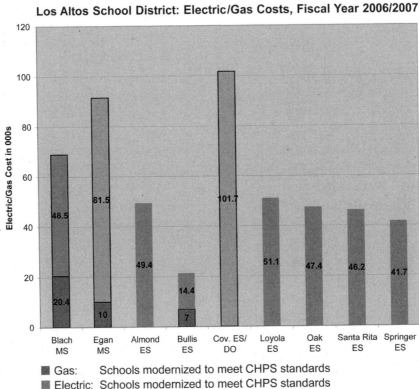

Los Altos School District: Electric/Gas Costs, Fiscal Year 2006/2007

Elementary school energy savings of high-performance schools averaged $50,000 per year, while middle school savings were $23,000 per year. *Los Altos School District*

■ Gas: Schools modernized to meet CHPS standards
■ Electric: Schools modernized to meet CHPS standards
■ Electric: Schools modernized to meet California Title 24

related to instruction. Saving money on heat and electricity means having more money for student supplies, teachers, and books. In the United States, school energy spending amounts to $8 billion a year, or 2% to 4% of school budgets, more than schools spend on textbooks. Improved operations and maintenance practices could save up to 20% of that in existing facilities, with major additional savings also available in design of new construction and modernization.

In addition to energy, other operating costs include water and landscape maintenance as well as maintenance of equipment and materials. Sustainable strategies lower water use with appropriate plant selection and high-efficiency irrigation; reduce the need for fertilizers and pesticides by appropriate plant selection and

uses of on-site compost; and match equipment with its engineering requirements to improve efficiency.

Many of the aspects green schools address also address risks that cost schools money to insure. Benefits in worker health and safety and reduction of mold issues through appropriate waterproofing and ventilation are particularly direct and should be brought to the attention of insurers.

Increased Student Attendance

A healthier environment is reflected in fewer sick days on the part of both employees and students. The emphasis on better indoor air quality in sustainable design is a direct approach to reducing asthma and other respiratory problems in schools. Displacement ventilation, one of the potential heating, ventilating, and air-conditioning (HVAC) strategies in sustainable schools, is directly linked to reduction of absentee rates. In Howell Township, New Jersey, absentee rates declined 60% after displacement ventilation was installed.[5] Even more limited improvements in indoor air yield measurable results; for example, changes in operations methods at Charles Young Elementary School in Washington, D.C., increased average daily attendance from 89% to 93%.[6]

Enhanced Teacher Performance and Satisfaction

Teacher retention affects both quality and operating costs of education. Gregory Kats, currently managing director of a green investment company, served as the Director of Financing for Energy Efficiency and Renewable Energy at the U.S. Department of Energy (1996-2001). In Kats' cost-benefit analysis of green design, the benefits of teacher retention alone exceed the cost of greening.

Financial Benefits of Green Schools ($/ft^2)	
Energy	$9
Emissions	$1
Water and Wastewater	$1
Increased Earnings	$49
Asthma Reduction	$3
Cold and Flu Reduction	$5
Teacher Retention	$4
Employment Impact	$2
Total	**$74**
Cost of Greening	**($3)**
Net Financial Benefits	**$71**

Green schools give positive financial returns. *Source: Courtesy Gregory Kats, Capital E*

Improvements can be made in schools of all ages. *Source: Claire Takacs, © 2009*

Increased Building Life

Beyond new construction, the real challenge in changing the impact of the building sector is in making existing buildings more sustainable. Extending the service life of existing buildings contributes to sustainability, as does construction of new buildings with a goal of permanence. In addition to the choice of durable materials, systems, and assemblies, the commissioning, operations, and maintenance of sustainable buildings keep systems running efficiently. Monitoring of building system performance creates the opportunity to catch problems in filters, balancing, or controls that can shorten system life. Preventive maintenance is built into the sustainable school, along with design and monitoring features that make efficient maintenance easier to accomplish.

Lower Environmental Impact

Schools are a large sector of the building market, which itself is a large contributor to the impacts people have on the planet. But it is salutary to note the direct reduction of impact the operation of each individual green school could accomplish. According to the Kats report,[7] each year one green school could save:

- 1,200 pounds of nitrogen oxides—a principal component of smog
- 1,300 pounds of sulfur dioxide—a principal cause of acid rain
- 585,000 pounds of carbon dioxide—the principal greenhouse gas and the principal product of combustion
- 150 pounds of coarse particulate matter—a principal cause of respiratory illness and an important contributor to smog

In addition, substantial water and wastewater benefits would vary by school and locality. Because of the large physical footprint of school campuses, these benefits could be significant, along with reductions in fertilizer and pesticide use.

Changing Attitudes

Schools have an influence on their community that extends beyond the education that occurs inside the four walls of the classroom. A sustainable school will work with its community to reduce driving, change eating habits, and demonstrate energy saving behavior. These influences can be very strong. Many solar panel installers give good prices for panels they put on a school because they know that seeing the panels will bring business from parents. As students grow up in a sustainably run organization, they will carry those habits and expectations into the workplace and into their own homes as adults.

Changing the mind-set of people who have grown up with a habit of waste, the advantages of the new, and an assumption of unlimited abundance is hard work. But sustainable schools can take part in readjusting these expectations and in resetting the base expectations of the next generation so that its members are much more cognizant of their impact on the world.

Teachers in California have done wonderful work with our children in the elementary grades, instilling in them a deep respect for the environment. By the time the kids reach us, they have really bought into the conservation ethic, intellectually and emotionally. The junior high years for many students mark the start of a phase of intense questioning of parental and societal values. Children at this age develop an exquisite sensitivity to any suggestion of hypocrisy or inauthenticity on the part of their elders. The inclusion of serious energy-conserving technologies at Blach makes a powerful statement to our youth that our commitment to environmentalism comes not only from our hearts, but also from our wallets.

—Arthur Harris, Principal,
Georgina Blach Intermediate School[8]

Bacich School in Kentfield, California, generates 100% of its electricity from roof-mounted photovoltaic panels.[9] *Source: Reproduced courtesy Mill Valley Herald*[10]

ELEMENTS OF SUSTAINABLE SCHOOLS

Community-Based Planning

Schools are entrusted with the care of the children of a community. It is an enormous responsibility. The school has a special status in the community. It forms the basis of the social life of the children, friendships that teach children how to have friendships, and often extends a web of connectivity into the whole family. Schools cannot be successful without the support of the families, friends, and neighbors who make up the school community.

The decision to create a sustainable school, whether by modernization or by new construction, is one that helps define the school community. The planning and design process for the school defines both the holistic approach and the sustainable features that are incorporated in it. Those choices reflect the values and priorities of the school community. Community participation in the process, at the site level and at the governing level of school boards or boards of trustees, is vital in engaging the passion, imagination, and commitment of the school community.

Just as the students will one day graduate with an understanding of sustainability nurtured by their experience in the school, the members of the community who are involved in building a sustainable school "graduate" from that process with knowledge and skills that they carry to their own homes and businesses. Involvement in design workshops, working groups, community outreach, or the legacy of sustainable operations offers scope for a range of individual commitments. A school is an ideal place to plant an idea that is meant to propagate throughout a community.

Community-based planning is the first step in creating the sustainable school. Through the policies and priorities that are developed, a program can be defined for the school. Especially when looking at the breadth

Workshop-style events involving the design team, community members, and even children can be fertile occasions for sustainable ideas. *Source: Sharon Danks*

and multivalent interpretations of sustainability, it is vital for the community to define its priorities for itself. Whether it is preservation of habitat, energy efficiency, or indoor air quality, the top concerns of the community need to be identified.

LEED and CHPS

For many organizations, achieving a certain level of performance as measured by a scorecard system such as LEED (Leadership in Energy and Environmental Design) or CHPS (Collaborative for High Performance Schools) satisfies their need to define sustainability. Cities, states, and school and university systems target a level, such as LEED Silver. The checklist systems include various categories of green design and define targets, documentation, and verification. In 2009, the U.S. Green Building Council (USGBC) finalized a specific LEED for Schools product that acknowledges the important ways in which schools differ from other building types.

LEED for Schools is a modification of the well-known LEED system, now such a standard in green design that product manufacturers include in their marketing literature how many LEED points their product can help achieve. Companies making products such as steel lockers that may always have been high-recycled-content steel are now putting that information on the front page of their brochures.

By their nature, scorecards reward features, or narrowly defined performance parameters. CHPS, originating in California, has created another sustainability checklist, along with an array of excellent best practice manuals and resources for planning sustainable schools.

Initially created by a committee with funding from California utilities, CHPS gave high importance to energy efficiency but also took an education-based look at other categories, based in part on the LEED system. The successful refinement of its criteria in California led to their adoption as an acceptable standard of sustainability for federal high-performance school funding. Other CHPS programs have included further regional refinements in nine states and various cities, including New York.

LEED and CHPS scorecards are the main vehicles for tracking sustainability goals. *Note: LEED and related logo is a trademark owned by the U.S. Green Building Council and is used by permission. CHPS is a registered trademark of the Collaborative for High Performance Schools.*

The International Code Council is developing a green building standard to be consistent with international building codes. The building code in California includes a voluntary green section. It is subject to review but if adopted in full in 2010 would require building performance roughly equal to LEED Silver. Already the building code in California requires energy and water conservation that meets LEED prerequisites.

Working through the categories of the CHPS or LEED checklist can help define the goals a school should meet, focusing on site, energy, materials, indoor air quality, water, construction, operations, and innovation. Most goals can be met at various levels. That way a design team can match goals to the situation.

Integrated Design

Integrated design is the most essential strategy in the sustainable design approach. But if it was hard to agree on a checklist, and indeed it was hard enough that US-

GBC in 2009 has nine separate LEED checklists, it is almost impossible to define a single holistic measure of building sustainability. And without measuring it, how can one know what has been achieved?

One solution is to separate the design process and approach, which must be synergistic, from the measurements of performance, which can be as simple as reading the utility bill before and after. Program goals, sustainability approaches, site and community needs and opportunities, and the resources available for the project all converge in the solution. A single decision, such as raising a part of the roof for a new clerestory, can be part of structural needs (new plywood, new framing), daylighting improvements, ventilation improvements, and a new appearance. Such an integrated solution cannot be separated easily into different budget items—the sustainable improvement does not increase the cost of the structural and appearance change. Using this kind of approach can mean that sustainable design is achieved at limited or no additional cost.

New light monitors added during a modernization at Almond School emphasize doors, bring in daylight, ventilate, and introduce better scale and rhythm along the building face. *Source: Gelfand Partners Architects*

Before modernization, Almond School classrooms needed seismic upgrading, reinforcement of daylighting, and better use of outdoor space. *Source: Gelfand Partners Architects*

Naturalistic plantings enrich the playground at Sherman School.
Source: Miller Company Landscape Architects. Photo Jeffrey Miller

The Sustainable Building Industry Council, with a history of working with the federal government, created a useful resource in developing integrated design strategies. The *Whole Building Design Guide* offers a wealth of online information to help teams think through integrated design approaches.[11] It helps to demystify the need for design strategies to do several things at once.

School as Campus

Schools differ from other building types in the frequency with which they are not just buildings but campuses composed of multiple buildings and a variety of site uses. This large footprint increases the need to look at the site impacts in terms of water and habitat as well as transportation impacts. The sustainable school can attempt to have a low impact, but it can also go further, using its open space to extend or connect areas of surrounding native habitat.

Building design on campuses takes into account the orientation to the sun and wind, not just of the individual building but of the spaces between the buildings. Buildings and planting can shade each other; planting can moderate building exposures to the setting sun or deciduous tree planting can shade classrooms in the summer but allow heat gain in the winter. Buildings can be used to screen outdoor areas from direct wind or unwanted sun or can be sited to avoid shading areas where full sun is desired. By integrating buildings with each other and the site design, a varied campus can still honor the differences between easily controlled north and south sun and more difficult east and west exposures.

Environmental Curriculum

The whole campus also contributes to supporting an environmental curriculum. Depending on the grade level, environmental learning can range from small children touching the leaves of lambs' ears and learning about the various textures in the natural world, to experimental farms at the primary and secondary level, to learning about ecological connections and

◀Children assist in planting and caring for their garden. *Source: Miller Company Landscape Architects. Photo Jeffrey Miller*

▼The rain garden at DaVinci Arts Middle School helps kids see how water moves through its cycle.[12] *Source: Portland Public Schools, 2004*

consequences in natural systems. The relationship of buildings to grounds is also a wordless lesson in the relation of our works to the works of nature and to the potential for partnership that always exists.

Flexibility for Multiple Uses

Many schools are the largest community facilities in their area. They represent large investments of money, space, and energy. The sustainable approach is to employ those facilities for many more uses than the school, cutting down on the need to build more facilities or cause more sprawl. Involving joint-use partners can also improve the quality of the facility further than either partner could have afforded separately.

Water Efficiency

The sustainable school reduces or eliminates potable water use for irrigation and cuts use of potable water in the buildings. The huge quantities of potable water going down toilet and urinal drains can be reduced by using gray water or roof water or waterless urinals. Making visible the collection of rainwater and its ultimate use to water gardens, for example, can be part of the sustainable curriculum.

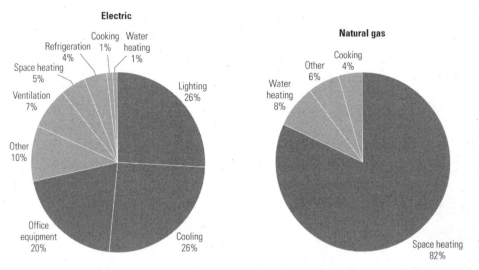

Electric

- Cooking 1%
- Water heating 1%
- Refrigeration 4%
- Space heating 5%
- Ventilation 7%
- Other 10%
- Office equipment 20%
- Cooling 26%
- Lighting 26%

Natural gas

- Other 6%
- Cooking 4%
- Water heating 8%
- Space heating 82%

Large energy uses are larger opportunities for savings. *Source: Used with permission, ©1999 E Source Companies LLC*

Courtesy: E SOURCE; from Commercial Building Energy Consumption Survey, 1999 data

Energy Efficiency

Twenty to 30% of a building's life cycle energy use occurs during construction. Modernization of existing buildings and design of new buildings for longevity make immediate energy savings. Energy efficiency in building operations attacks the other 70% to 80%.

Energy efficiency is more than saving money on utility bills. Energy use is the factor most directly tied to greenhouse gases, climate change, and the school's carbon footprint. To cut these major impacts, school managers must first understand where the energy uses are. Lighting and cooling are more than half the average electricity consumption, with office equipment providing another major load. Air conditioning, for schools that are not in use in the summer, is an area that must be examined with an eye toward using more natural ventilation systems or more efficient strategies, such as displacement.

In schools without air conditioning, lighting by itself is more than half the electric load. And schools have primarily daytime use. Good daylighting coupled with a daylight compensation electric light control system can cut electric use by 40% to 60%. Further, student test scores will rise.

Office equipment, including computers, is a major draw on power even when it is not in use. Replacing office equipment such as copiers with machines that power down and turning off computers, televisions, and other electric equipment when not in use saves another large bite of the power pie.

The other major energy load is space heating. Heating systems have greatly increased in their efficiency. Many choices are available from better package units, to more exotic systems such as geo-exchange heat pumps. Making the right choice is part of the integrated building design process.

Resource Efficiency

As in energy efficiency, the first place to look for gains in resource efficiency is in existing buildings. Even if a building must be stripped to its foundation and structure, 20% of the building is still there.

◀Foundation, structure, roof and wall sheathing, and windows remain for reuse. *Source: Gelfand Partners Architects*

▼The San Francisco Friends School is housed in an adaptive reuse of the historic original Levi Strauss factory. *Source: Gelfand Partners Architects*

Buildings that are reused do not go to landfills. In looking at existing buildings that did not start as schools, however, caution is required. Schools need wide hallways and column and wall spacings that allow larger spaces, such as classrooms. Classrooms should have access to daylighting. School entries need convenient access for students arriving in large numbers all at once. Most schools need to be adjacent or close to sport and recreation areas.

In addition to adaptive reuse, good use of the facilities also limits resource use. Small is better. Driven more by budget than sustainability, many high

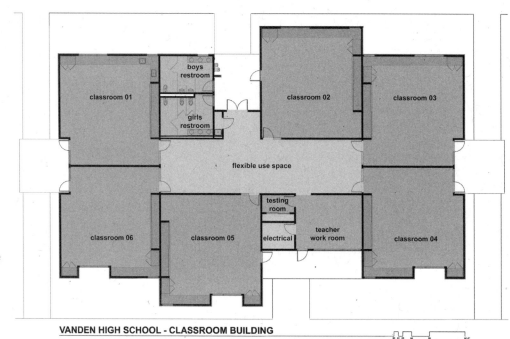

The teacher workroom allows teachers who teach six periods of students' seven-period day to have prep space without tying up an entire classroom. *Source: Gelfand Partners Architects*

VANDEN HIGH SCHOOL - CLASSROOM BUILDING

schools are unable to give teachers exclusive use of a classroom. If classrooms are used during the entire school day, then teachers need prep areas. Part of the sustainable school is working with the site to develop appropriate staff support spaces while encouraging full utilization of the facility in order to build less floor area.

High-recycled-content materials are part of the picture, too. As the industry adapts to changing economics and to the market created by LEED, these materials are more readily available. Contractors may choose to recycle asphalt on site, for example, or to contract with haulers that will do it off site for another project.

High-Performance Learning Spaces

The chief hallmark of the sustainable school is the quality of its classrooms and other learning spaces. Integrated design and energy efficiency contribute to

sustainability and contribute to an improved learning environment. With the heavy use of power in cooling and lighting, the incentives are strong to develop good daylighting and ventilation. These strategies will contribute to high performance in learning—the core mission of the school.

Daylighting

Good daylighting admits light but not heat or glare. The sky opposite the sun—north in the northern hemisphere—is an ideal source of cool, diffuse light. When evenly spread over the walls and ceiling of a room, it provides calm, appealing light. Sun from other angles is handled with various design techniques. The electric lighting is either separately switched or automatically controlled to go off or dim when not needed. Accompanied by views, daylighting is the single most effective combination of energy saving and classroom improvement the design can accomplish.

Excellent daylighting and automated window controls make this Vanden High School classroom energy efficient as well as comfortable. *Source: Mark Luthringer*

The Blach library was built between two existing buildings and admits daylight over one of the roofs. *Source: Mark Luthringer*

Improved Air Quality

US EPA studies of human exposure to air pollutants [indoors] may be two to five times— and occasionally more than 100 times—higher than outdoor levels.

—Environmental Protection Agency[13]

Indoor air quality is tied to the materials in the room, maintenance procedures, and ventilation. An integrated approach to specifying low volatile organic and nontoxic compounds, no added formaldehyde, and appropriate airing or flushing procedures before occupancy can turn over a building with good air quality from the beginning. Maintaining it depends on appropriate maintenance for materials such as carpet, which cannot be left wet, and in the choice and use of appropriate cleaning supplies.

But the other major influence is ventilation. New approaches such as heat or energy recovery ventilation can bring 90% to 100% outside air into the space continuously, flushing out pollutants, contaminants, and germs, without losing energy efficiency.

Indoor air quality in portable classrooms is so suspect that the California Department of Education has issued specific advisories of mitigation measures districts can adopt. *Source: Gelfand Partners Architects*

Thermal Comfort

One of the limitations of sustainability Version 1 in the 1970s was that it seemed to depend on discomfort and a lot of attention. If building inhabitants could accept discomfort, they would save a lot of energy— just expand that comfort range (with a sweater) before turning on the heat. In contrast to the unsustainable oversized mechanical systems that ran with no intervention, they could manually lower insulating blinds at night and turn on fans to blow heat down and then switch them to suck air out and then do all that again. Sustainability Version 2 right-sizes mechanical systems and depends on smart controls to maintain comfort with very little user input. The automatic system can be responsible for many more adjustments than a basic thermostat and can maintain higher levels of comfort than many conventional systems.

For many schools, though, the choice of whether to air-condition or not still may depend on tolerance for discomfort. If heating is best accomplished through a radiant system, air conditioning imposes either a different system or a redundant one. In climates where non–air-conditioned spaces with good ventilation are uncomfortable for several hours a day during 10 days in the year, is that acceptable? Even in Palm Springs, in the desert of California, many hours of every average day of the school year are at exactly the right temperature outside as inside. With a highly efficient ventilation system, the hourly need for additional cooling is greatly reduced and in some climates eliminated.

Improved Acoustics

The CHPS criteria include acoustics because of its vital role in creating a high-performance learning environment. In the terms of the Brundtland Commission sustainability definition, good acoustics is part of meeting the needs of the present. A classroom where children can hear the teacher and each other is very important.

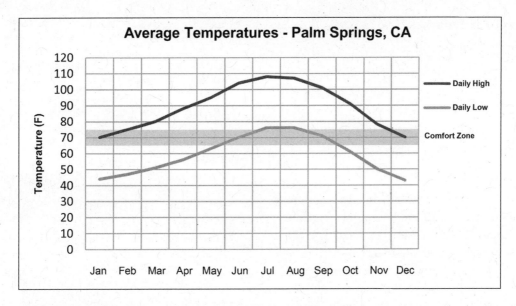

Even in Palm Springs, California, the daily low is always below or within the comfort zone, demonstrating that round-the-clock cooling should never be necessary. *Source: Gelfand Partners Architects*

In an integrated approach to design, acoustic performance is part of the envelope, the HVAC system, the finishes in the room, and the choice of natural ventilation system. The HVAC system must be designed so that noise does not drown out the teacher or the children when it kicks on. The room must cut reverberation times, which interfere with the intelligibility of speech, by installation of sufficient absorptive surfaces, typically the ceiling and the walls if there is no carpet or just the ceiling and the carpet. And ventilation must come in through acoustic louvers or windows that open onto quiet areas. If the school is near a noisy highway or railroad, the walls and even closed windows probably will need improvement to cut environmental noise.

Commissioning

Commissioning is an integrated strategy that helps define the expected performance of building systems, measures their performance after construction, and takes an interdisciplinary approach to troubleshooting problems. CHPS and LEED both require basic commissioning and give extra points for enhanced commissioning.

Commissioning is a good idea in any building program. The initial step of assuring that the building user has chosen an expected performance (e.g., light level or temperature comfort range) is invaluable in solving postoccupancy issues. The interdisciplinary approach of commissioning coordinates sophisticated control and HVAC systems so that their interactive performance meets design goals before the various contractors leave the job. It is not good enough to have the HVAC balancing check out and the system fail. Commissioning works so well that retro-commissioning—going back to existing buildings and systems on a regular basis—is also recommended.

PUTTING IT ALL TOGETHER

Sustainability is no luxury. It is an approach whose time has come. The building sector of the economy is responsible for a large percentage of energy and resource use, dispersed across millions of projects. But the only way to reduce the impact of the sector is to design and run each project in a sustainable way.

Any system designed into a project is useful only if it is maintained and operated as intended. Schools are a unique operating environment. They are busy, chronically underfunded, and house often rambunctious children. Systems, materials, and assemblies need to be designed to work in that environment. The people responsible for running the buildings are invaluable resources in keeping the design real. When they have participated in the design, they are also better prepared to manage the buildings.

Schools that tie sustainability and education into a way of inhabiting the campus support both the running of the facility and the educational activities. As buildings and landscapes that are found in every community, schools constitute a piece of the building sector that is uniquely suited to provide leadership in sustainability.

- Schools are a major construction activity.
- Schools can model long-term changes in attitudes.
- Schools are used by entire communities.
- Sustainable design makes better schools.

NOTES

1. USGBC, "Green Building Research" (April 2009), www.usgbc.org/DisplayPage.aspx?cmspageID=1718, accessed June 16, 2009.

2. Joe Agron, "34th Annual Official Education Construction Report," *American School & University*, May 1, 2008, http://asumag.com/Construction/34th_annual_construction_report, accessed June 12, 2009.

3. Heschong Mahone Group, "Daylighting in Schools: Reanalysis Report," California Energy Commission Technical Report, 500-03-082-A-3 (October 2003), www.newbuildings.org/downloads/FinalAttachments/A-3_Dayltg_Schools_2.2.5.pdf June 16, 2009.

4. Global Green USA, "Healthier, Wealthier, Wiser: A Report on National Green Schools," March 12, 2008, www.globalgreen.org/docs/publication-82-1.pdf, accessed June 12, 2009.

5. California's Coalition for Adequate School Housing, "Displacement Ventilation for Improved Air Quality and Energy Use in Schools" (February 2006), www.cashnet.org/resource-center/resourcefiles/603.pdf, accessed June 12, 2009.

6. Connecticut Foundation for Environmentally Safe Schools, "Green Cleaning in Schools Is Cost Effective," February 19, 2009, http://pollutionfreeschools.org/docs/greencleanschoolscosteffective.pdf, accessed June 16, 2009.

7. Gregory Kats, "Greening Americas Schools: Costs and Benefits," *Build Green Schools*, October 3, 2007, www.buildgreenschools.org/documents/pub_Greening_Americas_Schools.pdf, accessed June 12, 2009.

8. Collaborative for High Performance Schools, "Demonstration Project: Georgina Blach Intermediate School," April 2, 2004, www.chps.net/chps_schools/pdfs/Blach_summary-final.pdf, accessed June 16, 2009.

9. SPG Solar "Bacich Elementary School Case Study," (2007). www.spgsolar.com/assets/BacichElementary_SPG_casestudy.pdf, accessed June 16, 2009.

10. Chris Rooney, "San Rafael Firm Powered by Solar Award," *Mill Valley Herald* (June 21, 2007), www.marinscope.com/millvalleyherald/detail_page.php?rdate=2007-06-21%2013:53:20&pcode=NWP&scode=Mnl&ldate=2007-06-12%2013:02:03, accessed June 12, 2009.

11. National Institute of Building Sciences, *The Whole Building Design Guide* (2009), www.wbdg.org, accessed June 16, 2009.

12. Doug Pushard, "Oregon School Showcases Demo Rainwater System," Harvest H20.com, www.harvesth2o.com/davinci.shtml, accessed June 12, 2009.

13. Environmental Protection Agency, "EPA Reports and Factsheets: Air Contaminants," June 5, 2009. www.epa.gov/aging/resources/epareportsa.htm, accessed June 26, 2009.

chapter 2

PLANNING STRATEGIES

INTRODUCTION

IN 1962 RACHEL CARSON'S *Silent Spring* produced a revolution in awareness of chemicals in the environment and their effect on ecology. Now climate change threatens to devastate habitat for plants, animals, and human beings alike. Spikes in oil prices produce periodic bursts of conservation and alternative energy development. The burning of fossil fuels at any price generates a blanket of greenhouse gases. Many believe that scarcity of water will drive the geopolitics of the twenty-first century. These positions are strongly held. And these contrasting priorities present a challenge to anyone who would like to design a sustainable school.

In the face of these diverse interpretations of sustainability, how does a sustainable school come about? General statements are not enough to direct a project. Advocates of cost-based analysis will emphasize energy over indoor air quality. Advocates of stewardship will emphasize hydrology over daylighting. And advocates of education will emphasize daylighting above all.

One solution to this challenge is to embrace all positions under an umbrella of "integrated design." Another solution is to focus more narrowly on one goal while reducing impacts in other areas. But for many important allies in the school community, one goal or another is *the* priority. They believe it holds the urgency of saving the world for the next generation. And the ability to accomplish a sustainable school rests on the engagement and passion of the local community.

In order to begin translating talk into action, planners must first determine what the most salient goals are for their community. But who are the planners doing the asking? And who is the community? Planning any school is a complex multiyear process. Planning a sustainable school raises the stakes. Such a school is expected to be an integrated whole and to function permanently in a healthy, energy-efficient manner. The sustainable school will incorporate practices that are new to districts and even to many designers. The process of planning and building the school will differ from standard construction and management practices.

In an ideal world, a sustainable school would be created by a team that begins by developing a shared vision and stays consistent through the entire process. For example, architects and contractors would help select a site, educators might come into schools under construction and help tune acoustics in music rooms, and engineers and contractors would be engaged for a full year after a school opens to ensure that mechanical systems are functioning properly, users are comfortable, and operations staff are fully trained.

Putting together a *process* that will set a vision, achieve the vision, and live the vision is the first design task in creating a sustainable school.

These school buildings opened the same year Silent Spring was published and were modernized as a high-performance school in 1999. *Source: Gelfand Partners Architects*

SELECTING THE TEAM

Goal Setting

The challenge in goal setting is to maintain the long view. The school built when *Silent Spring* was published is probably still in use today as glaciers melt and seas rise.

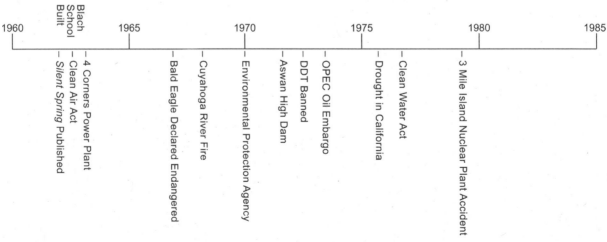

1960 — Blach School Built — 1965 — 1970 — 1975 — 1980 — 1985

- Silent Spring Published
- Clean Air Act
- 4 Corners Power Plant
- Bald Eagle Declared Endangered
- Cuyahoga River Fire
- Environmental Protection Agency
- Aswan High Dam
- DDT Banned
- OPEC Oil Embargo
- Drought in California
- Clean Water Act
- 3 Mile Island Nuclear Plant Accident

The idea of sustainability might first arise as saving energy or reducing the school's carbon footprint. It might mean getting a higher LEED (Leadership in Energy and Environmental Design) or CHPS (Collaborative for High Performance Schools) score than a competitor. It might mean protecting or restoring habitat or the hydrology that serves habitats. It might mean using recycled or renewable materials that contribute to indoor air quality and reduce the web of impacts that extend from a construction project. Or it might mean using sustainability features and measures to support curriculum.

What are the criteria that can be used to help choose among these goals? The ideal answer is that everyone in the school community has a voice, and the decisions reflect the values they most strongly hold. No professional can substitute.

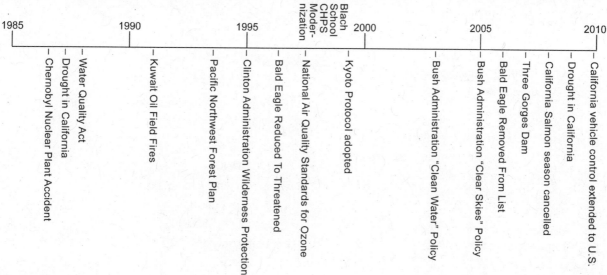

Community organizing is a skill that schools traditionally have had. School activities rely on parent and community involvement. The same methods of reaching out to the stakeholders can be part of planning the sustainable school. But where the issues are technical and the potential expenditures are large, the process tends to become increasingly confined to professionals. Such professionals (e.g., design consultants, contractors, attorneys, real estate developers or agents) might be involved in the community only for the duration of the project. This situation can sever decision making from what may be extremely strong school communities and the creative ideas and commitment they offer.

In a traditional school construction process, sites are selected by one entity, staff is hired and curriculum is set by another, the campus is designed by a third, and the whole is built by a fourth. Then the contractor turns the school over to people who were never consulted in its design. This process is obviously flawed for any school; for a sustainable school, it practically guarantees that opportunities will be missed.

If it is community members who first recognize that their school should be sustainable, they must seek professionals who can help them refine and achieve their goals. In hiring professionals to assist, community members should seek both the specific qualifications necessary to perform technical duties and experience in working with communities in defining their goals and in understanding their options.

Professionals hired through bureaucratic processes often compete based on qualifications such as successful design of schools in the past or successful control of schedule and budget. But organizations such as the American Institute of Architects have been encouraging their members to consider it part of their job to bring broader goals to the attention of the school community and to encourage clients to reach out for broader participation on the part of end users, neighbors, and family members. The qualifications necessary for planning and designing a sustainable school should include experience and skills in community outreach and community-based design.

Interview or Proposal Topics for Design Team Selection

INDOOR AIR QUALITY
- Approach to indoor air quality
- Experience controlling moisture, contamination, managing ventilation
- Lessons learned

ACOUSTIC COMFORT
- Acoustical consultant on team?
- Acoustic performance in previous projects
- Strategies to ensure acoustic quality
- Application of strategies: classrooms, multipurpose, hallways
- Approach to controlling heating, ventilating, and air-conditioning (HVAC) noise

THERMAL COMFORT
- Approach to maintaining thermal comfort
- Teachers' control over classrooms

VISUAL COMFORT
- Approach to ensuring visual comfort in terms of light level and source
- Examples to visit

DAYLIGHTING
- Previous daylighting examples
- Strategies used
- Occupant satisfaction
- Energy saved

ANALYSIS TOOLS FOR OPTIMIZATION OF SAFETY AND SECURITY

- Experience with CPTED (Crime Prevention Through Environmental Design)
- Previous projects incorporating CPTED
- Balance of security technology and CPTED

LIFE CYCLE COST ANALYSIS

- Included in the contract?
- Cost methodology used
- Methodology to reduce total ownership costs
- Methodology applied to school design? Results?
- Methodology proposed for current project

COMMISSIONING

- Previous buildings commissioned?
- Detail?
- Agent?
- Results?

ENERGY ANALYSIS TOOLS

- Tools team uses
- How do tools reduce consumption?
- Applied to school design? Results?
- Tools proposed for current project

ENERGY-EFFICIENT BUILDING SHELL

- Examples of energy-efficient walls, floors, roofs
- Key techniques, materials, products. Results?
- System still performing as designed?

ENVIRONMENTALLY PREFERABLE MATERIALS, PRODUCTS

- Experience specifying environmentally responsible materials and products
- Experience specifying recycled content materials

- Knowledge of procurement, delivery timelines, installation
- Knowledge of performance over time
- Applied to school design?

WASTE REDUCTION

- Experience designing for materials efficiency
- Experience specifying construction waste management

ENVIRONMENTALLY RESPONSIVE SITE PLANNING

- Experience creating environmentally responsive site plans
- Key features, performance

HIGH-PERFORMANCE HVAC

- Specify high-performance HVAC standard practice?
- Tools used to analyze and optimize performance
- High-performance HVAC used in previous projects, schools
- Energy savings generated
- System performance over time
- Provided quiet, comfortable learning environment?
- Design-build or independent mechanical engineer?

HIGH-PERFORMANCE ELECTRIC LIGHTING

- Experience with high-performance electric lighting in schools
- Providing high-quality visual environment, saving energy?
- Experience integrating daylighting and electric lighting systems
- Tools used to analyze and optimize combined performance of daylighting, electric lighting

(continued)

WATER EFFICIENCY

- Experience with water-efficient landscaping, water use reduction, innovative wastewater treatment
- Applied to schools? Results?

Source: Collaborative for High Performance Schools, Best Practices Manual[1]

RENEWABLE ENERGY

- Experience designing/installing renewable energy systems
- Specific systems used/installed. In schools?
- Energy saved
- System still performing as intended?

Architectural Contract Considerations

Once the architect has been selected, an agreement between the owner and the architect needs to include both the conventional services and the services that are part of a sustainable design process. The agreement defines the services and deliverables expected of the architect and the information, access, and compensation to be provided by the owner.

Most architectural fees for school projects are tied to the owner's construction budget and have been developed around an expected scope of services that includes a predesign period, where the architect is helping the owner refine their program needs, sometimes the budget itself, and consider alternative approaches on a particular site. This period is followed by schematic design and the progressive refinement of the design through contract documents. During construction, the architect assists the owner to determine if the contractor is meeting the intentions of the contract. At the end of the project, the architect helps the owner make sure that the contractor has cleaned up all the details, provided all training and warranties, released all liens and claims, and that the permits are closed out and final.

When the architect's services extend beyond these basic roles, the agreement should include a description of the additional services and related additional

Typical Extended Services for Sustainable Schools

- Master planning district enrollment and school location
- Facilitating sustainability design workshops with the extended school community
- Analysis and comparison of potential school sites
- District facility standards
- Grant, foundation, and utility rebate research and applications
- Life cycle cost analysis of various material and equipment options (usually requires district maintenance and operations staff to participate)

- Extensive daylight and energy modeling
- Coordination with commissioning authorities during the design phase
- Application for green certifications, such as LEED or CHPS
- Application for incentive funding from agencies or government
- Retro-commissioning existing systems in modernizations
- Coordinating commissioning extending into a full year postoccupancy
- Postoccupancy studies

fees. Some of the listed services also can be provided in house by sophisticated school districts or by separate consultants to the team. However, the most successful teams have continuity throughout the project.

Once the community has reached out for the professional skills it needs and the professionals have connected with the community they will serve, community-based brainstorming can focus the energy of the community onto the specific goals that are possible for the project and that engage community values.

Design is inherently a process of thinking about something that does not yet exist. It depends on inspiration, risk, testing, and communication. When a designer sketches or models an idea, he or she is testing it. A designer skilled in working with the community can help a broad range of people put their ideas forward,

---

Potential Workshop Participants

SPONSORS
- Project champion
- School and community college board members
- Community stakeholders and media
- Utility companies
- Research/universities
- Government agencies (federal, state, local)

BENEFICIARIES
- Students
- Teachers
- Administrators
- Curriculum planners
- General public (who might also use facilities)
- Taxpayers (who benefit from lower energy bills)

IMPLEMENTERS
- School and community college facility planners
- Green building consultants
- Energy specialist (conservation/generation)
- Maintenance and operations staff
- Construction finance/legal counsel (energy)
- Site selection team (environmental consultant, soils and geotechnical engineering)

- Design consultants
- Architectural and engineering team (mechanical, structural, civil, electrical)
- Major subcontractors
- Builder
- Construction team
- Energy service company
- Potential suppliers/energy equipment manufacturers
- Commissioning agent

MISCELLANEOUS
- Custodians
- School and college site staff (information technology, cafeteria, after-school, administration)
- Local fire marshal or city fire official
- Waste management/recycling expert
- Labor union, workforce development team
- Joint use partners (local governments, jurisdictions)
- Certified inspector
- Law enforcement
- Educational organizations
- Legislative representatives

Source: Courtesy California Division of the State Architect [2]

Children at Bryant Elementary School help envision playground. *Source: Sharon Danks*

test unexpected combinations, and communicate their findings. The challenge for the community-based designer is to create a safe place for wild ideas.

One workshop will not be enough. The first should help develop goals for the project, but later workshops should focus on site design, building design, finishes and operations, the construction and commissioning process itself, and finally the next steps the school community can take in using the new facility to help create a more sustainable way of life. The team should include in the work plan a schedule of workshops for the design of the school and create milestones when decisions that influence sustainability can be made. Such decisions start at a campus level but focus later on specific decisions such as carpet vs. resilient flooring.

Goal-setting Topics

- Campus location and community interface
- Campus design and ecosystem interface
- Carbon footprint
- Energy savings/independence
- Indoor environment
- Measurement and verification

Roles of School Boards, Districts, and Individual Schools

Initial goal setting may not be tied to a particular school or project. School boards adopt goals such as making future projects more energy efficient, or greening schoolyards, or conforming to a certain level of LEED or CHPS criteria. Sustainability can be part of the platform of candidates for school boards or part of the expertise sought among school trustees.

School boards set policies for school districts. Such policies cover everything from textbooks to lunches. In almost all of these areas, sustainability can be part of the decision-making process. It is the role of the school board to provide direction in matters such as whether lunches will be prepared at a central kitchen and distributed to the sites, or whether school garden programs will be integrated with school lunches. The board leads the district in decisions that affect all of the schools.

The district staff also includes academic staff, maintenance and operations people, and administrators. Such staff members can provide benchmarking data on the performance of students, buildings, systems, and district employees. Such benchmarks can be compared to the performance of school systems nationally and internationally, providing important feedback about practices the district could improve.

Education continually struggles between the need to create generally similar skills and knowledge and the need to work with individual children so that each child can flourish. The specifics of the learning place as it relates to its particular students, families, teachers, and community are the responsibility of the school. Just as individual children learn differently, each school community will invent a personality, approach, and linkages for itself that will outlast the individual families who pass through as their children advance.

Working Group

In setting goals, an inclusive process with as many people and ideas as possible is necessary. But such a large group is unwieldy in developing the details of a project. A core group meeting throughout the process is needed to maintain focus, efficiency, and continuity. It can pull in additional points of view, experts, or community involvement at key points. The core roles that need to be filled include:

- Representative responsible to the school board or other governing body
- Strong academic leadership, such as a principal or vice principal

- Teachers who can represent other teachers
- Parents
- Representative from maintenance and operations
- Architect
- Construction manager or contractor

A project manager might come from the consultants, district, or school site. The responsibility of the project manager is to coordinate and communicate the information, logistics, and decision making throughout the process. Ideally this person is committed to sustainability as a goal. But it is also workable if the project manager is one of the technical resources, and the sustainability advocate is one of the other members of the group. In such a situation, the scorecard systems such as CHPS and LEED have particular advantages. Project managers who come from a construction background are oriented to achieve measurable results, such as meeting schedules and budgets. Such a quantitative approach can also be applied to meeting a target number of points for sustainability.

Planning a school is complex, but it is undertaken in a step-by-step way. Final authority for decisions is always vested in the governing body (such as a school board or board of trustees). But the board consults the working group, blue ribbon panels (in the case of certain kinds of bonds), and the public. These advisory groups help the board set direction. The planning path branches into big decisions—site location, for example—and further out into the ramifications of all the small decisions—carpet versus linoleum in the office, for example. The working group is together through all those decisions and organizes the input of the larger community. The brainstorming workshops should occur at the points where alternative paths lead in different directions.

When the sustainability goals are clearly set out—by defining a mission, by targeting points on

Sustainable Design Process

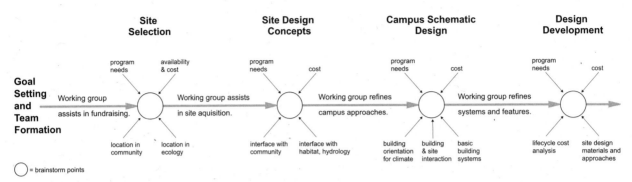

Brainstorming nodes help advance the sustainable design process. *Source: Gelfand Partners Architects*

a scorecard, or by adopting a narrowed focus, such as reducing carbon footprint—the working group can reference their decisions and progress. The task of the working group is to consider all the needs a school facility must meet, and to select strategies that will meet those needs most effectively. Sustainable design is best served by a design approach that integrates program and educational needs, campus design, building orientation and form, and building materials, assemblies, and systems. Such an approach is also most likely to achieve a high-quality educational environment. In order to integrate all the information and decisions that must be considered, the working group should:

- Meet consistently throughout the project.
- Be small enough for efficiency.
- Define sustainability as one of its roles.

INTEGRATED DESIGN

Site Selection

In the case of a new school, the first job for the working group is selecting a site. All the decisions that go into making a sustainable campus or building follow.

Location defines the impacts of development both to the site itself and to surrounding neighborhoods, transportation, habitat, and hydrology.

The location of a school is an emotionally charged issue. School boards will hear from parents, neighbors, and real estate interests. Families buy houses based on the attendance boundaries for public schools. Many of these issues overlap with sustainability concerns. Transportation impacts, habitats, and water must all be seen in the framework of the concern parents have for children's safety, the concerns neighbors have for traffic congestion, and the concern school staff and parents have for easily maintained, tidy school grounds.

Schools produce noise when active children are outside playing. Schools are also places where the most vulnerable population is concentrated—should they be next to highways, factories, pipelines, or high-voltage lines? Schools may not be the functions best located on a brownfield or other seriously degraded site unless the team is ready to prove that an extraordinary level of thoroughness has been applied to removing potential dangers. A school site choice must meet a commonsense test. Is this the right place for children to spend their day?

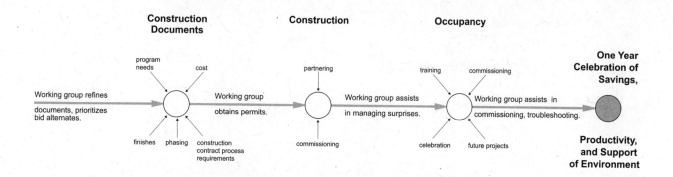

Environmental considerations include both positive and negative impacts. Positive impacts could include on-site provision of needed hydrological detention areas for the entire surrounding area. School landscape planting could help link flyways and provide habitat for native fauna. A school project could include improvement of existing infrastructure or mitigation of an existing degraded site.

Negative impacts might include disruption of an existing habitat, park, or prime farmland. Unless the open space of the school can be shown to mitigate such a disruption, such sites should be avoided. But transportation/traffic to and from school probably will be the most significant impact and the most difficult to isolate. The temptation exists to say that this problem is too much a part of the greater society's way of life for a school to solve. But it is major; for most California schools transportation accounts for half their current energy use. They could be off the electric grid entirely and half their energy use would remain.

The percentage of students walking or biking to school in the United States has dropped steeply since 1969. *Source: Department of Health and Human Services, Centers for Disease Control and Prevention[3]*

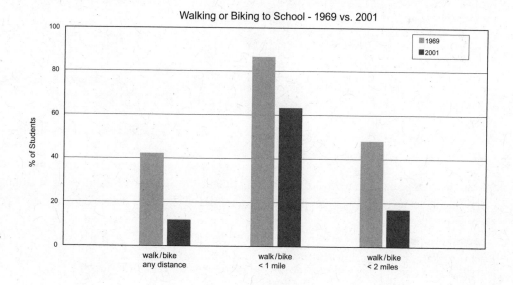

▲ Even children walking, taking buses, and biking have neighborhood impacts. *Source: Gelfand Partners Architects*

▶ Community assistance helps promote students leaving school under their own power. *Source: Gelfand Partners Architects*

The U.S. Safe Routes to School program began in local districts seeking to reverse the trend of students arriving at school one by one in private automobiles. Organizations are now active in 40 countries trying to get children back on their feet or their bikes to get to school.[4] Parents' perception of the dangers to children from both traffic and predatory adults have no doubt influenced the decline in children's walking to school. But it is possible to create safety improvements and to raise consciousness about the advantages of children who learn to navigate the streets and get themselves to school.

Planning for children to get to school on foot or bicycles should be part of choosing a school location. At the very least, the site selected for a new school should not make it more difficult to walk to school. Ideally it will be easier.

Other operational issues affected by location include hours of school operation and community use outside of school hours. Will high school students drive and need to park? How will food deliveries be made and garbage picked up? What impact will such service traffic have on surrounding residential neighbors?

Depending on jurisdiction, the bureaucratic process for developing open land will differ, but in most areas, some oversight exists. Usually impacts of the kinds just discussed will need a formal study and report. Sometimes the impacts of a school might have been included in the process for a larger development with housing, workplaces, shopping, and transportation links.

It is easy to say that the sustainable school location is in the neighborhood where the children live. But social, educational, and historical realities may mean that neighborhood schools in a given community are not equitable or no longer provide the range of choices in educational approaches that can help different children thrive. Alternatively, new housing may be developed at low density or in sensitive areas where additional development could be problematic. For these reasons, a sustainable approach to school location could include school busing, cooperation with municipal busing, biking, and carpools.

School locations often outlast the specific circumstances that exist at the time of their creation. Thus, family needs might require greater distances to be traveled now. At a planning level, a reasonable distribution of schools throughout residential neighborhoods, and perhaps even with some specialty schools in center business districts, offers a community the infrastructure that could make it possible to reduce car trips to school in the future. Similarly, in many suburban communities that are short on parks, such distribution also can ensure that the school grounds are available for sports and play after school and can serve the wider community.

The sustainable school site is:

- Central to the community it serves.
- Linked to walking and bike-friendly routes.
- Outside sensitive habitat.
- Coordinated with existing transportation, water, waste, and energy networks.

Social Forces

In 1954, the United States Supreme Court ruled in *Brown v. Board of Education* that racially separate school systems were inherently unequal. The majority opinion argued:

> Today, education is perhaps the most important function of state and local governments. Compulsory school attendance laws and the great expenditures for education both demonstrate our recognition of the importance of education to our democratic society. . . . Today it is a principal instrument in awakening the child to cultural values, in preparing him for later professional training, and in helping him to adjust normally to his environment.

This is just one example of the way schools have served both as a vehicle and as a battleground for social change. Any school reflects the ideological viewpoint of its community. Whether that community seeks to create an inwardly reflective place where students are sheltered from their surroundings, a strictly functional place where students meet standards and

▲ An outdoor gathering place will focus the school community at Druk White Lotus School in Ladakh, India. *Source: Arup Associates*

▶ Repetitive classroom wings embody the functionality, efficiency, and conformity of 1950s California. *Source: Google Earth*

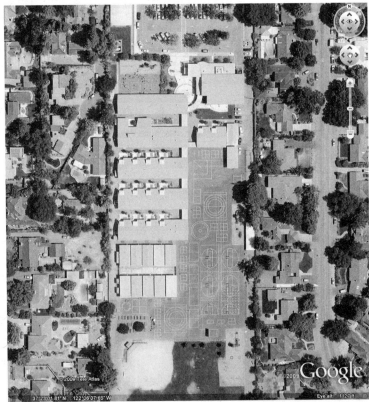

The Bows & Beaus Square Dance Club meets in the Loyola Elementary School multipurpose room. *Source: Bows & Beaus Square Dancing Club*

learn to fit into organized society, or the grove of trees where Plato and Socrates met to learn through questioning, school forms are loaded with ideas.

Many of the organizations active in the community have missions that overlap with those of schools. After-school programs providing both recreation and tutoring are obvious examples. Such programs extend the usefulness of the significant investment of money, resources, and embodied energy that is a school. Joint use of elements of the campus may extend beyond programs for children if adults use the facilities at night; if fields, playgrounds, gyms, auditoriums, and libraries are used during the weekends and summers. Such intensified use reduces the number of facilities that must be built to serve the entire community, saving energy and saving money.

The sustainable school brings its own ideas. Through sustainability, human beings hope to adapt themselves to their surroundings in a way that will enable them and the plants and animals around them to continue to thrive over many generations. This idea, in the tradition of the other ideas that have given schools form, will cause a different kind of campus to take shape.

School as Campus

School design differs from many other building types in that it commonly involves a substantial surrounding site. Sustainable site design decreases the impact of the development on local and regional hydrology, climate, and habitat. Just as a school could be neutral with respect to the electric grid, a school site could be thought of as neutral with respect to existing hydrology and habitat. But while electric grid neutrality is a straightforward equation of energy demand versus energy conservation and on-site energy generation (e.g., solar panels), environmental neutrality is rarely simple. The ecological web is deeper, denser, and much less understood. Research into the location of the site within the local natural world should be as

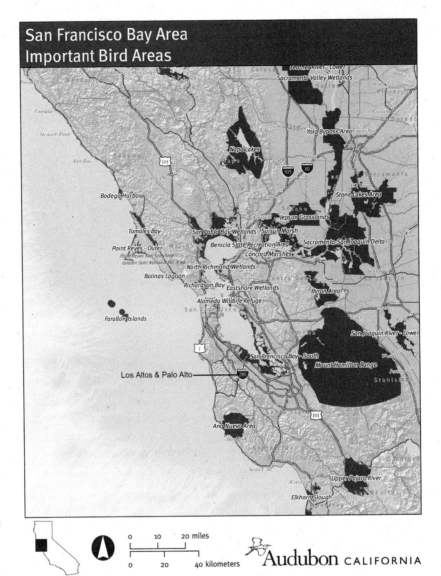

San Francisco Bay Area
Important Bird Areas

Los Altos & Palo Alto

0   10   20 miles

0   20   40 kilometers

Audubon CALIFORNIA

Los Altos School District and Palo Alto Unified School District are also home to the threatened western snowy plover. *Source: Audubon California*

much a part of site analysis as access, views, and wind and solar orientation.

This approach opens an opportunity for the design of the campus to express a relationship between the built environment and the natural system within which it occurs. Actions such as siting buildings and grading to disturb less of the existing topography, preserving existing trees and streams, planting more and paving less uniquely teach that sustainability is broader than a reduction in utility bills. The design of the school site and building can demonstrate a partnership with the physical place at a regional and a climatic level and in the specifics of coexisting with native plants and animals.

Roof forms evoke the mountains beyond.
Source: Patkau Architects, John Patkau

According to Patkau Architects, the design of the Seabird Island School in British Columbia responded to the belief of the Seabird Island Band "that the first purpose of their educational program is to foster the aboriginal culture of the Salish people of the Pacific Northwest."[5] The band's rootedness in the site is a major influence on the form of the school and the design of both buildings and grounds. In its connection to the adjacent village open space and to the mountain environment, the school could be in no other place.

In addition to the conceptual qualities of the site, school sites can have large practical impacts. Depending on the climate, the campus may use extensive water for irrigation. Extensive blacktop areas create heat islands. Site lighting is a substantial portion of the electricity consumed, much of it wasted in lighting up the sky rather than the ground. Weed and pest management on the campus introduce volumes of chemicals. Limits on these impacts should be established in the goal-setting portion of the project.

It is commonplace to think about the impacts the site will have on the building: views, prevailing winds, solar gain or daylighting, noise from highways or other neighboring uses. Buildings also have impacts on the site. Buildings can screen open areas from too much sun or wind. Building roofs can be a source of water or, as in green roofs, a part of the ecology. There is an argument to be made for multistory buildings because of their reduced footprint, but there is also an argument to be made for single-story buildings with their potential for integrating interior and exterior space and easier daylighting.

The hierarchy of spaces outside the building can range from expansive playing fields to more intimately scaled outdoor rooms where a small group of children can read or play. Sensitive use of the buildings to define the spaces around and between them is a key part of the design of successful campuses. At the scale of most schools, the character of a building as an object may be less important than its defining effect on the spaces that it and other buildings surround.

The buildings of this school are all connected internally. *Source: Google Earth*

Note chairs set up for an outdoor graduation. *Source: Google Earth*

Climate Considerations

Campuses that are truly adaptive to their climates look different. In a cold climate, the most energy-efficient building form is a compact, well-insulated building, often multistory to avoid extensive heat loss through the roof. A large multistory building surrounded by playing fields is the traditional solution.

In a mild climate, a pavilion approach to building could be the most energy efficient. By avoiding heat retention and surrounding buildings with shaded areas, air conditioning could be avoided. Such schools often are spread-out one-story buildings connected by outdoor walkways with outdoor lunch areas.

Hot and humid climates call for avoidance of heat gain, appropriate mechanical systems, insulation, and perhaps trying to gain benefits through excavating buildings into the cooler earth.

Climate is also a consideration in site selection. The microclimate of a site may differ from the regional climate because of wind, shade, proximity to water, or proximity to built-up or planted areas. The building/site strategy responds to climate, and ideally site selection can too. In hot climates, breezes are good; in cold climates, winds are bad; and in all climates, the immediate surroundings need to be considered.

Solar Orientation

Solar orientation is a major influence on building design, but it is also a factor in designing the integrated site. Most schools incorporate a recreational break into the school day. In a moderate climate, lunch and recess can be primarily outdoors. In a continental climate with extremes of heat and cold, there will be seasonal needs for interior eating and play. But where

Semirecessed buildings take advantage of the reduced temperature swings of the earth. *Source: Loretta Hall, SubsurfaceBuildings.com*

there is play, there is the need to provide a variety of microclimates: warm and sunny enough for sitting and socializing and shady enough for relief in hot weather. Coordinating planting, building siting, and context contributes to the variety of spaces.

Additional uses of the site, such as for edible school gardens that need direct sun or for photovoltaic panel arrays that also need direct sun, may add other factors to solar orientation considerations. The specifics of adapting building site and form to solar orientation to optimize daylighting, solar heating, or solar heat gain avoidance also influence the site.

Small Schools

In a one-room schoolhouse, the teacher knew every child and every child's family. Each child progressed at his or her own rate, because there was no delineation

Children eat lunch outdoors under umbrellas. *Source: Gelfand Partners Architects*

◀ This flow battery can store 2000 kilowatts of energy with deep discharging and rapid recharging. *Source: Prudent Energy Inc. VRB-ESS™*

▶ Swing classrooms (center) can serve either learning community, depending on enrollment. *Source: Gelfand Partners Architects*

by class or grade level. But options to advance into specialty areas of which the teacher had no knowledge were limited. Sports, music, and art were nonexistent or had to take into account vastly different capabilities on the part of the population of children.

Schools have swung between the ideal of the very small school to the ideal of extremely large comprehensive high schools with thousands of students. The arguments in favor of increasing size include economies of scale in everything from administration to procurement of supplies and services. In terms of sustainability, the very large school might be more capable of running sophisticated HVAC and electrical systems. It might be seen as having more impact and therefore deserving more attention and investment.

As an example, the Los Angeles Community College system plans to take itself entirely off the grid through a sophisticated combination of central plants generating electricity through solar hot water that also runs heating and absorptive air conditioning, gener-

ating electricity through roof-mounted photovoltaic panels for lighting and plug loads, and a further selection of wind turbines and room-size batteries. This plan requires a highly professional operations and maintenance group.

In educational terms, large schools are seen as having the potential to offer greater numbers of classes, programs, and services. But this view is now conflicting with research that shows that the greatest predictor of K–12 student success in the United States after family income, especially in urban areas, is a smaller school, defined as one with fewer than 400 students. Students in smaller schools may even outperform students in smaller classes.[6]

This research has encouraged many districts to develop new, smaller schools and to experiment with breaking down large schools into smaller ones on the same site. The strategies that a designer might take to reinforce the identity of these smaller communities can be a powerful force in planning the school cam-

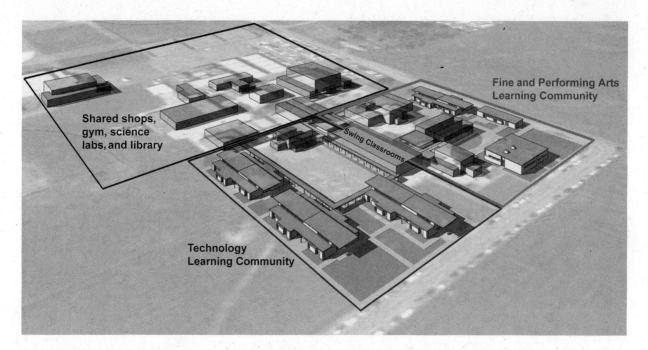

Shared shops, gym, science labs, and library

Fine and Performing Arts Learning Community

Swing Classrooms

Technology Learning Community

pus. Creating a hierarchy of spaces on the campus can be the designer's contribution to the creation of a more personally scaled environment.

Trends in education have changed over time. Part of sustainability is designing a school site that can adapt to changing ideas. This is sometimes described as the mitten fit rather than the glove fit. Rather than design a site that can be used only as three small schools, it might be better to design a site that offers three smaller communities that could relate to the larger one in a number of ways.

FUNDING THE SUSTAINABLE SCHOOL

The priority of school construction programs typically has been housing students in new schools quickly enough to accommodate rising enrollments in growing communities. This effort must be consistent with a budget that is acceptable to the tax- or fee-paying developers, homeowners, businesses, and voters. Even independent schools rarely have a rate of financial return that makes construction of a school a profit-making enterprise for the sponsoring body. The arguments that are put forward to justify sustainable design in other building types—lower life cycle costs, marketing advantages, quick payback in maintenance or energy costs—all run into structural problems in the way schools are funded, built, and run.

Capital Funding

Like politics, planning schools is mastering the art of the possible. Public schools are funded through a variety of mechanisms, almost all of which draw a bright line between the investment necessary to build a new school or perform a major modernization and the separate ongoing costs of maintaining and operating the school. The resources necessary to make a capital investment could be borrowed (bonds) or come from general funds (taxes) or from fees levied on developers of other real estate that might generate impact such as higher enrollments (impact fees).

From the sustainability viewpoint, the salient characteristics of all these mechanisms are that they predate sustainable thinking, come with various limitations, and are difficult to connect with life cycle cost analysis. This kind of capital funding is also infrequent and imposes real restraints on the ability of school designers to use anything experimental or potentially difficult to replace.

Private schools differ in the sources of their capital, from institutional sources within large organizations such as parochial schools, to the capital campaigns of individual independent schools. But they share some of the same traits: infrequency, restrictions, and concern for the consequences of requiring expensive

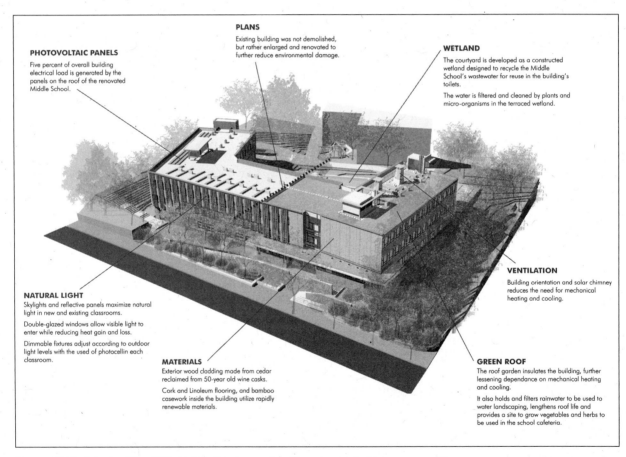

PLANS
Existing building was not demolished, but rather enlarged and renovated to further reduce environmental damage.

PHOTOVOLTAIC PANELS
Five percent of overall building electrical load is generated by the panels on the roof of the renovated Middle School.

WETLAND
The courtyard is developed as a constructed wetland designed to recycle the Middle School's wastewater for reuse in the building's toilets.

The water is filtered and cleaned by plants and micro-organisms in the terraced wetland.

NATURAL LIGHT
Skylights and reflective panels maximize natural light in new and existing classrooms.

Double-glazed windows allow visible light to enter while reducing heat gain and loss.

Dimmable fixtures adjust according to outdoor light levels with the used of photocellin each classroom.

MATERIALS
Exterior wood cladding made from cedar reclaimed from 50-year old wine casks.

Cork and Linoleum flooring, and bamboo casework inside the building utilize rapidly renewable materials.

VENTILATION
Building orientation and solar chimney reduces the need for mechanical heating and cooling.

GREEN ROOF
The roof garden insulates the building, further lessening dependance on mechanical heating and cooling.

It also holds and filters rainwater to be used to water landscaping, lengthens roof life and provides a site to grow vegetables and herbs to be used in the school cafeteria.

Stewart Middle School at Sidwell Friends School makes a point of its many sustainable features. *Source: Courtesy Sidwell Friends School*[7]

maintenance or replacement in the future. Private schools may be more capable than public institutions of accounting for reserves for such predictable future needs as replacing roofs. They may also have a greater need to compete for enrollment through attractive new facilities and programs.

Conflicts that must be recognized exist in both private and public situations. A real estate developer may want to hold school impact fees to the minimum to protect profits while at the same time making a new school look good to potential homeowners. A private school may compete for students with other schools and have a fundraising campaign based on providing the science labs and computers that parents feel their children need to get into the right college. Facilities staff may have a fixed financing capability and a job that is defined by delivering projects where the first cost is on budget.

Still, there is little conflict in the dream of a school or school district to use capital investment in facilities to lower operating and maintenance costs. Lowering these costs frees general funds for expenses related to the core mission of the school: learning. In this dream, sustainability plays a part. In particular, as sustainable school campuses lower energy costs, they pay back their institutions year after year after year.

Life Cycle Costing

The analysis that supports such choices is life cycle costing. This analysis compares the costs of installation, operation, and disposal over the entire life of a material or system to the total costs of another material or system. Life cycle costing reveals real costs in a way first-cost analyses do not. First-cost analysis is simply a comparison of the immediate price tag for furnishing and installing particular items.

While it is obvious that life cycle costs are more accurate in terms of the economic burden of a system, this analysis is often difficult to apply. The first increase in investment is the analysis itself. Typically, the design team has expertise in specifying systems and features but not so much in predicting the cost of their operation and maintenance. Assistance is available: the facilities group at the school, some utilities, and some foundation grants to support a professional performing the analysis. Alternatively, the costs of doing the analysis are added to the design fees for the project and come out of the project budget.

Most analyses require a projection of conventional energy costs and an estimate of the amount of maintenance time and materials. These projections and estimates are often subjective and always concern events in the future. With a building that is meant to last a generation, the projections extend into an unknowable future.

These limitations are addressed by shortening the time period. Perhaps it is not the entire life cycle that is decisive. Five- and 10-year horizons can be more convincing. But even when the logic of a low life cycle cost is undeniable, it is difficult to overcome a pure lack of money on the front end of a project. The savings in operation do not automatically pay back the fund that pays for construction. That is where life cycle analysis can help in setting fundraising goals and strategies such as rebates, philanthropic support, and the like.

In planning sustainable buildings, the argument often is made that a dollar spent today will save two dollars in the future. Over the life of the project, energy efficiency may pay back an investment many times. In a broader sense, the life cycle of a construction material includes its extraction, manufacture, transportation, use, and later disposal or reuse. The

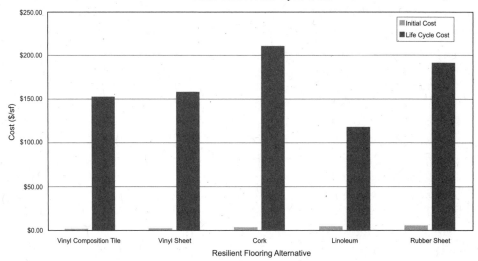

First cost is a minor component in the life cycle costs of these flooring materials. *Source: Helena Moussatche and Jennifer Languell* [8]

From "Flooring materials – life-cycle costing for educational facilities," Helena Moussatche and Jennifer Languell, *Facilities,* Vol. 19, No. 10, 2001, p. 341. MCB University Press. ISSN 0263-2772

costs implicit in all these phases are real costs to the society as a whole. But it is challenging to build them all into the decision process for a school project.

Supplementary Funding for Sustainability

Integrated design does not cost extra and indeed may save money. But some sustainable features or materials do add initial costs to the project. Supplementary funding sources can help make sustainable features affordable. Most utilities offer incentive or rebate programs for energy-efficiency improvements either specifically targeted at schools or within commercial construction programs. Some states have high-performance school grants. Through tax-credit incentive programs, for-profit corporations can get savings on installation of alternative energy sources, such as photovoltaic panels.

A mechanism known as a Power Purchase Agreement allows a corporation in the United States to in-stall photovoltaic panels on the roofs of a school at little or no cost to the school in return for a guaranteed rate of power purchase on the part of the school, thereby holding energy costs at or below market for the period of the agreement, and leaving the campus with the panels at the end. This does not directly transfer capital investment into large operating savings as does, for instance, installing photovoltaic (PV) panels with school money and then ceasing to pay electric bills. But it allows the school to use its own money where it was originally allocated.

Reform of utility rate structures would assist schools, which could generate a lot of extra power during the summer when their own needs are low and when demand in the marketplace, due to air conditioning, is high. If they actually could sell that energy, or at least offset winter needs, at the summer rates, this would be a major change in the feasibility of PV generation. As discussions continue in the realm of carbon offsets, opportunities may arise to help schools.

John Swett High School, built in 1927, needs a modern heating system. *Source: Gelfand Partners Architects*

An example is the expansion of the Conoco Phillips refinery in California; the project was allowed on the basis that the corporation would make investments to offset the production of greenhouse gases that its expansion would entail. One of those grants may finance high-performance upgrades on a new heating system at John Swett High School.

In addition to the major sources of capital and institutionalized utility rebates and incentives, sustainability is an attractive feature for which to seek individual, community, or foundation support. School gardens, farms, environmental study areas, and tree planting are all areas where individual support can make things possible. A popular school fundraiser—selling individual imprinted bricks—can help substitute permeable paving for asphalt while also netting extra dollars for the project.

Local businesses often provide schools with important support. Such support usually is characterized by a certain amount of visibility. Businesses may have a desire to hire workers requiring little investment in

Blank bricks also can be swapped for personalized bricks as the campaign goes on. *Source: Gelfand Partners Architects*

training, a desire to show parents who may be customers that they support the kids, or the desire to keep employees who may be parents committed to their jobs. For these reasons, local business support may be more easily recruited for PV panels than for insulation.

Fundraising is an area where school communities have experience and capabilities. Usually the local school scale is more appropriate to funding supplementary features than funding the bulk of the project. The community organizing and brainstorming part of defining sustainability can naturally transition into community-based fundraising. Community organizing, and sometimes fundraising itself are commonly funded through small community foundation or civic grants.

In addition to the bake sales, school fairs, dinners and auctions, Christmas tree sales, direct appeals, and other events that are staples of school fundraising, sustainability offers a specific hook. Buying and naming trees, bricks, solar panels, bike racks, shade structures, raised planter beds, and the like can all tap into the support that a community feels for its sustainable school while making sustainability more pervasive in the school design.

As the community develops a real stake in the ideas that will become a part of the sustainable school, their ownership can extend to helping raise money. It does not need to go to a specifically sustainable feature but may free money to be spent on things like lighting controls, which are hard to fund in a unitary way. For example, after a highly participatory design process for Claire Lilienthal School in San Francisco, engaged neighbors whose children were long grown contributed the money necessary to stock the new school library with books.

A community that is excited about creating a sustainable school is a powerful thing. Money should not be the reason to exclude sustainability.

- Grants are available to support technical assistance in community organizing.
- Grants are available to support technical assistance additional to base design tasks.
- Public/private and profit/not-for-profit partnerships can make large systems possible.
- Fundraising opportunities should be part of early project planning.

Neighbors stepped up when the new campus opened with no additional funding for books. *Source: Gelfand Partners Architects*

Seabird Island School, Agassiz, British Columbia, Canada

Patkau Architects

PLANNING: A COMMUNITY-BASED PROCESS

Sea Bird Island is the home of the Seabird Island Indian Band. The island is located in the Fraser River Delta 120 kilometers east of Vancouver and three kilometers northeast of the town of Agassiz. It is the service hub for several First Nations communities. The client was the Seabird Island Band Department of Public Works. The majority of the construction workers came from Seabird and neighboring communities. The architects used the traditional language of heavy timber construction in design and created a 1:20 scale model of the school to clarify the framing for the community team.

The school forms one side of a loose village commons. The school is by far the largest structure there, and mediates the scale change with an extended low front porch. The vertical extension of its columns gives it a strong personality where creating a tall arcade would have been overbearing. Viewed from a variety of angles, community members see "a canoe, an eagle, a clam, an owl and a salmon" suggested in the design

The Seabird Island School is a vital presence on the community commons. *Source: Google Earth*

▶ The existing swale passes across the front of the school.
A pedestrian bridge lines up with the entrance to the school.
Source: Patkau Architects

▼ Circulation space in the school provides informal gathering
space for the school and the larger community. *Source: Patkau
Architects*

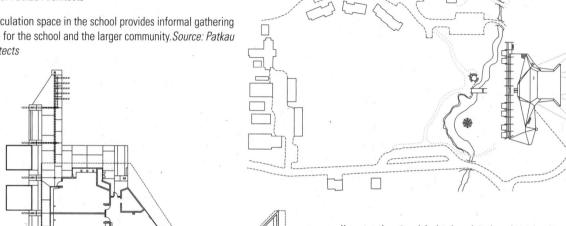

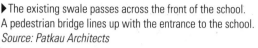

according to the Seabird Island School Web site.
The architect also felt a need to bring something
to life in the project. "The space of the island, a
flat delta of agricultural land, seemed very much
like a great room. We felt that the building which
was to inhabit this room should have an animated
personality, something that could be perceived on
a naïve level as a 'being' of some kind."[a]

DESIGN: INTEGRATION OF EDUCATIONAL, CULTURAL, AND SUSTAINABLE VALUES

The school serves K–10 children and satisfies the
ambition of the band to bring education into local
control. It is 23,000 square feet. The children can
use the commons for play. The kindergarten also
has a dedicated play area. Various elements of
band life are built into the school landscape, including salmon drying racks and a fire pit.

The structure is an interpretation of the traditional
system used by the Pacific Northwest peoples.
To achieve the greater scale of the modern
function, it incorporates a concrete beam and pile

▶ Extension of the columns at the front portico of the school create a strong presence while the comfortable height of the portico is scaled to the school users and daylighting scheme. *Source: Patkau Architects, James Dow*

▼ Most of the construction workers were members of local communities. The wood construction detailing is based on the heavy timber construction heritage of the Pacific coast. *Source: Patkau Architects, James Dow*

foundation and steel connections as well as the heavy timber parallel columns and beams. The organization of the school is a simple linear layout. The double-loaded diagram does not limit the design to banal corridor space but allows formal and informal breakout and gathering spaces, views out, and opportunities for the school community to share activities within the spaces.

Daylighting is a major consideration, affecting not only the openings but the materials adjacent to them. The cladding system uses translucent white-stained plywood panels to reflect light from the snow-clad mountains into the building. On the south side, a large clerestory with an overhang gathers daylight for the building. On the east and south sides, large overhangs block sunlight from entering in the summer to limit the amount of heat in the building.

Large roof overhangs also shelter the school from the extreme winter winds common to the area. These winds also led the architects to locate the gym at the back of the school, where its mass can help block them.

[a]Mark Dudek, *Architecture of Schools: The New Learning Environments* (St. Louis. Architectural Press, 2000), p. 138

Druk White Lotus School, Ladakh, India

Arup Associates

PLANNING: AN INTERNATIONAL PARTNERSHIP MATCHES VALUES

The school creates a comfortable courtyard within the expansive landscape of Ladakh.
Source: Christian Richters

Druk White Lotus School is located in Ladakh, India, a high-altitude area sometimes called Little Tibet. It is one of the few remaining areas where a traditional Tibetan Buddhist way of life is practiced. The school serves students whose families wish them to receive an education that is both grounded in local traditions and inclusive of modern science and ideas. It was designed on an essentially pro bono basis by Arup Associates. Throughout the design and construction of the school, volunteers from Arup have spent six-month periods as resident architects or engineers working with Ladakhis to help make sure that what is designed and drawn in London comes to fruition in Ladakh.

Floor levels of the buildings
and courtyard help
articulate the space and
provide separation from
the classroom windows.
Source: Arup Associates

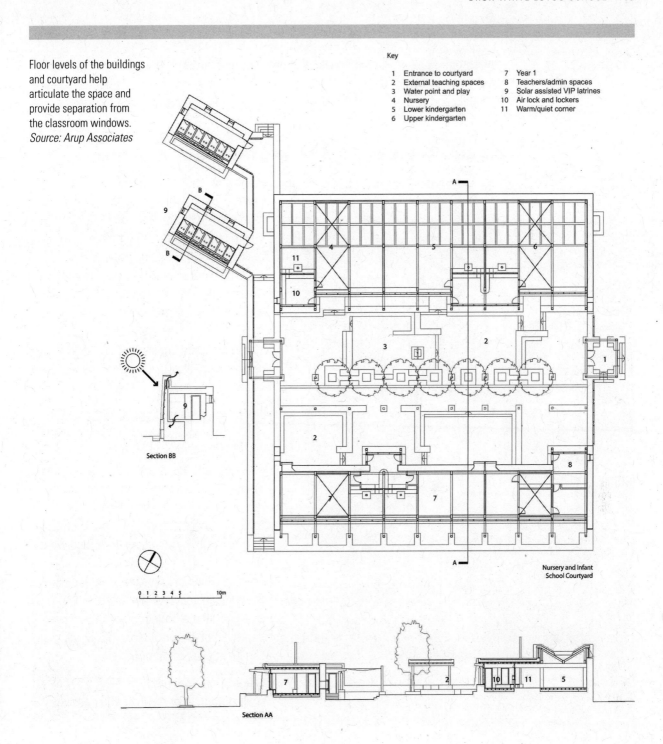

Key

1	Entrance to courtyard	7	Year 1
2	External teaching spaces	8	Teachers/admin spaces
3	Water point and play	9	Solar assisted VIP latrines
4	Nursery	10	Air lock and lockers
5	Lower kindergarten	11	Warm/quiet corner
6	Upper kindergarten		

Section BB

0 1 2 3 4 5   10m

Nursery and Infant
School Courtyard

Section AA

The school is being built in phases in an area so remote that snow cuts it off by road for up to nine months of the year. Arup engineers have worked to refine traditional building materials and systems to improve their earthquake safety, comfort, and hygiene as well as to create a campus that reflects the local culture.

DESIGN: MODERN ENGINEERING AND TRADITIONAL MATERIALS

The school is designed to be entirely sustainable by creating a completely self-regulating system for water, energy, and waste management. Like the vernacular buildings of the region, stone and mud for walls are found nearby. Arup designed a timber frame with cross bracing to greatly increase the seismic performance of the structure in this active earthquake zone. The wood used consists of timber from poplar and willow trees sourced from nearby producers.

The envelope is traditional, with a few important changes. Cavity walls are finished with granite blocks in mud mortar on the outside and traditional mudbrick masonry on the inside. This high thermal mass buffers the large day/night swings of the Ladakh climate. The roof material is made from a mix of mud and locally found wood. In addition to this, rock wool and felt are added to insulate. An aluminum and sand covering protects it from sun damage. One goal of the project is to demonstrate improvements to traditional methods that can be applied in other buildings.

The school is oriented to maximize the solar potential for daylight and passive

Daylit classrooms are created from locally sourced wood and stone.
Source: Christian Richters

The airlock and locker space helps keep classroom spaces tempered when children go in and out. *Source: Christian Richters*

solar heating. The heavy masonry walls act as trombe walls to store heat at night in cold weather and to remain cool in the day in hot weather. These features, along with the utilization of natural ventilation, greatly minimize the need for artificial heating and cooling. Arup also has helped install solar panels that charge batteries and provide energy for lighting and equipment.

Because there is very little rainfall in the area, solar energy is used to power a water system that pumps groundwater from a deep water table into a 16,000-gallon tank. This water, along with captured rainwater, is gravity fed to gardens, other planted areas, faucets, and other plumbing. The system then reuses water for irrigation so that it can be recycled. Finally, the toilets use a VIP (ventilated improved pit) system. This toilet system creates humus, which is then used as a fertilizer. No water is used in this system; instead, a solar-driven flue minimizes insects and smells.

NOTES

1. Collaborative for High Performance Schools, *Best Practices Manual*, vol. 1, 2006 ed., p. 129. www.chps.net/manual/documents/BPM_2006_Edition/CHPS_I_2006.pdf, accessed June 16, 2009.

2. Division of the State Architect, Northern California, "Grid Neutral: Electrical Independence for California Schools and Community Colleges," February 1, 2009, www.documents.dgs.ca.gov/dsa/pubs/gridneutralpub.pdf, accessed June 17, 2009.

3. Department of Health and Human Services, CDC, "Then and Now—Barriers and Solutions," February 25, 2008, www.cdc.gov/nccdphp/dnpa/kidswalk/then_and_now.htm, accessed June 12, 2009.

4. Walk to School in the USA, "Why Walk or Bicycle to School? Talking Points," June 4, 2009, www.walktoschool.org/downloads/WTS-talking-points-2009.doc, accessed June 22, 2009.

5. http://www.patkau.ca/ Seabird Island School text.

6. Bill & Melinda Gates Foundation, "Making the Case for Small Schools" (2003), www.washingtonsmallschools.org/makingthecase.pdf and www.washingtonsmallschools.org/GatesSmallSchoolsBrochure.pdf, accessed June 16, 2009.

7. Sidwell Friends School, "Transforming Sidwell Friends Middle School," October 20, 2009, www.sidwell.edu/images/support_sfs/wisconsinave_campus/greenfeatures.jpg, accessed June 12, 2009.

8. Helena Moussatche and Jennifer Languell, "Flooring Materials—Life-Cycle Costing for Educational Facilities," *Facilities* 19, No. 10 (2001): 341.

chapter 3

DESIGN STRATEGIES

INTRODUCTION

ELIZABETH BLODGETT HALL named her early college Simon's Rock after a rock on her family farm where she founded the school. From the rock one could observe all of the activities of the valley below from a peaceful and thoughtful vantage point. The rock develops meaning from context and knowledge as well as the thing itself. The rock is architecture, in the sense that it provides a place in the physical world from which to experience an idea.

People experience architecture, and the ideas of architecture, through all their senses. Their visual, aural, and tactile impressions may never rise to the level of conscious articulation, but people still have strong feelings about architectural space and architectural objects. When thinking about architecture and design, cerebral problem solving needs to be balanced by sensitivity to the highly sensory and emotional responses people have to buildings.

Elements that contribute to the perception of buildings include building form and its references, the spatial logic of the activities in the building, and the sensory qualities of the spaces.

For young children, sensory exploration is a particularly important way they understand their sur-roundings. Visual impressions and daylighting, fresh air, acoustics, textures of surfaces, and the experience of moving through a school are particularly rich ingredients in the experience of children.

Subsequent chapters analyze specific technical elements of sustainable schools, such as envelope design, heating and ventilating, daylighting, and site design. But before reducing the design to its various pieces, it is critical to look at design comprehensively and at the variety of sources that give rise to form.

INTEGRATED DESIGN

Integrated design is a key part of sustainability—all parts influence each other, as in an organic body. However, the way people experience a building is through movement and memory, not awareness of the mechanical or structural systems at work. The three-dimensional modeled bird's-eye view of a building is a great drawing for explaining relationships, but our view is closer to the worm's eye. Perhaps the fact that we almost never see an entire building at one time contributes to the difficulty in conceiving of a building as a whole.

This computer model, from a child's-eye level, also provides an X ray of the building structure. *Source: Gelfand Partners Architects*

Despite the conceptual challenge, considering the building as a whole body is a useful metaphor. Building structures provide the skeletal infrastructure or protective exoskeleton. Building skins keep out water but let through air; buildings metabolize fuels or energy inputs and maintain homeostasis within with respect to temperature, humidity, and mixtures of gases. Building sensors communicate with systems that act to adapt to changing outside conditions. Pushing and pulling the form of the building changes the amount of skin and the amount of space, the amount of energy in and out, and the amount of transparency and permeability of the skin. Integrated design balances all these consequences in optimizing a solution.

Although mechanical systems, building envelopes, and lighting are areas that are subject to specialist design, they all influence each other. Integrated design not only avoids conflicts but also amplifies the effectiveness of the constituent parts. One reason that architects model their buildings three-dimensionally during design is to test the holistic success of the design. The three-dimensional model can be viewed from many directions and in motion. It can be used to help understand how structural, mechanical, and electrical systems interact and bypass each other in space. It can help a designer understand how a single decision—creating a roof monitor, for example—affects the entire building experience and performance.

Compared to the simplest creature, buildings are primitive indeed. But rather than designing machines for learning, turning our minds to the body of learning can be a useful way to think more responsively, adaptively, and holistically.

FORMAL CONSIDERATIONS

One of the obstacles that sometimes is raised to sustainability is the notion that a sustainable school must have a certain appearance and that that appearance will not fit into the neighborhood or context. But sustainability is not limited to any one style or formal approach. Before modern engineering, modern travel, and the availability of imagery from around the world, traditional architectural styles developed in the context of local cultures, climates, and resources. The forms of buildings took very diverse paths.

Precedent

Traditional architectural styles developed before electric light and powered heating, ventilating, and air-conditioning (HVAC) systems, and by necessity they took daylight and ventilation into account. So, for example, when borrowing the form of an Italian palazzo for a school, the contemporary architect borrows a form that included a need for daylight and ventilation in its original iteration. The building works because the building form had been optimized over the years for high ceilings, cross-ventilation, and a narrow aspect from window to corridor wall. In the Mediterranean climate, the mass of the masonry also buffered temperature swings, holding the night coolness into the morning and the afternoon warmth into the evening.

Borrowing a historical style may also be meaningful for other reasons. In the example just given, the Italianate form helps to tie the idea of education to a European Renaissance precedent, itself tied to a classical original. The James Ward Public School, a Chicago landmark, is an Italianate building still in use as a public school. Chicago could not be farther from a Mediterranean climate. In this case, the formal choice was much more strongly based on the cultural reference than the functional one.

Historical precedents are still a source of formal inspiration in schools. They may refer back to European precedents such as Gothic, classical (ancient Greek or Roman), or Spanish. But they may also refer back to a country's own history, as in the Aga Khan Award–winning Sidi El-Aloui Primary School in Tunisia.

The choice of historical precedent may also be suggested by the immediate surroundings of a school, such as a location in a district where most of the buildings date from a particular era. It is not necessarily a problem for the sustainable architect to work in one of the historical languages. As noted, the form, if developed in an analogous climate, may already have useful characteristics. The style is unlikely, however, to take into account modern systems and structural approaches.

James Ward Public School, built in 1875, is the oldest Chicago school building still in use as a school. *Source: City of Chicago, IL*

The facade of the Sidi El-Aloui Primary School resembles that of a house located opposite the school. *Source: Aga Khan Award for Architecture*

Context and Function

Another approach to developing building form begins with the site context and develops an integrated response of building form, materials, and systems. Another Aga Khan Award–winning school demonstrates this approach while still making allusions to the cultural context of the school.

This three-room primary school in Gando, Burkina Faso, uses concrete beams to span the larger dimensions of the classrooms and mud walls. A lightweight steel roof that shades the building provides for air flow. It is raised from the ground, as are traditional granaries. The form is simple and elegant and clearly demonstrates, without the need for literal references to other buildings, that this is an important community building. In this example, orientation to the sun and wind, available materials, available skills, climate, and the site context influence the formal parameters for the building.

The building is not determined by its constraints or context, but the range of possibilities is narrowed.

The roof, walls, and frames are all distinctively expressed. Their logic is both structural and visual. The additional refinements of the steel roof also suggest the benefits to be gained through education and access to new materials and technology.

The designer of the school, Diebedo Francis Kere, was the first person from Gando to study abroad. His approach can generate form in campuses with much more complication. Solutions to daylight, shading, and ventilation create a visible language of screens and louvers, shelters, shelves, and roofs. The structural system can be hidden or expressed, but it will influence the form of the building because it controls the openings in the walls. A campus including a variety of functions—classrooms, multiuse building, office, library—will require different sizes of spaces, different openings, and therefore different building types. Often different requirements coexist within a single building to house these functions. They will also influence the choice of structural systems.

The air space between the roof and ceiling of the primary school provides for cooling air flow. Spaces between the classrooms evoke traditional arbors (known as *zandi*) characteristic of Gando. *Source: Aga Khan Award for Architecture*

The classroom in the primary school has a step up to make the blackboard more visible. *Source: Aga Khan Award for Architecture*

Glazing on the Blach Gym is articulated differently in response to its orientation toward the sun. *Source: Gelfand Partners Architects*

Building Type

Building type is different from building form. In building codes, *building type* describes the structural system and its combustibility. Building type in a broader sense influences form most strongly in the contrast between the two dominant structural types, frame buildings and bearing-wall buildings. Frame buildings generally use wood, steel, or concrete framing. Structural steel and concrete frames can be systems with posts and beams welded or braced together in a variety of ways, while wood or steel studs generally are used in frame walls made of many studs that are connected so as to distribute building loads among them or to provide lateral bracing to wood posts and beams. Bearing-wall buildings are generally concrete, masonry, or brick. The choice of building type needs to respond to the needs of the school rather than the other way around.

The effect of building type on the form and approach to the building is chiefly in the cost, flexibility, and amount of openings possible in the walls. If the walls are holding the building up, they are diffi-

cult to change later, and may also have limited area that can be open. The technical problem of spanning large open spaces or holes in masonry walls gave rise to domes and arches as well as building types where floors or roofs could be of light frame construction bearing on masonry walls. But in addition to their structural characteristics, masonry buildings have markedly different thermal performance and often offer great durability and fire resistance.

Buildings that reproduce the look of masonry domes and arches can be accomplished in light frame construction. Like the Italianate school in Chicago, these choices are not made because of the functional characteristics but because of the associations of the form. A building of this type remains frame construction. It will function thermally and structurally as a frame building. Thermal and structural performance can be separated. A frame building can also have a masonry, rammed earth, or adobe infill wall system that makes it operate thermally like a bearing-wall building.

Visual Expression

The surrounding buildings and landforms are often cited as another inspiration for building form. The expanses of the prairies of the American Midwest inspired Frank Lloyd Wright to develop the horizontal Prairie style of architecture, while the presence of nearby mountains sometimes can seem to call for an architecture where the vertical is accentuated.

In established towns and cities, the neighboring buildings can provide either a pattern into which a new building can recede or a background from which the building can stand out. In school design, such an expressive choice relates to the way the school itself is seen. Schools are in an ambiguous relationship to the public realm. In a sense, children are the most private part of a family, even when they are out of the home and in a school. Many schools are concerned that children should not be exposed to prying eyes or to dis-

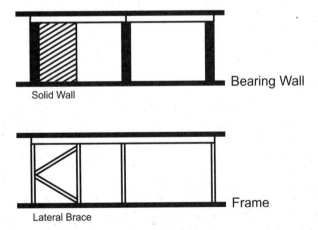

Solid Wall

Bearing Wall

Lateral Brace

Frame

In bearing-wall buildings openings are limited. Frame buildings offer more flexibility. Wood-frame buildings also limit openings due to plywood over walls that provide lateral bracing. *Source: Gelfand Partners Architects*

traction or temptation. Yet schools are frequented by many members of the community, serve the community, and reflect the community's values. Whether the conclusion is to blend in with existing neighbors or to stand out, the building form helps both express and achieve the desired relationship.

Sustainability itself is a source of formal inspiration. In addition to the functional benefits of sunscreens, ventilation, solar panels, wind scoops, and the like, the visible commitment to sustainability has its own appeal. Biophilia, biomimicry, and organic forms are examples of design approaches that make apparent the commitment to an ecologically based sustainability. Such formal choices can also be highly personal while still being meaningful to many people beyond the author. The organic metaphors of Friedrich Hundertwasser's work transform a prosaic German Democratic Republic prototype in Wittenberg into a romantic evocation of the richness of the biosphere.

The form of the Seabird Island School recalls the surrounding mountains. *Source: Patkau Architects, James Dow*

This Hundertwasser school is a remodel. *Source: Doris Antony, under GFDL*

SPATIAL CONSIDERATIONS

Space planning of sustainable schools adds a number of factors to the functional space planning of schools. Without attempting to review all of school space planning, the functional adjacencies that derive from an analysis of the program and schedule of school activities also affect the ease with which sustainable strategies can be adopted.

A primary strategy in saving energy is to run systems only when they are required. One's body does this by prioritizing the brain and the torso when it is cold out and sending increased circulation to the limbs only when needed. Lights, heat, and cooling are not needed, or are needed in a very limited way, in unoccupied spaces. At one extreme, school buildings with boilers and radiators or convectors could have heating systems that run 24/7 365 days a year. At the other extreme are schools where every space has its own HVAC system and the opportunity to control each one separately.

Zoning building spaces by functions so that those with similar schedules are close to each other facilitates keeping only the appropriate parts of the building lit and thermally comfortable. Even if a classroom has its own controls, the lighting and comfort systems for halls and restrooms still need to be on when that classroom is in use. Separating spaces that are used frequently by the community is helpful not only for energy conservation but also for security. Such spaces include multipurpose rooms, gyms, auditoriums, libraries, and after-school daycare or tutoring spaces. Associated restrooms are usually part of the management challenge.

If a recreation program is running on school grounds after school hours, there is often a desire to have access to restrooms or a rainy-day multipurpose space. That space should be able to be accessed without opening the entire school building to unsupervised use. It should also be conditioned separately. Turning on and off the systems either remotely or on a timed basis confines conditioning to the required hours. In extreme climates, the timing needs to take into account warm-up and cool-down lag time.

Decades-old assumptions about "traditional" separation of uses and the need for dedicated spaces for intermittent uses can lead to overbuilding of a school. Building less can be the most sustainable solution of all.

It is good sustainable practice to facilitate joint use of school facilities as much as possible because joint use reduces the number of facilities needed to serve the various community needs and enables the entire community to build less. Even if community uses do not exist at the time that a school is designed, they are very likely to be desirable sometime in the life of the

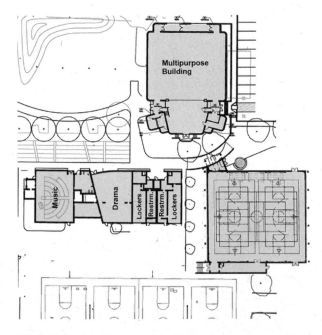

The Blach Gym is a joint-use facility for the school and community. Lockers and restrooms, or restrooms only, can be opened for community use. *Source: Gelfand Partners Architects*

building. Structures that are designed so that the entire building must be opened and conditioned in order to use part of it are often a hindrance to the efficient use of parts of the facility outside normal hours.

UNIQUE K–12 CONSIDERATIONS

Budget

Design for schools faces a set of competing needs. Schools are institutional buildings, assumed to have a service life of a generation or at least equal to the term of the bond raising the money, but generally they are not given the kind of investment that is made in other institutions, such as universities or museums. Schools typically have limited funds for maintenance and operations and a user group that is constantly testing their surroundings, if not occasionally indulging in destruction for its own sake. Additionally, schools need to assure safety from natural disasters (earthquakes, tsunamis, etc.), and security from predatory people either within or without. Schools stand in for parents and homes by providing warmth and guidance during the school day. All of this adds up to a high demand for robust construction and strong and humane design accomplished with just enough resources.

Robustness

There should be no wrong way to use a classroom just as there should be no wrong way to use a play structure. Teachers and children inhabit school spaces very thoroughly, hanging artwork from every projection, taping or pinning projects and posters to every wall surface available, raising plants and animals in the windows and in front of the vents, storing arcane ephemera on every horizontal surface.

Such active use impacts choice of windows, glazing, and other materials. Children throw baseballs at

Projects and inspirations occupy every space in this active classroom
Source: Gelfand Partners Architects

louvers to check their aim and to hear the noise when they hit them. Windows get yanked open, dangled from, and shoved. If thermally broken, do they have the same structural integrity? Window glazing gets broken all the time. Can the envelope be improved without depending on specialized glass that needs to be ordered?

Hygiene

School restrooms are also subject to amazingly hard use. In focus groups for high school restrooms, children said that their parents taught them to kick the flush valves rather than touch any of the surfaces in a public restroom. Potential solutions to vandalism such as stainless steel mirrors offended parents who thought they made schools look like prisons. Maintenance people said there should be no mirrors over sinks because of the hair products that clog drains. These are all attitudes that need to be considered along with the embodied energy, renewables, and recycled content.

Acoustics

CONTRIBUTOR: Ethan C. Salter, Charles M. Salter Associates, acoustical consultants in many building types and environments including wide experience in sustainable schools. Mr. Salter's paper "Achieving Acoustical Satisfaction in a Green Building" has been published in *The Journal of the Acoustical Society of America* 120, No. 5 (November 2006): 3185.

1. INTRODUCTION TO SUSTAINABLE SCHOOL ACOUSTICS

High-performance "green" building design has been one of the most progressive steps for the architecture, engineering, and construction industries in decades. This initiative has been compelled by the imperatives of climate change, carbon footprints, and other external factors but also in part due to research into building occupant safety, comfort, and satisfaction in green buildings.

In addition, everyone involved in the design and construction of buildings has become more aware of the life cycle costs of various equipment, building materials, and methods; now, informed decisions can account for not only first costs, but also life cycle investments for buildings.

However, projects can be highly rated (by green building rating systems) in terms of energy efficiency, materials reclamation, or indoor air quality but receive low marks from their occupants in post-occupancy evaluations, due to poor acoustics. This is due in part because the acoustical design "constituency" was not adequately considered in the formation of the rating systems, whereas other constituencies, such as energy use reduction, site selection, or indoor environmental quality, were involved.

This lack of demonstrated acoustical performance has led to a certain level of dissatisfaction with the acoustical environment in these new cutting-edge projects. School design standards have now been developed, based on extensive research into how the acoustical environment affects learning, speech communication, and knowledge retention. As green building rating systems have diversified and become more sophisticated, these school acoustical standards have been incorporated as prerequisite requirements for certification.

Adopting acoustical standards for green buildings is not the end of the process but merely one step in the continuum from design through occupancy. Ongoing education into acoustics design is still necessary for green building owners, designers, and builders. Each choice made by the designers and owners to support the project's sustainability mission can have acoustical consequences.

2. ACOUSTICAL DESIGN CONSIDERATIONS IN SCHOOLS

An acceptable acoustical environment is obviously important to a high-performing learning environment. As a part of school design, the three primary acoustical issues for classroom design are: background noise, room acoustics, and sound isolation. These issues affect speech comprehension and related factors.

2.1 Background Noise

Excessive noise in classrooms interferes with knowledge retention, concentration, mental health, and ongoing success of students and teachers. Studies show that high background noise levels can affect student test scores, and also may cause students to become disinterested or discouraged.[1]

When background noise in a classroom becomes excessive, students have to expend greater effort to hear and understand what the teacher or their classmates are saying. Researchers have determined that speech intelligibility strongly correlates with the signal-to-noise ratio. Listeners must discern the "signal" (i.e., their teacher) over the "noise" (i.e., other students, mechanical ventilation systems, or vehicular traffic outside). Over time, extra effort due to high levels of noise causes fatigue, distraction, and loss of concentration. Classrooms with such acoustical deficiencies can pose barriers to communication and student development.

Comprehending speech in noisy environments can be even more challenging for students who are learning English as a second language or have hearing impairments. High background noise levels in classrooms cause teachers to raise their voices, leading to vocal fatigue. Students in the back of the room, or near air outlets or windows, still may not hear information adequately.

Primary sources of background noise in schools are mechanical systems (e.g., ventilation systems, plumbing) and exterior sources (e.g., vehicular traffic, trains, or aircraft). Controlling ventilation system noise can be challenging for school owners, in part due to budgetary considerations or "standardized" designs. Technically, engineering quiet-enough ventilation systems is not difficult.

Schools in urban areas are susceptible to excessive environmental noise intrusion. Noise transfer through exterior windows is the typical weak link in the exterior building envelope.

Research by the American National Standards Institute (ANSI)[2] shows that to improve speech intelligibility, classroom background noise levels should be limited to 35 dBA[3] or less. Assuming that a teacher at the front of the classroom has an average speech sound level of 67 dBA at three feet away; in the back of the classroom, the teacher's speech sound level would be reduced to about 50 dBA.

For "optimum" speech intelligibility, background noise levels in schools should be at least 15 dBA quieter than the speech level (i.e., the signal-to-noise ratio). Since a 10 dBA change in noise level is perceived as a doubling of loudness, this would result in the teacher's voice being more than twice as loud as any other source of steady noise.

Background noise: This figure shows that high background noise level causes the teacher to shout yet students in the rear of the classroom still cannot hear. *Source: Charles M. Salter Associates*

(continued)

2.2 Room Acoustics

Reverberation is the persistence of a sound in a room after a sound source has ceased. Acousticians quantify the reverberant qualities of a room by measuring the time it takes for sound to decay to near-inaudibility; the time is dependent on both the room's size and its surface materials. One can hear this effect by clapping your hands in a room: In smaller rooms with lots of absorptive finishes, the clapping sound will vanish almost immediately; in large rooms with mostly hard surfaces, the sound reflections created by clapping can be audible for a second or more. Now imagine someone talking in the reverberant room. The effect of this reverberation degrades intelligibility of the signal, as students are trying to discern the speech.

ANSI standard S12.60, "Acoustical Performance Criteria, Design Requirements and Guidelines for Schools," recommends that reverberation times, especially in the speech frequency bands, be controlled to 0.6 seconds or less for standard-size classrooms under 10,000 cubic feet in volume and 0.7 seconds or less for larger classrooms up to 20,000 cubic feet in volume. Larger rooms, such as auditorium, cafeterias, and other spaces, should be reviewed on a case-by-case basis.

Reverberation can be controlled by reducing the large areas of acoustically reflective materials, such as glass, stone, and gypsum board to the project design. Other means, such as adding absorbing material to ceilings (e.g., lay-in acoustical tile, stretched fabric, acoustical plaster) and walls (e.g., fabric-wrapped panels, perforated wood or metal), must also be considered. Carpeting is also used, although there are sometimes concerns about maintenance.

Music classrooms, performance halls/auditoriums, and mixed-use spaces such as cafeterias require greater attention in terms of appropriate finish materials and room shape. Due to budgetary and space constraints, not every school can have a dedicated performance hall; multipurpose facilities are becoming the norm (e.g., a room that is a cafeteria by day and a theater by night).

2.3 Sound Isolation

Because schools have many disparate uses, adequately isolating one space type from another is important so as to minimize distractions to occupants.

ANSI S.12.60 recommends sound-isolating values (i.e., Sound Transmission Class [STC] ratings[4]) for particular demising assemblies depending on specific adjacencies. For example, the recommended STC rating for a wall separating classrooms is STC 50. However, if the classroom is to be used for

SOUND ISOLATION BETWEEN SPACES: This figure shows two enclosed rooms where sound isolation is important. *Charles M. Salter Associates*

PARTITION ASSEMBLIES: These figures show different partition assemblies and their laboratory-tested STC ratings. Partitions are wood single stud, staggered stud, double stud, masonry and combined masonry/stud, and metal studs. *Source: Charles M. Salter Associates*

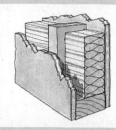
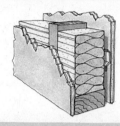
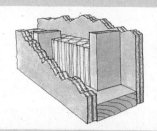

3a STC 40: Single 2x4 wood stud, insulated, with 2 layers of ⅝" gypsum board

3b STC 50: Single 2x4 wood stud, insulated, with 2 layers of ⅝" gypsum board; one side attached to resilient channels (RC)

3c STC 55: Staggered 2x4 wood studs on a 2x6 plate, with four total layers of ⅝" gypsum board

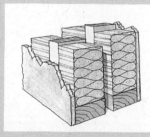
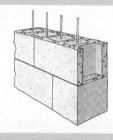
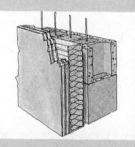

3d STC 59: Double 2x4 wood studs with batt insulation in each stud bay and one layer of ⅝" gypsum board on each side

3e STC 55: 8x8x18" hollow grout-filled masonry units, 33 pounds per square foot (psf); both sides sealed with paint

3f STC 60+: 8x8x18" hollow grout-filled masonry units, 33 psf; both sides sealed with paint; additional furred gypsum board stud wall

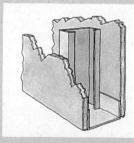
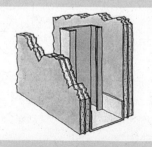

3g STC 44: 3⅝" light-gauge metal studs, stud bays insulated, with one layer of ⅝" gypsum board on each side

3h STC 56: 3⅝" light-gauge metal studs, stud bays insulated, with two layers of ⅝" gypsum board on each side

(continued)

music rehearsal or is located near a mechanical room, restroom, or other noisy space, then the rating should be increased to STC 60 or more. Other adjacencies (e.g., restroom to corridor) require partitions that are less sound isolating than the typical classroom example.

Achieving acceptable sound isolation between core learning spaces also depends on the activities of the users in each room. It is important for the design team to understand how spaces will be used and for the owners to convey this information accurately to the designers. Will there be singing time every day in a room next to a study hall? Will activities in the above-grade multiuse room involve children jumping on the floor? What is the noise level in the wood shop next to teachers' offices?

2.4 Development of Comprehensive Classroom Acoustical Guidelines

The committee that developed the ANSI S12.60-2002 guidelines is comprised of various government stakeholders, architects, and acousticians. The S12.60 comprehensive standard outlines means to identify and control noise within school facilities, based on international research conducted over many years. The ANSI S12.60 classroom acoustical design guidelines could be considered optimum.

As green design features in a building increase its energy efficiency, reduce its carbon footprint, and minimize overall construction waste, they can negatively impact the acoustical qualities of the building. Because of these potential impacts on occupants, green building rating systems, such as Leadership in Energy and Environmental Design

(LEED) and the Collaborative for High Performance Schools (CHPS) have standards that require that school projects achieve minimum levels of background noise, reverberation control, and sound isolation. These requirements are based on the ANSI S12.60 guidelines.

3. HOW CAN HIGH-PERFORMANCE GREEN SCHOOL DESIGN AFFECT ACOUSTICS?

Green design has engendered new ways of thinking about the impacts of buildings on the environment and their occupants. Optimization for energy and resource use, daylighting, and improving indoor air quality affects many of the same systems and assemblies that affect acoustics. High-performance design includes the three main factors in acoustical performance: background noise, room acoustics, and sound isolation.

The CHPS and LEED for Schools acoustical requirements are described on page 70. Since the inception of the original ANSI S12.60 guideline and the two leading green building systems that followed, the acoustical design community has been debating how best to promulgate design guidelines that make substantive improvements in school acoustical design within the ever-present budget constraints.

3.1 Materials and Room Acoustics

3.1.1 MATERIALS: CONSERVATION AND COORDINATION

Green schools strive to provide comfortable places for students and teachers. The evolution of materials selection in such buildings has affected acoustical design in various ways. One of these effects is on the overall reduction in material usage for a project. Sustainable design strives to reduce the total materials used in a project, and decrease the amount of construction waste and scrap materials sent to landfills.

Building materials used in school projects often reflect regional or time period–based methods, some of which may not be readily duplicated in today's school projects. For example, California and West Coast areas of the United States with greater risk of earthquakes use predominantly wood, steel-frame, or concrete buildings; by contrast, schools in lower-risk seismic zones use more brick, stone, or masonry.

There are also the cost control considerations of a school project. As a school building proceeds through design and construction, partition assemblies that are considered acoustically upgraded may be downgraded to save money (e.g., deleting layers of gypsum board, changing stud thicknesses, deletion of certain door hardware). Without an analysis of the acoustical consequences of these changes, the end result may not be satisfactory to the end users. Replacing the lost sound isolation of the originally designed partition assembly can be very expensive to implement after a project is completed.

3.1.2 ROOM FINISHES

Green design often induces projects to have more areas of sound-reflective surfaces (e.g., glass, concrete, wood, etc.). Designers emphasize improving indoor air quality by selecting nonfibrous materials; additionally, other green design features, such as increased areas of glazing for daylighting, and energy-efficient mechanical systems (both described below), can adversely impact the sound-absorptive qualities of a space.

Mitigating excessive reverberation provides absorptive materials on available wall, ceiling, and floor surfaces. This not only reduces the overall level of reverberation but also reduces "flutter echoes," which occur when two hard, sound-reflective surfaces are parallel to each other.

Since schools have many types of rooms (e.g., classrooms, counseling rooms, activity centers, gyms, music rooms, etc.), one "solution" typically is not always appropriate when selecting sound-absorptive, reflective, or diffusive finish materials. Certain soft materials, such as a standard fabric-wrapped wall panel, may not always be appropriate for classrooms, given the need for abuse resistance.

Some green designs do away with conventional lay-in acoustical tile ceilings to increase classroom ceiling height and expose structural components, such as beams and joists. By deleting what is often the largest and most inexpensive available area for absorptive finishes, the exposed structure look can have significant acoustical drawbacks and result in excessive reverberation.

Green building rating systems such as LEED for Schools use prescriptive means to help designers control reverberation in core learning spaces. These means include requiring 100% coverage of the ceiling with sound-absorptive finishes.

3.2 Mechanical Systems in Green Buildings

Green design has precipitated a revolution in the performance and efficiency of mechanical systems. In the past, school mechanical equipment consisted of relatively inefficient constant-volume systems, or in-the-wall air-conditioning systems. First cost was often the main criterion when

(continued)

selecting school mechanical systems; life cycle costs typically were not considered. The recent imperative of minimizing energy use in buildings is the one of the cornerstones of the sustainability movement. More efficient methods of moving air and water throughout a building are becoming commonplace. These newer systems include variable-air volume boxes, chilled beams, radiant-floor heating, and geothermal.

Some mechanical heating and cooling systems have significant acoustical drawbacks and must be carefully analyzed to reduce possible impacts on adjacent spaces. An example is radiant-floor heating systems. These systems must be installed under finish floors that do not affect their heat transfer efficiency. However, such hard-surfaced assemblies can have poor impact sound isolation and lead to excessive impact noise transmission (e.g., walking, dancing, or furniture movement) to spaces below. Impact noise transfer problems can be particularly acute when there is no dropped ceiling assembly in lower-level classrooms. Impact noise transfer can be very annoying and disruptive if not effectively mitigated by design elements or administrative controls. Area rugs or wall-to-wall carpeting (which would reduce impact noise transfer) cannot be used with some radiant-floor systems.

Plumbing system noise also needs to be analyzed and mitigated if predicted to be excessive. Many new high-efficiency mechanical systems use water to transfer heat; additionally, "green roof" designs, which use runoff for landscape watering, have entirely new piping runs that sometimes are routed through learning spaces. Plumbing chases need to be adequately isolated from surrounding sensitive locations.

Natural ventilation (i.e., operable windows) is sometimes used to provide fresh air to a space and save energy. When windows are opened, the noise reduction of the facade is substantially reduced. Even seemingly small openings in a facade can degrade its noise reduction to a point where environmental noise intrusion is a problem.

3.3 Effects of Site and Daylighting Design on Environmental Noise Intrusion

Environmental noise can cause problems when schools are located near roadways, railways, or airports. Since a goal of sustainable design is to provide incentives for projects located near transit (thus reducing car trips to the school), environmental noise impacts can be acute in these locations. Factors such as building setback distance, areas of exposed facade, room size, and facade assembly type have significant effects on the level of environmental noise that students are exposed to.

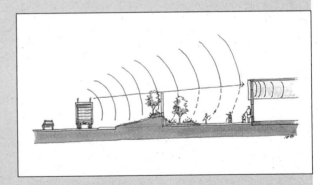

ENVIRONMENTAL NOISE IMPACTS: This shows a noise barrier and roadway next to a school with an outdoor use space. The barrier can reduce noise by about 5 to 10 decibels in the shadow zone. (The *shadow zone* is the area on the school side of the wall where the line of sight to vehicular traffic is blocked.) *Source: Charles M. Salter Associates*

Green building rating systems have specific requirements (i.e., STC ratings) for sound-rated windows in schools. For schools in rural areas or areas where environmental noise sources, such as roadways or aircraft flyovers, are less significant, relatively robust window assemblies probably are not necessary to meet interior noise goals. By contrast, schools near busy arterial roadways, freeways, rail rights-of-way, or airports would be improved by providing window assemblies with greater sound-insulating qualities (e.g., laminated glass or deeper window assemblies).

ANSI standard S12.60 acknowledges that "there is no single answer for the proper amount of noise isolation to include in the design to shield a learning space…from outdoor noise sources."[5] It recommends that environments be assessed on a case-by-case basis.

Outdoor-use spaces often are located near classrooms and other learning spaces. High noise levels can be generated in play yards, gardens, sandboxes, outdoor hallways, and other outdoor gathering spaces. This noise can disrupt classroom activities nearby, particularly during exam time.

Insufficiently sound-isolating glazing assemblies can also cause significant acoustical problems. For example, a glass-walled hallway may satisfy certain daylighting goals and allow light to penetrate farther into the building but lead to significant acoustical issues due to the relative acoustical weakness of typical glazing assemblies as compared to typical wall constructions. Noise from students running down the corridors could prove to be disruptive to classes. ANSI guidelines provide means to calculate the STC ratings[6] of each component of a facade (e.g., glazing assemblies and solid façade assemblies) that would be necessary to meet noise intrusion goals.

4. MEANS TO ADDRESS ACOUSTICAL CHALLENGES IN SUSTAINABLE SCHOOLS

School design needs to provide an acceptable acoustical environment for all students. If classrooms are too loud, education can be severely compromised.

The ANSI S12.60 classroom standards should be strived for when designing and developing green schools. Green building rating systems such as LEED for Schools and or the Collaborative for High Performance Schools (CHPS) acoustical standards are not exactly the same as ANSI S12.60; for example, ANSI guidelines for background noise control are more stringent (i.e., quieter) than the requirements of the leading green building rating systems. ANSI S12.60 is also more prescriptive than in CHPS or LEED for Schools when addressing sound isolation between classrooms.

Green building rating systems attempt to achieve greater market share by demonstrating that green design is not excessively expensive while achieving real, substantive changes in the building design and construction markets. For school owners to participate in these programs, these systems must be sensible and not make the credits or standards too onerous to achieve within budget or other constraints. If achieving a certain level of green certification is a project requirement, then the design team must carefully review the acoustical prerequisites and credits and determine their impact on the project's budget and scope.

(continued)

Since acoustical performance is a requirement for achieving project certification in both the LEED for Schools and CHPS rating systems, designers and owners are compelled to address the noise environment of school projects. As a project develops, the owner, design team, and other key stakeholders should evaluate the overall goals of their green school and how each affects the acoustical environment in the core learning spaces.

5. ACOUSTICAL DESIGN GUIDELINES FOR GREEN SCHOOL RATING SYSTEMS

5.1 LEED for Schools[7]—Earlier Version 1.0

When the U.S. Green Building Council (USGBC) released the initial LEED for Schools rating system in August 2007, its acoustical requirements were based on ANSI S12.60. These acoustical requirements were placed in the Indoor Environmental Quality section, and divided into prerequisite minimum performance and credits for enhanced performance.

The LEED for Schools acoustical prerequisite addressed items discussed above, namely sound isolation, environmental noise control, room acoustics and reverberation control, and ventilation system noise reduction.

Ventilation noise must be controlled to 45 dBA to meet the LEED prerequisite requirements. Airborne sound isolation between rooms was addressed by specifying partitions with STC ratings similar to the ANSI requirements. The rating system also sought to reduce exterior noise intrusion by requiring minimum STC ratings for window assemblies if the site environmental noise levels were shown to be above a threshold of 60 decibels. Additionally,

projects control reverberation by analyzing overall room absorption on a room-by-room basis, using the materials specified in each room.

In 2008, after the initial rating system had been implemented, the USGBC published a memorandum[8] explaining alternative, more prescriptive compliance paths for projects to achieve LEED for Schools prerequisite requirements and enhanced acoustical performance credits for the issues described above.

LEED for Schools requirements[9] have been changed recently as a part of the LEED 2009 system-wide comprehensive update. The prerequisite requirement for sound isolation (i.e., specifying assemblies which achieve specific STC ratings for) has been removed.[10] Requirements for reverberation control and background noise remain similar to the earlier version of the rating system.

Another change between the versions of the LEED for Schools system is the removal of one of the enhanced acoustical performance credits. In the older system, a project can gain one additional point for reducing background noise to 40 dBA and two points by controlling background noise levels in classrooms and other core learning spaces to 35 dBA. In the new LEED 2009, the stricter 35 dBA option has been removed.

5.2 Collaborative for High-Performance Schools (CHPS)

CHPS grants up to three Indoor Environmental Quality points (one prerequisite and up to two additional points) for controlling reverberation and ventilation noise.[11] Similar to LEED for Schools, the CHPS criteria are based in part on the ANSI S12.60 standards.

Developmental Considerations

From preschool to the end of high school, children pass through rapid and uneven physical, emotional, and cognitive changes. The learning environment is also the growing environment, where children mature into young adults. In the course of the school years, quiet, well-lit, comfortable environments are the safe havens from which a child embarks to explore ideas, sensations, and his or her own potential. Avoiding intrusive noise, glare, heat, cold, damp, dirt, and danger allows the child the security to be open to new experiences.

Children in preschool spend a great deal of their time investigating space and the physical world through all their senses. A rich visual and tactile environment stimulates the development of the child's mind as well as body. As children enter grade school, they enter a problem-solving age and begin to try to understand the world around them. The fascination children have with rules and boundaries is part of the enduring interest of hopscotch, four square, and other games that are mostly about being inside or outside of lines. As imperfect as asphalt is for hydrology, it can be a great material for the horizontal blackboard where kids learn to play together.

This rooftop playground safe above a gritty urban environment gives Tenderloin Childcare kids sand and grass to play in. *Source: Donna Kempner Architectural Photography © 2002*

Children's play is a huge part of their growth. *Source: Gelfand Partners Architects*

Across all ages, children need more physical activity. A 2009 report by the American Academy of Pediatricians notes that "an estimated 32 percent of American children are overweight. . . . Policies that promote more active lifestyles among children and adolescents will enable them to achieve the recommended 60 minutes of daily physical activity."[12]

In middle school, children spend more and more time paying attention to the social situation and their peer group. Adolescents need to perform for each other. Areas where groups can hang out together, preferably while keeping an eye on what the other kids are doing, are popular. Schools can be very short of places where a small group can gather in relative quiet as opposed to 300 kids in a cafeteria or in libraries or study halls, where they are supposed to be silent.

Children want and need to socialize. They will find undercover ways if they must—meeting up in the restroom or by texting on often-forbidden phones. Perhaps the cafeteria/student lounge needs a second look to accommodate smaller groups without losing supervision. High school students can be a great source of information for the design team and often notice things that the staff may have missed. One of the reasons schools show no signs of disappearing is that youngsters cannot learn to work and play well with others by sitting alone in front of a computer.

In addition to addressing the needs of the growing and developing child, schools must also provide a truly healthy place. This is more important than in other kinds of buildings, since children have greater sensitivity than adults to many environmental toxins. They get more colds than adults do, and they share them with each other through the air and all the things they handle. They are more prone to ear infections that may cause temporary hearing problems. The sustain-

Middle school kids meet up at a campus tree during lunch.
Source: Gelfand Partners Architects

able school addresses these issues through improved indoor air quality and healthy materials.

Systems choices in schools may stress health more strongly than energy efficiency as compared to other sustainable building types. Displacement ventilation is a strategy that offers schools particular advantages. It provides low-velocity air that rises and gently moves germs and stale air up and away from the children rather than traditional forced air that blows downward at high velocity, stirring up dust and allergens and keeping germs right where the children are breathing.

The teacher controls the lighting and comfort in a classroom. This is rarely a problem in terms of comfort, because adults seem to have a narrower comfort zone, and adults need more light to see. But it can limit potential energy savings. Lowering the ambient light levels in a classroom is fine for the children, who have better sight in dimmer conditions, but it can seem dim to a teacher. It can be a good strategy to locate an extra light and heater in the area where the teacher's desk is expected to be. Simply giving teachers the means to control their immediate environment is often enough to increase their perception of comfort.

The developmental differences among children of different ages, and between children and adults, should be part of the thinking in designing a sustainable school. There is a tremendous potential synergy between sustainability and the needs of a healthy school community.

▲ Air enters at a comfortable temperature, picks up more warmth from the occupants, and rises through convection to a high air return. *Source: Architectural Energy Corporation*

▶ Extra lighting at the whiteboard focuses children's attention and gives the teacher additional brightness. *Source: CHPS*

CONCLUSION

The cumulative effect of investigating form through site concept, context, function, and sensory experience is design. In the sustainable school, climate and ecology considerations beyond the internal and cultural needs of the school have strong influence.

It is inaccurate to say that climate alone determines form. It is equally inaccurate to say that the design context of the building determines its form. Space plans respond to functional connections, scheduling, acoustics, and accommodations for different stages in children's development. Designers make choices all the way through the process of the design. These choices balance the adaptations required by climate or urban or natural context; by the structural, mechanical, and electrical systems in the building; by the cultural connotation that the school is desired to have; and by the resources of the community.

Certain key strategies influence the design of the sustainable school regardless of the formal approach:

- Provide a varied building and campus that accommodates the needs of growing children.
- Combine energy-efficient strategies and healthy strategies.
- Optimize acoustics to help children with hearing problems and reduce teacher fatigue.
- Integrate design strategies to amplify their effects.

Stewart Middle School at Sidwell Friends School, Washington, DC

KieranTimberlake Associates, LLP

PLANNING: SUSTAINABILITY IS AN EXPRESSION OF THE VALUES OF THE SCHOOL

Sidwell Friends describes its commitment to environmental stewardship on its Web site:

Guided by its Quaker values, Sidwell Friends is committed to practicing responsible environmental stewardship. Our curriculum is grounded in teaching students about the natural world and their relationship to it. With the decision to construct a new green Middle School, Sidwell Friends chose sustainable design as a logical expression of its values. This commitment continued with the renovation of our Lower School campus. We believe that green design provides an opportunity to achieve an outstanding level of integration between the curriculum, values, and mission of the School.

◀ Sunscreens vary depending on solar orientation and interior uses.
Source: © Halkin Photography

▼ Storm water is led through a reclamation system for reuse.
Source: KieranTimberlake Associates

DESIGN: LEED PLATINUM

The new middle school building itself is a teaching tool in sustainability and other environmental education. En route to saving 90% of the municipal water of the base case, the school constructed a wetland to treat the building's wastewater. The water then is recycled so that the building can reuse the gray water. A green roof contains vegetation that holds and filters rainwater. This filtered water is then directed to the biology pond to support the native habitat. This entire cycle is visible to students.

Energy-saving strategies for the building include active measures such as PV and solar thermal. The classrooms use skylights and light shelves and also are situated so that the maximum amount of daylighting can be used instead of artificial lighting. Classrooms also utilize natural ventilation and solar chimneys to minimize the necessity for air conditioning and heating of the rooms.

Finally, the materials used to construct the school are environmentally friendly. The wood cladding on the outside of the building and the sunscreens are produced from reclaimed western red cedar. The vertical sunscreens balance thermal performance with daylighting. Wood flooring inside the school and wood decking are made of reclaimed greenheart timber while the copings, walls, and walkways use reclaimed stone. Other materials used for finishing, such as the linoleum and bamboo, are recycled and/or rapidly renewable, and locally produced. The selected paints, carpets, and adhesives emit low levels of volatile organic compounds (VOCs). New planting on the site includes 80% native species.

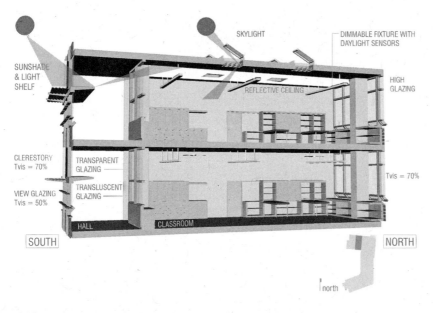

MIDDLE SCHOOL SYSTEMS: natural lighting in science classrooms

Excellent daylighting at Sidwell is the result of integrating systems, envelope, and massing. *Source: KieranTimberlake Associates*

Chartwell School, Seaside, CA

EHDD Architecture

PLANNING: PUBLIC-PRIVATE COOPERATION

Chartwell School, a private school providing services to students with language-related learning challenges, is located on 29 acres that were part of Fort Ord, a decommissioned military base. A first attempt to transfer property for educational use was made with the Monterey Peninsula Unified School District. Following that, with school district support, Chartwell was able to gather private financing and foundation and government grant resources to create a new home for itself and a new model of sustainable school design as it relates to supporting education.

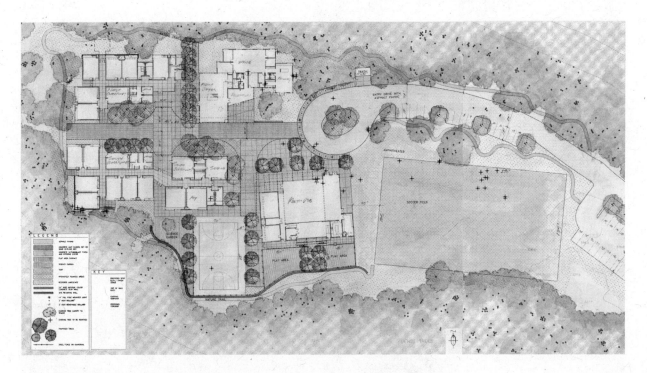

Interlocking courtyards reduce scale and provide daylight opportunities. *Source: EHDD Architecture*

Large amounts of glazing occur on north faces. *Source: EHDD Architecture*

Intermediate sunscreening reduces the scale of the multipurpose building facade. *Source: EHDD Architecture*

Students travel from wide distances to study at Chartwell. The program is intended to equip them to return to more conventional schools within a few years, having developed the confidence and skills they need to succeed. Chartwell also has active outreach in professional development for other school professionals in their area of excellence. Modeling an idea and approach that can spread beyond Chartwell itself was part of its approach to the planning of the new campus.

DESIGN: LEED PLATINUM, CHPS, ZERO NET ENERGY

The executive director of Chartwell, Doug Atkins, broke ground with a new description of sustainability and its connection with education. "Sustainability is the defining term for a new type of thinking that connects what was once unconnected in a way that produces surprising achievements. If this sounds like what Chartwell has been doing for 22 years with literacy and the learning processes of children, then you would be right."[a]

Chartwell School is 21,200 square feet. It is the first LEED platinum K–12 school campus, U.S. Green Building Council LEED-NC, v.2/v.2.1—Level: Platinum (57 points). The primary concern was excellence of the learning environment, leading the designers to maximize daylighting throughout the campus and reduce ambient noise in the classrooms. Natural ventilation in this seaside environment helps reduce the need for ducted HVAC systems. And with daylighting reducing the schools' expected electricity use by 50%, planners decided to go the rest of the way to zero by installing photovoltaic panels to handle the remaining load.

The multisensory educational approach at Chartwell can extend outside the classroom, with a network of trails, planting, and outdoor spaces that stimulates the children, reduces the hydrological impact of the buildings, and protects the native coastal woodland. Rainwater is harvested on the roofs, with a 70% reduction in the use of potable water expected on the campus.

The school also uses a 70% slag concrete mix, which minimizes the carbon dioxide emissions by 50%. Other materials include: salvaged wood siding, wall paneling from Terramai and Pacific Heritage Lumber, Shaw carpeting, Plyboo flooring, Forbo Marmoleum, ICI zero-VOC paints, and Walltalkers Tac-wall. The project also received an Environmental Protection Agency research grant to study methods for easing the use of recycled or salvaged material in the future.

[a]http://www.chartwell.org/index.cfm?Page=75

Woodward Academy Middle School, College Park, Georgia

Perkins + Will

PLANNING: NEW MIDDLE SCHOOL PART OF CAMPUS MASTER PLAN

Woodward Academy Middle School is located in College Park, Georgia. The original campus has been improved to include a new classroom building, dining hall, and art building. The three-story building has been designed as a two-story brick base with glass top story to reduce the apparent scale of the building. All the art rooms also have glass walls and face to the north to admit the maximum amount of natural lighting.

DESIGN: THE FIRST K–12 LEED CERTIFIED PROJECT IN GEORGIA

Daylighting is a priority of the new buildings. Second, a geothermal field of piping is constructed under the courtyard to reduce energy required for heating and cooling. Bioretention gardens and a green roof serve as stormwater management strategies. Recycled finish materials contribute to the sustainability of the building.

The new middle school is part of the greater Woodward Academy site.
Source: © Perkins+Will

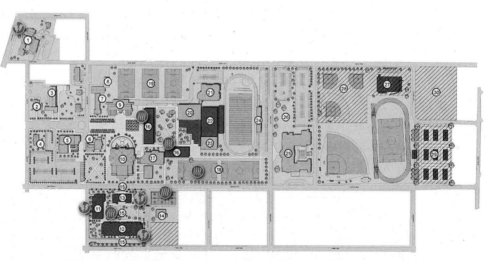

Green Energy at Woodward Academy

Buildings Using Green Power
Primary School 1
Middle School Dining Hall 11
Brand-Tucker Hall Classroom Building 12
A. Adair Dickerson Jr. Arts Center 13

Locations of Geothermal Wells
Campfield Building 14
Jordan N. Carlos Middle School Courtyard 15
New Upper School Buildings (future) 16
Lacrosse and Football Practice Fields 18

Both the general academic building and the art studios have easily controlled north and south facades. *Source: © Perkins+Will*

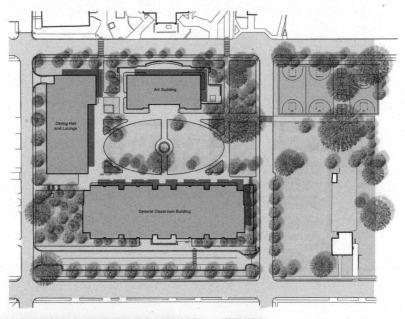

This academic quadrangle is also the location of one of the geothermal wells on the site. *Source: © Perkins+Will*

NOTES

1. B. Shield and J. Dockrell, "The Effect of Environmental and Classroom Noise on the Academic Attainments of Primary School Children," *Journal of the Acoustical Society of America* 123, no. 1 (January 2008), pp. 133–144.

2. ANSI S.12.60, Acoustical Performance Criteria, Design Requirements and Guidelines for Schools," Table 1, p. 5.

3. dBA: A-weighted sound pressure level (or noise level) represents the noisiness or loudness of a sound by weighting the amplitudes of various acoustical frequencies to correspond more closely with human hearing. A 10-dB (decibel) increase in noise level is perceived to be twice as loud. A-weighting is specified by the U.S. Environmental Protection Agency, Occupational Safety and Health Administration, Caltrans, and others for use in noise measurements.

4. STC is a single-figure rating standardized by ASTM and used to rate the sound insulation properties of building partitions. The STC rating is derived from laboratory measurements of a particular building element and as such is representative of the maximum sound insulation. Increasing STC ratings correspond to improved noise isolation.

5. ANSI S12.60, Annex D, Subsection D2.3, p. 24.

6. ANSI S12.60, Annex D, Subsection D2.3.3, p. 25.

7. LEED for Schools: www.usgbc.org/DisplayPage.aspx?CMS PageID=1586.

8. LEED for Schools ACP document, published by USGBC, April 23, 2008, www.usgbc.org.

9. www.usgbc.org/ShowFile.aspx?DocumentID=4121.

10. www.usgbc.org/DisplayPage.aspx?CMSPageID=1849.

11. www.chps.net/, CHPS Best Practices Manual Criteria 2006 Edition, p. 89.

12. PEDIATRICS, Vol. 123, No. 6, June 2009, pp. 1591–1598 (doi:10.1542/peds.2009-0750).

chapter 4

DAYLIGHTING

A room is not a room without natural light.

— Louis Kahn (1971)

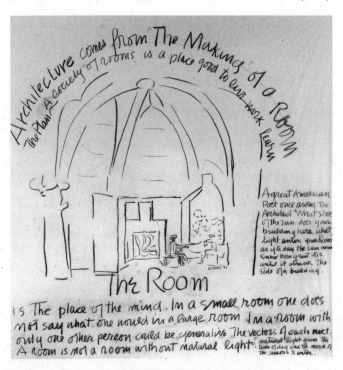

Louis Kahn's 1971 sketch crystallizes his thinking about the place of rooms and the place of light in architecture. *Source: Philadelphia Museum of Art: Gift of the Artist, 1972*

INTRODUCTION

The vast majority of schools see their most intense use during the hours when the sun is shining. Yet up to 60% of their electricity powers artificial illumination. By combining the controlled light of the sun and sky with appropriate electric lighting, much of this energy use can be saved. This practice, called daylighting, improves health and productivity and also provides comfort and pleasure.

BENEFITS OF DAYLIGHTING

Daylighting is the foundation of a sustainable school. Daylight can be the primary illumination source, with electric lights available merely to back it up for nights and dark days. By reducing (or possibly eliminating) the use of electric lighting, daylighting offers energy savings and can be integrated with opportunities for fresh air and natural ventilation.

The extensive use of natural daylight benefits students and faculty in both obvious and sublim-

Daylighting in Schools

An Investigation into the Relationship between Daylighting and Human Performance by Heschong Mahone Group

SUMMARY OF RESULTS

Capistrano Unified School District, California

Classrooms with maximum daylight are associated with 20% to 26% faster learning than classrooms with minimum daylight.

Classrooms with maximum window area are associated with 15% to 23% rate of improvement than classrooms with minimum daylight.

Seattle, Washington

Classrooms with maximum daylight exceed classrooms with minimum daylight by 13% of district averages in reading and 9% in math.

Classrooms with maximum windows exceed classrooms with minimum windows by 13% of district averages in reading and 15% in math.

Classrooms with maximum skylights exceed classrooms with minimum skylights by 7% of district averages in reading and 6% in math.

Fort Collins, Colorado

Classrooms with maximum daylight exceed classrooms with minimum daylight by 7% of district averages in reading and 7% in math.

Classrooms with maximum windows exceed classrooms with minimum windows by 18% of district averages in reading and 14% in math.

Classrooms with maximum skylights exceed classrooms with minimum skylights by 3% in math.

Source: Heschong Mahone Group, "Daylighting in Schools. An Investigation into the Relationship between Daylighting and Human Performance," August 20, 1999. www.coe.uga.edu/sdpl/research/ daylightingstudy.pdf, accessed June 29, 2009.

inal ways. The relative importance of the spectrum, the brightness, the variability, or our associations with the passing of the time of day or seasons are still unknown, but many studies have shown that the holistic effect of natural light correlates with greater health and productivity. In 1999, a landmark study by the Heschong Mahone Group on daylighting in schools showed student performance ranging up to 20% better in daylit classrooms than in nondaylit classrooms. Results of the study are summarized here.

Daylighting performance benefits extend beyond school. Wal-Mart's experimental Eco-Store in Lawrence, Kansas, included skylights. Wal-Mart tracked higher retail sales in the daylit portions of the store. Furniture manufacturer Herman Miller found measurable increases in production in its daylit factory.[1]

Other studies indicate that exposure to daylight improved mental functioning, reduced depression, reduced aggressive behaviors, and led to better sleep in dementia patients.[2] Daylight correlated with reduced absenteeism on the part of office workers.[3] Exposure to very bright light has been linked to treatment of maladies such as seasonal affective disorder (SAD), also known as winter blues.

In addition to the amount of exposure to daylight, human experience of the world is profoundly affected by the qualities of light. Light shows us all we see. Both in the perception of buildings and the experience within them, light is the medium for the art of architecture. We build buildings as a sign of our presence and as solutions to our need for protection from predators and the weather. We also identify with our creations, commonly thinking of doors and windows as the mouths and eyes of our buildings. Such body images, territorial marking, and frank shelter create a literal reality that the enlivening and dematerializing effects of light can boost into a magical intensity.

Light is a metaphor for learning (enlightenment) and a way of creating sacred space. This less tangible benefit should not be neglected as we quantify the importance of daylight. While the benefits of higher test scores and lower energy bills can help justify the specific cost of adding daylight windows, we should feel no embarrassment in embracing the simple happiness that comes from a well-lit space. Daylight helps us feel better. **Daylighting is one of the best investments you can make in the design of a learning environment.**

Different religions have sought inspiration under the Hagia Sophia dome.

Benefits of Daylighting

■ **Better light quality.** Learning requires visual tasks (writing, reading, observing) for both students and teachers. For young children, learning to read the faces and bodies around them is as important as learning to read text. Successful daylighting engages the entire space of the classroom, not just the work surface.

■ **Lower operational costs.** Decreasing the 40% to 60% of power going to electric lighting is the first cost saving. Daylighting, with less waste heat from lights, can also contribute up to 20% to energy savings due to decreased cooling loads in schools with air conditioning.

■ **Decreased carbon footprint.** Nearly 60% of electricity production comes from the burning of coal and its attendant emission of carbon. Every watt of energy saved reduces the amount of carbon emissions released into the atmosphere.

■ **Reduced peak usage.** Daylight provides its benefits during the daytime, when the demand for electricity is at its peak. Reducing energy usage during the day reduces the strain on the electricity grid infrastructure.

■ **Connection to nature.** Daylighting changes with weather and time and is the spectrum human beings are biologically adapted to perceive. Daylighting can enhance a connection to nature and directly improve the mood of the students and faculty.

■ **Improved student performance.** The addition of natural daylight has been shown to improve student test scores by up to 20%.

Successful daylighting requires integration of building location, shape, size and orientation of openings, internal space planning, building envelope design, and technicalities of glazing, shading, and detailing at windows and skylights. Daylighting strategies include simple things, such as windows, but may also include complex energy management controllers. Even when all these qualities are optimized, occupants must understand the systems and learn not to habitually flip on the lights when not required. By making daylighting a priority, the design team can find solutions that fit the project budget and schedule.

EARLY PRECEDENTS

Before the advent of air conditioning and electric lighting, builders explicitly used light and air to determine site design. Florence Nightingale linked light and air to health and hygiene. She argued that the excessive mortality that occurred after wounded soldiers were put in dark, airless hospitals could be avoided. She advocated narrow wards with windows on both sides, cross-ventilation, and spaces for light and air between parallel wings. This plan, the "finger plan," came to be applied to other hospitals, to factories, and to thousands of postwar schools.

San Francisco General Hospital is an example of the finger plan. *Source: Google Earth*

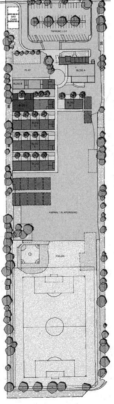

NORTH

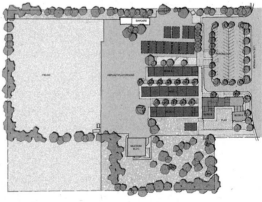

Los Altos school site plans preserve solar orientations even when orientation toward the street changes. *Source: Gelfand Partners Architects*

This school, in Green Bay, Wisconsin, was designed to save heating energy by having the fewest possible windows. *Source: Gelfand Partners Architects*

Early twentieth-century reformers linked light and air to social issues. Adding light to the halls of early 20th-century tenement buildings was advocated for reasons of morality as well as safety.[4] The importance of light and air is noted cross-culturally. Families relocated to western-style apartments in Tunisia were seen to suffer from the loss of the access they had to light and air in their traditional courtyard homes.[5]

However, as electric lighting and mechanical systems were adopted, the need for natural light and ventilation was seen to decrease. In fact, the energy crisis of the 1970s gave rise to a wave of windowless schools where a closed box was seen as more energy efficient and easier to manage. These schools are now among the most difficult to retrofit to create more appealing and better-functioning learning environments.

In contrast, finger schools of the 1950s with their normative barracks-style repetition are easy to retrofit for good daylighting. But however well the finger plan may address the quantitative exposure to light and air, it does not address all site planning needs. Simply arraying narrow east-west buildings in a grid can create deadly repetition and waste the potential of the spaces between the buildings both for learning—outdoor classrooms—and for recess and sport. The fact that schools are often multibuilding environments calls for an expansion in thinking beyond the footprint of each building to their possible synergies on the campus.

SITE DESIGN AND DAYLIGHTING

School site design is subject to many pressures. For most schools, the daily circulation of masses of students can have the same intensity as a fire drill for another kind of building. Schools also house a variety of functions. The plan will be strongly affected by required adjacencies. Outdoor learning, gathering, playing, eating, and parking all influence the campus layout. But within these imperatives, considering daylighting first at the campus level can simplify building design.

Depending on latitude and season, the sun is seen to describe varying arcs across the sky. In almost the direct opposite of solar heat gain used to reduce the need to provide other sources of heat, for daylighting we are interested in the parts of the sky where the sun is not. In the northern hemisphere, the northern sky is the source of diffuse, cool light. In the southern hemi-

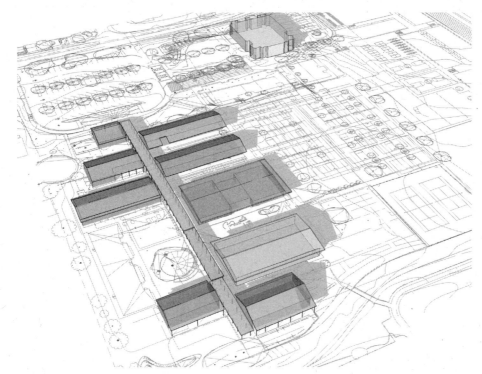

◀ Blach School was originally designed as a finger plan with a covered walkway down the middle. *Source: Gelfand Partners Architects*

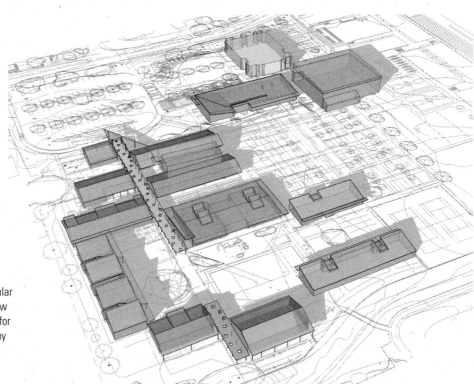

▶ Removal of an obsolete modular building and construction of new additions created a new focus for the campus and a new hierarchy of outdoor spaces. *Source: Gelfand Partners Architects*

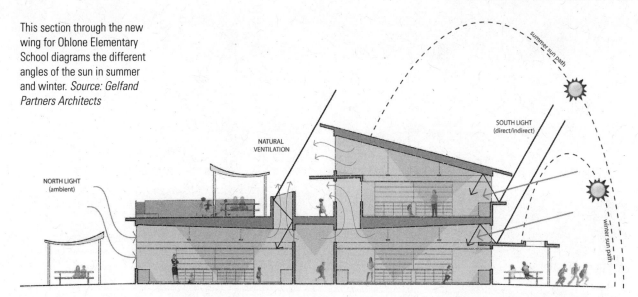

This section through the new wing for Ohlone Elementary School diagrams the different angles of the sun in summer and winter. *Source: Gelfand Partners Architects*

sphere, the southern sky is the source. Having bounced around the particles in the atmosphere, the light in the sky opposite the sun is an even, broad source.

Locating a building with its long axis east and west offers the longest potential window walls along the most easily controlled faces (north and south). In a hot or mild climate, solar heat gain is almost never desirable. In a cold climate, passive solar gain may be desirable, but the heat generated by a classroom full of active children, their computers and other machines, and whatever lights are on must be considered. In an extreme climate, solar heat gain could be welcome in the winter but needs to be excluded in the summer.

The advantage of the north and south faces is that the sun is highest at midday, and even the sunny side can be easily screened by overhangs that can be calibrated to shade windows in summer, when the sun is highest, while allowing the low winter sun to shine directly in, when its heat gain is welcome.

Low east and west sun is more problematic. Other buildings on a campus may provide shading, which they almost never do from the high-noon sun. Trees may help, creating screens that will be seen as ame-

nities rather than obstacles. Studies in healthcare settings showed better patient outcomes in rooms with views of trees compared to rooms with views of walls.[6] But preventing heat from entering an east- or west-facing window directly almost always means reducing the view from the window as well.

Buildings shade spaces and other buildings, and attention to preserving both sunny and shady outdoor spaces will affect the plan. In site planning schools, daylighting should certainly be a factor, and the long narrow east-west building can be a natural response, but building design can assist the site design and accommodate a less-than-optimal orientation.

Site planning factors include:

- Efficient circulation and educational adjacencies
- Variety and potential of outdoor spaces
- Desirability of narrow east-west orientation for buildings housing daylit spaces
- Potential for locating functions requiring less daylit spaces on east and west faces
- Screening east and west windows with planting

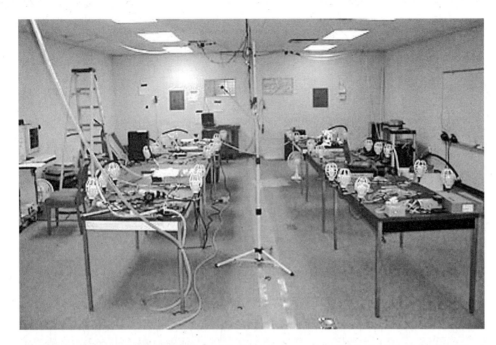

Lawrence Berkeley Lab experimental modeling for new portable classroom mechanical systems substituted light bulbs for kids. *Source: Lawrence Berkeley National Laboratory*

The west-facing wall on the Vanden music room has vertical windows facing north, screening direct glare or heat gain. *Source: Mark Luthringer*

DAYLIGHTING LIGHT REQUIREMENTS

Lighting requirements typically are defined by task. According to the Illuminating Engineering Society of North America (IES), classrooms need 50 foot-candles (fc) on the task (reading) while dining areas require only 30 fc.

As discussed, classroom tasks include both reading and interaction that is much more similar to dining. Learning goes on in many modes: auditory, physical/kinesthetic as well as visual. In part, the variety of tasks and modes indicates the need for light levels to be adjustable. But it also means that ambient light levels could very well be closer to 30 fc than 50 fc as a base case. Achieving lighting levels that can be manipulated usually includes using artificial lighting along with the daylighting solution. New artificial sources are coming on the market rapidly. The likelihood that incandescent and even fluorescent lighting will be replaced by new lamps in the near future is high. But whatever the source, directing and distributing artificial lighting must be consistent with the daylighting design.

A soft, even light can be comfortable even at a reduced light level. Reducing ambient light does increase the need for a careful lighting design. Even children, whose eyes adjust to changing brightness more quickly than adults, find their task area dark after staring at a bright window or skylight. Inappropriate spots of brightness in the room increase the level of lighting required at the task and ironically make the entire space look darker. Improperly diffused skylights that introduced areas of glare into classrooms in the Heschong Mahone study had small negative effects on student performance.

Our visual perception system also directs our attention to the brightest thing in the scene. IES recommendations for retail are:

Circulation areas: 30 fc

Merchandise: 100 fc

Feature displays: 500 fc

To convert from	into	multiply by...
Lumens	Candela steradian	1.0
Lumens	Candle power (spherical)	0.07958
Lumens	Watts	0.0015
Lumens per square centimeter	Lamberts	1
Lumens per square centimeter	Lux	10000
Lumens per square centimeter	Phots	1
Lumens per square foot	Foot-candles	1
Lumens per square foot	Foot-lamberts	1
Lumens per square foot	Lumens/square meter	10.76391
Lumens per square foot	Lux	10.76396
Lumens per square meter	Foot-candles	0.0929
Lumens per square meter	Lumens/square foot	0.0929
Lumens per square meter	Phots	0.0001
Lumens per square meter	Lux	1
Lux	Foot-candles	0.0929
Lux	Lumens/square meter	1
Lux	Phots	0.0001

Orson Welles's dramatic and selective lighting in *The Third Man* directs the viewer's attention within the chaos of broken Vienna.
Source: Orson Welles, The Third Man, *1949*

When classrooms have the same ranges of illumination, the same kinds of direction of attention occur. This may help explain why so many teachers permanently obscure their classroom windows. It is the designer's job to position the windows and balance the lighting so that the classroom is comfortably uniform and the teacher can direct student focus on teaching walls, projected material, or other learning activities.

The ideal school daylighting solution would:

- Admit sunlight but not summer heat.
- Admit solar heat in winter where needed.
- Allow views but exclude glare.
- Include electric lighting controls that adjust electric light to respond to available daylight and user needs.
- Preserve the liveliness and full spectrum of natural light.

Control Direct Sunlight Penetration

- Admit diffuse or reflected light. Bright and hot direct sunlight can create great visual and thermal discomfort. Daylight, from the sky, from clouds, or from diffused or reflected sunlight, efficiently provides excellent illumination.

Avoid Glare

- Excessively high contrast (as between a light source and a dark wall) causes glare. Glare causes discomfort or loss in visual performance.

Provide Gentle, Uniform Illumination

- Place daylight apertures at the edge of a sloped or perpendicular surface so the daylight washes either a ceiling or a wall plane and is reflected deeper into the space. For greatest efficiency and visual comfort, paint surfaces white or a very light color that has a high light reflectance value.

Provide Control of Daylight

- Daylight varies throughout the day and the year. Teachers need to be able to darken rooms too. Blinds and shades should be reliable and economical to clean and repair. These systems should not be relied on to solve intrinsic problems of orientation.

Integrate with Electric Lighting Design

- The daylight and the electric light systems should complement each other. Electric illumination should light surfaces using a similar strategy as daylighting. The electric lighting should be controlled so that the lights can be manually or automatically turned off or dimmed in areas where daylight is abundant and left on where it is deficient.

BUILDING DESIGN FOR DAYLIGHTING

The classic one-room schoolhouse accommodated all functions in the same space. The modern school of the last century included classrooms, libraries, cafeterias, gyms, music rehearsal spaces, science labs, shops, studios, auditoriums, and administrative and support spaces. Even a contemporary school focused on project-based learning and the widespread use of technology will have some highly differentiated spaces. These varying functions have varying needs for daylighting.

The daylighting described earlier is broadly applicable to classrooms, libraries, and studios. In smaller spaces, such as offices or individual practice rooms, it is possible to achieve good daylighting throughout the room with a single window. It might be argued that the time-limited use of rooms such as conference or practice rooms makes daylight less of a priority. But within the life cycle of a school, today's practice room could be tomorrow's office.

Specific functions do have specific constraints. An ensemble music space (band or orchestra room) needs bright enough lighting to read sheet music that may have been used many times and is oriented nearly vertically instead of on a horizontal surface. Too much light behind the conductor makes it hard for musicians to look back and forth between the conductor and the music and will raise the perceived need for light on the music stand.

Science labs have varying requirements depending on the discipline. Biology classes may study plants and animals that need light to thrive. Physics classes study light itself and may need labs that can be darkened completely. The same kind of analysis can be applied to all the individual spaces in a school. But another reality of school design is that today's elementary school might be tomorrow's high school. An extreme degree of differentiation—the "glove fit"—is less flexible over the life of an institution that the "mitten fit" of the one-room schoolhouse.

Beyond the one room, certain general approaches exist. In looking at school plan types, single-loaded bars (finger schools), double-loaded bars (wing schools), courtyard schools, and a variety of open-plan or pod schools, radial panopticon schools, mall types, and multistory complex section schools cover most of the variations. Only finger schools were really driven by daylighting. For other plan types, ideology or educational theory (courtyards and pods), supervision (panopticon and mall), space constraints and harsh climate (wing schools and multistory) drove the plan type.

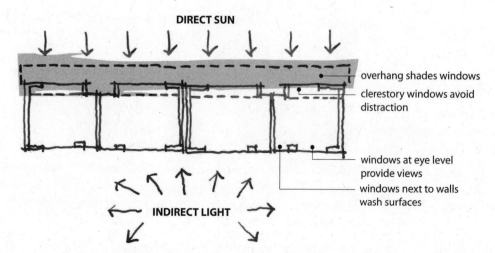

Single-loaded bars can easily be oriented for maximum daylighting.
Source: Gelfand Partners Architects

DIRECT SUN

overhang shades windows

clerestory windows avoid distraction

windows at eye level provide views

windows next to walls wash surfaces

INDIRECT LIGHT

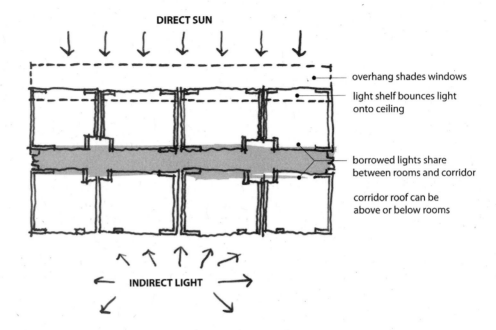

DIRECT SUN

overhang shades windows

light shelf bounces light onto ceiling

borrowed lights share between rooms and corridor

corridor roof can be above or below rooms

INDIRECT LIGHT

Double-loaded bars require different solutions on each face and a strategy for corridor lighting. *Source: Gelfand Partners Architects*

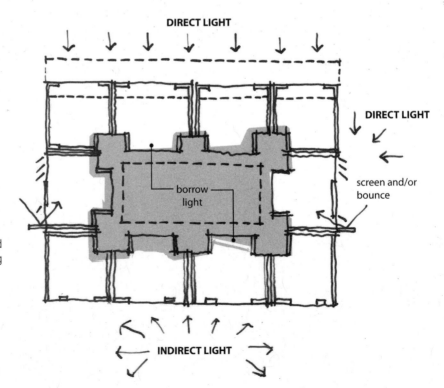

DIRECT LIGHT

DIRECT LIGHT

borrow light

screen and/or bounce

INDIRECT LIGHT

Courtyard schools look inward and need different daylighting solutions for all outer walls. *Source: Gelfand Partners Architects*

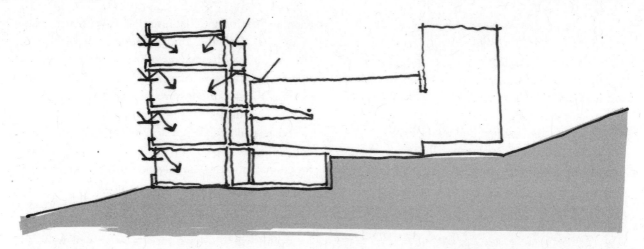

The multistory building offers some opportunities when functions have different ceiling heights. *Source: Gelfand Partners Architects*

This auditorium has daylighting opportunities on three sides. *Source: Gelfand Partners Architects*

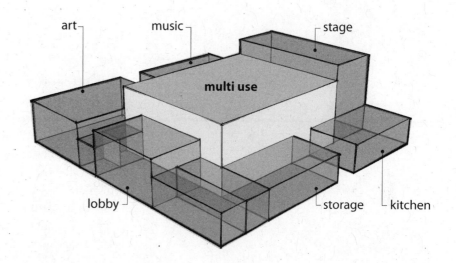

Louis Kahn's notion of served and servant spaces can be a useful paradigm in looking at any of the various school plan types. Almost all the major spaces in a school will be "served" spaces and will have ancillary "servant spaces." For example, a gym has locker rooms, coaches' offices, equipment storage, and possibly its own mechanical systems. An auditorium will have a lobby, restrooms, backstage or green room, or possibly adjacency with music rooms and art studios that can double as servant spaces to the performance space. These ancillary functions usually require less volume than the main space, creating the potential for clerestory windows, to bounce light off roofs, and, conversely, to borrow light to smaller spaces from the well-lit major space.

But even the servant spaces in a school can have great importance in a child's day. Corridors can be more than spaces that connect other spaces. In an active school, they can be galleries for student work or social spaces where kids meet up at each other's lockers to walk home together. Corridors need light that fits those tasks too, not just finding the exit.

School restrooms deserve special consideration. A dark, airless restroom is vulnerable to graffiti and oth-

The classrooms at Strawberry Vale "borrow light" from the central spine. *Source: Patkau Architects, James Dow*

er vandalism in ways that bright, well-ventilated spaces are not. While the control of graffiti depends on a large number of factors, including the general culture of the school, the level of maintenance, and the culture at large, the impulse to save energy by underlighting restrooms probably should be avoided.

Solar building design and orientation principles help organize served and servant spaces to support functional efficiency but also to integrate a system of daylighting throughout a complex plan. Because comfortable spaces also have volumes that are proportional to their floor area, school plans, with their spatial hierarchy, will also have varying heights of walls. In general terms, the larger the floor area, the higher the ceiling should be.

SPECIFICS OF OPENING DESIGN

Building form and massing create opportunities for apertures to bring in light. Openings are also a major element in the composition of building façades. Apertures for daylighting include skylights, clerestory windows, windows, and borrowed light from other spaces. Both skylights (through roofs) and clerestory windows (high on walls above vision windows) allow light into a space from above the occupied area. Windows also allow view outside. Borrowed lights are windows or clerestories into other spaces—for example, the window on a private office that brings in light from an open office area.

Baffled skylights, clerestories, dormer windows, and windows offer more opportunity for achieving heat and glare-free daylighting than skylights in the middle of a ceiling. The ceiling is often more than half of the visual scene. This is one reason that direct/indirect lighting is so successful—although only a small percentage of the light from the fixture

Light penetrates the room roughly 2.5 times the height of the window opening. These windows are optimized for daylighting. *Source: Gelfand Partners Architects*

These windows are optimized for view. *Source: Gelfand Partners Architects*

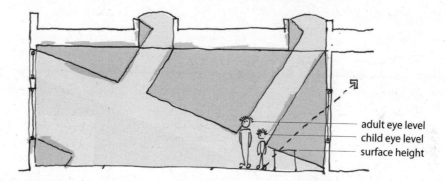

Skylights in the middle of the room create bright spots while skylights next to walls help balance room lighting. *Source: Gelfand Partners Architects*

is shining directly on the task. The brightness of the ceiling reduces contrast so that the entire room does not need to be as bright to be equally comfortable.

Windows perform a variety of functions. The Collaborative for High Performance Schools (CHPS) program, in developing criteria for the daylighting credit, analyzes the amount of light available through each kind of opening.[7] Windows with sills 7.5 feet or more above the floor are optimized for daylighting. They help light penetrate deeply into the classroom because

of the angle of the light. A larger opening admits more light—more is more.

Windows or clerestory windows that are directly under the ceiling offer the potential for raking light along the ceiling surface. Even small detailing changes are important. The top of the window should be as snug as possible to the ceiling.

Another way to light the ceiling is to bounce direct light from a light shelf. This can turn south-facing walls into a great source of indirect light.

These images from a Public Interest Energy Research study for CHPS contrast the effect of direct versus indirect lighting on a classroom while providing equal lighting on the work surface. *Source: CHPS*

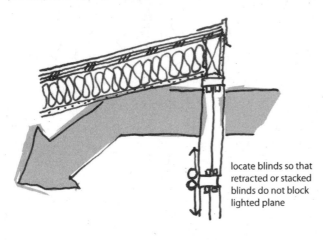

locate blinds so that retracted or stacked blinds do not block lighted plane

◀ Flush framing allows light to wash the ceiling. *Source: Gelfand Partners Architects*

▲ Stacked framing blocks light. *Source: Gelfand Partners Architects*

▼ The roof overhang blocks direct light and heat while the light shelf reflects light onto the ceiling. Note that the angle with which the light hits the surface (incidence) equals the angle of reflectance. *Source: Gelfand Partners Architects*

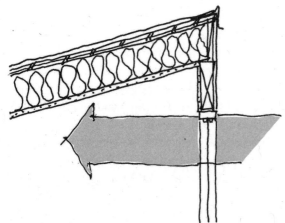

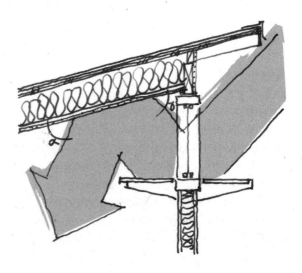

Both windows and clerestories wash the wall surfaces next to them with light. *Source: Mark Luthringer*

Eye-level windows also allow views. That is important in allowing people to fix their eyes on distant things once in a while and to maintain connections with the environment. Such windows need to be located to minimize distraction, or teachers may defeat the daylighting system by blocking the windows. The classic finger school had view windows on the north facing the space between the fingers and daylighting windows high on the south under the overhang where the walkway was, above the heads of people passing through the walkways.

View windows can be placed next to walls to create the same raking effect as clerestories do for ceilings, with vertical fins creating a bounce analogous to light shelves.

With the rising interest in sustainability, window systems with integral sunshades, blinds, and sophisticated glazing have become more commonly available.

Schools can be dangerous places for fragile materials, and it is the rare school maintenance group that will replace broken glazing with special-order glazing that must be delivered from a distant factory. More maintenance-friendly solutions, rather than relying on a coating or special glass, are rugged sunshades and proper orientation and placement to minimize heat and glare.

Strategies for design of windows include:

- Locate a variety of windows at heights that allow light to reach the whole space.
- Prevent glare and heat from entering the window through shading outside rather than inside.
- Limit use of exotic materials.

Skylights require extremely careful design. They are open to the direct rays of the sun at the hottest times of day. They are located on roofs and penetrate the waterproofing membrane. In some urban areas, they may cause concern if they are a potential point of entry for criminals or vandals. They are at the top of a space, where heat is rising. Often they are less well insulated than surrounding ceiling areas, creating cold surfaces where humidity inside the space can condense. Many a "leaking" skylight is damp because of moisture from air inside in the building.

Strategies for designing skylights include:

- Translucent insulating glazing
- White surfaces for bouncing light in skylight wells

- Provision for ventilation at the high point of the well
- Integral shading
- Coordination with artificial lighting

Building design can support daylighting by providing openings that:

- Distribute daylight throughout the space.
- Diffuse light across large surfaces.
- Avoid hot spots that amplify total brightness needs.
- Bounce direct sun at least once—off the sky, a shelf, a fin, or a skylight well.

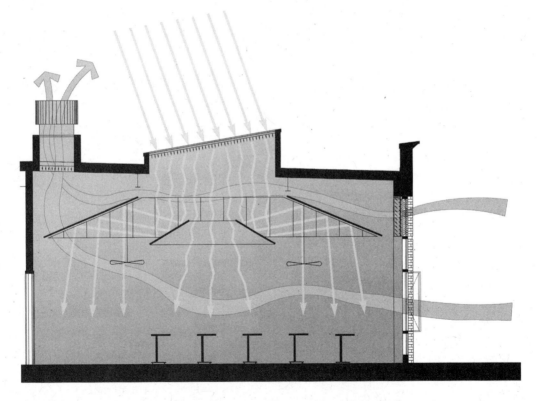

The Mt. Angel prototype classroom in Oregon admits light through an automatically adjusting skylight and reflects it around the room. *Source: Mt. Angel High Performance Classroom Daylight and Ventilation Diagram, project designed by SRG Partnership*

The Mt. Angel skylight admits less light to control glare in overly bright conditions, as in this view. *Source: Oregon Department of Energy*

The Mt. Angel skylight admits more light in indirect conditions, as in this view. *Source: Oregon Department of Energy*

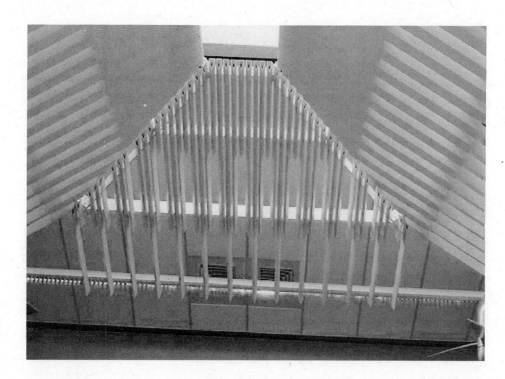

A diffusing screen of aluminum distributes light evenly around the Mt. Angel classroom. *Source: Oregon Department of Energy*

ARTIFICIAL LIGHTING

In designing the artificial lighting that coordinates with the daylighting scheme, many of the same goals exist. For most school spaces, the artificial lighting should light whole surfaces rather than create points of glare. It should distribute light evenly with the exception of those areas where attention is intended to be directed. But assuming that the lighting design is correct, the sustainability benefits come chiefly from the type of light source and the type of controls.

If nothing else is done, replacing the bulbs or lamps in existing fluorescent fixtures can provide instant energy savings. In some cases incandescent bulbs are still being used. Replacing them with compact fluorescents provides immediate savings in both energy use and maintenance time.

High-bay lighting has become available using fluorescent lamps that avoid warm-up time and increase efficiency. Light-emitting diode (LED) lamps are improving daily; soon LED fixtures probably will expand broadly throughout the industry, with increased efficiency and long life.

The simplest controls are on and off. Controls could include occupancy sensors that switch off the lights when no one is in the room. At the next level, switching lights so that a bank of lights next to windows can be off while lights toward the inside of the room are on saves half the energy. It assumes that the teacher is thinking about it, though, and rarely achieves even light distribution.

A variety of systems exist for daylight harvesting. In concept, such systems look down on the work surface with a light sensor and automatically control the

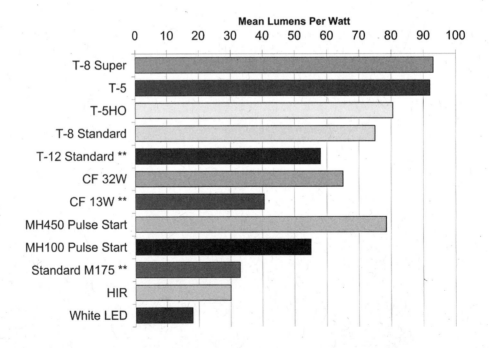

Mean Lumens Per Watt

Electronic ballasts except where noted by **

Source: CHPS

brightness of the light fixtures to maintain the same illumination on the work surface. Stepped ballasts were cheap and changed the light levels in noticeable increments. They were not popular because they drew attention to themselves.

Continuously dimming ballasts are available for fluorescent fixtures. While (in 2009) it is very expensive to dim all the way to zero, systems that dim only to about 10% of the light output are increasingly affordable. Ten years ago, the systems were proprietary combinations of controls, ballasts, and light fixtures. Such systems are still available, but the market has expanded to include systems that use more standard light fixtures and provide only the dimmers and the sensors. While the systems can be set to operate completely automatically, they also can be controlled by the teacher. Borrowing a strategy from theater lighting, some systems have preset "scenes" that combine a variety of light settings (on, off, dimmer) that can be selected with one switch or button rather than adjusting settings and fixtures independently.

Teachers can control the lights to direct attention (e.g., focus light on the whiteboard) or to control mood. Children coming in from the playground may benefit from a calmer, dimmer light to help quiet down and refocus. Such a "scene" could also be appropriate for audio-visual use.[8]

Although light sources and controls have been developing rapidly, the most energy-saving solution of all is the use of daylighting as the primary source of daytime illumination. When designing for sustainability, the most important decisions are the longest-lasting ones. The building that is designed to admit daylight in the most effective way can have many different lighting systems in its service life. It is a better choice to save money by using basic controls that can be upgraded later than by eliminating the windows that admit daylight. It is also the choice that

LEED for Schools

Daylighting contributes to these points on the proposed (2009) LEED (Leadership in Energy and Environmental Design) for Schools checklist.

CATEGORY: ENERGY AND ATMOSPHERE

- EA Credit 1: Optimize Energy Performance
- EA Credit 3: Enhanced Commissioning

CATEGORY: INDOOR ENVIRONMENTAL QUALITY

- EQ Credit 6.1: Lighting System Design and Controllability
- EQ Credit 7.1: Thermal Comfort: Design
- EQ Credit 8.1: Daylight & Views: Daylighting
- EQ Credit 8.2: Daylight & Views: Views for 90% of Spaces

will create the most healthy and productive learning environment.

Basics for Artificial Lighting

- Coordinate with daylighting.
- Turn off when not in use.
- Provide dimming for daylight harvesting and for classroom mood control.

Organizations and Associations

INTERNATIONAL COMMISSION ON ILLUMINATION

Commission Internationale de L'Eclairage, an international forum for research, standard setting, discussion, and interchange of information relating to the science, technology, and art of light and lighting.

www.cie.co.at/index_ie.html

ILLUMINATING ENGINEERING SOCIETY OF NORTH AMERICA (IESNA)

Organization whose mission is to advance knowledge and disseminate information for the improvement of the lighted environment for the benefit of society.

www.iesna.org

LIGHTING RESEARCH CENTER (LRC), SCHOOL OF ARCHITECTURE, RENSSELAER POLYTECHNIC INSTITUTE

University-based research and educational institution dedicated to lighting research and education.

www.lrc.rpi.edu

DAYLIGHTING COLLABORATIVE

Practical information on why and how to daylight, supported by the Energy Center of Wisconsin.

www.daylighting.org

TOOLS

Sensor Placement and Optimization Tool (SPOT)

Free software to assist a designer in establishing optimal photosensor placement.

www.archenergy.com/SPOT/

Radiance

Free software for UNIX computers for lighting ray tracing. Radiance user interface for windows available.

http://radsite.lbl.gov/radiance/HOME.html

Whole Building Design Guide: Daylighting

Good summary of many more tools available to assist designers.

www.wbdg.org/resources/daylighting.php

NCEF's Daylighting Resource Guide

More tools and studies for designers.

www.edfacilities.org/rl/daylighting.cfm

Blach Intermediate School

Gelfand Partners Architects

PLANNING: CHPS PILOT

Blach Intermediate School is located in Los Altos, California. It was under design for modernization and additions in 1999 when the architects made contact with the local utility, PG+E. PG+E was looking for a pilot school for the new CHPS program. Because

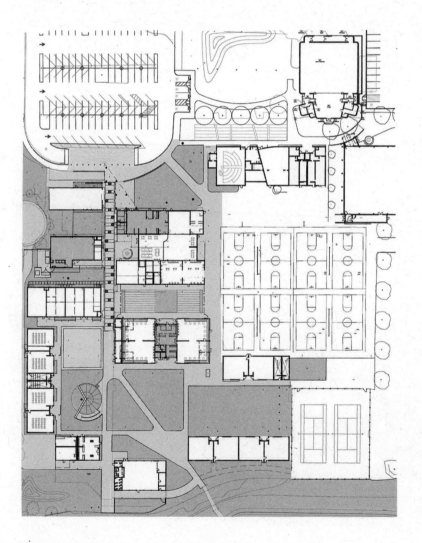

The site design limits paving to areas where it is functionally required.
Source: Gelfand Partners Architects

Blach included both modernizations and new buildings, and was already focused on improved daylighting, the school was ideal to demonstrate aspects of the high-performance approach. The district received extra funding and the design team received extra technical support and was able to do more energy and daylight modeling than on a conventional project. In return, the campus has been made available for many tours and presentations regarding sustainable features.

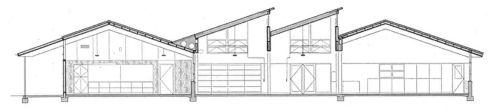

Library - Section

▲ The library reuses two existing classroom wings and infills additional daylit space between. *Source: Gelfand Partners Architects*

◀The new quad surrounds an existing tree and creates a student stage. *Source: Mark Luthringer*

The student store, a school feature much valued by the students, becomes a campus landmark. *Source: Mark Luthringer*

DESIGN: NO SECOND-CLASS CLASSROOMS

The Blach project saves 35% of energy over California's minimum energy requirements. Half of the school is modernized, half new construction. The modernized classrooms have all been retrofitted with new light monitors and upgrades that make them of equal quality to new classrooms. Heating, ventilating, and air-conditioning (HVAC) systems are high efficiency, but the bulk of the energy savings come from the daylight-harvesting system.

Site planning reduced the impermeable areas on the campus, creating a new turf quadrangle. Sensors in each room automatically shut the HVAC off when a window or door is opened for a period of time. Occupancy sensors turn lighting off in empty rooms.

Bronx Charter School for the Arts, Hunts Point, Bronx

Weisz + Yoes

PLANNING: ADAPTIVE REUSE REPROGRAMS FACTORY SPACE

Bronx Charter School for the Arts is located in the Hunts Point section of the South Bronx in New York. Weisz + Yoes adapted the remains of a 23,700-square-foot meat-processing plant into a colorful elementary school. This repurposing made it possible to develop the new school where it needed to be on a limited budget.

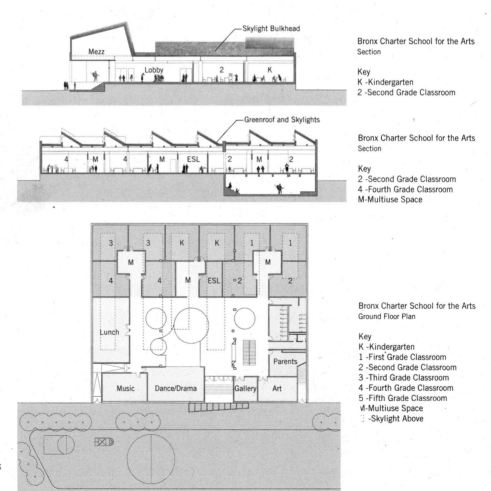

Bronx Charter School for the Arts
Section

Key
K -Kindergarten
2 -Second Grade Classroom

Bronx Charter School for the Arts
Section

Key
2 -Second Grade Classroom
4 -Fourth Grade Classroom
M -Multiuse Space

Bronx Charter School for the Arts
Ground Floor Plan

Key
K -Kindergarten
1 -First Grade Classroom
2 -Second Grade Classroom
3 -Third Grade Classroom
4 -Fourth Grade Classroom
5 -Fifth Grade Classroom
M -Multiuse Space
◌ -Skylight Above

The rehabilitation brings natural light into all spaces in the plan. *Source: WXY Architecture*

A new facade completely changes the impression of the building. *Source: © Albert Vecerka/ESTO*

DESIGN: TRANSFORMATION

The design converts two buildings with masonry bearing walls and structural steel into a cheerful learning environment. Inside the school, floor patterns and wall paintings are very bright and colorful, as is a high-gloss brick veneer applied to the front of the school. The facade structure also helps insulate the building. Many of the materials used in this project are a minimum of 80% recycled content.

Daylight improvements include six new skylights and large new windows at street level. In addition, the school uses large amounts of natural fresh air. To limit the amount of space used, many units, such as heat and air conditioning units, were placed on the roof.

New skylights integrate daylighting and ventilation improvements *Source: WXY Architecture*

Brightness and openness characterize the school interiors. *Source: © Albert Vecerka/ESTO*

NOTES

1. Herman Miller Company Brochure, November 14, 2007, www.policy53.com/policy53.pdf, accessed June 29, 2009.

2. Rixt F. Riemersma-van der Lek, MD, "Effect of Bright and Melatonin on Cognitive and Noncognitive Function in Elderly Residents of Group Care Facilities," June 11, 2008, http://jama.ama-assn.org/cgi/content/abstract/299/22/2642, accessed June 29, 2009.

3. National Lighting Bureau, "Case History: Pennsylvania Power & Light Saves Almost $250,000 Annually Because of Better Lighting," 2009, www.nlb.org/index.cfm?cdid=10394, accessed June 29, 2009.

4. Robert Weeks De Forest and Lawrence Veiller, eds., *The Tenement House Problem* (New York: Macmillan, 1908), "The Proposed Code of Tenement House Laws," p. 313, http://books .google.com/books?id=fc0JAAAAIAAJ&pg=PA131&lpg =PA131&dq=tenement+light+and+air&source=bl&ots= uy2UXBKr4N&sig=bCnzkt0vXb-WzuyOpczGBPGHeA E&hl=en&ei=8t4iSo6YEKWKtgPYscz4Aw&sa=X&oi=bo ok_result&ct=result&resnum=1.

5. John W. Berry, Ype H. Poortinga, Marshall H. Segall, Janak Pandey, and Çiğdem Kağitçibaşi, eds., *Handbook of Cross-Cultural Psychology: Social Behavior and Applications*, vol. 3, 2nd ed. (Boston: Allyn & Bacon, 1997, 1980), p. 276, http://books.google.com/books?id=Z0L7dwJKel8C&pg= PA276&lpg=PA276&dq=social+behavior+light+and+ air&source=bl&ots=hBlQMdymdI&sig=BzKDnlNKB-OiDVok1p69ZvNH5Ns&hl=en&ei=E-AiSrjAK5S6tAOan bT4Aw&sa=X&oi=book_result&ct=result&resnum=2, accessed June 29, 2009.

6. Roger S. Ulrich, Ph.D. "Health Benefits of Gardens in Hospitals," 2002, http://greenplantsforgreenbuildings.org/ pdf/HealthSettingsUlrich_copy.pdf, accessed June 29, 2009.

7. Collaborative for High Performance Schools, Daylighting Chapter, Best Practices Manual, Part II, Volume II, Design, www.chps.net/dev/Drupal/node/31, accessed October 5, 2009.

8. "Back to School: Advanced Lighting Systems for Classrooms," *Energy Design Resources E-News* (October 2006), www.energydesignresources.com/Portals/0/documents/ Newsletters/EDR_eNews_055.pdf, accessed June 29, 2009.

chapter 5

BUILDING STRUCTURE AND ENVELOPE

BY ERIC COREY FREED, LEED-AP

Principal, organicARCHITECT

Author, *Green Building & Remodeling for Dummies* (Wiley, 2007)

The world of the made will soon be like the world of the born.

—Kevin Kelly, 1994

INTRODUCTION

Toby the cat has a musculoskeletal system that can withstand forces applied from all directions and at many times her weight. She can wake up and respond to dangers such as smoke or noise sensed while she is sleeping. She can maintain internal equilibrium over a broad range of external conditions. Thermoreceptors in her skin sense heat and cold. In cold weather, the hairs in her fur stand up straighter, trapping more air and improving their insulation. She seeks out sunny spots and lies in them to stay warm. In hot weather, only her paws sweat so she licks herself to produce evaporation over more of her body.

This cat maintains an internal body temperature of 102 in spite of a wide variation of external temperatures. *Source: Gelfand Partners Architects*

111

Building systems try to handle these kinds of tasks through the structure, the skin, and various automatic sensors and alarms. As building design changes to take advantage of our growing engineering and instrumentation capabilities, we can get a little closer to the capabilities of the cat. Concepts of flexibility and adaptability to changing external conditions have become part of building design. Buildings that move and dissipate energy throughout their structure do better in earthquakes than rigid structures. Building skins can insulate, exclude liquid water, and manage water vapor. Mechanical systems and envelope systems can work together to maintain a healthy mixture of gases and comfortable temperature and humidity. The sustainable building handles these tasks with an efficient use of resources and limited ongoing energy inputs.

Sustainability concerns for envelope systems include:

- **Resource efficiency.** In terms of weight, the structural systems make up a large portion of the school. Alternative construction methods, such as prefabricated insulated panels, or efficient framing, reduce waste.

- **Insulation.** Heat or cooling lost through the building envelope is energy wasted.

- **Weatherizing.** Gaps between wall materials, and doors and windows, allow heat to escape.

- **Water and moisture control.** Moisture should not penetrate the envelope from outside or build up within walls or ceilings.

- **Openings.** Daylighting requires a variety of large openings in the walls or roof. Heat gain and loss through doors and windows may exceed all the solid areas of roofs and walls.

- **Acoustics.** School spaces should not be subject to distraction from outdoor noise or from adjacent rooms and should not be excessively reverberant.

- **Durability.** Durable materials lower operation costs and improve school security.

- **Flexibility.** Schools evolve over time. Bearing and shear walls are difficult to remove, penetrate or relocate.

- **Thermal comfort.** Insulation reduces conduction, but sometimes when materials absorb and reemit heat, they help buffer temperature swings. If used correctly, high-thermal-mass materials such as concrete and stone can help maintain a consistent temperature.

- **Recyclability.** Recycling can occur at many levels, from reusing crushed aggregate from concrete, to disassembling and reassembling prefabricated panels.

INITIAL CONSIDERATIONS IN WALL DESIGN

Architects and engineers begin wall design by analyzing the structural choices and fire separation requirements for the walls and roof. Building codes have evolved in response to disasters, and until the current environmental crisis, most building-related disasters have occurred through fire or building collapse. In the case of schools, in most jurisdictions particularly stringent requirements govern both fire resistance and structural strength for educational occupancies. Children are vulnerable, valuable, and less capable than adults of reacting independently to an emergency such as fire or earthquake. Therefore, the building should allow its occupants a longer time to evacuate in safety, or the building should be able to withstand more powerful disasters.

These design standards often appear to be overly restrictive. But they have proven their worth in actual disasters. School buildings were disproportionately damaged during the 1933 Long Beach earthquake in

This school building collapsed in the 1933 Long Beach earthquake. *Source: Historical Society of Long Beach*

California (magnitude 6.3). That was the impetus for California's "Field Act," which essentially required that California school buildings meet the same requirements as facilities such as police and fire stations. In 1940, the Imperial Valley earthquake (magnitude 7.1) tested 15 new public schools built to the new standard. None had apparent damage.

Performance of school buildings around the world has shown that where such elevated building standards are not in place, schools are intrinsically vulnerable to events such as earthquakes. As a building type, they usually have large spaces that require more carefully engineered structural systems. Because classrooms, auditoriums, and gyms ought not to have columns in the middle of them, the beams, trusses, or floor systems spanning them need to be properly sized. The one-room schoolhouse in the country that may have been built by local families with the same technology and materials as a home has been replaced in most areas by buildings whose scale makes it necessary to use engineered structural systems.

The implications of fire safety are less visible. One basic strategy is to separate exits from spaces where a fire might start by walls that can keep fire out long enough for people to get out of the building. Other lines of defense include automatic fire sprinklers and fire alarms. Fire sprinklers can stop a small fire from getting to be a big fire, and fire alarms can alert occupants to get out while the danger is still localized.

Both the higher level of performance of structural systems and the additional fire safety provisions of school buildings interact with green design. The simplest structural system is a doorless windowless box. Achieving the right amount and location of openings for daylighting must be integrated with the structure. Fire safety depends on separating smoke and fire from exit paths. Ventilation depends on moving air throughout the building. Both structure and ventilation must be reconciled early in the design to avoid extra costs, such as large structural members over openings or motorized fire dampers in ducts. Integrated design avoids unnecessary additive fixes.

Traditional structural systems include a significant amount of redundancy so that if mistakes are made, or accidents happen, the building continues to perform. In reexamining framing materials and methods and masonry unit design, the industry is beginning to re-duce the excessive resource use that accompanied this safety factor.

ALTERNATIVE WALL CONSTRUCTION METHODS

In conventional U.S. wood stud framing, walls are made of small section wood members placed at 16 inches on center and held together by more small wood members at the top and bottom of the wall. In platform framing, they sit on wood-framed floor plat-forms and serve as the support for the floor or ceiling/roof above. In earlier times, walls ran past interme-diate floors in a framing style called balloon framing. Metal studs have become an increasingly popular vari-ation on wood studs. They tend to be installed using platform-framing techniques.

Both kinds of frame walls use the studs as arma-tures for an assembly that also includes insulation, sheathing, waterproofing, siding, drywall, taping, and paint. Plumbing and electrical runs have to be routed through the studs. Wood studs are notched or drilled to accomplish this, while metal studs have punch-outs. A whole sequence of construction has grown up around the installation of the rough framing, the rough-in of the electrical and mechanical and plumbing systems, the subsequent installation of insulation and finishes, and the return trip of the plumbers and electricians to finish installing their fixtures. A system that pro-duced a more resource efficient building structure and a more compressed schedule would be advantageous for the environment and the budget.

In residential construction alternative framing methods such as 2×6 studs at 24 inches on center (o.c.) lined up directly under floor or roof joists re-duce thermal bridging through insulation and reduce the amount of wood used. School structures, due to their higher ceilings, are generally already framed with 2×6's 16 inches o.c., and have longer spans in floor and roof assemblies, also typically calling for joists that are 16 feet o.c. A more promising direction is to look at the potential to lay out buildings systematically, so that contractors can optimize their material use and their schedules and keep all trades moving through the project steadily.

Sixteen inches is a magic number (spacing of studs, nominal size of concrete blocks): three 16s equal 48, and many building materials come in 4×8-foot mod-ules. In brick and block work, the courses of the ma-sonry help set up dimensional systems. Metric coun-tries have similar dimensioning relationships. These systems help materials to be placed whole, with no time wasted cutting and no material wasted as scrap. Creating repetitive modules also facilitates the use of panelized wall and floor systems. With the panels fab-ricated off site in controlled circumstances, they can be more efficient, less expensive, and take much less time to install on site.

Walls are also built out of heavy materials, such as brick and concrete block, precast concrete, and tilt-up slabs. A commonality among these conventional systems is that the exterior finish is the waterproof-ing surface and the surface where the sealants create a tight building envelope.

Another approach is to use a rain screen concept, where the exterior surface stops most of the rain, but there is a cavity behind it that allows ventilation, pre-vents heat and vapor buildup, and protects the actual waterproofing surface. In hot weather, air circulates be-hind the outside material, cutting down on heat build-up. In cold weather, air flow in the cavity helps dry out condensation. Similar cladding materials can be used in conventional or rain-screen approaches so that they may look similar while performing very differently.

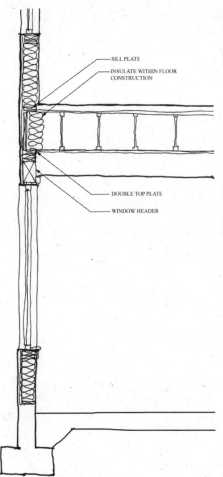

SILL PLATE

INSULATE WITHIN FLOOR
CONSTRUCTION

DOUBLE TOP PLATE

WINDOW HEADER

▲ Glass Fiber Reinforced Concrete (GFRC) wall panels helped accelerate construction on this gym. *Source: Gelfand Partners Architects*

▲ Wood studs used in platform framing remain a typical form of American school construction. *Source: Gelfand Partners Architects*

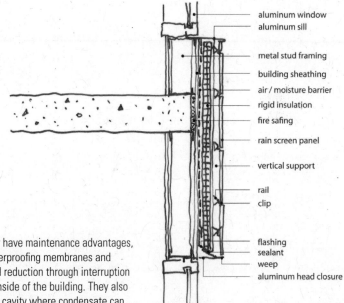

aluminum window
aluminum sill

metal stud framing

building sheathing

air / moisture barrier

rigid insulation

fire safing

rain screen panel

vertical support

rail

clip

flashing
sealant
weep
aluminum head closure

▶ Rain-screen systems may have maintenance advantages, extending longevity of waterproofing membranes and contributing to cooling load reduction through interruption of heat conduction to the inside of the building. They also place the vapor barrier in a cavity where condensate can evaporate or drain away without damaging the insulation. *Source: Gelfand Partners Architects*

Design Strategies

The environmental impact of wall systems can be improved through the use of:

▦ Preengineered materials, such as engineered lumber, glulam beams, and engineered joists

▦ Sustainably harvested wood products

▦ Panelized wall systems, including Structural Insulated Panels (SIPs)

▦ Dimensioning the walls to the module of the material to reduce construction waste

▦ Coordinating and stacking openings, electrical, and mechanical systems

▦ Durable materials

▦ Materials whose structure can be left as the final finish

▦ Thermal mass materials (stone, brick, concrete) to stabilize the temperature of the school

▦ Thicker walls to allow extra space for insulation

▦ Healthy, natural, or nontoxic materials, such as formaldehyde-free plywood

Sheathing

In wood or steel stud walls, the lateral resistance (to forces such as wind or earthquake) is provided by sheathing. Sheathing may also be used in an infill wall as a backing for cement plaster or wall finishes such as shingles, clapboard, or tile. Most standard plywood uses formaldehyde as an adhesive. Specify formaldehyde-free plywood. Since wood is a diminishing natural resource, the greenest option is to specify wood certified by the Forest Stewardship Council (FSC). The FSC seal is a trusted mark of sustainably harvested wood products. Not all wood products are yet available certified by FSC.

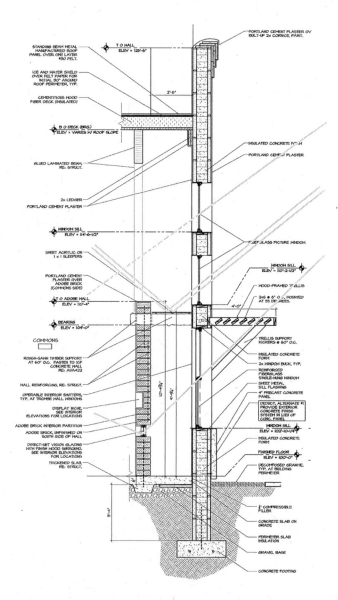

This wall section for Centennial School in San Luis, Colorado, combines a modern insulated concrete form wall with an interior adobe wall. Sunlight shining through the windows onto the interior adobe heats it up. The insulated exterior wall keeps the warmth that is reemitted by the adobe inside the building. *Source: SLATERPAULL Architects*

Wall Finishes

A variety of environmentally friendly siding options are available. Preference should be given to materials that contain:

- High recycled material content
- Reclaimed materials
- Durable and maintenance-free materials

Some sustainable options for siding include:

- **Exposed wood.** Sustainably harvested or reclaimed wood is a natural material and a renewable resource. Keep it out of direct sunlight. Certain species of wood are naturally resistant to pests. Redwood, cypress, and ipe are naturally rot resistant.
- **Fiber cement panels.** These strong, fire-resistant panels are available as shingles, panels, and boards. Certain manufacturers produce integrally colored panels. They may be installed as siding or as rain screens.
- **Stucco.** Available in an incredible palette of colors, stucco creates a durable and forgiving surface. Dark colors will absorb heat; light colors will reflect the sun and keep the school cooler. Integral color stucco can be left alone or painted only when needed, and then with less need for repainting.

INSULATION

Perhaps no other green building feature has more impact for less cost than insulation. Where temperatures outside are either uncomfortably cold or uncomfortably hot, to maintain a constant comfortable temperature inside, one must maintain a high temperature differential between the inside and the outside of the building. Heat is transferred by conduction, convection, or radiation. When it is cold outside, the building wall becomes cold too. If it is a solid material, people on the inside will lose heat to the wall through conduction, if they are touching it, or through radiation, if they are standing near it. Conduction of heat from the air to the wall will cause cold air to fall and hot air to rise—convection.

Insulation interrupts all these mechanisms. If there is insulation, or an air gap or void between the inside surface and the outside surface, such as an insulating window, heat cannot be conducted, and the inside surface will maintain the temperature of the inside space. Thus, there will be no loss of energy to the surface through radiation and no differential to set up convection. Convection occurs whenever there is a temperature differential in a space, with warm air rising. This causes insulation in the roof to be the most important first step in reducing heat loss. Often the requirements for the roof/ceiling insulation are higher than for the walls, which is also convenient because there tends to be more space for insulation in the ceiling than in the walls. Insulation comes in many forms,

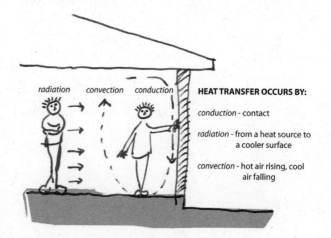

radiation   convection   conduction

HEAT TRANSFER OCCURS BY:

conduction - contact

radiation - from a heat source to a cooler surface

convection - hot air rising, cool air falling

Heat transfer follows three paths. *Source: Gelfand Partners Architects*

each with a different R-value. Higher R-values indicate more insulating efficiency.

Batt Insulation

Batts are the most common type of insulation. Consisting of light, fluffy blankets, batt insulation is sold in long rolls in standard widths. They easily fit within the spaces between either wood or metal wall studs or floor joists. The rolls typically come in 16- or 24-inch widths to match the standard spacing of framing.

Although fiberglass is most common, batts are available in several materials, including cotton, rock wool, and recycled materials. Formaldehyde is normally used as an adhesive but is a known carcinogen and poses a health risk. Most insulation companies now provide formaldehyde-free versions of their batt insulation. Other choices exist, including recycled cotton batt insulation sourced from scraps of denim. This clever use of a waste material is also naturally formaldehyde free.

The rolls of batt insulation are available unfaced or "faced" with heavy kraft paper or foil. The reflective barrier increases the R-value and energy efficiency and can serve as a vapor barrier within the wall. In walls where space is tight, faced batts are a way to achieve a higher R-value in less space. The facing needs to be on the warm side of the wall so that moisture-laden air does not penetrate the insulation and condense on the cool side of the insulation. When the warm side and the cool side switch, unbacked insulation can avoid the difficulties of condensation.

Loose-Fill Insulation

Loose-fill insulation consists of shredded bits of insulation, which is then blown into place using a piece of equipment resembling a leaf blower. The advantage to loose fill is that it can get into hard-to-reach areas and fill up the voids and cavities. In areas where installing rolled batt insulation would be difficult, such as in existing buildings or a low attic, loose fill simplifies the task. Loose fill is available in the same materials as batt insulation (fiberglass, cotton, and rock wool) and also in cellulose, often from recycled sources. Specify only formaldehyde-free products.

Spray Foam Insulation

Just like loose fill, spray foam insulation requires special equipment to blow the material into the wall. During installation, foam insulation typically expands like shaving cream to fill the entire space between the studs. This creates a dense and well-insulated wall with a much higher R-value than batt insulation in the same thickness. Spray foam is ideal for walls and around windows, as it seals the walls completely, preventing air leaks.

Spray foam products range from healthy to toxic. Recent healthy products include a soy-based foam. The initial cost may be steep, but circumstances such as difficulty of access for batts or an open wall where loose fill will not work could make spray foam the appropriate choice. These spray foams will work with either wood or metal studs. They are not cost effective for horizontal areas, such as roofs and attics. For

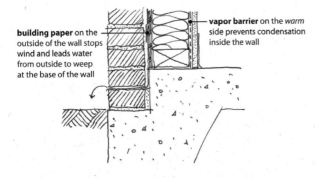

building paper on the outside of the wall stops wind and leads water from outside to weep at the base of the wall

vapor barrier on the *warm* side prevents condensation inside the wall

This brick veneer wall assembly includes both building paper and a vapor barrier. *Source: Gelfand Partners Architects*

any spray foam product, specify only water- and air-based blowing agents. Avoid petrochemical blowers for health reasons.

Rigid Foam Insulation

Rigid foam insulation comes in stiff, solid panels of dense hardened foam. The boards have up to double the R-value of standard batt insulation in the same thickness. Sometimes rigid foam can be used to add slope to a flat roof. Due to their higher cost, rigid foams are best used in places with limited depth, where other insulation will not work, or where they are needed to create extra slope. Rigid boards often are used between exposed ceiling beams or over a concrete wall.

WEATHERIZING

Filling the gaps between different materials and assemblies in the wall is *weatherizing*. If air is leaking through a wall or ceiling, conduction and convection can lead to significant energy losses even if the bulk of the wall or roof is insulated and there is no contact for conduction. Caulk and various kinds of compressible fillers are the mainstays of this task.

As discussed earlier, foam insulation products create tight seals in floors, walls, and ceilings and around such items as electric outlets and plumbing penetrations. Larger joints require specialized joint filler materials, such as closed cell neoprene or insulated expansion joints. New energy audit methods such as infrared thermography can help locate energy leaks in existing buildings.

One consequence of closing up the gaps and improving doors and windows is that air infiltration, once a significant source of indoor air changes, will no longer provide needed ventilation. Any well-sealed building requires a well-designed ventilation solution. Within rain-screen assemblies, the interior of the building is still well sealed, with the additional air gap provided beyond the sealed part of the envelope.

This thermographic image demonstrates differences in heat loss through walls and windows. *Source: Architectural Energy Corporation*

WATER AND MOISTURE CONTROL

Protection from the elements is one of the primary requirements of the building envelope. Water infiltration can damage the structure, leading to rust and corrosion of metal elements and to rot, warping, and swelling of wood. Moisture can reduce the effectiveness of insulation. Growth of mold and mildew, encouraged by the presence of moisture, can create serious health problems. Roofing eaves and overhangs push rainwater away from the walls of the school. In addition, the ground around the school should slope away, carrying runoff away from the walls and foundation.

Warm air can contain more water vapor than cool air. As warm air cools, at its dew point, water that was in a vapor form condenses out into a liquid form and falls or coheres onto cool surfaces. Through surface tension, water has a tendency to stay connected with itself, giving it the capability of following surfaces

Building waterproofing layers should overlap just as hats, raincoats, and rain pants overlap the tops of boots. *Source: Gelfand Partners Architects*

up and around where gravity would not take it. The temperature differential that causes water to condense should not occur within a wall. By placing the vapor barrier on the warm side of a wall, the moisture-bearing air cannot get to the side where its temperature would fall and water would condense.

In climates with high humidity and air conditioning, it may be difficult to identify the warm side of the wall, and vapor barriers may do more harm than good. Unbacked insulation exists for these situations. An additional precaution to avoid mold growth is to provide ventilation in concealed spaces. Attics, soffits, crawl spaces, and roof ridges should be ventilated to reduce the risk of mold.

OPENINGS

Windows

School windows present different challenges from the windows in other building types. The glass area is large because the floor area of the rooms is large. Operating windows require robust hardware to survive constant use over many years of service. Window lights (glass panes) should be of manageable size because windows on school campuses get broken.

A variety of materials have been developed for use in residential windows. Because of the size and usage of school windows, the material choice is more limited. Aluminum windows are the standard choice. Aluminum takes a great deal of energy to create but is relatively easy to recycle. Aluminum windows can be specified with a high percentage of recycled content without degradation in quality.

Windows lose energy in much the same way walls do—through conduction, radiation, and convection/infiltration. Conduction through the window frame can be reduced by using thermally broken frames.

parts of a window

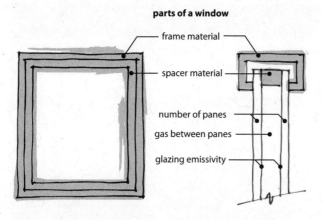

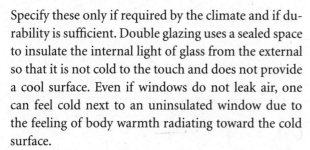

- frame material
- spacer material
- number of panes
- gas between panes
- glazing emissivity

Typical window elements include the frame or sash, the lights or glazing or panes, and the materials used to fit the lights into the frame. *Source: Courtesy* Whole Building Design Guide

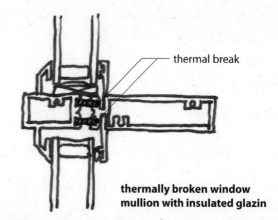

- thermal break

thermally broken window mullion with insulated glazin

Thermally broken windows with insulating glazing reduce heat loss through both conduction and radiation. Tight installation and good weatherstripping on operating windows prevent air infiltration and resulting convection. *Source: Gelfand Partners Architects*

Specify these only if required by the climate and if durability is sufficient. Double glazing uses a sealed space to insulate the internal light of glass from the external so that it is not cold to the touch and does not provide a cool surface. Even if windows do not leak air, one can feel cold next to an uninsulated window due to the feeling of body warmth radiating toward the cold surface.

Windows have their own performance metrics. Where insulations are calculated using R-values (higher means more insulating value), windows use U-values that indicate the rate of heat flow through the window due to conduction, convection, and radiation. The higher the U-value, the more heat is lost. The Solar Heat Gain Coefficient (SHGC) is a new value intended to replace the Shading Coefficient. It indicates how much of the sun's energy striking the window is transmitted through as heat. Zero means that none of the heat goes through, and 1 means that all of the solar energy is transmitted through the window as heat.

In climates where heat gain is desired to offset heating loads, a higher SHGC is good. In climates where air conditioning or other cooling loads should be limited, heat gain should be limited and a lower SHGC is good. Low-SHGC windows might be considered for east- and west-facing windows. The third factor is Visible Transmittance (TVIS-glass). Sunlight contains ultraviolet (UV) wavelengths, visible wavelengths, and infrared (IR) wavelengths. In general, greater than 70% visible transmittance is desirable. Where windows are accessible to children and play areas, the likelihood of glazing replacement should be part of any cost-benefit analysis.

Compared to glazing, the performance characteristics of aluminum frames have fewer variations. The main choices concern methods of installation: nail-on, replacement, or window/wall systems, such as curtain walls or storefronts. These choices are made based on budget, sequence of construction, size of opening, and number and type of operating sashes. For sustainability, the salient performance point is whether the window does anything to reduce heat loss through the frame, (i.e., is it thermally broken?). Like glazing, a cost-benefit analysis of the frames should be made.

Glass Type (Product)	Glass Thickness (Inches)	Visible Transmittance (% Daylight)	U-factor (Winter)	Solar Heat Gain Coefficient (SHGC)
Single-Pane glass (standard clear)	0.25	89	1.09	0.81
Single White Laminated w/Heat-Rejecting Coating (Southwall California Series®)	0.25	73	1.06	0.46
Double-Pane Insulated Glass (standard clear)	0.25	79	0.48	0.70
Double-Bronze Reflective Glass (LOF Eclipse®)	0.25	21	0.48	0.35
Triple-Pane Insulated Glass (standard clear)	0.125	74	0.36	0.67
Pyrolitic Low-e Double Glass (LOF Clear Low-e®)	0.125	75	0.33	0.71
Soft-coat Low-e Double Glass w/Argon gas fill (PPG Sungate® 100 Clear)	0.25	73	0.26	0.57
High-Efficiency Low-e (Solarscreen 2000 VEI-2M™)	0.25	70	0.29	0.37
Suspended Coated Film (Heat Mirror™ 66 Clear)	0.125	55	0.25	0.35
Suspended Coated Film w/Argon gas fill (Azurlite® Heat Mirror SC75)	0.125	53	0.19	0.27
Double Suspended Coated Films w/Krypton (Heat Mirror™ 77 Superglass)	0.125	55	0.10	0.34

Source: Courtesy Whole Building Design Guide

Performance information was calculated using Lawrence Berkeley National Laboratory WINDOW 5.2 computer analysis program.

California Series® and Heat Mirror™ are trademarks of Southwall Technologies.

LOF Eclipse® is a registered trademark of Pilkington/Libby-Owens-Ford Co.

Sungate® and Azurlite® are registered trademarks of PPG Industries.

Solarscreen 2000 VEI-2M™ is a registered trademark of Viracon.

Shading Devices

Part of the window design is the shading device. Shading devices serve two purposes. One is to prevent heat gain or glare from outside. The other is to allow the teacher to control views or light level inside the classroom depending on the learning activity. Roller blinds are still in use in schools, either manual or motorized.

Venetian blinds can survive in offices and libraries but are fragile for classroom use. Blinds built into the gap between two lights of glass have advantages in that the blind will not be vulnerable, but the entire unit remains vulnerable. Because of the size of classroom windows and the variety of locations for operating sash, the blinds need to be considered at the same time that the windows are detailed.

Bottom-up blinds avoid interfering with clerestory light on the ceiling. *Source: Mark Luthringer*

Exterior shading prevents heat from entering the building. *Source: Mark Luthringer*

Doors

Doors have less impact on sustainability than windows. Materials include aluminum or steel, with the occasional wood door still in use. The biggest issue is an interlock between the door and the heating, ventilating, and air-conditioning (HVAC) system. Teachers prop doors open, and systems should shut down when that occurs. When a large group of children is pouring through a door, it will remain open for a significant period. In some climates, generous vestibules with two sets of doors could cut the heat loss from doors that remain open.

ACOUSTICS

Two aspects of acoustic performance influence the design of the building wall. Sound transmission through the wall is the first, and reverberation is the second. Sound transmission varies due to the wavelength of the sound. High frequencies are blocked by strategies such as staggering studs so that sheathing materials on one side of the wall are attached to one set of studs and sheathing materials on the other side to another, rather than transmitting directly through the stud, using resilient channels to block vibration, and filling walls with insulation. Low frequencies need mass to block them.

Sound transmission and reverberation are reviewed in the acoustics section in Chapter 3.

ROOF DESIGN

The selection of a roofing type depends on the roof structure, slope, height, wind load, and installation requirements. Flat roofs have been implicated in many health problems due to the tendency of standing water to pond and become home to microbes. All flat roofs must slope a minimum of ⅛ inch per foot. It is good practice to slope "flat" roofs closer to ½ inch per foot to avoid ponding. Roof finishes for such roofs include built-up roofing (BUR), consisting of multiple plies of fiberglass-reinforced felts laid in hot tar; single-ply roofing, either membrane or liquid applied and made of various synthetics; and modified bitumen, or "torch-down" roofing that is heated as it is placed. BUR and torch-down roofs are black and absorb heat, becoming culprits in the heat island problems of urban areas. With light or reflective coatings or cap sheets, these problems can be reduced.

In air-conditioned buildings, use a roof surface that is light in color (high reflectance) yet has a non-metallic finish (high emissivity). Asphalt roofs with a cap sheet and modified bitumen roofs should be coated with a material having an initial reflectance greater than 0.7 where 0 means that the roof absorbs all solar radiation and 1 means total reflectivity. Their emittance, or ability to release absorbed heat, should be greater than 0.8. Single-ply roofing material should be selected with the same surface properties.

Roofs with a minimum slope of 3" per foot can be asphalt composition shingle or metal. Similar to flat roofs, color is a major influence on heat performance. Such roofs are visible from the outside of the school, and designers may find that the light colors that perform the best in keeping buildings cool meet resistance in terms of building aesthetics.

Cool roofs can save demand charges and energy charges. They are highly cost effective, especially in desert climates. However, there are other benefits as well. Since solar radiation (especially ultraviolet light) is a major cause of roof deterioration, cool roof coatings can significantly increase the life of the roof membrane. Smaller daily thermal cycles in surface temperature will reduce the wear on the roof membrane caused by material expansion and contraction.

Different roofing materials offer a wide array of reflectance factors. Higher numbers are better for cool roofs.

Roof Type		Reflectance	Emittance	Cost ($/ft²)
Built-up	With white gravel	0.30 – 0.50	0.80 – 0.90	1.2 – 2.15
	With gravel and cementitious coating	0.50 – 0.70	0.80 – 0.90	1.2 – 2.15
	Smooth surface with white roof coating	0.75 – 0.85	0.85 – 0.95	1.2 – 2.15
Single-Ply	White (EPDM, CPE, CSPE, PVC)	0.70 – 0.78	0.85 – 0.95	1.0 – 2.05
Modified Bitumen	White coating over a mineral surface	0.60 – 0.75	0.85 – 0.95	1.5 – 1.95
Metal Roof	White, painted	0.60 – 0.70	0.80 -0.90	1.8 – 3.75
Asphalt Shingle	White	0.25 – 0.27	0.80 – 0.90	1.2 – 1.5
Liquid Applied	Smooth white	0.70 – 0.85	0.85 – 0.95	0.60 – 0.80
Coating	Smooth off-white	0.40 – 0.60	0.85 – 0.95	0.60 – 0.80
	Rough off-white	0.50 – 0.60	0.85 – 0.95	0.60 – 0.80
Concrete Tile	White	0.65 – 0.75	0.85 – 0.90	3 – 4
	Off-white coating	0.65 – 0.75	0.85 – 0.90	3 – 4
Cement Tile		0.70 – 0.75	0.85 – 0.90	3 – 4

Source: H. Akbari et al., "Inclusion of Cool Roofs in Nonresidential Title 24 Prescriptive Requirements," Code Change Proposal, PG&E, 2002.

Cool roofs also can help make the whole community cooler by reducing the heat island effect.

Comparison of standard roofing materials and their cool roof reflectance

Because cool roofs can significantly reduce cooling loads, allow for the use of smaller air-conditioning equipment, or, in some cases, eliminate air-conditioning entirely in favor of natural ventilation, various incentives to use them have been adopted.

The cool roof must be certified by the Cool Roof Rating Council with a minimum initial solar reflectance of 0.70 and minimum initial thermal emittance of 075. This organization has a rating procedure, CRRC-1, for certifying cool roofs. The standard allows for a trade-off for cool roof products, such as metal-

lic surfaces that have an emittance less than 0.75, if their solar reflectance exceeds 0.70. Cool roofs are also considered in American National Standards Institute (ANSI), American Society of Heating, Refrigerating and Air Conditioning Engineers (ASHRAE), Illuminating Engineering Society of North America (IESNA) Standard 90.1-2001 and state energy codes in Georgia, Florida, and Hawaii. Credit may be realized for cool roof products that exceed minimum requirements if the whole building performance method of compliance is used.

LEED (Leadership in Energy and Environmental Design) requires low-sloped cool roofs to have an initial solar reflectance of 0.65, an aged solar reflectance of 0.50, and a minimum thermal emittance of 0.9.

This environmental green roof has been in place for 10 years. *Source: Gelfand Partners Architects*

Green Roof

Looked at from above, cities are very impermeable places, with paving and roofs accounting for the majority of surfaces. These areas rush storm water into drains, cause flood dangers, and create heat islands that change the local habitat until it is unrecognizable. The area represented by roofs is extensive, and the appeal of covering it all in greenery is intense. An established green roof is a piece of the local habitat. Water is absorbed into the planting and transpired, greatly reducing the speed and quantity of run-off. The roof is habitat to plants and animals. The assembly of insulation and soil needed to support the plants reduces temperature swings and increases the longevity of the roof membrane.

Green roof systems may be modular, with drainage layers, filter cloth, growing media, and plants already prepared in movable, interlocking grids, or, each component of the system may be installed separately. This green space could be below, at, or above grade, but in all cases, the plants are not planted in the "ground." Planting may be extensive, as in the grasses shown, or intensive, as in trees or large shrubs.

For schools, green roofs have the same assets as for other buildings but are also an opportunity to take advantage of roof areas that are visible from other parts of the school as demonstrations for students. They can replace areas that might be lost to asphalt on the ground. Green roofs may be adjacent to usable parts of roofs, but they are rarely designed for high traffic. They can be designed to attract butterflies or birds.

Plant selection for green roofs depends on a variety of factors, including climate, type and depth of growing medium, loading capacity, height and slope of the roof, maintenance expectations, and the presence or absence of an irrigation system. Preparing for maintenance needs to be a part of the selection of green roof system. With conventional low-slope roofs, when a leak occurs, roofing contractors usually can go up onto the roof, find the leak, and repair it. With a green roof, a leak may be more difficult to find if the membrane cannot be examined or if water has migrated through the green roof assembly. Visual inspection and repairs can be done only after removing vegetation, soil, and the assorted drainage and filter layers present with most green roofs. At least one green roof system addresses this concern through a modular design that allows planting areas to be lifted like tiles to access the roofing membrane.

Roofs can serve other functions besides supporting vegetation with an environmentally friendly building, and some of these other uses may be incompatible with plantings. For example, a roof can support a photovoltaic or solar-thermal array, producing electricity or hot water for a building. Or a roof can serve as a rainwater harvesting system to serve the water needs of the building and surrounding site. Green roofs in Seattle were found to produce very limited amounts of runoff—the plants were using all the rain that fell on them!

Most low-profile (extensive) green roofs are not designed to be walked on. For applications in which rooftop gardens and patio space is desired, providing the most cost-effective and most environmentally attractive low-profile green roof may not make sense— or the area for such a roof may be limited. So-called garden roofs tend to be designed for much more intensive human use.

Green roofs are a sophisticated sandwich of materials.
Source: Living Roof Section provided with permission by CETCO

LEED for Schools

Building Structure and Envelope contribute to these points on the LEED for Schools 2007 checklist.

Category: Sustainable Sites
- SS Credit 6.1: Stormwater Design, Quantity Control
- SS Credit 6.2: Stormwater Design, Quality Control
- SS Credit 7.2: Heat Island Effect, Roof

Category: Water Efficiency
- WE Credit 1.1: Water Efficient Landscaping, Reduce by 50%
- WE Credit 1.2: Water Efficient Landscaping, No Potable Use or No Irrigation

Category: Energy and Atmosphere
- EA Credit 1: Optimize Energy Performance

Category: Materials and Resources
- MR Credit 3.1, 3.2: Materials Reuse
- MR Credit 4.1, 4.2: Recycled Content
- MR Credit 5.1, 5.2: Regional Materials
- MR Credit 6: Rapidly Renewable Materials
- MR Credit 7: Certified Wood

Category: Indoor Environmental Quality
- EQ Credit 4: Low-Emitting Materials
- EQ Credit 5: Indoor Chemical and Pollutant Source Control
- EQ Credit 9: Enhanced Acoustical Performance
- EQ Credit 10: Mold Prevention

Category: Innovation and Design Process
- ID Credit 1: Cradle to Cradle certification
- ID Credit 3: School as a Teaching Tool

Whitman-Hanson Regional High School, Whitman, Massachusetts

Architecture Involution LLC

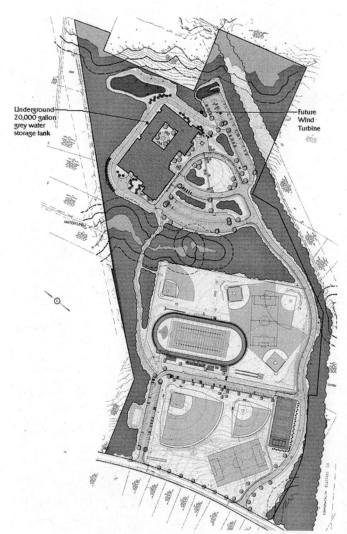

Underground 20,000 gallon grey water storage tank

Future Wind Turbine

This multistory building has a compact footprint.
Source: Ai3 Architects, LLC

PLANNING: NEW TECHNOLOGY PUSHES REPLACEMENT DECISION

The Whitman-Hanson School is a 234,500-square-foot comprehensive high school. It replaces a 60-year-old building that was deemed too expensive to renovate. Ambitious performance and technology standards for the new school were part of the decision. Some site features, such as paved areas and existing athletic fields, were reincorporated.

DESIGN: HIGH-PERFORMANCE FEATURES CALCULATED TO SAVE $100,000 IN ENERGY ANNUALLY

High-performance features were arrived at using full life-cycle cost analysis. They contribute to a 39% energy use reduction from code allowable levels. Energy-related features include high-performance glazing, increased insulation, a cool roof, and energy-efficient mechanical and electrical systems and appliances. Daylight harvesting controls integrate with efficient lighting systems and much natural lighting. The library, lecture hall, classrooms, performing arts center, and double gymnasium all take advantage of natural lighting.

In addition to energy conservation, there is a 38% water savings compared to other schools. The school features a 20,000- gallon rainwater collection tank. Stored water is used in the toilets and urinals. The toilets and sinks are low flow, which require less water, and the plants included in the landscaping are very tolerant of the local weather and require reduced irrigation water consumption.

▶ Exterior walls have continuous R-10 insulation on the outside of the sheathing in addition to the batt insulation. *Source: Ai3 Architects, LLC*

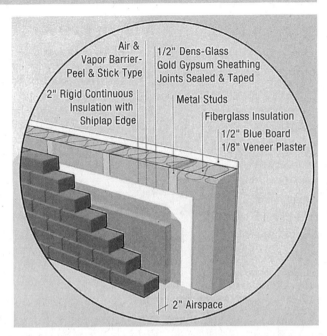

Air & Vapor Barrier- Peel & Stick Type

1/2" Dens-Glass Gold Gypsum Sheathing Joints Sealed & Taped

2" Rigid Continuous Insulation with Shiplap Edge

Metal Studs

Fiberglass Insulation

1/2" Blue Board 1/8" Veneer Plaster

2" Airspace

▼ The school image is not determined by its systems. *Source: © www. brucetmartin.com*

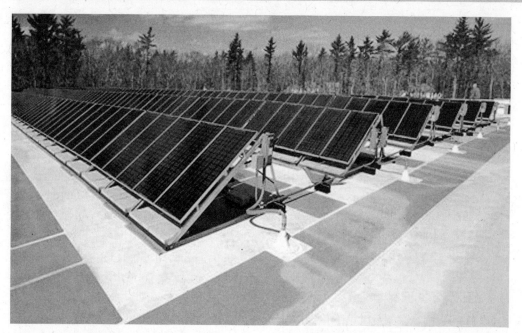

▲ The school roof accommodates a 49.5-kilowatt photovoltaic power generation system. It supplies the school with about 5% of all energy used. *Source: © www. brucetmartin.com*

▶ Daylighting reduces the need for electric lighting throughout the building. *Source: © www.brucetmartin.com*

Tarkington Elementary School, Chicago, Illinois

OWP&P

PLANNING: PILOT SCHOOL FOR DISTRICT-WIDE SUSTAINABLE COMMITMENT

Tarkington Elementary School is a 134,000-square-foot, three-story building located in Chicago. It is the first school in the Chicago Public Schools to meet the U.S. Green Building Council green standards. It will stand as a model for other Chicago public schools to come, which will be required to go green. The school district regards the decision as equally important in terms of teaching the students about sustainability as the impact of the building itself.

The new Tarkington school is also a community anchor that reflects the strong partnership between the Public Building Commission of Chicago, the Chicago Public Schools, and the Chicago Park District. Tarkington houses a Chicago Park District office and shares its athletic facilities with the community after school hours.

DESIGN: LEED-NC CERTIFIED

Green features in the school include low-toxic paint, glues, and caulking so that concentration and health are not affected. Daylighting is maximized through very large windows and a lighting system that regulates the amount of light entering the room. A key feature that Tarkington possesses is the roof garden that blooms almost year-round and helps buffer building temperature swings. On the remaining third of roof that the garden does not cover, there is a white coating to create a cool roof.

A stormwater management system drains the clean runoff into the lagoon beside the school. The school also has low-flow toilets, which should reduce water usage by 20%. In addition, one-quarter of the materials were locally sourced, 90% of the steel is recycled, and 82% of the construction waste from the building was recycled.

▶ Park district uses are adjacent to the gym and can be secured separately from the rest of the building.
Source: OWP/P

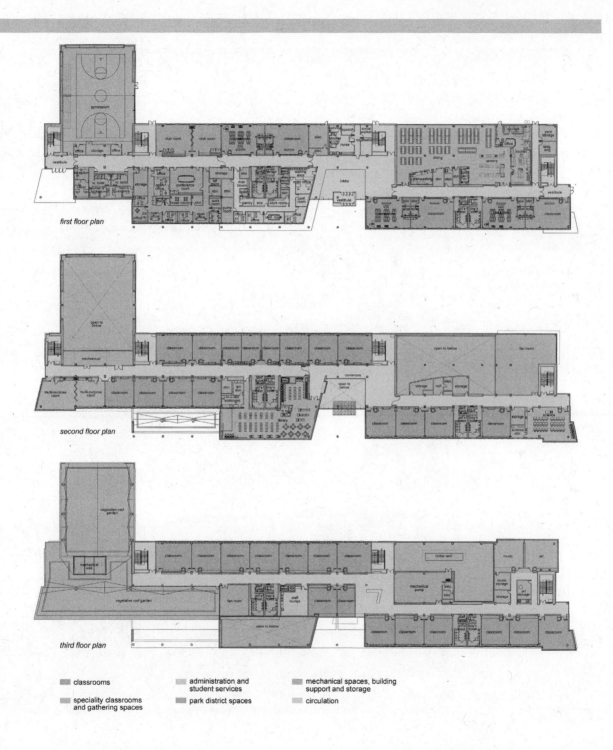

first floor plan

second floor plan

third floor plan

classrooms

administration and
student services

mechanical spaces, building
support and storage

speciality classrooms
and gathering spaces

park district spaces

circulation

▲ Tarkington Elementary School has a strong civic presence. *Source: James Steinkamp*

▶ A green roof extends across the length of the building. *Source: James Steinkamp*

Interior spaces are brightly lit. *Source: James Steinkamp*

chapter **6**

HEATING, VENTILATING, COOLING, AND PLUMBING

BY RON BLUE, PE, LEED-AP

Ron Blue is a principal with List Engineering Company located in Monterey, California. He has spent over 35 years as a consulting mechanical engineer and is LEED accredited and licensed in six states.

INTRODUCTION

Buildings historically used a variety of passive systems, envelope design, and daylighting to create a usable and comfortable interior environment. Modern buildings rely to a greater or lesser extent on heating, ventilating, and air-conditioning systems, often referred to as HVAC, to keep the occupants comfortable. Ideally, this is accomplished automatically, without their noticing how it happens.

The availability of running water throughout the building is the other modern convenience we take for granted. With as little thought as given to the comfort systems, building occupants feel that water at the tap is endlessly available. But water, like energy, is a finite resource. The plumbing part of the project, when combined with the fire protection system, rounds out what is referred to as the mechanical trades or the Construction Specifica-

tion Institute's Division 15 (1995 format). Fire protection systems are static and, when considered in terms of life safety, not very negotiable. In contrast, HVAC and plumbing have significant consequences for sustainability.

This chapter considers a number of items mechanical engineers evaluate in completing their portion of the project.

COMFORT

Comfort describes the degree to which people are not distracted by outside influences. They are able to focus or concentrate without being annoyed by noise, odor, or being too warm or too cool. The space is not drafty, and there is little tendency to become sleepy. These are all desirable characteristics for the classroom environment.

Not everyone will be comfortable with the same conditions. The American Society of Heating, Refrigeration and Air Conditioning Engineers (ASHRAE) Standard 55-2004 has defined comfort as conditions acceptable to 80% or more of the occupants. LEED (Leadership in Energy and Environmental Design) for Schools reinforces this by awarding a point for that accomplishment. Does this mean that the uncomfortable 20% will accept the definition? No. In classrooms, there is the added complication that adults and children seem to have different tolerances. What it does mean is that up-front discussion needs to occur involving end users, maintenance, and operations staff, so that the target range of conditions is understood by all.

Several factors contribute to make a space comfortable. The list includes:

- **Temperature.** Is the space too warm or too cool? Even if the room thermostat reads a perfect 72°F, is the occupant's chair located in the direct, glaring sun?

- **Relative humidity.** Air can hold a different amount of moisture depending on the temperature. Relative humidity compares the amount of moisture in the air to the maximum it could hold at that temperature. Both high and low relative humidity create comfort problems.

- **Air velocity.** People do not enjoy sitting in a draft, yet they do not appreciate a stuffy space either. Air velocities that are higher than necessary can make an occupant feel cooler than necessary due to the evaporative cooling that will occur. Proper air distribution techniques can handle this issue.

- **Acoustics.** Machinery makes noise, air movement makes noise, and reflective surfaces affect room acoustics. The noise criteria (NC) is a single numerical value that interprets how the human ear hears various frequencies. Various design guides identify NC design limits for the various spaces. Libraries and classrooms should have NC 30 to 35; a gymnasium, NC 35 to 40.

- **Odor.** While odor can be a warning of a health hazard, in the typical school application, it is usually more of a distraction. People sweat, and the released moisture needs to be removed. Science classrooms and locker rooms can have special requirements. Placing an outside air intake near a loading dock or too close to a plumbing vent or boiler flue can create a problem. Increasing outside air can be a solution, but increasing outside air can also lead to greater energy consumption. The use of an energy recovery device may aid, but some climates are too mild to make the economics work. ASHRAE 62.1 and the various Mechanical Codes prescribe minimum outside air quantities.

- **Carbon dioxide.** Carbon dioxide is the gas people exhale. It may build up in rooms with inadequate ventilation. Too much carbon dioxide may cause headaches and drowsiness.

These factors should be considered as a checklist when reviewing a project based on sustainable design.

SYSTEM TYPES

Selection of the HVAC system depends on its mechanical characteristics, its requirements for location and distribution of its components, and the capabilities of the maintenance staff who will keep it running. A primary question is whether a system must heat and cool and ventilate or whether a combination of systems will handle the three requirements. Because HVAC is a major energy load, selection of an efficient system or combination of systems is a key part of energy conservation.

HVAC can be designed with heating or chilling occurring at a central place and either heated air or heated fluids circulating to temper the various rooms. Alternatively, each room can have its own single unit that handles all necessary functions.

These decisions should be made early in the design of the building so that the needs of the mechanical system are integrated with the rest of the design. How much floor space will be required? How much ceiling space will be required? How much space is available between the ceiling and the structural framing? The answers to these questions will have an impact on whether a central system or an individual system is to be used and on the mode of distribution.

Central versus Individual System

A central system means that a significant part of the HVAC system energy exchange is concentrated in one location. A boiler room contains boiler(s) and pump(s) that send heating hot water out to the various rooms where it is used to temper the space through some kind of terminal device. In an individual system, each classroom might have its own individual gas-fired furnaces located inside the classroom or furnace closet. A large central packaged rooftop unit sends tempered, filtered supply air, including the required outside air component, out to the various rooms where terminal devices meter it into the space as necessary to maintain comfort. Individual packaged rooftop gas packs or heat pumps serve only one space each.

In the central boiler case, a boiler room is necessary, and that takes floor space. In some climates, boilers can be mounted outdoors, but that reduces equipment life and makes maintenance more difficult. When a large rooftop unit is used, floor space requirements may be reduced, but the designer's desire to hide the equipment must be matched with the maintenance department's need for access.

CENTRAL SYSTEM

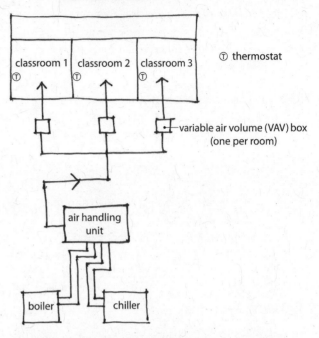

This diagram illustrates a central system with an air-handling unit that receives heated and chilled water from central sources and delivers tempered air to variable air volume (VAV) boxes that mix the air entering the room. *Source: Gelfand Partners Architects*

INDIVIDUAL SYSTEMS

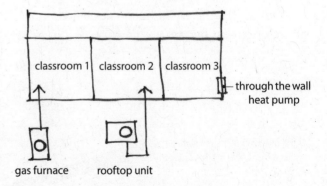

This diagram illustrates three different individual systems scaled for each classroom. *Source: Gelfand Partners Architects*

Factors in Favor of a Central System

- Moving heating or cooling energy through a pipe takes less space and energy than that required by a duct.
- Frequently, larger unitary pieces of equipment will have better performance and life expectancies than smaller, residential-grade furnaces or light commercial-grade packaged rooftop units.
- Maintenance takes place outside of the occupied space.
- More system options are available to the mechanical engineer.
- Cooling load diversity is a fact in most structures. When that occurs, less equipment capacity is required, thus providing first cost savings.
- Outside air and combustion requirements, such as flues and combustion air, are integrated more easily into the facility design.
- Multiple-story structures are designed more easily.

Factors in Favor of Individual Systems

- There is an inherent simplicity in equipment. Every maintenance person can troubleshoot a furnace, and most can work on a gas pack.
- Lower first costs exist.
- Loss of one unit does not affect heating or cooling in more than that room.

Radiant Systems

In many areas, radiant heat transfer can be used to heat the space. Often a radiant floor can be used, provided system limitations are not exceeded. Another method of delivering radiant heat to the occupants is to use a radiator or heated panel. In both cases, heated hot water is delivered to the space where a room thermostat controls the temperature.

Radiant floors allow maximum flexibility for furniture placement but are not great systems in cases where future remodels are expected. Typical school floor coverings, such as wood, tile, or thin carpet, pose a problem. A 6-inch wall cavity somewhere around the classroom is required for the manifold (the control device that interconnects the floor tubing with the Hot Water Supply / Return (HWS/R) piping). Heat loss will determine the tube (cross-linked polyethylene, or PEX) spacing. On multiple floor structures, the 2-inch gypcrete used to bury the PEX tubing also contributes to the sound transfer coefficient between the classrooms. The tubes in use today have overcome

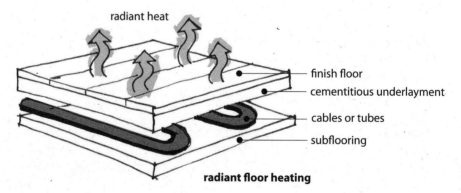

A grid of tubing heats the surface of this radiant floor system. *Source: Gelfand Partners Architects*

radiant heat

finish floor
cementitious underlayment
cables or tubes
subflooring

radiant floor heating

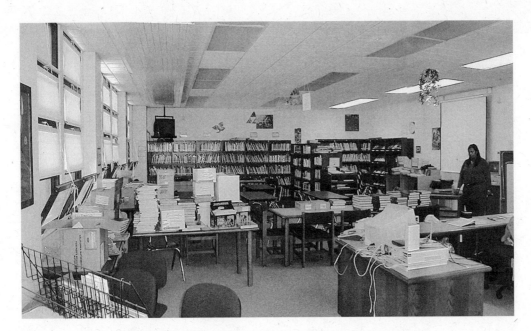

A radiator mounted on the ceiling next to the wall heats this library without using floor or wall space. *Source: Gelfand Partners Architects*

many of the maintenance and durability issues that put radiant floor systems out of action when the tubing was copper with multiple joints. But the tubing is still vulnerable to holes in the floor or ceiling or to remodels that relocate partitions.

The most common radiator used today offers a fair amount of flexibility also. Units can be ceiling or wall mounted, color selection is almost infinite, and besides the control valve, there are no moving parts.

With radiant heat, the system is quiet and control is good. With a thin gypcrete topping, response time is reduced and overheating is minimized. Radiant systems can provide cooling in addition to heating. But just as cool surfaces can be a problem in walls and lead to condensation, radiant cooling needs humidity control or a dry climate. If a radiant heating or cooling system is used, the ventilation air requirement must still be provided either directly through windows or louvers, or using equipment that will temper the outside air before it is admitted to the space.

Forced Air Systems

Forced air systems rely on either turbulence or convection to distribute warm or cool air around a space. When turbulence is the main mechanism, air is delivered either warmer or cooler than the ultimate comfortable temperature but in such a way that it mixes with the air in the room and reaches a comfortable temperature. Where convection is the primary mechanism, as in displacement, air close to the desired temperature is delivered at floor level, picks up warmth from people and machines in the room, and rises as it warms. The warming or cooling of the air before distribution in either mode can be either central or individual.

Individual systems usually are gas-fired furnaces mounted inside a classroom enclosure (see www.benoistco.com/images/products/teamair.pdf for examples) or inside a dedicated furnace closet. Another typical individual system is a packaged rooftop unit,

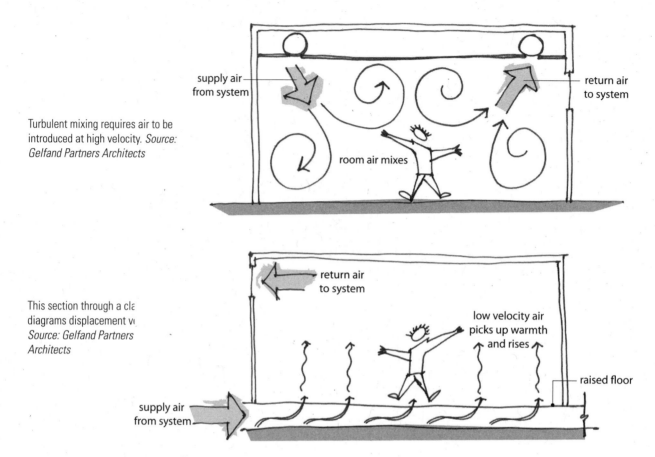

Turbulent mixing requires air to be introduced at high velocity. *Source: Gelfand Partners Architects*

This section through a cla diagrams displacement v *Source: Gelfand Partners Architects*

either gas fired with electric cooling, or a heat pump, either air source or water source.

The gas-fired furnace is easiest to apply in a single-story structure where the flue, combustion air, and outside air source can go through the roof. Multiple stories are possible but are more complicated. Another solution places the furnace on the outside wall with flue, combustion air, and outside air going out through the wall. Separation between outside air intake, flues, and other openings into the building required by building codes must be considered.

Packaged rooftop units can make sense with a single-story structure as all construction occurs outside. Split-system technology can be applied to multiple-

story structures with the compressor/condenser on the roof and the blower coil above the classroom ceiling, provided separation limitations are not exceeded (typically 35 feet vertical and 75 feet total). The split system distributes hot or cold water, so the outside air requirements for the system still need to be addressed.

Recent equipment developments in have introduced a system called the variable refrigerant flow or variable refrigerant volume (VRV) system. The VRV system uses a single compressor/condenser unit that can provide up to 16 tons of cooling and heating capacity and support numerous blower coil terminal units. While technically a split-system air source heat pump, these systems use high-grade controls and very clever engineering to arrive at very high efficiencies and greatly improved distance and vertical lift. They should be considered a high-end HVAC solution, and they are priced accordingly. Outside air still needs to be addressed.

Yet another system feature that may be discussed during the schematic phase incorporates what is known as *displacement ventilation*. The concept here is that if the new, clean, fresh, tempered air is introduced at the space floor level, closer to the occupant, less airflow may accomplish more good. The reasoning is this: If the lower 4 to 6 feet of a space can be made a comfortable environment, we do not need to concern ourselves with the upper third of the volume. By moving less air, acoustics probably will be easier to control and energy usage will be less. The downside is that the system usually requires thicker wall sections and/or a recessed floor space (effectively a raised floor) to provide space for the air to enter the room at very low velocity. If the room is going to contain student computers, the recessed floor may be desirable for other reasons and may not be a detractor at all. The recessed floor may also be coordinated with the high ceiling desired for daylighting.

Displacement ventilation has been associated with lower absentee rates. Because the system does not depend on achieving comfort by mixing all the air in the room, it reduces the tendency of turbulent systems to broadcast dust and microbes around the room.

DESIGN FOR NATURAL VENTILATION

Fan use is second only to lighting as an electricity use in buildings. If air could circulate without fans, much energy could be saved. What can be more sustainable than opening the window? And under many circumstances, that is all it takes to ensure air circulation. But there are considerations that make operable sash less attractive. Building codes establish a minimum amount of open area, typically 5% of the space floor area. For a 1,000-square-foot (sf) classroom, the open area is significant: 50 sf. Codes also limit the distance an occupant can be away from the opening, typically 20 feet. If a classroom is 30×32 feet, both sides of the classroom will need openings. Openings also must connect directly to the outside, with no atriums or other occupied spaces in between. Security may be a concern.

But presuming none of these concerns is an issue, inclement weather may be. When it is nice outside, it can be pleasant to open windows. When it is snowing outside, it may be considered a nuisance to open windows. If a space is designed to use natural ventilation, provisions must be made to provide tempering, and in some cases filtering, for that air during all seasons. Perhaps a storm-proof louver/backdraft damper/heating coil/filter/grille assembly can be placed in the exterior wall to provide a controlled source of outside air. With all that equipment, an opening high in the space or exhaust fan will be required to get the air moving.

Another consideration for the naturally ventilated room is fresh air distribution. For those not sitting near the window or outside air grille, a ceiling fan will aid in moving air throughout the space, helping to keep all breathing fresh air.

What moves air through a space? Windward/leeward pressure on the building pulls air through, and buoyancy resulting from temperature stratification and negative pressure moves air vertically. The wind blowing at an open window will move air into a space, provided it has somewhere to go once inside. Be sure to provide for cross ventilation. Normally, a design will work to decrease stratification. Why heat the ceiling when the occupied zone is the six feet closest to

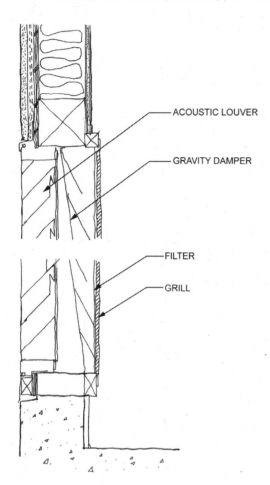

ACOUSTIC LOUVER

GRAVITY DAMPER

FILTER

GRILL

Natural ventilation systems can get air moving fast enough to require filters so that the air does not bring dust and pollen from outside with it. *Source: Gelfand Partners Architects*

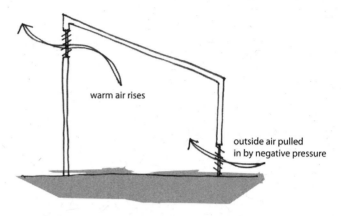

warm air rises

outside air pulled in by negative pressure

Stack ventilation works due to the pressure differences as rising warm air sucks outside air in behind it. *Source: Gelfand Partners Architects*

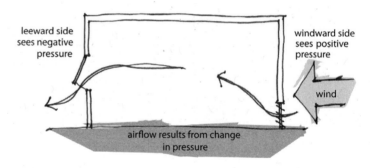

leeward side sees negative pressure

windward side sees positive pressure

wind

airflow results from change in pressure

Cross ventilation works due to the pressure differential on the opposite sides of the space. *Source: Gelfand Partners Architects*

the floor? And, in reality, a typical classroom ceiling height will not generate enough force to move air. If cross ventilation cannot be provided, an exhaust fan probably will be required.

Architectural features that can enhance natural ventilation include solar chimneys. Basically, the greater the height difference and the greater the temperature difference, the greater the "stack effect" for ventilation. A solar chimney provides a higher stack and a greater temperature difference. The chimney has glazing that faces the sun, with a black or dark surface to increase the heat. A louver at the top of the stack lets the rising warm air out, pulling room air from below (assuming there is a source of air to the room). Pulling in the ventilation air through a shady planted area can enhance the effect.

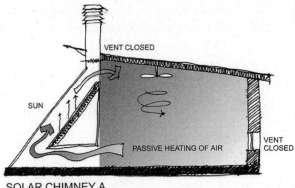

SOLAR CHIMNEY A
HEATING
TYPICAL WINTER DAY

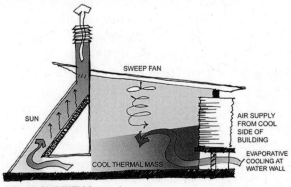

SOLAR CHIMNEY A
VENTILATION + EVAPORATIVE COOLING
TYPICAL SUMMER DAY

This solar chimney helps create positive ventilation in the Chum Creek Outdoor Education Centre. *Source: FMSA Architecture and Construction*

HIGH-PERFORMANCE STRATEGIES

High-performance strategies are those that strive to get more from less. Characteristics of high-performance strategies include:

- Oversize condenser coils that lead to higher equipment efficiencies
- Water-cooled condensers in lieu of air-cooled condensers
- Mechanical systems that recover unwanted heat or water in one part of the building and get it to another part that requires heat
- Systems that provide for extended periods of economizer cycle operation, such as displacement ventilation
- Systems that capture otherwise unwanted or waste heat
- Clear thinking that carefully examines approach temperatures, temperature differentials, and friction pressure loss rates

High-Efficiency Equipment

Higher equipment efficiencies can be specified in most products. A typical gas-fired furnace or boiler will be rated at 80% efficient (useful energy out divided by gross energy in). But both furnaces and boilers with greater than 90% efficiency can be specified. Caution: When going above 88% to 90% efficiency, acidic moisture condenses in the flue gases and must be addressed in equipment material chemistry. These higher-efficiency boilers or furnaces are often referred to as condensing. Condensing technology includes upgrades in material chemistry, to better deal with the acidic moisture, and provides drainage at appropriate places to remove the condensate. Rated boiler efficiency will also increase with lower entering (return) water temperatures, but a return water temperature less than 140°F on a noncondensing boiler will lead to very early equipment failure unless tempering or recirculation measures are taken during the installation.

Equipment cost and need for maintenance attention will increase and energy requirements will decrease with the higher-efficiency selections. A life cycle cost analysis of the various system alternates should be used to verify, justify, or eliminate the choices. While a private sector owner might require a simple payback in less than three years, nonprofit, institutional owners should be satisfied with a simple payback in less than 10 years. Results within 10% should be considered equal.

Chilled Beam Cooling

Another HVAC system gaining acceptance uses a terminal device called the chilled beam. There are passive chilled beams and active chilled beams. The concept relies on running chilled water through a ceiling-mounted "radiator" that cools the air within. Through buoyancy, the cooler air drops into the occupied space. The cool air is replaced by rising, warmer room air, and the cycle continues. The heat gain in the space is transferred into the chilled water and removed from the space.

When air is cooled, its ability to hold moisture is reduced. Cool the air to its dew point and the moisture will condense. Since the lowest part of a chilled beam is the ceiling surface, there is no opportunity to drain condensate from the terminal device. This means that there can be no condensate. In order for the chilled beam system to be applied successfully, the engineer must consider the latent heat load in the space and the incoming ventilation or outside air and the operating temperature of the chilled beam. Typical room conditions have a dew point around 53° to 55°F. To be safe, the chilled water supply temperature is increased from the typical 45°F to 57 or 58°F. This does two things:

1. It helps prevent condensation from occurring.

2. It means that the chiller uses less energy.

Note that this does *not* mean condensation is no longer a concern. Operable windows, room relative humidity sensors and alarms, and ventilation air cooling must be considered. In some climates, chilled beams are just not a good idea.

The passive chilled beam system contains no moving parts. All heat transfer occurs through natural convection. Because natural convection is used, more fin space is required, so a greater amount of ceiling space is necessary to meet the load requirements. Heating and outside air requirements still need to be considered.

There are no moving parts in the active chilled beam either, but here the ventilation air is ducted into the terminal device in such a way that room air is induced to flow. This turns natural convection into forced convection, and the heat transfer rate increases. The induced airflow also increases the overall air movement in the space. Since active beams are more effective than passive beams, less ceiling space is required for the chilled beams. With the addition of heating hot water, the space heating requirement is met.

Another benefit of the chilled beam system is that the central air system is moving less air than a typical VAV system, so the air-handling unit and distribution ductwork is smaller. This can lead to lower equipment costs and possibly lower structure heights or higher ceilings.

Classrooms, libraries, and offices make good candidates for a chilled beam system. Cafeterias, locker rooms, and indoor swimming pools do not. Because of the dew point concerns in these areas, natural ventilation is not a good match for chilled beam systems.

Geoexchange Heat Pumps

One system that is gaining better acceptance, especially when cooling is required, is the geoexchange, ground loop, or ground-coupled water source heat pump system. The terminal equipment consists of extended capacity (meaning the condenser works with warmer- or colder-than-normal water temperatures) heat pumps, typically one per zone (thermostat). This part looks like an individual system. The

PASSIVE CHILLED BEAM

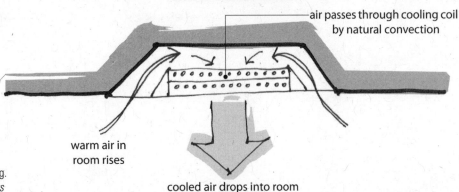

air passes through cooling coil
by natural convection

warm air in
room rises

cooled air drops into room

The passive chilled beam terminal
unit can be quite large, requiring
coordination with the lighting and
acoustic requirements of the ceiling.
Source: Gelfand Partners Architects

ACTIVE CHILLED BEAM

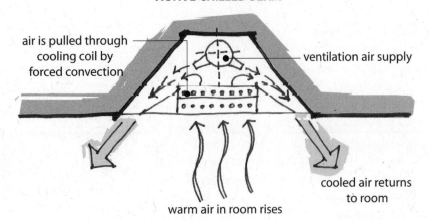

air is pulled through
cooling coil by
forced convection

ventilation air supply

cooled air returns
to room

warm air in room rises

Active and passive chilled beams both
depend on heat transfer between the
air and water in the piping. *Source:
Gelfand Partners Architects*

heat pumps are connected together by a tempered water supply/return piping circuit, with this part looking like a central system. The tempered water piping then extends to the bore field, where the excess heat is rejected or the cool water is warmed by the earth.

Many variables need to be considered in applying a geoexchange system, but computer-aided design (calculations) help reduce the mystery. The bore is typically a 6-inch-diameter hole, drilled between 200 and 400 feet into the earth. A PEX tubing loop is inserted in the hole, connected to a circulation loop, and the hole is filled with Bentonite to assure good heat transfer between the PEX tubing and ground. The depth of the bore depends on the heat transfer required by the design, the capacitance of the earth, and the bore spacing. Another variable is the duration of the heating and/or cooling cycle, so careful temperature analysis of the structure's heating and cooling loads must be provided.

Typical rules of thumb include one bore per ton of building cooling, 20 feet spacing between the bores,

GROUND WATER

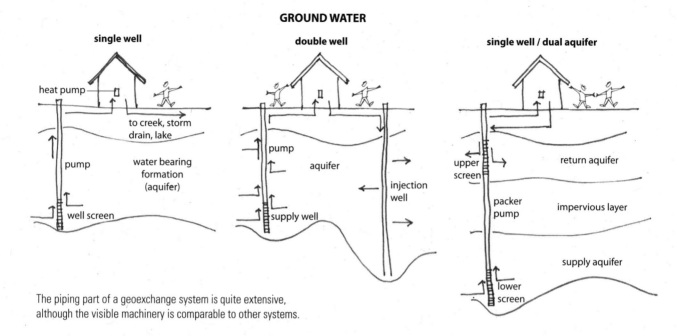

The piping part of a geoexchange system is quite extensive, although the visible machinery is comparable to other systems.

and 3 gallons per minute of tempered water flow per ton. Note that tempered water temperatures in a ground-coupled system can reach over 110°F and go below freezing. If freezing is a possibility, propylene glycol must be added to prevent the tempered water from freezing in case of a power outage. Propylene glycol will reduce system heat transfer and increase the amount of water and pump requirements.

In a perfect system, the bore field heat transfer capacity will match both the building heat rejection requirements and heating requirements. In some cases, the bore field may not meet this requirement. In this case, a supplementary boiler and/or closed circuit evaporative cooler may be required.

In the perfect system, the only central system equipment required is a circulating pump, preferably two 100% capacity pumps in parallel. If the supplementary boiler or cooler is required, additional mechanical space will be required.

Other requirements of geoexchange heat pumps:

- Insulate ground loop tempered water piping. A typical water source heat pump system uses tempered water that remains between 55°F and 85°F. Ground loop system water can get cold enough to go below the dew point in the ceiling space, causing condensation on the pipe exterior, possibly leading to a mold condition on the ceiling below.

- Do not specify PVC or PEX tubing for the circulation piping in the building. The fire marshal will probably take exception, and the water temperatures may cause problems.

- Provide for a 72-hour in situ test on the first bore drilled. This will determine the actual heat capacitance of the earth and remove much of the uncertainty of the bore field design. It may also lead to a construction change order, so prior to project bidding, review with the client whether a deductive change order or an additive change order is preferred. Also, consider asking for a unit price for bore depth in the bid.

- Be sure to allow space for the interface between the bore field and the pump room to allow to venting the bore field tubing.

- Review with the other design team members issues that may arise if the bores are placed under the building.

- A geothermal water source heat pump system will not get a LEED point per se. It is not considered on-site power generation nor particularly innovative. But the overall system efficiencies will most likely contribute to the LEED scorecard by increasing the supercompliance points given in EA 1 (LEED NC v2.2).

- The most recent equipment releases of water source heat pumps now include green refrigerants. R-22 is no longer required.

Solar Thermal Energy

Solar thermal energy is put to use with two different technologies: flat-plate collectors and evacuated tubes.

Flat-plate collectors have been heating domestic hot water and swimming pools for years. Flat-plate collectors circulate water through black-painted copper piping behind a glass panel. The highest water temperature is somewhat limited and works well with radiant floor heating systems.

The evacuated tube collector can generate the higher output temperature water needed by most other type heating systems, such as fan coils or air-handling units. The collector is an array of glass tubes containing a vacuum and a heat pipe. The heat pipe contains a liquid (often a glycol solution) that evaporates as it absorbs heat, then rises to the top of the heat pipe where it gives up its heat to a fluid flowing in the collector header. Once the heat is transferred, the heat pipe liquid condenses and falls to the bottom of the heat pipe, and the cycle continues. The vacuum, glass tube design, and chemistry in the collector allow for improved energy collection and efficiency. The fluid in the collector header is pumped to a heat exchanger in a storage tank, which in turn heats domestic hot water or is simply stored until the heating system calls for heat.

Considerations must include freeze protection, additional system components, storage capacity and loca-

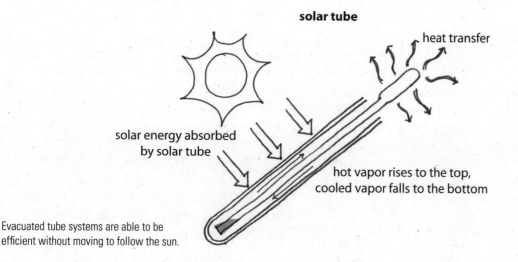

solar tube

heat transfer

solar energy absorbed by solar tube

hot vapor rises to the top, cooled vapor falls to the bottom

Evacuated tube systems are able to be efficient without moving to follow the sun.

tion, controls, and collector placement, especially with regard to vandalism or excessive curiosity. Because these systems are more complicated, verify with the maintenance department that they have the skills and budget to support the choice. If the answer is outsourcing, be sure there are resources in the community.

Cogeneration

Cogeneration refers to a system where electricity is generated and what would be waste heat from the fuel burned to turn the generator is captured for heating use. The electricity is distributed through the main electrical panel, and the waste heat is captured in a heat exchanger to make domestic and/or heating hot water. A small, packaged microturbine, a Buick V-6 engine, or a larger diesel engine can be used to drive the generator.

In projects that have simultaneous hot water requirements and electrical loads, cogeneration can be a win-win selection. Look for a project that includes an active physical education program with a shower room that is often in use, a swimming pool that requires heating, a full-service food service program, or even a laundry. Waste heat needs to be used every day. Mixed use projects such as schools with recreation centers or with adjacent multifamily housing can provide the mix of year round and all day and night energy use that makes cogeneration most effective.

The electrical side almost speaks for itself. Lighting, computers, and HVAC systems create an ongoing demand for kilowatts.

The successful project will match the heat rejected by the engine with that required by the hot water demand, without oversizing the generator. Making the electric meter run backward (selling power to the utility company) does not earn much of a payback. And rejecting heat out through a radiator because there is no demand for the hot water does not make any money.

Again, make sure the maintenance department is committed. In cogeneration systems, there are additional components that require attention. If they are not serviced, the system is not online. A life cycle cost analysis should be performed and consideration given to local utility company incentives. Since most schools are nonprofit or governmental organizations, tax incentives are of little value unless a complicated arrangement, such as a power purchase agreement, allows the power generation to be the responsibility of a for-profit entity. First cost cannot be ignored.

Controls

Maintenance departments are rejoicing at the demise of the old pneumatic temperature control systems. The days of the hissing thermostats, water-logged damper controllers, or torn operator diaphragms are passing, at least for those with direct digital control (DDC) systems. The age of the computer-savvy janitor or maintenance person is now with us. Just losing the air compressor and refrigerated air dryer is a sustainable event. Being able to rely on a communication network and software is even more so, making future HVAC system expansion or renovations easier to complete.

There are many DDC manufacturers, so the bidding climate is good. Many of the major HVAC equipment suppliers also offer DDC controls from the factory, using factory labor rates rather than field labor rates. There are also common communication protocols, so just because you started with Brand X does not necessarily mean that company has a stranglehold on your maintenance budget. If you selected a BACnet (or equivalent) capable system, you can switch brands.

Consider and discuss just how much control is needed. Many routines, such as an economizer cycle or hot water reset, will run blind to the user. Other routines, such as occupied/unoccupied periods and after-hours scheduling, will require more user participation. This can be a programmable room thermostat or a password-protected computer workstation in a locked room. Where would this workstation go? Who will be trained to operate it? Is the worker on site or out of the district office? Per-point costs have been decreasing, but first cost still can be noticeable in the budget.

One of the major features of the DDC-based system is that most are now web based. This means an alarm in one facility can be interrogated by the maintenance manager at the district office or an outside contractor in his or her office, often revealing the exact problem: a broken belt, a failed heating valve, or an active smoke detector. The repairperson can be sent to the field with the proper parts, thus reducing downtime and avoiding the cost of multiple trips. You just need a phone line near the DDC controller.

Building automation allows systems to be turned on and off or to operate at different temperature ranges according to preset programs or manual override. With sensor points in all zones, the controls also provide the capability to have enough heating or cooling where demand is high and not too much where demand is low. Different spaces in different parts of the building can be maintained efficiently in comfortable conditions.

WATER

The second major area that is included within mechanical systems is plumbing. In terms of sustainability, the main point is to reduce the use of potable (drinking) water. Currently most of the municipal water that is delivered and the water that is used in buildings has been treated to be safe for drinking. It is used for all purposes, including flushing toilets, watering lawns, and circulating in heating systems. While some utilities have started to distribute nonpotable water, in many cases reduction of potable water waste happens at the site level.

Use of Nonpotable Water

Reclaimed water is treated, disinfected, and filtered to tertiary standards and distributed in purple pipe for nonpotable uses. Gray water is water collected from shower drains, hand sinks, bathtubs, and drinking fountains and contains no human or food wastes. The first question to ask when considering the use of gray water is to the local Health Department. What is allowed in the jurisdiction? Some will allow seemingly anything stamped by an engineer. Others will allow nonpotable water for irrigation purposes, limiting it to belowground or allowing aboveground usage. Still others will not allow purple pipes within 75 feet of the structure. This is one area where the U.S. Green Building Council and our government(s) have some work to do on standardization. And even though the International Plumbing Code and Uniform Plumbing Code already make provisions, the final word always belongs to the authority having jurisdiction, and the Health Department may not be in agreement. Do not let your project get trapped.

According to the code, reclaimed or gray water can be used for subsurface irrigation but not where human contact can be made. If the gray water is treated on site, it may be able to be used above grade for irrigation. Rainwater and foundation drainage can also be collected and used for irrigation. Many schools include collection of rainwater in cisterns in visible areas

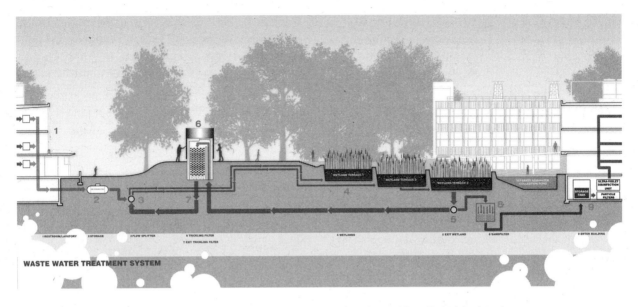

WASTE WATER TREATMENT SYSTEM

Part of the water recycling system at Sidwell Friends is available to student study. *Source: KieranTimberlake Associates*

so that children can make connections between water sources and water uses.

Points to consider: Gray water left unused can become black water and not desirable for use. Consider the implications of storing large quantities and the turnover rate. Collected drainage water is at atmospheric pressure and must be pumped in order to be reused. The importance of backflow prevention cannot be overlooked. Be sure the maintenance department is prepared to monitor controls, clean the strainers, and keep the pump seals operable.

Water used or produced in mechanical systems should be considered as a potential source of gray water. Condensate produced in air-conditioning equipment can be a significant amount of water. It can be a nuisance in the sense that it needs to be directed to a drain so that it does not pond on a roof or in a mechanical room. But it can also be an asset if reclaimed and reused for irrigation or another application. (Per-

haps if convenient it can serve as the automatic priming that all floor drains need to keep their traps full and block sewer gases.)

Water-Saving Fixtures

Choices that would have been considered green or sustainable a couple years ago may now simply be expected. A 1.6-gallon-per-flush (GPF) water closet or 1.0 GPF urinal probably will be required by the local building code. Also consider the flow rate at a faucet. If the sink is there to distribute water, such as a janitor's mop sink, a higher flow rate may still be allowed. But if the faucet is designed simply to wash hands, such as a toilet room lavatory, the flow rate can be much lower.

In a school situation, a flush valve is still the best choice for reliable operation. Several water closet manufacturers now offer fixtures with two flush rates, one designed for .8 GPF and another designed for 1.6

GPF, for obvious reasons. Also, the effectiveness of the flushing action has improved over the earlier water-saving water closet designs. The use of infrared sensors again improves the fixture performance and saves water. Retrofit projects can use battery-powered sensors that have a long life and do not tax the maintenance department. New projects can use line voltage sensors and avoid maintenance (almost) altogether. School toilet rooms can be tough neighborhoods, frequently abused by users. Be sure that any design decision made respects the durability requirements of the owner.

Though not a plumbing fixture, including a domestic hot water (DHW) recirculating system along with the DHW distribution is a very good way to save water. If the faucets and showers are kept within 30 feet of a circulating DHW line, the time the user waits for hot water is greatly reduced and less water is used. A paradox may arise with this choice: Recirculating DHW (DHWR) means an increased loss of heat that has to be made up at some point. To minimize the loss of DHW heat and the loss of not-so-hot water, include DHW and DHWR pipe insulation and some kind of control on the DHWR pump (typically, time of day or return water temperature).

Be sure to consider the branch run-out pipe size with low-flow faucets. Historically, a lavatory run-out would be a ½-inch pipe. At the new low-flow rates, the resulting time to get hot water may very well be unacceptable. Perhaps a ⅜-inch run-out should be used.

CLOSING

The term *life cycle cost analysis* (LCCA) has been used several times. The reason is this: While any number of clever or just plain obvious choices would lead to using less energy or water, when the increased first cost,

LEED for Schools

Building structure and envelope contribute to these points on the LEED for Schools 2007 checklist:

Category: Water Efficiency
- WE Credit 2: Innovative Wastewater Technologies
- WE Credit 3: Water Use Reduction
- WE Credit 4: Process Water Use Reduction, 20% Reduction

Category: Energy and Atmosphere
- EA Credit 1: Optimize Energy Performance
- EA Credit 2: On-Site Renewable Energy
- EA Credit 3: Enhanced Commissioning
- EA Credit 4: Enhanced Refrigerant Management
- EA Credit 5: Measurement & Verification
- EA Credit 6: Green Power

Category: Indoor Environmental Quality
- IAQ Credit 1: Minimum IAQ Performance
- IAQ Credit 2: Increased Ventilation
- IAQ Credit 6.1: Controllability of System, Lighting
- IAQ Credit 6.2: Controllability of System, Thermal Comfort
- IAQ Credit 7.1: Thermal Comfort, Design
- IAQ Credit 7.2: Thermal Comfort, Verification
- IAQ Credit 9: Enhanced Acoustical Performance
- IAQ Credit 10: Mold Prevention

added maintenance skill level or man-hours, quality of selected equipment, and ease of use is considered, a choice may not be economically wise. Institutional owners should be interested in the lowest LCCA, but first cost can be a very compelling consideration too. Human nature being what it is, a clever design that turns out to be unreliable, inconvenient, or annoying will be defeated. Where does that fit in the LCCA equation? And where does that leave the occupant?

If the point of the project is to demonstrate a principle or make a statement, then perhaps the LCCA is less relevant. But most school projects have to be paid for by a district that has competing forces for its limited resources. And most schools are maintained by departments with shrinking budgets and limited manpower. Be sure your client understands the implications of the choices.

Integration of ventilation and solar heat gain into the basic design of the building—before mechanical systems—is a key part of sustainability. Strategies that increase ventilation without fans, avoid solar heat gain where it will be uncomfortable, and increase solar heat gain where needed decrease the additional energy needed to keep buildings comfortable.

The increasing ability of systems to monitor conditions and selectively respond has helped reduce waste already. Sensors and controls are likely to continue to improve so that comfort can be achieved with increasing specificity. Mechanical systems may be replaced or modified over the life of a building, either to take advantage of such improvements or to replace worn-out machinery. The basic design of the building should take into account such potential changes as well as positioning the building's comfort and energy use to withstand the inevitable value engineering exercise that the design will undergo when the bids come in.

Centennial PK–12 School, San Luis, Colorado

Slater Paull Architects

PLANNING: A SCHOOL TO MATCH THE STEWARDSHIP AND INDEPENDENCE OF ITS RURAL COMMUNITY

Children in San Luis enter this school before kindergarten and continue until they graduate from high school. It will accommodate an enrollment of 400 in 64,000 square feet. The campus is 30 acres. It is also a community center. The functions are organized around a central space with a fireplace that can be used for school or community events. The fireplace has a tower that is reminiscent of a historic bell tower in the town but also serves as fireplace flue and cooling tower. At 8,000 feet in elevation, the town needs to adapt to severe mountain weather. Off-the-grid operation of the school was a goal.

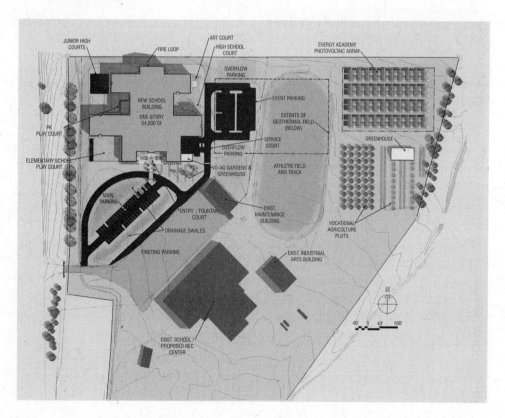

The site devotes significant space to sustainable power generation. It will also serve as a curricular tool. *Source: SLATERPAULL Architects*

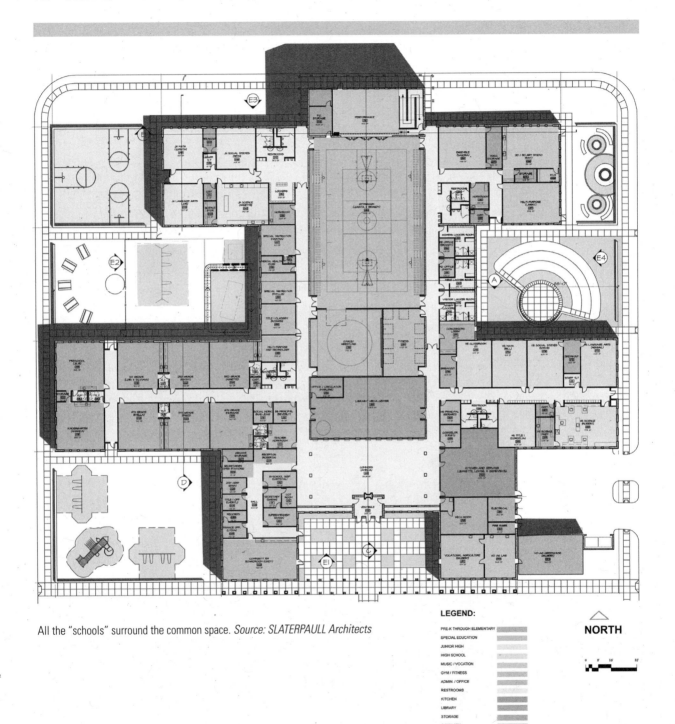

All the "schools" surround the common space. *Source: SLATERPAULL Architects*

LEGEND:

PRE-K THROUGH ELEMENTARY

SPECIAL EDUCATION

JUNIOR HIGH

HIGH SCHOOL

MUSIC / VOCATION

GYM / FITNESS

ADMIN. / OFFICE

RESTROOMS

KITCHEN

LIBRARY

STORAGE

AUXILIARY

CIRCULATION

NORTH

NEW CENTENNIAL R-1 SCHOOL
SAN LUIS, COLORADO

The school is designed to relate to the surrounding community. *Source: SLATERPAULL Architects*

DESIGN: ZERO NET ENERGY USE

The school community prioritized the environment in this affordable building. Sustainable goals set in the beginning of the project include:

- Improved R-value of envelope
- Additional mass for thermal storage: adobe and/or concrete
- Alternative building strategies: insulated concrete forms, adobe
- Extensive daylighting throughout with controls
- Light-colored roof
- Energy recovery in south walls
- 100% solar heated (passive and active: photovoltaics)
- Construction of "solar" field
- Natural cooling and ventilation: tower and operable windows
- Water-conserving plumbing fixtures
- Use local materials and labor
- Use materials with high recycled content
- Reduce quantity of material
- Significantly reduce construction waste

- Salvage and reclaim materials from existing buildings
- Building commissioning
- Storm water reclamation
- Bioswales to clean water runoff
- Electric vehicle recharging at the solar field
- Displacement ventilation
- Solar domestic hot water
- Research use of ground source and heat pumps
- Set goal for net zero energy use
- Demonstration green roof
- Radiant heating in slabs
- Wood-powered boiler?
- Waste management postoccupancy
- Xeriscaping and reclamation of natural site vegetation
- Demonstration gardens and greenhouse (grow produce for cafeteria)

Loyola Elementary School, Los Altos, California

Gelfand Partners Architects

PLANNING: STUDY SHOWS BENEFITS OF MAJOR MODERNIZATION OVER RECONSTRUCTION

Loyola Elementary School is located in Los Altos, California, and originally was built in 1948. A condition and cost-benefit analysis established that the existing foundations, slabs, and structural system remained in good condition and that the site plan was conducive to good daylighting. The decision was made to modernize but to aim for the same level of performance expected in a new building.

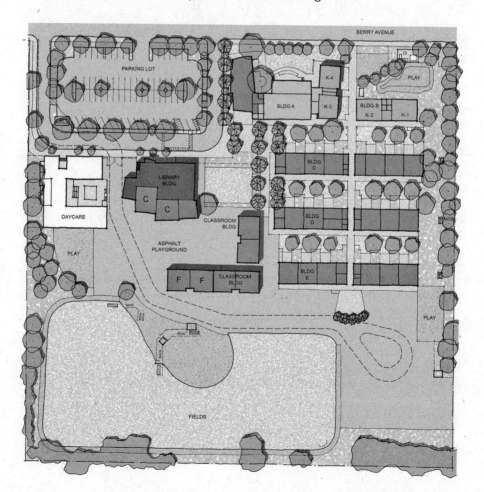

Master planning for a future new library and portable classroom replacement was considered in designing the site plan for the modernization. *Source: Gelfand Partners Architects*

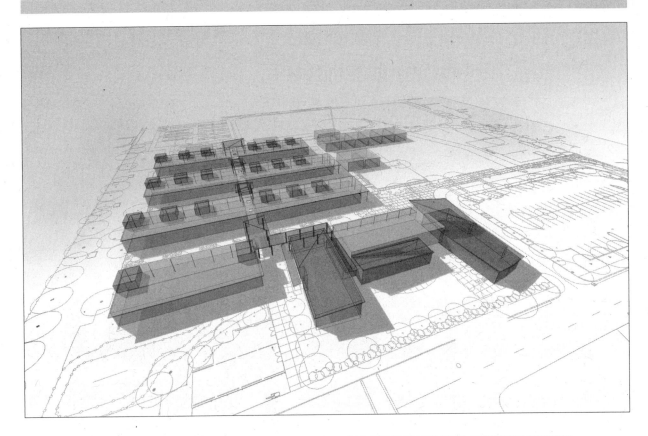

This diagram shows the limited extent of new additions to the campus in Phase I. *Source: Gelfand Partners Architects*

DESIGN: CHPS MODERNIZATION MEETING NEW CONSTRUCTION STANDARDS

Building envelope improvements were aimed at improved seismic performance, improved daylighting, and improved ventilation. An innovative HVAC system ties clerestory window operation to the energy management system, reducing the need for fan-powered ventilation.

To achieve and rebalance additional daylight, new roof monitors were added, along with clerestory windows, which are placed adjacent to the ceiling to maximize reflected daylight. There are also project display windows on the new shear walls. Spaces between the buildings were redesigned to extend learning space into the outdoors.

The louver that admits outside air can be seen next to the classroom door. *Source: Gelfand Partners Architects*

The automatic window operator can be seen below the clerestory window. *Source: Mark Luthringer*

chapter 7

LANDSCAPE AND SITE DESIGN

The Third Teacher

CONTRIBUTOR:

Susan Herrington, Associate Professor, Landscape Architecture, University of British Columbia

Susan is a licensed landscape architect in the United States and consults professionally in Canada and the United States. Her research concerns the design and history of landscapes. Susan led a five-year-long research program called "Outside Criteria" as part of the CHILD project, which is funded through the Social Sciences and Humanities Research Council of Canada.

For many adults, their fondest childhood memories are drawn from experiences outdoors. These include navigating the rugged terrain of an open ditch, piling fallen leaves to untold heights, building a snow fort, or catching fireflies on a summer night. Unfortunately, children today rarely have access to the types of landscapes that afford these experiences. Children not only spend increasingly less time outdoors, but when they are outdoors, the landscapes they experience are often highly controlled, and much of nature has been removed. Schoolyards are typified by large expanses of paving, rubber-matted play areas with fixed equipment, and monoculture sports fields restricted to single-use, organized play.

Yet there is a movement afoot to keep and restore natural elements in the play landscapes of learning environments. School greening projects have been launched throughout North America. These projects return trees, gardens, water habitats, and social spaces to the schoolyard and are beneficial not only to the ecological environment but to the children using these places as well. Many green schoolyards are linked to learning programs that consider the yard as a third teacher. Children and teachers use the schoolyard as a resource to learn from, resulting in diverse educational experiences and improved academic outcomes. For example, the National Environmental Education & Training Foundation (NEETF) studied the effects of environmentally based education programs on student learning in 60 schools. It found that students participating in these programs performed better on "standardized measures of academic achievement in reading, writing, math, science, and social studies," and there was a reduction in disciplinary actions. In addition, there was an "increased engagement and enthusiasm for learning, and greater pride and ownership in accomplishment."[a]

The benefits of using natural systems as third teachers are not limited to school-age children. Observing changes in nature, such as plant growth, improves all children's awareness, curiosity, observational skills, and reasoning.[b] A study of preschool-age children's outdoor play behavior at 17 child care centers found that they had more frequent and longer verbal exchanges when they encountered something living in their outdoor play environment. These encounters included interactions with plants, worms, and bugs and often involved ethical discussions, such as the merits of preserving or killing a worm.[c]

Green campuses are also valuable to children with learning disorders. For example, a study of 10- to 11-year-old children with attention deficit disorder (which effects over 2 million children in the United States) determined that exposure to green landscapes increased their attentional functioning. As part of the study, parents observed their child's attention after playing in different types of outdoor environments. These observations were analyzed by researchers who found that the children functioned "better than usual after activities in green settings and that the 'greener' a child's play area, the less severe his or her attention deficit symptoms."[d] Thus, providing green schoolyards that ensure contact with natural systems also helps children whose disorder has yet to be cured.

Importantly, keeping the schoolyard landscape green as part of the design process is a fundamental dimension of sustainable landscape architecture. The preservation of existing site features, such as soil, mature trees, and wildlife habitats, means less importation and transportation of materials onto the site. Construction on previously disturbed areas and the reuse of building materials from former on-site buildings also substantially contribute to the sustainability of landscapes. When landscape architect Cornelia Hahn Oberlander and architect Eva Matsuzaki designed the C.K. Choi Institute of Asian Research at the University of British Columbia campus, pioneering measures were taken to recycle every aspect of the existing site. The C.K. Choi building was made from materials and framing systems from an adjacent building slated for demolition. The new building's footprint matched the size and location of the existing parking lot, the most disturbed area of the site—thus preserving a grove of mature evergreens. The building contains compost toilets. All water is retained on site and is filtered using plant material. During the construction process, there was no soil importation, and even the construction workers were required to recycle their own materials— from building scraps to former lunch containers.

Green campuses are certainly attainable, and they benefit not only the ecological environment but also the children who use these places on a daily basis. According to Richard Louv, the author of *Last Child in the Woods,* children need visceral interactions with nature—experiences obtained through direct contact with natural systems and when learning is accompanied by feeling.[e] The logical location for these visceral interactions is the outdoor learning environment, a place that can contribute not only to children's minds and bodies but to their memories yet to come.

REFERENCES

a. National Environmental Education & Training Foundation, "Environment-based Education," Washington, DC, 2000, pp. 4–5, http://74.125.95 .132/search?q=cache:QDyFe6cIb7gJ:www.neefusa .org/pdf/NEETF8400.pdf+National+Environmental +Education+%26+Training+Foundation+(2000).+ Environment, accessed April 9, 2009.

b. R. C. Moore and H. Wong, *Natural Learning: Rediscovering Nature's Way of Teaching* (Berkeley, CA: MIG Communications, 1997).

c. S. Herrington, C. Lesmeister, J. Nicholls, and K. Stefiuk. *An informational Guide for young children's outdoor play spaces: Seven C's* (Vancouver: University of British Columbia, 2006), www.wstcoast.org/playspaces/ outsidecriteria/7Cs.html, accessed April 10, 2009.

d. A. F. Taylor, F. E. Kuo, and W. C. Sullivan, "Coping with ADD: The Surprising Connection to Green Play Settings," *Environment & Behavior* 33, No. 1 (2001): 54–77.

e. Richard Louv, *Last Child in the Woods: Saving Our Children from Nature-Deficit Disorder* (New York: Algonquin Books, 2006).

Biofilter at the C.K. Choi building. *Source: Cornelia Oberlander, ©2002*

Tomorrow you will see a campus with plenty of opportunity to build and sustain a community of learners. By simply moving through the thoughtfully designed series of courtyards, trails, recreation and gathering places, students, faculty, families and visiting community members will know a sense of place that causes us to belong, to take ownership and to care. This belonging will extend beyond our own campus into all of our neighboring communities through the new capability this campus will afford our outreach effort....We know by listening and by practice that sustainability is not something that can survive in isolation.

—Doug Atkins, on the occasion of the groundbreaking for the new LEED Platinum Chartwell School[1]

INTRODUCTION

In conventional urban schools, a multistory building occupies much of a school site, with paved playground adjacent, surrounded in a courtyard, on a roof, or entirely absent. In suburban or rural schools, the site usually has large areas of paved playground and often athletic fields, as well as a variety of miscellaneous functions, such as parking, pickup and drop-off, fire access lanes, storage, bicycles, gardens, lunch areas, trash enclosures, transformers, and space between buildings. These school sites are as paved and/or open as possible, with features located for easiest monitoring, and surfaces, even turf, chosen for their ability to stay flat and clean.

This urban middle school has paved all of its play space. *Source: Gelfand Partners Architects*

Such a campus is not the inevitable response to the security and maintenance pressures schools face. It is certainly not the most sustainable way to design acres of land. An integrated approach to the educational/developmental needs of children and to sustainability in paving, planting, and the location of buildings produces a very different campus. That campus could influence the experience of students, their families, teachers, and the community in a manner greater than the influence of any single building.

But campus design is the area where most sustainability rating systems are weakest. Quantifiable issues are included in LEED (Leadership in Energy and Environmental Design) and CHPS (Collaborative for High Performance Schools): site selection, areas of site disturbance, efficient irrigation, parking for carpool or alternative energy vehicles, and controls on storm water runoff quality and quantity. These issues are significant, but the larger opportunity afforded by sustainable school campuses is less quantifiable. Such campuses provide an opportunity for children to develop attitudes and knowledge they will carry with them forever, to develop empathy with other living beings, and to learn about the life that goes on outside us.

Concentrating here on suburban and rural schools, the challenge is to advance thinking about the entire campus ahead of thinking about the needs of individual buildings. The restorative potential of sustainable sites, the opportunity to create diverse settings for diverse school activities, and the visibility of the changes all argue for close consideration of site planning and landscape.

The Strawberry Vale School is designed to take advantage of its adjacency to a mature woodland. *Source: Patkau Architects, James Dow*

The site creates the first impression. Imagine a school accessed by safe sidewalks with improved intersections and the additional planting, speed control, and improved parking that calm traffic. Imagine walking into the school without interference from cars maneuvering into parking lots and with bikes wheeling in on their own convenient path. Imagine a garden in the front of the school, perhaps using area that might once have been parking but is available because there are better ways to get to the school.

The campus has a variety of places to gather in shade and in sun. The playground has area for kids to run and areas for them to build, perform, dig, find insects, and climb. Runoff from roofs soaks into planting. The site is visited by migrating birds and butterflies and is home to a diversity of plants and animals. Lunch is growing in the garden. Neighbors visit for ideas about how they can make their homes as sustainable as the school.

There is no technical reason such a campus could not exist today. Nothing needs to be invented. But habitual approaches need to be changed.

STORMWATER/GROUNDWATER MANAGEMENT

One of the major regional elements in habitat, climate, and human needs is water. Although often people in developed areas are using water that fell as rain a long distance away, the rain that falls in the immediate area also joins the water cycle. Before development, surface water passes over rough surfaces, is filtered through soil, and is absorbed and transpired by plants. A landscape of buildings with hard roofs and impermeable asphalt parking lots and playgrounds sheds water rapidly into drains and ultimately into streams and rivers. Speeding water into rivers is a major cause of flooding when that water exceeds the ability of the rivers to transport it within their banks.

Streams and rivers do require replenishing flows from surrounding land. The goal is not to eliminate runoff but to manage its quality and quantity in a manner consistent with the health of receiving water-

When water exceeds the carrying capacities of riverbeds, floods occur. *Source: U.S. Geological Survey*

This bioswale improves water quality and slows down run-off from the school parking lot.
Source: Gelfand Partners Architects

ways. Most simply, a sustainable hydrology design is either no net change to a site and its receiving waterways or restoration of a degraded site and its receiving waterways to their original runoff quantity, quality, and velocity—or to an even healthier state.

School campuses are often large enough to play a significant role in improved water quality, quantity, and velocity beyond their boundaries. The sustainable approach is based on reversing the modern civil engineering goal of rapid drainage from developed areas. While paving certainly can be improved, the biggest impact will be gained by reducing the amount of paved or impermeable area. The traditional approach of catching water in pipes and gutters was a direct way to avoid mud, unhealthy standing water, erosion, and

inconvenience. Fortunately, the alternatives not only improve hydrology but provide other benefits. Planted retention areas and bioswales avoid unhealthy pitfalls, slow water transport as natural surfaces did, can reduce flood dangers, reduce disruption of aquatic habitat, and reduce load on water treatment facilities.

Bioswales combine a sloped watercourse with appropriate planting and often rock mulch. Bioswales and planted retention or detention areas also purify water running off paved areas, improving the water quality that enters the storm drain system. They are a cost-effective strategy that can help reduce the costs of other drainage structures. They do require space.

Strategies for reducing the impact of paved areas on hydrology also include purposely sizing pipes leading

If this downspout is clogged, water pours out of the dragon's mouth.
Source: Gelfand Partners Architects

out of paved areas small enough that stormwater will collect on the paving and drain at a rate that the receiving pipes, streams, and rivers can handle without flooding. This method clearly accepts the inconvenience of temporary standing water and may be a better strategy for occasional large storms than for typical rains.

In addition to paved areas, roofs and athletic fields typically are designed to shed water as quickly as possible. Green roofs do drain, but some of the water falling on them is used by the plants and transpired without ever entering the drainage system. Roof drains and stormwater leaders should get water away

from where it can damage the building, but that water need not directly enter piped drainage systems. Running roof water through planted areas helps filter it, slow it down, and use it. Making this transition visible is also a potential teaching tool.

HEAT ISLANDS

Black pavement absorbs and reradiates more heat than light pavement. In addition to the discomfort of running around on a surface that increases the heat around the active children, when asphalt is located next to classrooms, it increases the heat load on them. This problem can be addressed through shade, limitation of paving use, or selection of a less heat-absorbent paving.

Higher solar reflectance and SRI values are preferable.

Material Surface	Solar Reflectance	Emittance	Solar Reflective Index (SRI)
Black acrylic paint	0.05	0.9	0
New asphalt	0.05	0.9	0
Aged asphalt	.1	0.9	6
"White" asphalt shingle	.21	0.91	21
Aged concrete	0.2 to 0.3	0.9	19 to 32
New concrete (ordinary)	.0.35 to 0.45	0.9	38 to 52
New white Portland cement concrete	0.7 to 0.8	0.9	86 to 100
White acrylic paint	0.8	0.9	100

Source: Courtesy Architectural Precast Association[2]

The other major contributor to heat islands on the school campus is the roof. Dark bituminous roofs may serve needs such as ease of repair, lower initial cost, and consistency with existing school or other district roofs. Various coatings can mitigate heat island effects and may also extend the service life of the roof.

Often asphalt is regarded by maintenance departments as the default surface for school grounds. It does not need to be kept alive, short, or weed free. It does not get muddy, and if it gets wet, teachers keep the children inside and eventually it dries out. Fire trucks can drive on it, and maintenance workers can access the whole campus with their vehicles at will.

Combating this pressure to pave everything that is not a playing field includes broadening playground ideas as well as solving the practical problems and helping maintenance workers do their work.

PAVING

Even with an increase in alternative uses of school sites, large areas of pavement may be desirable for games such as basketball, hopscotch, and four square and for parking. Asphalt is a contributor to heat islands, a petrochemical product, and an impermeable surface. No single material replaces asphalt in all its uses, but a variety of materials can improve on asphalt in some of its uses.

Paving itself can allow water to penetrate below the surface through such materials as bricks or blocks (unit pavers). These materials make attractive paved areas that are good for patios, gathering places, and picnic table locations. They can become part of fundraising campaigns (buy a block). Depending on

---

Paving Material Alternatives

Grass Pave uses buried plastic rings to maintain bearing for occasional vehicles while protecting grass root zones.

Gravel Pave is similar to Grass Pave but is filled with a gravel surface.

Grass Block is a system using precast blocks with open cells to allow plants to grow.

Unit pavers are bricks or blocks that are set on sand and allow water to percolate through in a limited way.

Porous asphalt allows water to drain through the surface.

Resin pavement can use local aggregates to create many different appearances.

Natural Pave resin pavement substitutes a recycled pine resin binder for the petroleum-based binder in asphalt.[3] *Source: Natural Pave Resin Pavement*

▶ Unit pavers improve the appearance and sustainability of this outdoor area. *Source: Gelfand Partners Architects*

▼ The National Asphalt Pavement Association details the construction of permeable asphalt paving. The figure shows a section through permeable paving. *Source: National Asphalt Pavement Association*

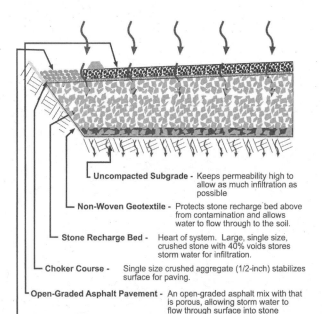

Uncompacted Subgrade - Keeps permeability high to allow as much infiltration as possible

Non-Woven Geotextile - Protects stone recharge bed above from contamination and allows water to flow through to the soil.

Stone Recharge Bed - Heart of system. Large, single size, crushed stone with 40% voids stores storm water for infiltration.

Choker Course - Single size crushed aggregate (1/2-inch) stabilizes surface for paving.

Open-Graded Asphalt Pavement - An open-graded asphalt mix with that is porous, allowing storm water to flow through surface into stone recharge bed.

Unpaved Stone Edge - A backup system in case the pavement surface should ever become sealed. Storm water can flow off pavement surface to stone edge and into stone recharge bed.

NATIONAL ASPHALT PAVEMENT ASSOCIATION

www.hotmix.org
www.PorousPavement.net
www.PaveGreen.com

the local labor market, they are more expensive than either concrete or asphalt.

In addition, new mixes for pavement can also create a permeable layer that allows water to penetrate. This could be a good retrofit for a playground at an existing school where the original surface did not slope and water problems have developed.

Portland cement paving, like sidewalks, is less of a problem from a heat point of view, but it does not resolve the adverse hydrology issues. Sidewalks help drivers know where to expect pedestrians and can help distinguish walking areas from playing areas on playgrounds.

FIELDS

School site plans often look very green due to the presence of athletic fields. But a school field designed for daily physical education class use, after-school sport practice and play, and weekend use by the community

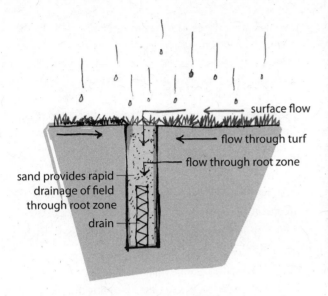

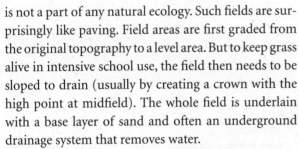

surface flow

flow through turf

flow through root zone

sand provides rapid
drainage of field
through root zone

drain

A grid of trenches and drains help accelerate drying of athletic fields. *Source: Gelfand Partners Architects*

Artificial turf has been manufactured to provide professional-level playing fields. *Source: Gelfand Partners Architects*

is not a part of any natural ecology. Such fields are surprisingly like paving. Field areas are first graded from the original topography to a level area. But to keep grass alive in intensive school use, the field then needs to be sloped to drain (usually by creating a crown with the high point at midfield). The whole field is underlain with a base layer of sand and often an underground drainage system that removes water.

Grasses are selected for athletic fields for their evenness and resilience. In most climates, irrigation will be required. Grass requires mowing (usually a noisy, dirty ride-on mower), fertilizers, and pesticides. Compared to this, in some cases an artificial turf field is an improvement in terms of environmental impact over a "natural" turf field. Such artificial turf fields involve the same grading and drainage and substitute the top level of planting with rubber and artificial grass–appearing fibers. By reducing or eliminating the need for water, fertilizing, and pesticide, in some climates, such fields may have less impact than grass. However,

each product should be researched for chemical content and dark (heat island) granules.

Natural turf playing fields are not intrinsically sustainable in most climates. But it is possible to reduce their impact. Drought-tolerant grasses have been developed that require less irrigation. Irrigation systems can be high efficiency. In some cases, site runoff, roof water, or gray water can be collected for use in irrigation so that the water budget for the site is closer to net zero.

Seattle University has instituted a series of measures to reduce the impact of athletic fields and other turf.[4] It has successfully maintained its campus since 1986 without the use of chemical pesticides. The university's integrated pest management program includes:

- Mechanical removal of pests with various traps and tools
- Choice of appropriate disease- and pest-resistant plants
- Release of beneficial insects

■ Use of natural compounds (i.e. insecticidal soaps, compost tea, vinegar, and citric acid)

Seattle University distinguishes between lawns for ornamental or social areas—quads and gardens—and turf for athletic fields. Lawns are less heavily used, and the grass is grown out of native soil. The university mixes in clover with the grasses, leading to a healthier, meadowlike system that needs less fertilizer. In contrast, the athletic fields grow out of sand, which needs an artificial source of nutrients for the plants. But even these fields can be managed in a more sustainable way.

According to the university:

In 2006, the sand-based athletic fields switched from synthetic fertilizer to a maintenance regime that includes applications of compost tea, mycorrhizal fungi spores and organic fertilizer to improve the root growing environment. The tea has good fungi and bacteria that attach themselves to the root zone and fix nitrogen. Grass clippings are also left on the field to break down and add nutrients to the soil. The first year saw a 26% reduction in water usage and healthier turf. The athletic coaches were thrilled with the condition of the fields.[5]

At Seattle University, even the compost tea is generated from its own waste. The scale of this opportunity may not be appropriate for all sites. Unlike products such as ENERGY STAR appliances, one size does not fit all in landscape management. Choices of turf, management of pests, fertilizers, and irrigation have to be designed carefully to fit the local conditions.

Seattle University playing fields. *Source: Andrew Gelfand Wright*

The Guilford Living Machine made it possible to avoid a costly sewer extension while creating a living laboratory. *Source: Guilford County Schools*

WATER-EFFICIENT IRRIGATION SYSTEMS

Irrigation systems range in efficiency from extremely thrifty to extremely wasteful, but the most water-efficient system is not having one at all. Select plants that thrive in the local environment and do not need supplemental watering. After that, the best irrigation system is one that does not use any potable water. In some areas, local water departments distribute reclaimed water on a municipal scale. The reclaimed water is typically the end product of the wastewater treatment facilities. These facilities provide cities like Tucson, Arizona, with irrigation water while saving groundwater for drinking water.

On-site storage of rainwater and runoff from roofs and paving is a potential source of irrigation water in some climates. The Living Machine is an on-site treatment facility that can transform even sanitary sewage into a usable outflow. It has been installed at several schools and colleges. Basically creating a controlled wetland, the Living Machine filters and purifies waste water. Rather than a costly sewer extension in Guilford, North Carolina:

> The Hybrid Wetland Living Machine®. . . uses a series of wetland installations to naturally cleanse the school's wastewater. That water then goes right back into use irrigating three athletic fields and re-charging their aquifer.
>
> For a fraction of the cost of sewer lines, the schools get added green space; they get a living laboratory to use in their studies of the environment; they get 5 million gallons of recycled water every year; and (here's what's got the other schools in the area envious), they've got the greenest athletic fields around, even during a drought.[6]

An issue of importance to school sites is the amount of interaction children have with the irrigation water if it is not potable. Local health departments may need to rule on this. In countries where it is assumed that water coming out of the faucet is good to drink, it may take thorough education for students to understand that outdoor irrigation water might be good for the plants but not for them.

If water is imported to the site to use as irrigation, getting it directly to the plant in the state and time the plant can best use it is the essence of water-efficient irrigation. The most efficient systems suit emitters to the kind of planting, using drip or low-volume spray to deliver water to the root zone of plants with the least evaporation. It is also possible to water turf with underground drip systems with good results, but the kind of soil and the amount of maintenance have a big influence on system success.[7]

Drip systems need to be maintained free of clogging and root infiltration. According to the Center for Irrigation Technology at the California State University at Fresno, chemical herbicides used in minute amounts in the drip tubing discourage root infiltration without adverse effects on the surrounding soil and have an expected life of 20 years. Porous or gravelly soils and lawns with competition from large trees with many roots are not good candidates for drip systems. Buried drip systems also need preventive maintenance or malfunctioning areas may announce themselves as areas of dead plants.

A mixture of drip emitters, microspray, and sprinklers can be handled by a single control system. Available systems now can automatically control each head or emitter individually, track evapotranspiration, and be programmed for activity times and levels. Automatic watering can thus respond to rain, or the lack of rain, and to variations in temperature and humidity. With the right system, a preference for

Student gardens bring children up close and personal with plants. *Source: The Edible Schoolyard New Orleans*

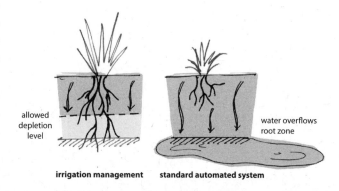

Evapotranspiration (ET) management limits irrigation to necessary amounts of water. *Source: Gelfand Partners Architects*

Irrigation System Resources

Techniques

- Reduce demand with native plants and mulch.
- Water only when needed and avoid midday.
- Zone the irrigation by planting location and type.
- Maintain valve heads and filters.
- Get smart controllers, starting with a switch to turn off irrigation during rain.
- Use low-volume irrigation for gardens, trees, and shrubs.

Resources

- www.epa.gov/watersense
- www.irrigation.org

sprinklers on grass does not rule out drip irrigation for trees, shrubs, or planting beds. Appropriate irrigation not only saves water but can contribute to preventing weed growth (e.g., underground drip irrigation of lawns cuts down on weed seed germination on the surface).

In addition to applying water to the plants where and when they can use it, use of compost and mulch prevents the water from draining or evaporating away before the plants can use it. Compost can come from on-site sources, as in the Seattle example, or from community programs. Mulch, lying on top of the soil, keeps down weeds and evaporation. Organic mulches also break down with time and feed the soil. They should be chosen with care that they will not wash away or blow around. Rock mulches stay in one place, but the size needs to be chosen to avoid providing handy projectiles.

This microemitter is scaled to apply water only where required. *Source: Gelfand Partners Architects, courtesy The Urban Farmers Store*

MISCELLANEOUS SITE USES

Part of promoting bicycling to school is providing a safe place to store bikes. For most schools, this is not a rack that can store five bikes but an enclosure where dozens or even hundreds of bikes can be kept. Given the attraction of bikes to thieves, it is a good idea to locate the bike enclosure where it can be seen from the school office. Since the office ideally is easy to find for visitors, the bikes need to be fenced or screened so that they do not become unsightly.

A patio area outside a classroom is a great place for science and art. It can be a pull-out space for a small group of children to read or do a special project. Grouped together, a number of outdoor spaces can provide the group meeting space once envisioned in open plan schools but without compromising the classroom itself.

School sites are used at night, but they are also abused at night. Sustainability argues for as little light as possible both to save energy and to preserve dark skies. Some schools find that the dark campus is a deterrent to vandals because they cannot see what they are doing and any flashlights show up immediately. Other schools provide enough lighting for patrolling police to see activity.

Lights cover the greatest area the higher they are mounted. In residential areas, neighbors often object to lights that shine in their windows at night, making it difficult to darken bedrooms. More and lower lights with good cut-outs to focus the light on the ground and keep it out of both the sky and the windows solve the problems but come at increased cost. If security needs can be met, minimizing the amount that lights are turned on saves on expensive installations. As in other areas of sustainability, smart controls—photo and motion sensors—can provide lighting only when needed.

Oak Elementary School patios are shared by four classrooms. *Source: Gelfand Partners Architects*

◀ Loyola Elementary School patios provide a pull-out space for each classroom. *Source: Gelfand Partners Architects*

▼ The higher the light source, the wider the spread of the light. *Source: Gelfand Partners Architects*

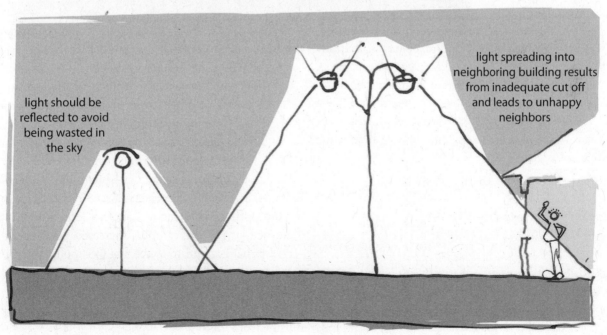

light should be reflected to avoid being wasted in the sky

light spreading into neighboring building results from inadequate cut off and leads to unhappy neighbors

This Dover Marathon equipment is ideally suited for power by DC-generating photovoltaic panels. *Source: Dover Marathon*

Distribution of power to distant features on school sites is expensive. Direct use of solar panels has already become a practical way of powering some lights. A commercial-scale solar garbage compactor is available. Taking snack shacks or press boxes for athletic fields off the grid might not save that much energy, but it would save trenching and be a visible gesture toward sustainability.

PLANTING THE PLAY ENVIRONMENT

A powerful synergy exists between sustainable site design and progressive educational thinking. A variety of environments—planted water courses and detention areas, slopes and rocky areas—can support more kinds of social spaces, imaginative play, and environmental study opportunities than a traditional campus.

The play environment for schools often consists only of a paved asphalt area with stripes, some basketball hoops or other games apparatus, and a prefabricated climbing structure installed with a rubber mat covering asphalt beneath. Sometimes the athletic fields are part of the playground too. A broader definition of playground would be beneficial not only to the environment but to the children. Including more naturalistic areas introduces another level of interest and activity to the campus. Increased planting increases habitat and frees the soil to support the microscopic flora and fauna that are vital to biosphere health. Tree planting creates shade that further moderates local heat islands, and trees remove carbon dioxide from the air.

The Garden City Park, by space2place, in Richmond, British Columbia, is located next to a public school and offers play and environmental opportunities for children of all ages. It combines industrial materials such as rubberized slopes and slides with natural materials such as old-growth stumps and log fingers to provide an enriched sensory, imaginative, and sustainable environment. The design accommodates a high density of children and provides refuges for quiet play as well as opportunity for active play.[8]

Playgrounds are being studied worldwide to increase educational and social benefits. The Swedes studied development and academic achievement of kindergarten children who played on a new climbing structure in a conventional playground compared with kindergarten children who played in a forest with logs, rocks, uneven surfaces, and water. At the end of the kindergarten year, the forest school children tested higher in balance, coordination, and reading.

Susan Solomon's book *American Playgrounds* traces the social development of playgrounds to their current risk management–driven state of limited interest and creativity for children.[9] Where playgrounds

Children and adults enjoy the forms and materials of the Garden City Park climbing structure. *Source: space2place design inc.*

once were seen as an important place to create an alternative to the hard urban world and as a place for children to learn to get along with each other, now they are seen as a place to control against lawsuits. This reduction to flat surfaces and singular equipment surrounded by large rubber mats is also a reduction in the idea of play.

The play opportunities offered by sand, water, and movable props such as blocks can ramify into complex group activities that can give imaginative children a place to shine as athletic children do in ball sports. Most school programs call for a "ball closet" to store balls to hand out during recess. Designing the "ball closet" explicitly favors playing with balls as the activity of choice.

The Rockwell Group in association with KaBOOM is developing a "playground in a box" that packages the elements needed to create an imagination playground similar to the Burling Slip playground in New York. Substituting the play elements in the imagination box for the traditional elements in the ball closet helps children develop new activities in the kinds of

The Rusk Institute, which serves severely disabled children, has created this varied and challenging playground for children in its program and for children in the neighborhood to enjoy. *Source: Gelfand Partners Architects*

▲ Children create an entire play environment from the props in the box. *Source: Rockwell Group/KaBOOM*

▶ This plant, which flourished when the dinosaurs did, can become part of a science lesson. *Source: Gelfand Partners Architects*

alternative environments that support more sustainable school landscapes.

Some children may find the presence of flowers, bugs, trees, and grasses other than turf stimulating both to their senses and to their scientific curiosity. Using planted mounds can create outdoor seating for performances or simply stimulate children to roll and slide and run up and over and around. Selecting appropriate plants attracts favorite creatures, such as butterflies and hummingbirds. Literal connections to curriculum—plants representing the biota of their state, or plants dating from the era of the dinosaurs—can help spark the interest of children, who learn by touching and smelling.

Children expand their knowledge, experience, and diet in this school garden. *Source: Source: Miller Company Landscape Architects. Photo Jeffrey Miller*

It is obvious that these educational opportunities are integral with the environmental benefits of treating school campuses as ecologically connected to their location. Even school aggression can be decreased by providing more variety in the playground.[10]

In addition to play, there is a movement to reinstate school gardens, sometimes for food, sometimes for pleasure, sometimes for study. The edible schoolyard movement in Berkeley has included bringing healthier food into the school lunch program. This is not only a way of reducing childhood obesity but also educates children for life about the sources of the things we eat. Children participate in planting and caring for the fruits and vegetables they will later prepare and eat. The program applies organic pest control strategies and teaches the children about the ecological connections among plants, the creatures that eat the plants, and the creatures that eat the creatures.

INTEGRATING SUSTAINABLE PRACTICES

Features such as bioswales and retention areas can be integrated in the kind of alternative play environments just described. They can buffer parking areas from the rest of the campus. Appropriate paving choices provide both better hydrological performance and design refinements that improve the attractiveness of the campus. When sustainable practices are incorporated in turf management, grass can become a feature of the campus used for more than athletic fields. Trees, which absorb carbon dioxide and provide shade and habitat, as well as providing beauty and pleasure, thrive better when they are not choked by areas of impermeable paving and can do all their important work.

Sustainable school campuses:

- Enrich the experience of everyone who uses them.
- Contribute to a less extreme hydrology.
- Support the soil biota without which no higher plants and animals can exist.

LEED Credits

Sustainable Sites

5.1 Site Development, Protect or Restore Habitat

5.2 Site Development, Maximize Open Space

6.1 Stormwater Design, Quantity Control

6.2 Stormwater Design, Quality Control

7.1 Heat Island Effect, Non-roof

 8 Light Pollution Reduction

Water Efficiency

1.1 Water Efficient Landscaping, Reduce by 50%

1.2 Water Efficient Landscaping, No Potable Use or No Irrigation

 2 Innovative Wastewater Technologies

Innovation

 1 School as a Teaching Tool

Strawberry Vale School, Victoria, British Columbia

Patkau Architects

PLANNING: A HISTORIC AND ENVIRONMENTALLY SENSITIVE SITE

The Strawberry Vale School takes a radically different approach to a site that has had an educational use since 1893. While the 1893 and 1950 sites were located consistent with the street grid, the new location puts the school immediately adjacent to a Garry Oak woodland, a rare and threatened species of tree, and at the top of a rocky protrusion. This natural site is clearly an asset, and the design capitalizes on it while preserving its environmental integrity.

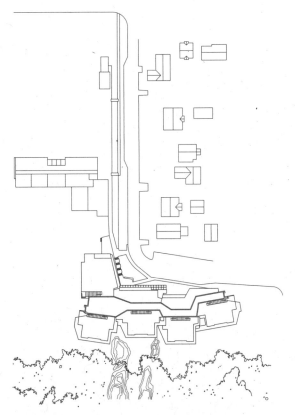

The new school has a compact footprint next to the woodland.
Source: Patkau Architects

This breakout area along the spine is a casual gathering space.
Source: Patkau Architects, James Dow

Rainwater is collected in concrete trenches below the eaves and directed to the lower north side of the school, where it joins an open watercourse. This in turn diffuses into a shallow marsh that is accessible to the children and suitable both for study and enjoyment.

DESIGN: DAYLIGHTING DIVERSE EDUCATIONAL SPACES

Strawberry Vale is an elementary school with an enrollment of up to 448 students. It is a steel and wood-frame building with wood cladding and a metal roof. Polished concrete floors are exposed in the circulation and wet areas. Classrooms are carpeted.

The 16 classrooms are designed in groups of 4, all facing the wooded area. They create small intermediary spaces both inside and outside the classrooms. The gym is located to the north. The slope of the site allows the floor of the gym to be lower so that its greater volume does not interfere with the massing of the school. The supporting functions, such as offices, computers, workrooms, restrooms, and recycling, string

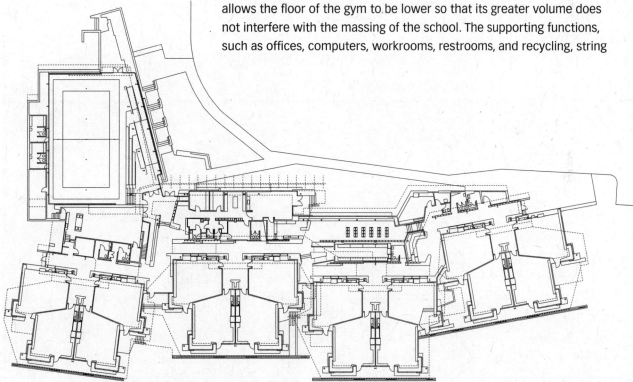

Daylight activates spaces all along the spine, providing flexible accommodation for varied educational uses.   *Source: Patkau Architects*

out along the linear spine that also mediates the changing levels of the site. In a reverse of typical school sections, the spine extends above surrounding spaces, admitting light that benefits both the uses in the spine and balances the classroom daylighting.

Each classroom is a well-defined room, while the uses in the spine are treated much more flexibly. Movable carts for art, science, and cooking can be wheeled around both inside and outside to take advantage of the many beautifully lit spaces created along the circulation of the building and in the interface with the outside. Daylighting and plan reorientations along the corridor transform it from waste space to an integral part of the educational scheme as well as a backbone of the daylighting approach.

Computer modeling helped refine the daylighting approach. Openings and reflective surfaces distribute daylight throughout the interior. Passive heat gain was also optimized. Much of the primary structure is exposed. Wallboard is used sparingly both to cut material use and to help develop expressiveness in texture and light quality throughout the school.

Sunscreening is an important part of the visual expression of the school. *Source: Patkau Architects, James Dow*

Pine Jog Elementary School

Florida Atlantic University Pine Jog Environmental Education Center, West Palm Beach, Florida

Zyscovich Architects

PLANNING: COORDINATION WITH TEACHER EDUCATION AND A NATURE PRESERVE

The Pine Jog Elementary School is 128,291 square feet, and the environmental education center is 17,105 square feet. The project is the first public school in South Florida to pursue a LEED certification. It is located within a 150-acre pineland preserve. The program will integrate the preserve as an outdoor classroom. The K–5 elementary school is also situated right next to the university. Students at the Florida Atlantic University Pine Jog Environmental Education Center can intern to become teachers and learn to include environmental experience throughout the curriculum.

The school accesses the entire preserve. Specialized areas include butterfly gardens, habitat and tree preservation zones, water-reuse demonstration areas, native pineland landscape, wildlife habitats, stormwater collection and conservation areas, soil composting, and a sundial. In addition, students can monitor a Solar Plaza that combines photovoltaic and hot water solar techniques.

DESIGN: EXPOSING SUSTAINABLE BUILDING MECHANICS

LEED features in the campus include alternative fuel and carpool parking, water-efficient plumbing and waterless urinals, student recycling stations and the use of recycled and locally available construction materials, highly efficient and visible mechanical equipment, and polished concrete floors at high-use areas. All the features the building utilizes, along with the preserve in which it is located, are available to students.

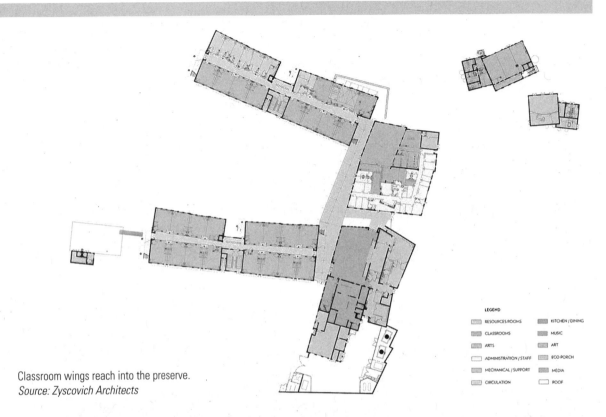

Classroom wings reach into the preserve.
Source: Zyscovich Architects

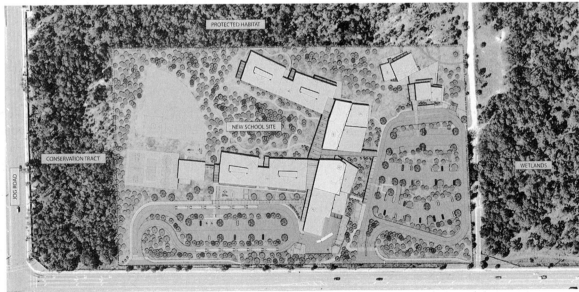

▲ The discovery porch engages both the site and the inner courtyard. *Source: Zyscovich Architects*

▶ School buildings help define outdoor spaces. *Source: Zyscovich Architects*

Chum Creek Outdoor Education Centre, Chum Creek, Victoria, Australia

FMSA Architects

PLANNING: CAMP IS REMOTE BUT INTRINSIC PART OF SCHOOL EXPERIENCE

Chum Creek is a compulsory school camp belonging to Wesley College, an independent school in Melbourne. The camp is based on a typical bush shelter updated to adhere to sustainable principles. The school focuses on hands-on learning for students to get up close with the environment.

The Chum Creek Camp fits into its rural site. *Source: FMSA Architects*

DESIGN: SIMPLE AND RUSTIC FEATURES ACHIEVE SUSTAINABLE PERFORMANCE

It features simple metal roofs, on top of corrugated iron cladding and recycled timber walls. The simple layout resembles a typical bush shelter and demonstrates how to increase sustainability through simple geometry, physics, and a good design.

The polished concrete floors and mudbrick walls incorporate thermal mass and are fully insulated. Outdoor areas are designed so that they can be shielded from the winds from the south, while the double-glazed windows face the north to maximize natural lighting and minimize the amount of heat that can escape them. All waste and food is reused on the campus, composted in the worm farm, or recycled.

Simple materials make a casually elegant gathering space. *Source: FMSA Architects*

Other efficient features include two solar chimneys, which heat the air in the winter and allow cross-ventilation during the summer. There is also a heat pump to heat the water and solar-drying facilities. Systems are deliberately not automatic. They require student and teacher involvement in changing the heating, cooling, and ventilation systems by manipulating windows, louvers, awnings, and the water drip system.

The plan provides a variety of interior and exterior spaces. *Source: FMSA Architects*

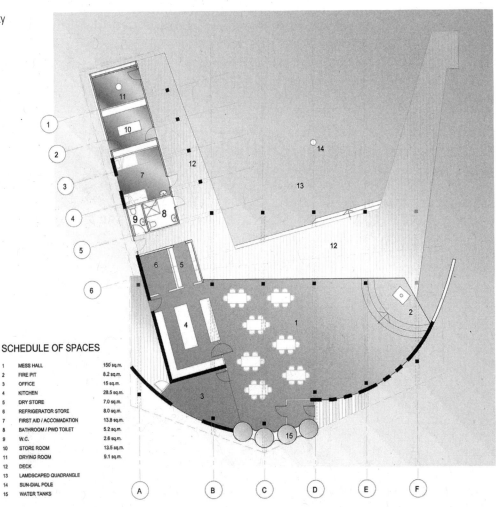

SCHEDULE OF SPACES

1	MESS HALL	150 sq.m.
2	FIRE PIT	8.2 sq.m.
3	OFFICE	15 sq.m.
4	KITCHEN	28.5 sq.m.
5	DRY STORE	7.0 sq.m.
6	REFRIGERATOR STORE	8.0 sq.m.
7	FIRST AID / ACCOMADATION	13.8 sq.m.
8	BATHROOM / PWD TOILET	5.2 sq.m.
9	W.C.	2.6 sq.m.
10	STORE ROOM	13.5 sq.m.
11	DRYING ROOM	9.1 sq.m.
12	DECK	
13	LAMDSCAPED QUADRANGLE	
14	SUN-DIAL POLE	
15	WATER TANKS	

FLOOR PLAN

Systems adjust to each season for heating and cooling. For example, the ceiling fans drive risen heat down in the winter, while in the summer the fans can cool the room. Natural light is maximized by orienting the windows toward the north. Backup electric lighting is high efficiency. Draw-out awnings reflect light away when there is too much daylight.

Water-saving strategies include mini-ecosystems used to biologically treat wastewater, which is cleaned and then reused for irrigation purposes. Rainwater can be collected, stored in tanks, and reused. An evaporative cooling system through a "wet wall" below the water tanks helps make the building more comfortable without spending additional energy.

Local materials demonstrate sustainability. Recycled timber and macrocarpa from local farm windbreaks are used in the wall claddings and veranda.

Zoning for climatic and solar orientation is integrated with activity needs. *Source: FMSA Architects*

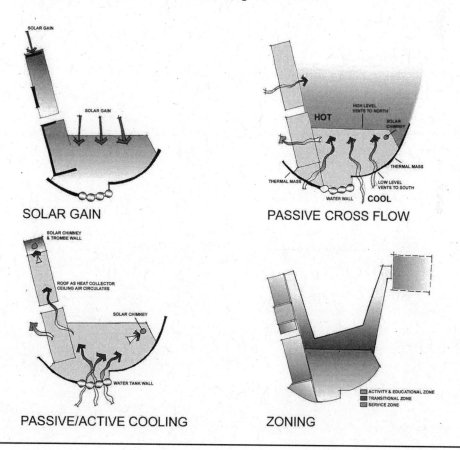

SOLAR GAIN

PASSIVE CROSS FLOW

PASSIVE/ACTIVE COOLING

ZONING

NOTES

1. Chartwell School, "New Campus," September 11, 2006, www. chartwell.org/index.cfm?Page=75, accessed June 12, 2009.

2. Architectural Precast Association, "Solar Reflectance (Albedo), Emittance, and Solar Reflective Index (SRI) of Select Material Surfaces," *Architectural Record* (April 2008), http:// ce.construction.com/article.php?L=109&C=396&P=7, accessed June 26, 2009.

3. Soil Stabilization Products Company, "Sustainable Pavement Technology for Road, Parking Lot and Trail Paving Projects," 2009, www.sspco.com/pdf/2092.pdf, accessed June 12, 2009.

4. www2.seattleu.edu/Sustainability/Inner.aspx?id=774.

5. Ibid.

6. Living Machine, Worrel Water & Living Machine (2009), http://www.livingmachines.com/images/uploads/resources /living_machine_guilford_brochure.pdf, p.4 accessed June 12, 2009.

7. Lauren Bonar Swezey, "Drip Irrigation for Lawns," *Sunset* (June 1995), http://findarticles.com/p/articles/mi_m1216/ is_n6_v194/ai_17149317, accessed June 12, 2009.

8. Space2Place, "Garden City Park Play Environment," June 13, 2008, www.space2place.com/public_garden-city.html, accessed. June 12, 2009.

9. Susan G. Solomon, *American Playgrounds: Revitalizing Community Space* (Lebanon, NH: UPNE, 2005).

10. (Herrington CHILD) S. Herrington, C. Lesmeister, J. Nicholls, and K. Stefiuk. *An informational Guide for young children's outdoor play spaces: Seven C's* (Vancouver: University of British Columbia, 2006), www.wstcoast. org/playspaces/outsidecriteria/7Cs.html, accessed April 10, 2009.

chapter 8

FINISHES, EQUIPMENT, AND FURNISHINGS

INTRODUCTION

When *Silent Spring* was published in 1962, author Rachel Carson drew attention to the toxicity of chemicals people were adding to the environment. Air pollution, water pollution, pesticides, and emissions of all sorts were poisoning plants and animals as well as humans. Countries that were the worst offenders at that time have made improvements in limiting emissions and pollution of the environment; now the worst air is found in newly industrializing nations or indoors in the West.

Volatile organic compounds (VOCs) vaporize (become a gas) at room temperature. VOCs include a large number of compounds found in building materials and cleaning materials and supplies. Some cause irritation, some cause neurological symptoms, some cause cancer. Indoor air typically contains VOC concentrations many times higher than outdoor air.

In addition to bad air, toxic materials often involve toxic production processes and contribute to toxic waste at the end of their use. Even materials that are not toxic in themselves can have toxic manufacturing processes or involve large amounts of transportation emissions in delivery from a distant source.

Materials, finishes, equipment, and furniture represent some of the myriad decisions that go into the sustainable school. Products are changing all the time, and it is important to think about how to make choices as the market changes and as it becomes time to make changes in the school.

The Cradle-to-Cradle (C2C) approach articulated by William McDonough and Michael Braungart offers a framework for looking at the entire process of making, using, and recycling things.[1] In Cradle-to-Cradle thinking, it is not enough to limit harm. Just as single organisms can provide a useful metaphor for the integrated design of a building, McDonough and Braungart encourage thinking about the life cycle of things as analogous to waste products in nature that are the nutrition of some other part of the ecological cycle, in an endless nutritive loop.

This idea is starting to catch on, and a few materials and products certified by C2C are available. But at this point it is more powerful as a philosophy than as a ratings system. Even when referring to other rating systems, thoughtful consideration of the entire cycle of use of a material can inform design. The waste products of one cycle should be the raw materials of the next.

Rating systems usually are not as holistic as C2C. Most times they focus either on the particles or gases emitted by the material and its contribution to indoor air quality or on the manufacturing/disposal process in terms of renewable or recycled/recyclable resources. Because of the interest on the part of schools in green buildings and healthy environments and the size of the market, quite a few rating systems aim directly at school needs.

This chapter reviews resources for product information and applications in finishes including flooring, ceilings, wall coverings, and paints as well as built-in casework, furniture, and some of the specialty items required in schools.[1]

PRODUCT INFORMATION

Using C2C-certified materials as a percentage of all materials has been accepted as the basis for a LEED (Leadership in Energy and Environmental Design) innovation point. C2C certification considers materials more holistically than the LEED materials and resources credits. For the LEED point and C2C Certification, these criteria must be met:

- Using environmentally safe and healthy materials
- Design for material reutilization, such as recycling or composting
- Energy efficiency and the use of renewable energy
- Efficient use of water, and maximum water quality associated with production
- Instituting strategies for social responsibility[3]

TYPICAL SOURCES OF INDOOR AIR POLLUTANTS			
Outdoor Sources	**Building Equipment**	**Components/Furnishings**	**Other Potential Indoor Sources**
Polluted Outdoor Air • Pollen, dust, mold spores • Industrial emissions • Vehicle and nonroad engine emissions (cars, buses, trucks, lawn and garden equipment) **Nearby Sources** • Loading docks • Odors from Dumpsters • Unsanitary debris or building exhausts near outdoor air intakes **Underground Sources** • Radon • Pesticides • Leakage from underground storage tanks	**Heating, Ventilating, and Air-Conditioning (HVAC) Equipment** • Mold growth in drip pans, ductwork, coils, and humidifiers • Improper venting of combustion products • Dust or debris in ductwork **Non-HVAC Equipment** • Emissions from office equipment (VOCs), ozone • Emissions from shop, lab, and cleaning equipment	**Components** • Mold growth on or in soiled or water-damaged materials • Dry drain traps that allow the passage of sewer gas • Materials containing VOCs, inorganic compounds, or damaged asbestos • Materials that produce particles (dust) **Furnishings** • Emissions from new furnishings and floorings • Mold growth on or in soiled or water-damaged furnishings	• Science laboratory supplies • Vocational art supplies • Copy/print areas • Food prep areas • Smoking lounges • Cleaning materials • Emissions from trash • Pesticides • Odors and VOCs from paint, chalk, adhesives • Occupants with communicable diseases • Dry-erase markers and similar pens • Insects and other pests • Personal care products • Stored gasoline and lawn and garden equipment[2]

SCS Environmental Certifications for Products for Schools cover more than construction.

School Designers, Builders, and Procurement Officers

- Indoor air quality performance for *paint and coatings, hard-surface flooring, furniture, and wallcoverings* is certified **SCS Indoor Advantage™ Gold, SCS Indoor Advantage™,** and **Floor Score®.***

- *Composite wood products* meeting California Air Resources Board (CARB) Airborne Toxic Control Measures (ATCM) requirements for formaldehyde emissions bear the **SCS calCOMPliant™** label.

- *Ceiling tiles, adhesives, and sealants* are certified for being manufactured with **No Added Formaldehyde.**

- Playground equipment, fabrics, architectural panels, cement, and insulation are certified for **Recycled** or **Reclaimed Content.**

- *Pressure-treatment processes for lumber used in playground equipment, gardens,* and other schoolyard applications, are certified **Environmentally Preferable.**

- *Doors, windows, furniture, floors, and playground equipment* bear the **Forest Stewardship Council (FSC)** mark, as certified by SCS.

School Facility Managers, Grounds and Maintenance Personnel

- Use *paint, adhesives, and sealants* certified to the highest indoor air quality standard in North America under **SCS Indoor Advantage™ Gold.**

- Cleaners, degreasers, and polishes are certified **Biodegradable.**

- *Flowerpots* made from boxes and newspapers collected by Boy Scouts are certified for **Recycled Content.**

- *Landscape plants* that have been certified sustainably grown bear the **VeriFlora®** label.

Faculty and Students

- *Paper notebooks and pencils* from responsibly managed forests are **FSC chain-of-custody certified** by SCS.[4]

* FloorScore® is an independent program developed by the Resilient Floor Covering Institute (RFCI). Independent certification for this program is provided by SCS.

Another group that provides holistic analysis is Scientific Certification Systems (SCS), which has been providing third-party assessment of a product's consequences for its full life cycle (in their terms, cradle to grave) for two decades. The U.S. Green Building Council furnished its new offices with SCS-certified furniture. SCS has analyzed school products in terms of their intended use as well as SCS' customary environmental analysis.

Another third-party certification group is GREEN-GUARD, a standards developer authorized by the American National Standards Institute (ANSI). GREEN-GUARD focuses on emissions and the improvement of indoor air quality. Their GREENGUARD Children and Schools standard recognizes the increased sensitivity of children to toxins in the environment.

CHPS (Collaborative for High Performance Schools) has prepared a reference Specification Section 01350 (included in the Appendix) as a basis for project documents for a school. It requires the contractor to:

- Require practices to ensure healthy indoor air quality in final project.
- Maximize use of durable products.
- Maximize use of products that are easy to maintain and repair and that can be cleaned using nontoxic substances.
- Maximize recycled content in materials, products, and systems.
- Require use of wood that is certified sustainably harvested by the Forest Stewardship Council.
- Maximize use of reusable and recyclable packaging.
- Maximize use of products with low embodied energy (including energy used in production, manufacturing, and transportation).

Green Label Plus by the Carpet and Rug Institute (CRI) is another certification that meets scientific standards in drawing distinctions among carpets. It can be substituted for Section 01350 in carpet specification for CHPS purposes. Green Label Plus testing includes carpets and adhesives and is the fourth time that the carpet industry itself has raised indoor air quality standards for its products.

The International Organization for Standardization (ISO) has developed environmental management standards (ISO 14000) that incorporate the LCA (Life Cycle Assessment) protocol (ISO 14040). The ISO 14001 environmental management standards exist to help organizations repetitively duplicate, measure and report, and improve how their operations impact the environment. Further, they enable compliance with applicable laws, regulations, and other environmentally oriented requirements.

LEED divides credits between a focus on where materials come from and a focus on the effect of materials on indoor environmental quality. Credits can be gained from materials that are recycled (no matter where) or from materials that are new, shipped long distances, but low emitting. Manufacturer literature includes information about LEED points that the material may help gain. With more and more government agencies requiring certification, LEED points are selling points.

As public and client support for environmentally beneficial products grows, manufacturers have been making claims for their products as part of their sales efforts. Some of these claims are made without research or testing, and give designers or clients a false sense that they are selecting beneficial products. Such deceptive advertising is called "greenwashing." Third-party certifications, such as C2C, SCS, GREENGUARD, or Green Label Plus, show that a rigorous level of testing has been completed on the product and that the team can specify with confidence that they are meeting their sustainable goals. Certification that a product must have earned should be included in specifications for that product.

FLOORING

Carpet

In addition to product characteristics in terms of production or contribution to indoor air quality, flooring has particular synergies with construction and maintenance. Many teachers love carpet for its acoustic properties, softness underfoot, and comfortable image, but carpet can have serious indoor air quality issues.

Specify a carpet system—including glues and pad, if applicable—that meets the CRI Green Label

Plus certification requirements, is constructed to prevent liquids from penetrating the backing layer where moisture under the carpet can result in mold growth, and can be removed easily without the use of toxic chemicals.

Install carpet per CRI recommendations (CRI 104, Standard for Installation of Commercial Carpet). Do not install while the school building is in use except in very small areas where direct ventilation can occur in the space for 72 hours before use.[5] Also air out large carpet installations for at least 72 hours before occupancy.

Install carpet well away from known sources of moisture, such as sinks, drinking fountains or doors to the outside. When classrooms have two floor coverings, such as carpet plus resilient flooring at sinks and doors, maintenance people have to use two different cleaning protocols in each room. Libraries and offices are easier to keep free of spills and therefore may be better choices for carpet.

If carpets are installed prior to painting or other construction processes that release VOCs, the carpets can absorb the VOCs and then reemit them later. To avoid this sequence, carpet and other soft materials should be installed following painting or application of other coatings. If this is not possible, cover the carpet during painting or coating and use direct ventilation until the coating dries. Carpets should also be installed after concrete slabs are thoroughly dry.

Unless carpet is properly maintained, even a carefully specified low-emitting carpet installation can become unhealthy. Particles must be removed by a properly functioning vacuum cleaner (CRI has a program to identify such vacuum cleaners) so that they do not build up in the carpet and get released by children's activity. The U.S. Environmental Protection Agency (EPA) recommends that clean water spills on carpet be extracted and dried out within 24 hours of wetting in order to avoid mold growth.

Resilient Flooring

The Resilient Floor Covering Institute, in collaboration with SCS, has developed the FloorScore IAQ certification program. It certifies hard-surface floorings for compliance with Section 01350 requirements and for CHPS low-emitting materials credits.

Resilient flooring comes in sheets and tiles. Vinyl composition tile has been a mainstay of school flooring for many years. The flooring industry has been working to reduce off-gassing, increase recycled content and recyclability, improve adhesives, and hold the price point for vinyl materials. However, the industry is starting with a product that is made using polyvinyl chlorides that have significant toxicity issues in both manufacture and disposal.

Significantly more expensive on a first-cost basis, linoleum is an all-natural resilient flooring choice. Linoleum has been around a long time and has proven its durability. Contributing to its long service life is the fact that, over time, linoleum spreads out to close cracks rather than shrinking to open them up. It is made from renewable resources: linseed oil (pressed from the flax plant), pine resin, wood flour, cork powder, limestone dust, natural pigments, and jute. Over its life cycle, it is less expensive flooring than vinyl due to its maintenance advantages. In schools accustomed to vinyl composition tile (VCT) maintenance, care should be taken to educate maintenance staff so that resource-intensive methods do not negate the life cycle savings. In a new project, be aware that floor slabs need to be dry before the linoleum can be installed.

Wood, concrete, and tile all have their uses in schools. Wood floors in gyms and dance rooms pro-

The linoleum floor in this 1920s school is an original finish. *Source: Gelfand Partners Architects*

vide resilient surfaces for exercise and performance. The wood in the flooring should be FSC certified. Exposed concrete can be sealed and waxed to provide a durable floor finish. It is an extra cost to specify a concrete slab that designers wish to see exposed, but sheet flooring cost is not needed.

Ceramic tile, terrazzo, and epoxy resins are used in restrooms. The choice of material for restrooms is particularly sensitive to the maintenance environment of the school.

WALL FINISHES

Walls in schools are used for display, projection, and acoustics. Many different finishes work in various places in the school. Most teachers would love it if every square inch of the wall surface were tackable. Many tackable surfaces are also sound absorptive, an added benefit. Especially if the flooring is resilient instead of carpet, sound-absorbent qualities are valuable attributes in a wall finish. Options include washable fabric-wrapped panels, systems where fabric is stretched across panels applied to the wall already, and rolled tackable linoleum goods. Tackable surfaces should be certified low emitting.

Gyms need durable finishes but could also benefit from sound absorption. Safety matting will reduce sound too.

If tackable wall surfaces are not used, many schools have used vinyl wall covering to provide a washable surface that is somewhat less vulnerable to tape. Sustainable alternatives to vinyl wall coverings include woven polyethylene. Look for the third-party certifications mentioned earlier, particularly in regard to low-emitting materials.

▲ Carpet tiles applied to the walls in this nursery school help quiet the classroom while leaving the floor washable. *Source: Donna Kempner Architectural Photography ©2002*

◀ Insulation behind perforated plywood helps reduce reverberation. *Source: Mark Luthringer*

CEILINGS

Ceilings are the first place to look for acoustic absorption. They are also a large part of the visual scene and a significant factor in room lighting. Commercial 2x4 lay-in ceilings are problematic in schools. Often a lay-in ceiling is used when access is required to wiring, ducts, or equipment above the ceiling. If ceiling tiles get wet, they may be subject to staining, sagging, and mold or mildew growth. Ceiling tiles should be replaced if they get wet. After repeated uses to access space above, tiles get broken or left open, and the ceiling can become an unsightly mess.

Sprinklers and lighting were added after the ceiling in this case, creating a condition very hard to modernize. *Source: Gelfand Partners Architects*

◀Raised ceilings help transform Bullis Elementary School classrooms. Exposed ducts and pendant lighting reduce access needs. *Source: Mark Luthringer*

▼ Before modernization, the Bullis classrooms were so discouraging that demolition was considered. *Source: Gelfand Partners Architects*

Finding solutions to air distribution without dropping ceilings can help transform classrooms by raising the ceiling and improving daylighting and the feeling of the space. 2×2 grids and reducing the need to access the ceiling space improve drop ceilings. Specify ceiling tiles with high sound absorption, recycled content, no added formaldehyde, and certainly no asbestos. A C2C Silver product exists with a jute backing, high NRC (noise reduction coefficient), Class A fire rating, high-recycled-content grid, and treatment to reduce water absorption and discourage microbes.

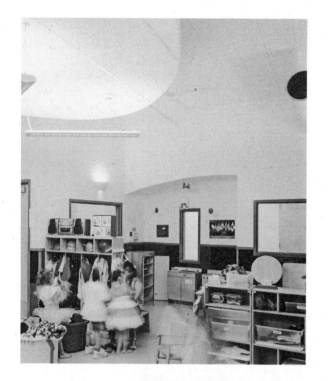

Ceilings may also be part of fire separations. Achieving a fire rating is possible with drop ceilings, but it is more common to use a gypsum wallboard ceiling. Acoustic tile is then adhesively applied to the wallboard to improve the acoustics in the room. Selecting an appropriate material involves verifying its sound absorption as well as the green characteristics of the material and its adhesives.

Other approaches to providing acoustic surfaces on ceilings include panels and integral steel acoustic decks. In music rooms, a combination of absorption and diffusion may be necessary.

◄Dropped ceiling areas can provide acoustic characteristics and help conceal unsightly pipes and ducts where needed. *Source: Donna Kempner Architectural Photography ©2002*

▼The Vanden music room uses thermal insulation for its acoustic absorption values, perforated insulation-backed wall panels, and diffusing panels suspended on a standard ceiling grid. *Source: Mark Luthringer*

PAINTS AND COATINGS

VOCs are added to many conventional paints to enhance product performance or shelf life. They can also be by-products of drying. Low-VOC and zero-VOC paints are available. They vary in performance in hiding capability and in durability. Specify the low-VOC or zero-VOC paint that meets the performance requirements of the project. Water-based acrylic latex paints generally have lower VOCs, and leftover latex paint may be recyclable.

Various heavy metals, such as lead and mercury, have been added to commercial and industrial paints and may be present even if they have been banned from consumer paints. Material safety data sheets detail these ingredients and should be referenced if the paint has not been otherwise certified.

The potential for VOCs to be absorbed and reemitted by soft materials, such as carpet and ceiling tile, has been noted. Sequence construction to paint first, or cover such materials and ventilate until the paint dries. Specifying prefinished materials can both increase the quality of the finish and decrease the amount of VOCs released on site.

CASEWORK AND FURNISHINGS

Built-in casework (counters, cabinets, etc.) and furnishings also contribute to indoor air quality. Traditionally they have not had the same number of problems that absorptive materials such as ceiling tile and carpet have had. But casework and furnishings still outgas if they are made with formaldehyde, vinyls, and the like. Many new materials are being developed to reduce their environmental impact.

Most of casework is some variation of a box. The sides of the box should be rigid, strong, and flat. The surfaces should be tough and washable. A common solution is plywood or particleboard covered with a veneer of wood or a layer of plastic laminate to provide the wearing surface. The inside and the outside of the box have different durability demands. Counters or desktops are different again.

Particleboard is made of compressed wood fiber that is an industrial by-product of the manufacture of other wood products. It is typically bound into a board with urea formaldehyde, a known carcinogen. MDF, medium-density fiberboard, another common material, typically also is bound with urea formaldehyde resins. Ongoing research is attacking the problem of the urea formaldehyde binder in particleboard and MDF.

Alternative binders containing no formaldehyde are available, especially on the West Coast of the United States. Phenol-formaldehyde bonding is an improvement. If you must specify any products containing urea formaldehyde, make sure they are third-party certified to meet the relevant ANSI formaldehyde emission standard. It is better to specify products with no added formaldehyde that are also certified low emitting.

Various rapidly renewable plant materials are being used to make boards. Wheat board is made from a waste product available after each year's wheat harvest. Millions of tons of wheat straw residue are available each year. Bales of wheat straw are milled into fine particles, sorted, dried, and then bound together with a formaldehyde-free resin. Rice straw is also being made into board. Another rapidly renewable material is a board made out of bamboo.

Besides the goal of seeking an environmentally preferable manufacturing process and final product, water resistance in these products is important. When the wearing surface of a particleboard cabinet is breached and water gets into the particleboard, the board swells, interfering with its appearance and functionality. Screws tend to pull out of fiberboards on active parts of cabinets (doors, drawers). These problems are less apt to occur with plywood. At present, plywood is readily available in a no-added-formaldehyde version. The plywood upcharge is usually not a huge increase in casework costs.

Counter materials are also made with plywood or fiber cores and wearing surfaces, although a variety of solid materials are available. Various counter materials are made of recycled glass, porcelain, and stone bound together by resins. Countertops need to be durable, stain resistant, water resistant, and workable. Solid materials have gained popularity because they do not chip or delaminate, or if they do chip, a similar substrate will show that will still be functional. Solid countertops often are more expensive than laminated materials.

Furniture comes as a complete product. Designers do not have the option to customize its various materials in the same way as they do with the built-in casework. As in the rest of the product selection, it is helpful to select environmentally preferable products based on research and testing others already have done. C2C work with the office systems manufacturer Herman Miller encompasses not only the materials but their potential for reconfiguration and their eventual disassembly and reuse. Look for third-party certifications from the sources discussed. At a minimum, specify low-emitting products.

COMPUTERS AND OFFICE EQUIPMENT

Computers and office equipment have impacts on both energy consumption and indoor air quality. U.S. EPA has ENERGY STAR–labeled computers and office machines. According to the U.S. EPA, "If all computers sold in the United States meet the ENERGY STAR requirements, the savings in energy costs will grow to more than $2 billion each year and greenhouse gas emissions will be reduced by the equivalent of greenhouse gas emissions from nearly 3 million vehicles."[6] The basic strategy is to limit energy use to when it is needed, reducing waste when the machine is idle. ENERGY STAR applies to computer peripherals and imaging equipment too, providing a database of environmentally preferable products from which to choose the machines that meet the school's functional needs.

Indoor air concerns are related to the chemicals used in printing and copying. It is recommended to ventilate all rooms with copiers separately. It is now possible to purchase ink or toner cartridges made with agri-based ink, such as soy-based inks. These avoid the VOC emissions found in conventional petroleum-based inks. They are also easier to de-ink in paper recycling. Compatibility with the school's equipment needs to be confirmed.

SPECIALTIES

Lockers

Lockers are a feature of many schools. They are more or less of a headache at most schools that have them. Students lose keys, forget combinations, and switch locks. They may leave old lunches or gym clothes in lockers for long periods of time. Sometimes they store contraband items. Some school districts are removing them entirely.

Almost all school lockers are sheet metal. They can have high recycled content, and they can be recycled when they are removed. As they age, they are dented, scratched, repainted on site, and often become very unsightly. They provide reflective surfaces that contribute to noise in school corridors.

Toilet Partitions

Toilet partitions have been made of sheet metal, composite laminated boards, and solid materials. Although upgrading school lockers to solid materials has been judged cost prohibitive, it is a real option for toilet partitions. Solid plastic or resin composite partitions can be specified with high recycled content—at least 20%—and meeting third-party certification off-gassing limits. The resins used should be identified for later recycling.

Toilet partitions should be specified for easy graffiti removal, resistance to gouging and scratching, impact resistance, fire resistance, and warranties against general corrosion, warping, and delamination. In particular, hardware should be robust and vandal resistant.

These lockers show typical surface problems, holes from former locks, and dents. *Source: Gelfand Partners Architects*

LEED for Schools

Finishes, equipment, and furnishings contribute to the following points on the proposed (2009) LEED for Schools checklist:

Category: Energy & Atmosphere
- EA Credit 1: Optimize Energy Performance

Category: Materials and Resources
- MR Credit 3.1, 3.2: Materials Reuse
- MR Credit 4.1, 4.2: Recycled Content
- MR Credit 5.1, 5.2: Regional Materials
- MR Credit 6: Rapidly Renewable Materials
- MR Credit 7: Certified Wood

Category: Indoor Environmental Quality
- EQ Credit 4: Low Emitting Materials
- EQ Credit 5: Indoor Chemical and Pollutant Source Control
- EQ Credit 9: Enhanced Acoustical Performance
- EQ Credit 10: Mold Prevention

Category: Innovation and Design Process
- ID Credit 1: Cradle to Cradle certification
- ID Credit 3: School as a Teaching Tool

Hazelwood School, Glasgow, Scotland

Gordon Murray & Alan Dunlop Architects

PLANNING: SPECIAL NEEDS CHILDREN NEED SPECIAL SCHOOL

Hazelwood School is located in Glasgow, Scotland, in a landscaped green area adjacent to Bellahouston Park. It is 28,686 square feet. The school is designed to provide an education for up to 60 students from age 3 to 19 who have multiple disabilities, which include visual impairment, hearing impairment, and mobility or cognitive impairment. Goals for the campus were to be safe and stimulating for the teachers and students, eliminate an institutionalized feel, and avoid standard details while entirely following the users' needs.

The school creates a special place within its neighborhood. *Source: Gordon Murray & Alan Dunlop Architects*

DESIGN: MATERIALS MEANT FOR ALL SENSES

The school is situated among lime trees and curves around the existing trees. The curve creates spaces for gardens to allow for outdoor teaching environments and also to reduce visual confusion by limiting the amount of space seen at any one time. Outdoor rooms with many windows and clerestories allow natural ventilation throughout the building.

The architects selected the project materials carefully in an effort to stimulate the children. Highly textured natural materials were used for the touch and smell inside. On the outside, naturally weathering timber siding, slate tiles, and zinc provide variety and contrast. Interior walls covered with cork provide warmth while also providing location information through a navigational tool children can feel so that they can move around the school freely.

1. Administration

2. Hydrotherapy pool / & Gym

3. Entrance / Assembly /
   Performance Space

4. Dining / Assembly /
   Performance

5. Nursery

6. General Classroom

7. Specialist learning Areas

8. Life Skills Home

9 Sanitary cluster

10 subject specific classrooms

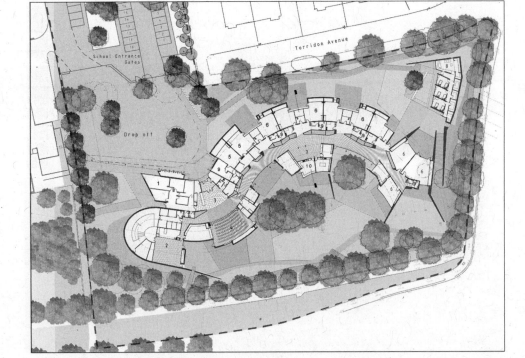

This lovely ground plan provides a simple double-loaded spine but creates many varied spaces. *Source: Gordon Murray & Alan Dunlop Architects*

▲ Exterior spaces have a cozy scale and both a visual and a tactile variety of materials. *Source: © Keith Hunter*

◀The daylit classroom has a complementary suspended light system. *Source: © Keith Hunter*

New Jersey City University Academy Charter High School, Jersey City, New Jersey

KSS Architects

PLANNING: BONDING WITH THE SURROUNDING COMMUNITY

This reuse preserves the best of the old building while updating where necessary. *Source: KSS Architects*

New Jersey City University wanted to create a school to help prepare students from disadvantaged educational backgrounds for college. To do this, the university pushed for a design engaging the students with the surrounding community in addition to their own education. By transforming an abandoned industrial laundry building on a contaminated site into the new charter school, the university reconnected it to the community that had grown around it.

The original building was not encouraging. *Source: KSS Architects*

The laundry building was a symbol of the area's former prosperity. Relatives of many of the incoming students had been employed there. The university and architects deepened the connection between the students and the building by opening the project's planning and design processes to community input. A series of "visioning" sessions were conducted along with an eight-week Architect-in-Residence program, where students learned about architecture and discussed what a "dream school" meant.

DESIGN: HISTORIC COMMERCIAL SPACE MORPHS INTO EDUCATIONAL SPACE

The charter school is 38,844 square feet and includes a unique floor plan, balancing openness and enclosure, with a layout placing classrooms with large rolling doors along the building perimeter and a community "living room" where students interact formally and informally at its center. The central lobby, modeled after an urban street lined with mixed-use spaces, connects the school with a business incubator and gives students an awareness of the opportunities that arise from education. With the focus on open spaces, the school's environment contrasts with the institutionalized atmosphere prevalent at many public schools and invites students to focus on learning.

The school not only inherited the building's legacy but also its existing interior finishes: concrete, steel, and brick. These nearly indestructible materials represent the strength of its community. New interior finishes are also durable and tough. All cabinetry is constructed with solid wood instead of plywood, and carpet tiles provide a versatile, environmentally sensitive flooring material. The design also converts a former double-height boiler room into a basketball court and multipurpose room.

The design creates transparency wherever possible. *Source: KSS Architects*

The contrast of old and new preserves a sense of the building's history and a suggestion of its trajectory. *Source: KSS Architects*

NOTES

1. William McDonough & Michael Braungart, "Cradle to Cradle/Remaking the Way We Make Things," North Point Press, 2002.

2. U.S. Environmental Protection Agency, *IAQ Design Tools for Schools*, "Typical Sources of Indoor Air Pollutants," www.epa.gov/iaq/schooldesign/controlling.htm, accessed January 7, 2009.

3. USGBC LEED Innovation Credit, "Cradle to Cradle Certification," 2007, www.mbdc.com/cert_innovation_credit.htm, accessed June 7, 2009.

4. Scientific Certification Systems, "Products for the School Earn SCS Environmental Certifications," March 20, 2009, www.scscertified.com/press_releases/SCSinSchools_PR_032009.pdf, accessed June 7, 2009.

5. U.S. Environmental Protection Agency, *IAQ Design Tools for Schools*, "Controlling Pollutants and Sources," www.epa.gov/iaq/schooldesign/controlling.html, accessed January 7, 2009.

6. ENERGY STAR, "Computers for Consumers," www.energystar.gov/index.cfm?fuseaction=find_a_product.showProductGroup&pgw_code=CO, accessed June 7, 2009.

chapter 9

COST AND BIDDING PROCESS

INTRODUCTION

Construction contracting is one of the most difficult businesses that exist. Builders are asked to predict, sometimes years in advance, the costs of materials they will buy, the amount of time it will take each of hundreds of workers to complete work, the conditions they will find when they start working, and sometimes even the weather. Yet with all these inherent risks, selecting a contractor in the public works arena often is based not on who is most qualified but almost solely on the lowest bid for the work.

The simplest bid process is to advertise the opportunity to do work, make plans and specifications available, offer contractors the opportunity to see the job, give them a period of time to review the documents, set a time and date for bids to be opened, and then open the envelope to discover the low bidder. The contractor probably will have been required to post a bond and provide evidence of insurance and required licensing. Once that is verified, for better or for worse, the contractor has been chosen.

During the design process, many cost estimates probably will have been made to forecast the outcome of the bid. But until the bids are opened, there is no way of knowing what the initial cost will be, and until the job is over there is no way of knowing whether unknown conditions or other surprises will cost more money. In this kind of bidding environment, contractors rarely communicate with architects regarding potential conflicts in the documents or issues they may see on the site. Instead, they may count on such issues to form the basis of change orders that will raise the final cost while allowing them to win the job by bidding low.

In order to give the team a range of scope to adjust for bidding variances, the documents may include bid alternates that the owner may select depending on the results of the competitive bidding process. Such decisions are made before contracts are signed and do not take into account potential change orders. Elements of the design that are considered to be optional may be shown as alternates. It is important to keep essential elements of the sustainable approach out of this category. Fortunately, it is also unlikely that basic sustainable strategies can be piecemealed in this way.

In most cases, the documents that describe the project consist of drawings and specifications. The drawings are carefully limited to describing the quantity, desired location, extent, relationships, and appearance of the construction elements while the specifications detail quality. It has long been the practice of architects and engineers to stay out of the means and methods that the contractor will employ. This is in large part to maintain clarity regarding roles and responsibilities, particularly with respect to safety on the job site. It also allows the imaginative contractor to come up with better ways to do the work and thus underbid competitors.

One of the implications of sustainability is that the construction process itself cannot be left out of consideration. Construction debris makes up 20% to 30% of the trash going to U.S. landfills. In addition, the process of building and clearing land not only destroys habitat but can lead to erosion, dust, and the subsequent pollution of streams and the air. Incorrect removal of hazardous materials risks contaminating much larger areas than the original locale. During the process of construction, the methods the contractor uses to install mechanical equipment and certain materials can have a lasting effect on the air quality of the completed building. Therefore, the methods that the contractor uses are critical to the sustainability of the project. Despite contracting precedents, the builder needs to be a part of the sustainable team.

It is invaluable to be able to engage the expertise of the contractor in the preconstruction phases of the project. If a contractor can be involved during design, the restrictions and requirements that are written into the bid documents can be as practical as possible and can be designed to have as little

The contractor is wetting down the debris to reduce dust. *Source: Gelfand Partners Architects*

cost impact as possible. Just as the best design is fully integrative, the best construction process is also an interlocking set of tasks, materials, and quality control. When issues of sustainability become issues of construction sequence, having a contractor involved helps preserve the sustainability intent and contributes to the project success. Clearly the typical public bid process does not do this.

Hiring a contractor based on qualifications for preconstruction services as a consultant causes the least change to the current system. In most public bidding situations, serving as a consultant will disqualify the contractor from bidding to do the actual work. The next variation is to hire a contractor based on qualifications first to consult during preconstruction, often including cost estimating, and then to divide up the job and put the various parts of the contract out to public bid to trade contractors who may act as prime contractors or subcontractors, depending on the contract details.

Even if one of those methods is used, some members of the contractor's team still will be subcontractors brought into the process at the end of design, through the competitive bidding of either the whole project or project components. Sustainable building changes the way contractors do their work and therefore requires that these changes be communicated to contractors as part of the conditions for the project detailed in the bid documents.

The team benefits greatly by the early involvement of a contractor versed in sustainable building, making it possible for a sustainable school to be built. The benefits include realistic cost estimating, practical information about construction strategies, and a well-informed management team as the project goes into construction. In order to put sustainable ideas into practice, the team must understand:

- Sources of high construction costs
- Potential methods of selecting a contractor and trade contractors
- Elements that must be included in contract documents
- How to structure the bid to protect project priorities

HIGH COST

The most frequent obstacle raised to sustainable school design is its assumed high cost. While it has been established that sustainable design and construction of academic buildings occurs at every budget, certain materials or systems may very well be seen as expensive. The most important part of sustainable design—integrated design—usually helps to control costs rather than add to them. Good daylighting, ventilation, site design and orientation, and integration of building systems should not cost more.

Where does the perception of high cost arise? Certain materials, controls, sensors, and other components of green design are expensive by themselves. Such components need to be considered within the context of the entire system—for example, more expensive controls may allow a mechanical system to be smaller, and the total result may be a saving. But the controls still will look expensive. Given the data we have that shows modest, if any, cost increases for sustainable design, it is still worth looking at where the perception might arise. Green design does interact with the sources of high costs in general.

Higher Building Standards

In part, the expense of school buildings is the understandable result of a higher standard of safety imposed by most building codes on educational occupancies. As

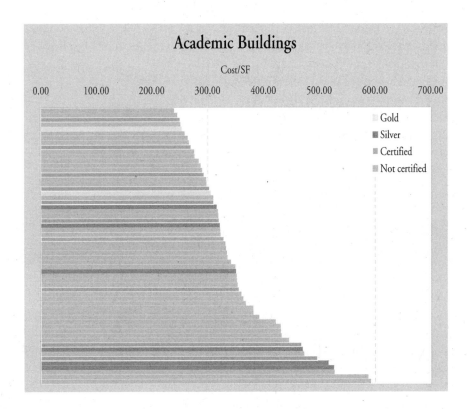

Academic Buildings

Cost/SF

Gold
Silver
Certified
Not certified

The 2007 Davis Langdon study analyzed 231 buildings and found no significant difference in average cost between green and nongreen buildings. *Source: Davis Langdon*

discussed, structural systems and fire and life safety systems are likely to be more expensive than in other building types. Where conflicts arise between the structural requirements and the requirements for large openings for daylighting, or between the fire requirements and the desire for ventilation, a contractor who understands the objectives can be a resource in suggesting less expensive ways to achieve the goal (value engineering).

Durability

LEED (Leadership in Energy and Environmental Design) for Homes includes a durability credit, addressing the short life cycle of many residential building materials and systems. There is no such credit in LEED for Schools. Schools need durability whether they are green or not.

When a building is planned to house thousands of children, adolescents, or even adults over decades of service, materials and fittings such as cabinets, plumbing fixtures, lockers, and hardware must withstand heavy use. According to industry sources, the typical cycle for remodeling a retail establishment in the United States is five to seven years.[1] In California, the state contributes to major school modernization only after 25 years. At the same time, the resources of local schools for maintenance must compete with the operating costs of instruction. In a situation of high use and low maintenance, great pressure exists to install rugged materials and durable equipment. This is an additional cost, but it is not an extra cost of green design. Green design must meet the same criteria of durability and in some cases ultimately saves maintenance costs.

Washable materials in this bathroom are not inexpensive. *Source: Gelfand Partners Architects*

Public Contracting

If it were more obvious that school buildings are built better than comparable commercial buildings, their costs would be less controversial. But some of the higher costs have nothing to do with materials, workmanship, or timeliness.

Over a yearlong period a task force of construction managers, architects, and contractors collected data from the United States as a whole and within California to develop a K–12 California Construction Report.[2] The group concluded that the three central areas affecting costs are:

1. State regulatory structures

2. School politics, practices, and design

3. Market conditions

Sustainable design can have impacts in all three areas. As states begin to require rather than simply target sustainable performance, regulators will begin checking documents and construction for compliance. Sealing the envelope of a building is an important part of energy conservation. Will inspectors require blower tests or thermography to determine if standards have been met? Although regulators have skills in structural and fire safety codes, many green measures are new to them and require new training.

Design elements may have the least cost impact, even as they change the design vocabulary, as shown in the track record of green construction so far. The accelerating application of green standards to materials, methods, and the industry in general have already changed the market considerably, making green design

Locating a window next to a wall costs the same as locating it in the middle of a wall but increases the effectiveness of daylighting. *Source: Gelfand Partners Architects*

an element that manufacturers tout for competitive advantage rather than an esoteric and costly addition.

Independent schools are affected by the design and market factors, but not as strongly by regulation as public schools. Public school construction is a big industry, and as such attracts regulation. Even though the level of spending is nowhere near that of military spending, there nonetheless exists a government/in-dustry complex to deliver school buildings. Because of the money at stake, rules of procurement attempt to ensure fair competition that helps avoid corruption and attempts to achieve the lowest reasonable price for the taxpayer.

In addition to the selection of the general contrac-tor who takes responsibility for delivering the entire project for a certain price, rules govern the various products and equipment that are specified for the project. The philosophy (and the law, with certain exceptions) is that competition should exist at all levels of the contract, down to the choice of carpet.

Additional pressure exists to ensure that public monies are spent both as planned and in a way that provides other public goods. School construction creates jobs. It is considered in the public interest that contractors be required to compete without sacrificing the interests of labor. In the United States, public contracting requires that workers be paid prevailing wages for their work. Prevailing wage differs regionally but consistently acts to level the playing field for union and nonunion contractors. The workforce for a nonunion contractor still must be compensated at regionally prevailing rates, which generally are comparable to union wages.

In order to hold contractors and local government accountable for a fair and competitive selection process, an open marketplace for materials and equipment, and fair compensation for workers, reporting requirements exist at all levels of the process. This amounts to paperwork. Inspectors make detailed regulatory visits to ensure that construction matches contract documents. Contractors also often must provide certified payroll documentation that all workers on the job are properly compensated. The reporting requirements add considerable cost as well as limiting the kinds of companies that are equipped to compete. As green design requirements, particularly commissioning, become incorporated in the process, inspectors will need to learn new skills.

The traditional public bid process relies on competition to lower prices. The contract documents are

Construction administration and oversight usually includes the design team and also government inspectors. *Source: Gelfand Partners Architects*

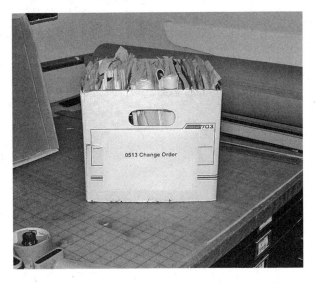

This paperwork relates to a single construction change order. *Source: Gelfand Partners Architects*

made available to any contractor who is properly licensed, can qualify for bonding, and responds properly to the invitation to bid. Sustainability, while built into the drawings and specifications, need not be a great concern of the contractor. The contractor has no prior knowledge or participation in the project.

Any product or material specified with no alternatives needs a defense that the single product specified has no "equal." This kind of specification often requires prior approval by the legal department of the school district, which can be prohibitive in tight schedule situations. Even when granted, it may be expected that various contractors, subcontractors, and suppliers will attempt to get approval for substitutions, forcing the design team to qualify or disqualify the substitution based on the detailed specifications provided in the bidding documents.

Commissioning requirements, especially enhanced commissioning, need to be spelled out clearly in contract documents. The largest construction claims often are built on assertions of "delay," or contractors'

inability to get the job done through no fault of their own, and thereby maintaining their overhead of supervision, trailers, equipment, and site control longer than anticipated in the bid. Adding additional testing and inspection before the contractor can proceed to the next step of the project needs to spelled out so that it is part of the contractor's initial schedule and bid.

ALTERNATIVE PROJECT DELIVERY METHODS

Partnering in Public Contracting

Even in the traditional design-bid-build method of public contracting, it is possible to develop relationships among the owner, design team, and contractor that can be efficient, equitable, and mutually beneficial. A formal process known as partnering was developed initially to facilitate the formation of these relationships for U.S. Defense Department procurement. While it does not change the legal relationships of any of the contracting entities, it is tied to lower costs and lower rates of litigation.

Partnering is a preemptive way to approach dispute resolution. It is also a method that can be employed to improve communication for any purpose, including enhancing the understanding of the responsibilities of everyone involved in a sustainable building project.

The first step is a daylong retreat involving all the key participants in the building project. Often this retreat is run by a professional facilitator. The goal of the retreat is to introduce all the players to one another, identify their goals, identify the concerns they may have with respect to the project, and make sure that everyone understands the communication protocols that will govern the project. For example, the partnering session will identify how quickly a concern or dispute should be brought to the attention of field personnel supervisors so that decisions can be made in a timely manner. It is easier to organize these decisions before there is a burning problem that must be resolved.

A contractor may have legitimate concerns about how a commissioning agent will go about testing installed systems. This is a good opportunity to make sure the commissioning agent's access and timing is understood and that the contractor and trade subcontractors know who should be present or copied on the commissioning agent's findings.

Part of the goal of the partnering process is to establish common ground. The public bid process forces together entities that may have no prior knowledge of each other. Built into the process is the mechanism

that the low-bid general contractor probably has already been looking for ways to claim extra money to make up for profit cut from the bid in order to get the job. To overcome this adversarial position and encourage cooperation, it is helpful to create more human connections among all the people who will be working together over a year or multiyear construction process. While it is true that at the end of the process no one will be a stranger anymore, it is helpful to accelerate getting to know one another.

At the end of the partnering session, it is customary for everyone to sign a joint document that describes their good-faith intentions to communicate so as to contribute to overcoming concerns participants

The team at this partnering retreat included school district employees, including the superintendant, facilities director, and construction manager, architect and subconsultant team, and the general contractor and subcontractor management team. *Source: The Covello Group*

have and accomplishing goals participants share. This document is not contractually binding but is a constructive way to embark on the high-stress business of building.

Innovative Project Delivery Methods

Although partnering is a step in the direction of creating a less adversarial method of accomplishing public works, there is a great deal of interest in more radical approaches. In the private world, an owner has the option to bring on the contractor and the design team at the same time so that cost estimating, constructability reviews, and feasibility discussions can occur during the design and decision-making process. This is all done from the point of view of reducing the risk that the cost of the work will be prohibitive or that the cost-benefit analyses that are done during the design process inaccurately represent the actual costs of the various features.

In public contracting, the goal has been to push the commitment on cost earlier and earlier in the process. The problem for the contractor is that early in the process, the scope of the work is not as tightly defined as it is when the contract documents are ready for final bidding. The primary vehicles for changing the project delivery process are *design build* and *construction manager at risk* and its related process, *construction management multiprime*. A relatively new process of privatizing the process is called lease leaseback.

In *design build*, the school district puts a schematic set of documents out to bid and design/build companies bid on completing the design and performing the construction. Such companies include architects and engineers within the contracted entity. This way the contractor gets to control the details of the project in order to meet the bid price. To use this process for sustainable construction, the schematic design needs to include all performance requirements related to sustainability, including the expected performance of the building systems, envelope, materials, daylighting, and construction processes. This means going beyond the level of design that the documents might include in other areas. Occasionally architects lead design/build teams, and this can put the design professional in charge. But more typically the contractor is in charge, and the contractor's focus is on schedule and budget.

Construction manager at risk and *construction manager multiprime* both allow a qualifications-based selection of the entity that will perform most general contractor tasks. Instead of simply going with the low bidder, the district can hire a general contractor (GC)/construction manager (CM) who will run the project and provide preconstruction services, including cost estimating, constructability reviews, and exploratory testing of existing sites and buildings. In most cases, the GC/CM is limited to management and cannot perform any of the construction with its own forces. The difference between the two methods is that in CM at risk, the CM has guaranteed a certain price. Controversy exists whether CM at risk is legal in construction of public works.

In either case the GC/CM can prequalify a pool of subcontractors along criteria such as capacity, skills, certifications (e.g., from manufacturers of specialty products), on-time performance, and claims history. The bureaucratic problem of running many separate prime contracts with each trade contractor is also usually handled by the CM. The trade contracts are then competitively bid among the prequalified bidders at the end of the design period. This is a popular method for controlling selection of trade contractors and obtaining the involvement of a GC early enough in the process to benefit from his or her expertise.

Because selection of the GC/CM can be qualifications based, it is possible in this process to include requirements such as successful completion of sustainable projects in the past or individual experience or expertise on the part of the contractor's staff. This can be important so that when the contractor is performing value engineering analyses, he or she does not automatically suggest things like eliminating the skylights. The GC/CM makes money through fees related to the eventual cost of the construction. These fees need to be carefully monitored so that they do not become an incentive for the GC/CM to allow multiple changes to drive up the price. Sometimes it is possible to build in incentives based on dividing cost savings between the GC/CM and the owner.

Last, "lease leaseback" is a process that was developed essentially so that a private entity would build a school and then turn it over to the district. The hope was to reduce the administrative burdens of public contracting and allow public works to function more like private construction. In California, it was originally intended to allow the lease leaseback entity to assist in financing projects as well. It works by having the district lease a school site to a general contractor; the terms of the lease are construction of the project, and then the district leases back the site at the cost of the construction.

As a result of all these options, there are more ways than ever before to build a team that can provide continuity throughout all phases of the project. As noted, the role of the contractor in managing the construction process in a sustainable way has long-term influence on the success of the sustainable measures incorporated in the design. When the contractor participates in the design, is fully familiar with the decisions made, has the expertise to implement them throughout construction, and has responsibilities extending into the postoccupancy period of the project, the project is most likely to succeed.

Potential Sustainable Requirements

- Preconstruction services to assist in cost-benefit analysis
- Preconstruction services to assist in refining construction techniques for new materials and equipment
- Preconstruction services performing exploratory demolition or testing
- Diversion of large percentages of the construction waste stream for salvage or recycling
- Limitation of areas of disturbance on sensitive sites
- Protection of existing plant and animal habitat
- Dust, runoff, and erosion control or prevention
- Salvage of usable items in areas to be demolished
- Protection of ducts and air-handling equipment during construction
- Flushing of air prior to project occupancy
- Storing carpets and other materials in heated areas to off-gas prior to installation in the project
- Coordination with commissioning authorities throughout construction, closeout, and the warranty period

CONTRACTS

The agreements between owner and architect and owner and contractor have important ramifications for each other. Unless the project is design build, there will be no independent agreement between architect and contractor. The American Institute of Architects has created a set of forms of agreement that specify the roles and responsibilities of each of the parties. It is the rare public agency that uses these forms. Most have forms of agreement that have been developed by their own counsel. These agreements have terms concerning compensation, dispute resolution, responsibility for project costs, and the like that are not specifically related to sustainability. But some specific considerations should be incorporated in agreements for sustainable projects.

Construction Contract Considerations

The construction contract will have many options depending on the project delivery method. However, some important conditions need to make it into the construction contract under any scenario. In multiprime projects, all the agreements need to reference these considerations. The proposed form of agreement is included in the bid documents and becomes part of the conditions of the contract. In many jurisdictions, various of the listed requirements have become part of all construction projects, not just sustainable ones.

BIDDING

Regardless of the project delivery method chosen, at some point contractors or subcontractors will be required to set a price to the work described in the contract documents. All the estimates and projections made prior to that point are moot if no contractor can be found who agrees to do the work at that price. In the various scenarios that require a GC/CM to guarantee a maximum price before bidding, the GC/CM is assuming some of the risk that prices may vary upward. In practice, the GC/CM will be very wary about guaranteeing any price that does not include a healthy cushion to deal with uncertainties in actually buying the job. That self-protection may result in seriously underdesigning the project and eliminating features that might otherwise be included.

The more typical scenario is a set of documents made available for bidding for a period that is related to the complexity of the project. A simple project could be made available for as little as two weeks, and a complex one, for six weeks or two months. The documents may be bid by a general contractor who also solicits bids from subcontractors, or they may be bid as prime by contractors such as roofers or plumbers or electricians, known as trade contractors, who also often bid as subcontractors to a prime or general contractor.

The contractors may be required to visit the site and will have a chance to make formal requests for clarification or substitutions. The answers to questions are made known to all bidders. On a given date and time, the bids are opened, and the low bidder advances to a verification period. The owner or owner's agent will then check on bonds and insurance and whether the bidder has met all requirements relating to experience, certifications, and paperwork. The owner then will have the option to accept or reject the bids.

This is the first time that the price for the project is real.

Flexibility

At this point, the school may have been in design for several years. The construction market may be nothing like it was at the beginning of the project. Prices go up due to escalation in the larger economy, local shortages of materials or labor, disasters, and huge competing projects such as airport terminals. Prices can go down when recessions reduce commercial construction and contractors and material suppliers are hungry. Pricing within the construction marketplace is very hard to predict.

In order to provide flexibility for changing market conditions, it is good practice to include some bid alternates in the job. The base documents include a scope of work that is estimated at less than the available budget. The documents then include a few upgrades that are estimated to exceed the budget. This method enables the pricing on the additions to be established as part of the competitive process rather than waiting for change orders when the contractor is already on site.

Easy-to-estimate upgrades are things like linoleum rather that vinyl composition tile or a higher quality of glazing in all windows. Difficult alternates involve complex assemblies or areas with multiple trades. Too many choices of that sort can drive all prices up just because they confuse the bidders.

The goal of including alternates in the bid process is that a bid can be awarded right away with the project at a scope that the working group has settled on and with alternates that have already been prioritized. Alternates are legally required to be ranked, and the criteria for awarding the bid must be set out ahead of time—for example, lowest bid on the base scope of work or lowest bid on the base scope plus selected alternate.

In the traditional design-bid-build process where a general contractor makes a single bid, the owner has no control over subcontractors. The general contractor has to list them and cannot "shop" the job afterward (trying to substitute subcontractors who may be low bidders to another contractor for those included in the GC's bid). There is actually very little flexibility after a public bid. Even changes of scope such as cuts to bring the project back to budget cannot exceed a certain percentage. This is considered unfair because the original higher scope may have excluded smaller contractors who could not bond high enough for the original scope. At that point, the owner might need to reject all bids and rebid, with the attendant costs and delay.

Because of these potential problems, it is important that the documents that go out to bid include alternates adequate to provide flexibility. Changing the scope after a competitive bid is difficult and is unlikely to be as cost effective as providing room to maneuver ahead of time.

Another advantage of providing for flexibility ahead of time is that the working group will be able to set priorities thoughtfully. The panic mode that goes with potentially missing a summer construction window is a bad time to make decisions about what can be cut from a project.

Where to Draw the Line

Sustainability is often vulnerable to cost cutting. The mission of the project is probably to put students in classrooms. Facilities that directly affect the mission—such as safety, support for the curriculum in the form of whiteboards, sinks, storage, or specialty labs and facilities in the case of middle and high schools—may appear more important than lighting controls.

Taking a hard look at sustainability measures so that the infrastructure is provided and the basic design of the building and campus is appropriate can make it possible to provide for the inclusion of specific features over time if they are not initially affordable. Coming back later to rework a building so that it uses daylight more effectively is clearly undesirable. But it may be possible to upgrade lighting controls later so that the electric lighting responds to the daylight and saves energy.

Likewise, it is expensive to wholly replace an irrigation system with a more efficient one; it is easy to add planting over time. Buildings can be made "photovoltaic ready" while waiting for solar panels to become more affordable. Alternatively, the decision may be made to build fewer or smaller permanent buildings and include some temporary buildings either to cut costs or to deal with enrollment bubbles or swings.

The bottom line is that the basic design of the campus and buildings must have an integrated approach to daylight, fresh air, and site design. Basic materials must be appropriate, and the contractor must use sustainable methods in construction. The building envelope—doors, windows, insulation—is critical to get right. Getting the last 5% of ultra-high performance through better machines and controls may cost a lot more than the first 95% of high performance. But worse than that, if the basic building is not right—if it gains too much heat and too little light, lacks operable windows, leaks heat through insufficient insulation and sealants, lacks ventilation and requires cooling even on cool days—then no amount of fancy thermostats will fix the problems.

The highest-yield strategies—daylight, adequate ventilation, and an appropriate envelope—should not be cut. But these strategies should not be particularly vulnerable once the design is done; they *are* the design.

NOTES

1. Telephone interview with Christine Milloff, Managing Partner at The Mosley Group, food and beverage consulting, 23 June 2009.

2. K–12 California Construction Report, http://web.archive.org /web/20071030230137/http://www.parsons.com/k-12-cc_ construction_cost_report.pdf, accessed 29 June 2009.

chapter 10
CONSTRUCTION

INTRODUCTION

In the planning of a sustainable school, the early participation of the construction contractor is highly desirable. Many of the contractor's methods and operations have impacts on the site, the building, and the success of the sustainable strategies. Where this is true, bid documents must spell out what the contractor needs to do. With the contractor's involvement in the early stages, parameters such as contractor staging areas, waste management, site protection, construction scheduling, and team submittal and verification information flow can be set in a way that is mutually beneficial and described in the documents to assure the smooth functioning of the team.

Looked at from the contractor's viewpoint, the project includes preconstruction (planning and design), bidding or "buying" the job, construction, closeout, and warranty and postconstruction. Despite the participation of a general contractor in preconstruction, there are many new players once the job is bid. Mobilizing the entire enlarged team is a key contractor responsibility. Once the contractor moves onto the site, he or she moves into control of the site and probably discovers more new information. Contractors are organized to optimize the construction period

and that is the part of the project in which they should be expected to be strongest.

In the traditional system, at the end of the job, after all the sign-offs from building inspectors, owner, and design team, contractors are paid their money and they leave. During a warranty period, they are called back to fix things that go wrong. There is such a strong expectation that things will go wrong and that the contractor must be incentivized to fix them that often long retention times for final payments are built into contracts.

In building a team that is less adversarial, thinking in a new way about the first year of occupancy is key. With systems that must work properly in all seasons, adjustments should be made when people move in and start using a building and as the weather changes. It is impossible to see whether waterproofing and drainage are working until they are tested by real storms. Maintaining a cohesive team that can solve these issues as they arise is an important contractual goal.

As construction adapts, like everything else, to a changing world, prefabrication and deconstruction may become much more important parts of the way we approach making buildings. Prefabrication and deconstruction offer potentially powerful new tools in reducing the cradle-to-cradle energy use of buildings and in increasing quality through the ability to optimize rather than create individual projects that make new mistakes each time. But it is important to remember that these methods apply to the built objects and that almost all buildings occupy sites. When considering anything on the scale of a school, no matter where it is fabricated, sensitivity to the site will always be part of sustainable construction.

The contractor starting a sustainable school today needs to give certain issues particular attention:

- Controlling impact on the site
- Ensuring safety of children on occupied sites
- Recycling and reducing waste
- Protecting indoor air quality
- Controlling quality and verifying methods, materials, equipment, and assemblies
- Facilitating commissioning

SUSTAINABLE JOB-SITE OPERATIONS

The first steps toward sustainability have already been taken when the site selected for the school is not a park, prime farmland, or sensitive habitat. But even if the site is not home to endangered species, it is still home to many plants and animals. Water falling on the site soaks into the ground and replenishes groundwater or is transpired by plants back into the atmosphere. These factors help shape the design of paving, planting, hydrology, and building location. But the construction period itself can have permanent impacts on the site. The greater the impact the contractor has on the site, the greater the disruption the local ecology will suffer.

At the same time, construction is a big logistical operation. Materials come on site and need to be

Grading and compaction creates potential for stormwater and air pollution and for the disruption of the soil as a medium for growing. *Source: Gelfand Partners Architects*

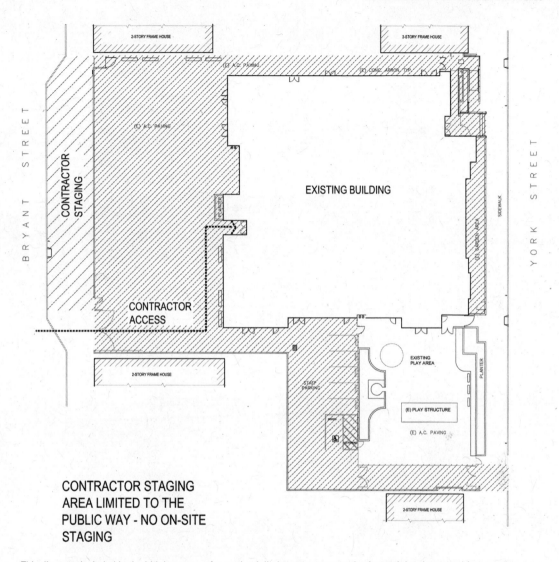

CONTRACTOR STAGING
AREA LIMITED TO THE
PUBLIC WAY - NO ON-SITE
STAGING

This diagram, included in the bid documents for a school, limits contractor staging beyond the playground fence and delineates the access route the contractor will need to take. *Source: Gelfand Partners Architects*

stored before installation. Sometimes certain construction elements are fabricated into assemblies on site. Contractors need to have space for all their staging, parking their vehicles, setting up a field office, and storing their machinery. LEED (Leadership in Energy and Environmental Design) sets limits around a building and confines the contractor's operations to that space. Such limits should recognize the extent of site work that will extend beyond the building for playgrounds, parking lots, and athletic fields. These areas, particularly areas destined to be paved, can be appropriate staging areas for the contractor.

Temporary portables remove children from the job site but disrupt additional site areas. *Source: Gelfand Partners Architects*

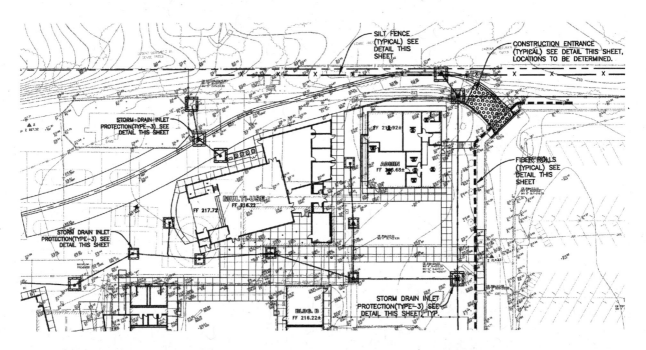

This drawing is a stormwater protection plan (SWPP) that details contractor responsibilities for water protection during construction. *Source: Gelfand Partners Architects*

On existing school sites where either modernization or additions are planned, the presence of children adds an additional safety concern. Contractor traffic (trucks, deliveries, off-haul of debris or dirt) needs to be separate from children. Ideally it is separate from all other traffic. Classes may need to be moved temporarily so that the contractor can get access to the building. If it is necessary to extend grading operations to create construction roads, or if temporary portables need to be placed on site, the project needs to include, and clearly describe, restoration or enhancement of the site to the ultimate design intent. During the bidding process, the sequence of the work needs to be clearly described to the contractor so that the inefficiencies of dealing with an occupied site become part of the contractor's pricing.

If grading and foundation work is part of the scope, the potential exists for increased stormwater pollution due to increased soil erosion in areas that are no longer either paved or planted. The two main strategies for controlling this are filtration (surrounding construction areas with materials such as hay bales) and retention and settling with the reinfiltration of groundwater on site. Retention can take up a significant amount of space and needs to be factored into the area of construction disturbance. The season (wet or dry, cold or hot) during which the work will occur influences the management of the site work and the sequence of tasks in the job.

Topsoil is valuable. Stockpiling topsoil for reuse when excavating is good sustainable practice. It needs to be stored so that it will not become a problem either by drying out—dust—or becoming a source of muddy runoff. Cover stockpiled topsoil until ready for reuse. Moving things twice is more expensive than moving them once; can the topsoil be moved to its ultimate location rather than moved to a stockpile and then spread out in a field?

Trees require special protection during construction. Trees get water not only from rain on leaves but from the water that soaks into the ground. If construction vehicles and materials get too close to a tree, even if they do not actually break limbs or damage the trunk, the compaction of the ground ultimately can prove fatal to the tree. Fencing an area as large as the drip line of the tree is a minimum protection. The drip line is the entire area below the crown of the tree that might be dripped on by the leaves. Fencing should be indicated on a plan, and the contractor should be required to submit a drawing with proposed materials and installation details.

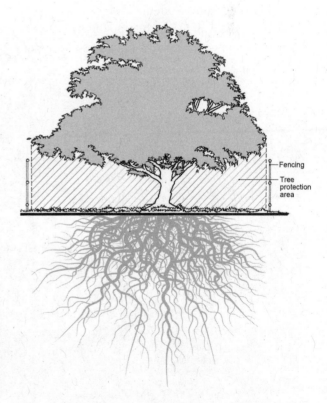

The roots of trees occupy an area roughly equal to the visible crown.
Source: Gelfand Partners Architects

CONSTRUCTION AND DEMOLITION WASTE MANAGEMENT

Recycling is necessary throughout construction. Provision should be made for recycling waste, packaging, and scrap as well as salvaging or diverting demolition debris if an existing structure is being removed or modified. Many local scavenger companies have begun sorting and recycling construction debris. A stepped process in sorting and salvaging may be the most efficient approach.

The contractor can salvage and protect usable items on site and also can do the first gross separation of debris. Finicky things, such as pulling nails out of lumber, may be better value if done off site by a different entity. Similarly, a scavenger company may be better able to coordinate crushing concrete for reuse of the aggregate and shipping off rebar for recycling with many other construction projects producing the same class of debris.

Construction debris can also contain hazardous materials. Soils next to heavily trafficked roads may contain lead from the many years of leaded fuel emissions, as may soils next to buildings where leaded paints were scraped over generations of repainting. Soils that were used in agriculture may contain heavy doses of pesticide. Hazardous material testing should be done early in the design process so that cost and schedule impacts are accounted for.

Interior and exterior use of asbestos requires special handling, as does the disposal of concentrated lead paint (paint scrapings). Lead-painted building

Reinforcing bars and crushed concrete await removal for recycling. *Source: Gelfand Partners Architects*

materials (often disposed of as standard construction debris) may be handled rather routinely for disposal but require expensive mitigation for salvage. If the project priorities include salvaging such materials, abatement of the hazardous materials must be included in the work.

INDOOR AIR QUALITY PROTECTION DURING CONSTRUCTION

Once the building is erected and enclosed, the indoor air quality of the permanent building can be strongly influenced by the air quality strategies taken during construction. Clean jobs, where dust control is implemented inside and outside, make it easier to turn over a project where the air quality at occupancy is acceptable. Door mats are an accepted part of indoor air quality protection in completed buildings, and some method of preventing construction debris, mud, and dust from being tracked in during construction is also important. Housekeeping even at the level of where workers eat and discard food waste influences the establishment of pest problems that may outlast construction, besides protecting workers from ingesting building materials along with their lunch.

Once ducts are installed, it is important to seal them from the dusty environment of construction. Cleaning the ducts afterward is much harder than keeping construction dirt out.

Even when materials are selected for their sustainable, nontoxic properties, there is still a cumulative effect from the materials, adhesives, solvents, and coatings that are used during construction. The project schedule should include airing out the various materials that might emit odors or gases. The materials themselves can be aired out prior to installation—for

Registers on ducts are sealed during construction. *Source: Gelfand Partners Architects*

example, by unrolling a carpet in a warehouse before installation.

Another strategy is flushing the building out before occupancy by running heating, ventilating, and air-conditioning (HVAC) systems at capacity for a period of time. These requirements must be included in bid specifications, or they will cause extra charges if they delay the contractor.

VERIFICATION

Both LEED and CHPS (Collaborative for High Performance Schools) have third-party verification options. To attain official recognition under these systems, the design team must submit calculations and specifications for selected points during design, and the construction process must include documentation of the sustainable strategies employed. Recycling points require verification from haulers. Duct protection requires dated photographs. Each system goes into detail about reporting requirements.

The contractor is a full-fledged member of the sustainable project team. Coordinating project contract submittals with sustainable submittals, scheduling contract and building code inspections and commissioning together, and working to integrate the process is as important as integrating design features. When sustainability verification is made part of quality control, it need not be an onerous or expensive addition to the construction process.

As sustainability becomes part of building codes, field inspectors will enforce requirements. Grade-stamped lumber is checked in the field by inspectors

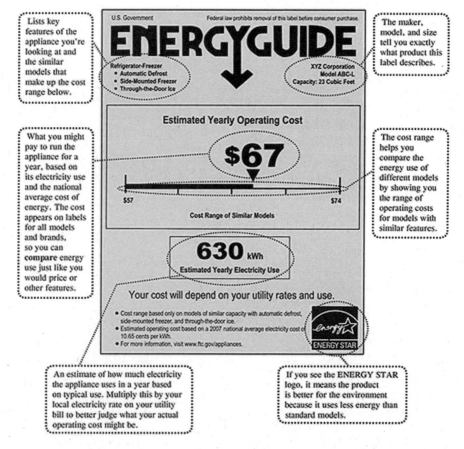

This ENERGY STAR label delineates both the model and the expected performance.

for structural values and may in the future be checked for certification of its sustainable harvesting and shipping. Equipment and appliances come with tags and labels identifying not only ENERGY STAR compliance but performance criteria. Many items, including insulation, filters, and fluorescent lamps, are labeled by type. All these are part of sustainable systems and are included in the specifications. During construction, such labels and contractor submittals allow the team to verify that the right products are being installed in the job in the right way.

Many labels and stamps are concealed behind finishes as construction progresses. It thus becomes part of construction scheduling that signoffs and inspections and documentation of compliance need to occur in a timely manner so that the contractor can proceed with a sequence that makes sense for construction and is consistent with the bid documents.

COMMISSIONING

Commissioning is the verification that system performance standards have been clearly described, the design is appropriate to meet them, the contractor has fulfilled the design requirements, and the system operates as required. Commissioning is defined as either "fundamental" or "enhanced." Fundamental commissioning verifies that the systems are performing as designed. It differs from the normal construction quality control in that it requires measurements of comfort or light conditions in the completed space rather than just verifying that system testing or balancing has taken place. It also requires the contractor to train the user to maintain and operate their new systems.

Enhanced commissioning includes the participation of the commissioning agent during design (setting performance requirements and doublechecking the design) and construction prior to closeout.

For LEED and CHPS, fundamental commissioning is a prerequisite. Enhanced commissioning is a way to earn points within those systems. Commissioning is also an excellent way to clarify what kind of performance is expected in the sustainable school and to have objective criteria to ensure that it is achieved. In lighting, for example, during design, the working group (including end users) decides how bright the ambient light in a classroom should be. The commissioning agent in enhanced commissioning can assist in setting those targets. The design team designs lighting and controls. In enhanced commissioning, the commissioning agent checks whether the design is likely to meet the selected target.

During construction, the commissioning agent checks the installation and is consulted on any design changes. Also during construction, the agent, along with the design team, checks submittals to be sure that the specified systems are being installed and that any substitutions are really equal. After construction, the agent checks the light levels to be sure that the target performance has been achieved. If this is not the case, the agent troubleshoots the installation. In enhanced commissioning, the agent can track whether the design remained as first verified and, if so, concentrate on installation issues.

Part of the sustainable construction process is the involvement of the subcontractors as well as the commissioning agent in turning over building systems to maintenance and operations staff. The contractors submit manuals on installed systems, but often these manuals are made by the manufacturers for individual pieces of equipment. With the involvement of the commissioning agent, a formal training process occurs to be sure that a fully operational system is turned over to a fully trained and informed staff. The commissioning agent may assist in preparation of a building systems manual that integrates all the building equipment into one logical, connected system.

POSTOCCUPANCY

An example of commissioning versus standard construction administration is a music room where the lights were turned off by occupancy sensors but kept coming on at random times when the room was not occupied. The lighting contractor was called back repeatedly and found nothing wrong with the system. The commissioning agent found that the HVAC nozzles were pointed directly at the music stands, and the movement of the paper was causing the sensor to switch on the lights. The nozzles were adjusted. Problem resolved.

Setting criteria during the design process, especially with the involvement of end users, helps handle complaints later. Comfort is subjective. If a room is too warm but it is within the target range, then the contractor does not have a problem—the system is operating as specified. It can help building managers to be able to tell occupants what the criteria were, why they were set that way, and how they have been met.

Sometimes it is difficult to know ahead of time what will really feel comfortable. Part of designing the system is designing a range of system performance. If the system is properly installed and if the operations and maintenance personnel are properly trained, it should be possible to make adjustments to the system. If people are still uncomfortable when the system is operating as planned, staff members need to be able to say that energy calculations were based on the performance as it is and that the district or school has a policy to vary only by a certain amount.

The commissioning agent stays involved in the project for a full year after completion of construction. This is typically the minimum contractor warranty period. It is important to test mechanical systems through both heating and cooling seasons. The school may be turned over to users just in time for the beginning of the school year, often still in cooling mode. The owner might not discover problems in heating until November or later, or whenever the system switches over and temperatures become extreme enough to test it.

One of the challenges in developing good teamwork during and after construction is determining how troubleshooting time and callback time is compensated. In the music room example, the lighting contractor spent a lot of time on something that was not its problem. The commissioning agent has a contract and is paid for his or her time; should postoccupancy become a part of construction contracts, perhaps with a savings for the owner and a bonus for the contractor if the job is one of those marvelous ones where there are no problems?

In a modernization, if some of the systems in the existing campus are not being replaced, it is good practice to include retro-commissioning in the building project. In essence, the commissioning agent does the same thing for these systems as for new ones: monitors their performance to see that they match their design criteria. Many existing systems have gone out of adjustment and use much more energy than necessary. Old systems should run at their own best performance too.

PREFABRICATION

Prefabrication has been advocated as a solution to the high costs of construction and to the quality problems that result from uncontrolled field conditions. For sustainability, prefabrication offers the advantages of a controlled manufacturing process and the ability to prototype buildings, optimize the prototype, and then reduce costs through volume. The significance of controlled manufacturing and optimization is that they make possible a reduction in the amount of material

The design of these portables has been upgraded to include daylighting and displacement ventilation while remaining affordable. *Source: Gelfand Partners Architects*

used in the building because of the reduction in safety factors that are otherwise built into field construction. More sophisticated engineering is theoretically possible because the price of construction should come down due to the factory process.

In practice, premanufactured school buildings have offered economy but not much in the way of either sustainability or design quality. "Portables" have targeted economy above any other consideration. This is not inevitable and does not invalidate the potential advantages of prefabrication. Sustainable prefabricated buildings could quickly find a market if they are priced right.

Prefabricated buildings are by definition generic. But sustainability depends on adaptation to local conditions. One size does not fit all. Even the current relatively unsustainable buildings practically double in price when the costs of site preparation, foundations, and connection to utilities and building fire, data, and phone systems are added.

One challenge in developing a sustainable product is to provide for good daylighting and ventilation as well an energy-efficient mechanical unit in a building whose orientation might be set in any direction. The more changes that are required on site, the fewer the advantages of prefabrication.

The potential on-site benefits in terms of a better building and lower cost are worth continued research in pre-fabricated buildings and assemblies. In addition, the site disturbance and the disruption to occupied school sites could be reduced by off-site fabrication. A mature industry in sustainable prefabricated classrooms could offer different models suited to different climates and orientations. Prefabricated panels are another direction for buildings too large to be transported as assemblies. This too could support the kind of site adaptation that is vital to sustainable schools.

DECONSTRUCTION VERSUS DEMOLITION

Beyond the kind of evolution of the existing system just described, extensive changes have been proposed to the construction system. One of these is decon-struction. In deconstruction, a building is designed from the beginning so that its materials can be reused more easily when it is eventually retired.

Deconstruction would replace demolition. For example, instead of tearing out plywood and framing so that the wood ends up splintered, broken, and full of fasteners, the idea is that the material is still intact enough to use again in its original form. At present, buildings are not designed to be deconstructed, and the work involved in pulling nails and preserving materials is generally cost prohibitive because of the labor involved. Recycled materials generally are reconstituted out of a much earlier state.

The invention of the "open office" system of movable workstations (cubicles) made reconfiguration of office interiors possible without demolition and reconstruction. This is analogous to the goal in designing for deconstruction—buildings would be made of reconfigurable components or would be assembled so that disassembly would be easier to accomplish.

This Herman Miller Intent office furniture is composed of environmentally safe and healthy materials, is designed for material reuse in a closed-loop system, such as recycling or composting, and is assembled using 100% renewable energy. It is warranted for 12 years and three shifts. *Source: Herman Miller*

This joint use gym was constructed on an occupied school site. Prefabricated steel components and prefabricated wall panels allowed the building to be erected with minimum disruption, and will ultimately be possible to disassemble. *Source: Gelfand Partners Architects*

Modular office furniture fits together to meet many different spatial needs although within the limits of office work. Expanding the concept to modular buildings is more complicated due to the different forces they must resist (wind, snow, earthquake, heat, cold, etc). The uses in buildings are also more varied. But designing system components for assembly and disassembly at finer levels allows them to be fit together in more varied ways. Building toys allow children to put together a great variety of structures. Is this idea scalable?

Deconstruction of prefabricated panelized buildings could be a natural consequence of the method of construction. If a building arrives in panels, it seems that the panels could be components, like the workstation components, and that reconfiguration would be possible. The full life cycle of a building should be considered during design instead of assuming that the building will be either a permanent monument or a temporary phase on the way to the dump.

Consciousness of the entire cycle of construction, including the eventual reuse of the materials, whether at the material, component, or assembly level, is ultimately where the industry will need to go. As in many other areas of sustainability, it may be possible to achieve only part of this goal on any given project. But as in the rest of sustainability, we cannot delay starting.

LEED Construction Credits

Sustainable Sites
    Prereq   Construction Activity Pollution Prevention
    Energy and Atmosphere

Prereq   Fundamental Commissioning of the Building Energy Systems
  3 Enhanced Commissioning

Materials and Resources
1.1 Building Reuse, Maintain 75% of Existing Walls, Floors & Roof
1.2 Building Reuse, Maintain 95% of Existing Walls, Floors & Roof
1.3 Building Reuse, Maintain 50% of Interior Non-Structural Elements
2.1 Construction Waste Management, Divert 50% from Disposal
2.2 Construction Waste Management, Divert 75% from Disposal
3.1 Materials Reuse, 5%
3.2 Materials Reuse, 10%
  7 Certified Wood

Indoor Environmental Quality
3.1 Construction IAQ Management Plan, During Construction
3.2 Construction IAQ Management Plan, Before Occupancy
  4 Low-emitting Materials
10 Mold prevention

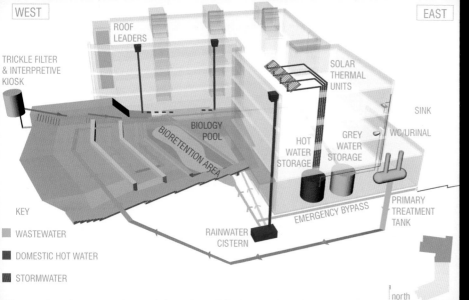

WEST

EAST

ROOF LEADERS

TRICKLE FILTER & INTERPRETIVE KIOSK

SOLAR THERMAL UNITS

SINK

BIOLOGY POOL

BIORETENTION AREA

HOT WATER STORAGE

GREY WATER STORAGE

WC/URINAL

KEY

WASTEWATER

DOMESTIC HOT WATER

STORMWATER

RAINWATER CISTERN

EMERGENCY BYPASS

PRIMARY TREATMENT TANK

north

▲ The Bruce B. Stewart and Andra B. Jurist Middle School at Sidwell Friends School in Washington, DC is a LEED-NC Platinum project. It is an independent school, and embraces sustainability as a basis of its educational mission.

◄ The project uses 60% less energy than a conventional school, has lowered municipal water use by 90%, and selecte 80% of the planting on site from native species

Sea Bird Island, near Agassiz, British Columbia, is the home of the Seabird Island Indian Band. Their new school answered a dream to bring education into local control so that it would be consistent with the band's values. As viewed from a variety of angles the community sees "a canoe, an eagle, a clam, an owl and a salmon" suggested in the design of the school.

The client was the Seabird Island Band Department of Public Works. The majority of the construction workers came from Seabird and the neighboring communities. The architects used the traditional language of heavy timber construction in design and created a 1:20 scale model of the school to clarif... framing for the communit...

The Strawberry Vale School takes a radically different approach to a Victoria, British Columbia site that has had an educational use since 1893. The new location places the school immediately adjacent to a Garry Oak woodland, a rare and threatened species of tree. This natural site is clearly an asset, and the design capitalizes on it while preserving its environmental integrity.

Strawberry Vale supporting functions such as offices, computers, workrooms, restrooms, and recycling, string out along the linear spine that also mediates the changing levels of the site. In a reverse of typical school sections, the spine extends above surrounding spaces, admitting light that benefits both the uses in the spine and balances the classroom daylighting.

▲ Hazelwood School is located in Glasgow, Scotland, situated in a landscaped green area that is adjacent to Bellahouston Park. The school serves students from age 3 to 19 who have multiple disabilities that include visual impairment, hearing aimpairment, mobility or cognitive impairment. The building specifically deals with stimulating all the senses and the imagination.

◀ The interior cork wall finish provides messages through a navigational tool that children can use to locate themselves in the school. They can move around the school freely and confidently. The finishes also provide warm and non-institutional qualities.

▲ Chartwell School in Seaside, California, is the first K-12 project to earn LEED Platinum classification. Doug Atkins, the executive director, broke ground with a new description of sustainability and its connection with education. "Sustainability is the defining term for a new type of thinking that connects what was once unconnected in a way that produces surprising achievements."

➤ The site captures all stormwater either through infiltration back into the ground or in a system that captures roof run off and stores it in a 9,000 gallon cistern. Water stored in the cistern may be used for children's activities during the rainy system or as irrigation for the adjacent science garden when required.

The Chum Creek Outdoor Education Center is a camp located near 300 acres of nature park near Melbourne, Austral It is modeled on simple bush shelters with sustainable refinements. First, the polished concrete floors and mudbrick walls incorporate thermal mass, and are fully insulated. Outdoor areas are designed so that they can be shielded from the winds from the south, while the double glazed windows face the north to maximize natural lighting and minimize the amount of heat that can escape ther

▼ Pine Jog Education Center in West Palm Beach, Florida in the Palm Beach County School District is located within 150-acre pineland. The school utilizes th entire preserve including butterfly gardens, habitat and tree preservation zone water-reuse demonstration areas, native pineland landscape, wildlife habitats, stormwater collection and conservation areas, soil composting, and a sundial.

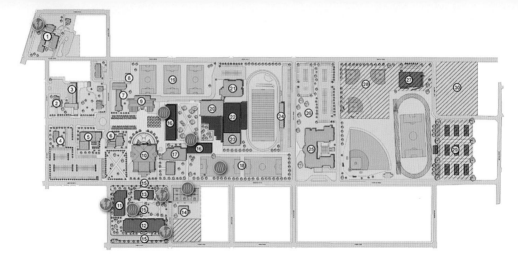

Green Energy at Woodward Academy

Buildings Using Green Power
Primary School **1**
Middle School Dining Hall **11**
Brand-Tucker Hall Classroom Building **12**
A. Adair Dickerson Jr. Arts Center **13**

Locations of Geothermal Wells
Campfield Building **14**
Jordan N. Carlos Middle School Courtyard **15**
New Upper School Buildings (future) **16**
Lacrosse and Football Practice Fields **18**

The Jordan N. Carlos Middle School at Woodward Academy in College Park, Georgia has earned a LEED Silver certification including an array of energy saving strategies, daylighting, and a green roof. Geo-exchange heat pumps reduce the energy load of cooling.

Different solar orientations receive appropriate screening within a consistent architectural design.

The Tarkington Elementary School project is a LEED-NC certified project. Its green standards will serve as a prototype for all new schools in Chicago to emulate.

A key feature that Tarkington Elementary School in Chicago possesses is the roof garden that blooms almost year-round and helps to insulate the building. Energy is saved by reducing the swings of temperature necessary to warm and cool the building. On the remaining 1/3 of roof that the garden does not cover, there is a white coating to reflect light so that it will not turn into heat

The traditional image of the Whitman Hanson Regional High School, in Whitman, Massachusetts, conceals a highly insulated wall with exterior and interior rigid and batt insulation, a 51-kW PV array, 1.15 w/sf lighting density, daylighting, and a 20,000 gallon greywater storage tank.

NEW CENTENNIAL R-1 SCHOOL
SAN LUIS, COLORADO

Centennial School is a Pre-K-12 school San Luis, the oldest town in Colorado. The school will serve as a community center as well as a school. While including state of the art sustainable strategies, including a geo-exchange heat pump system and photovoltaic power generation, the building is designed to meet the community's desire for a locally appropriate building that recalls a historic bell tower in the town.

The Druk White Lotus School in Ladakh, India, is in a region that is virtually cut off by snow for months at a time. The design is largely voluntary, on the part of Arup Associates. The campus is being built by local people with primarily local resources with strategic inclusion of technology for power generation, and a timber frame with cross bracing Arup designed to greatly increase the seismic performance of the structure in this active earthquake zone.

Druk White Lotus is designed to be an entirely sustainable school with completely self-regulating systems for water, energy, and waste management. Like the vernacular buildings of the region stone and mud for walls are found nearby.

The floating schools of Shidhulai Swanirvar Sangstha in northwestern Bangladesh bring a new meaning to "off the grid." These boat bring education to children cut off from land schools by flooding, and bring internet connectivity to an area with no electric grid.

By bringing school to the children, the project greatly increases access to education, particularly for girls, who may not have been allowed to travel distances to school. The PV panels also charge lanterns that children can bring home at night for use studying or for their families to use in microeconomic enterprises.

◄ The New Jersey CU Academy Charter High School is an adaptive reuse of an abandoned industrial laundry building. The laundry had employed many student family members in the more prosperous past. The school makes connectivity at all levels—of the school with the community, of activities within the school, and of the past with the present, an important feature of the design.

▼ Rugged industrial materials and fittings are part of the design approach for new elements too.

The Bronx Charter School for the Arts is an adaptive reuse of a 23,700 square foot meat processing plant in the Hunts Point section of the South Bronx in New York. The glazed brick exterior not only announces the new use but covers a new, highly insulated wall system.

New skylights and windows bring natural light into the teaching spaces in the old factory.

▲ Daylight is the unifying element for the CHPS major modernization and additions to Blach School in Los Altos, California. Major energy savings, as well as exceptionally comfortable spaces result from the careful design of indirect natural light in all habitable spaces.

▶ Existing buildings were reused where possible. A new library was inserted between two existing classroom wings, locating the library where it needed to be for educational uses, and reusing the existing structures.

▲ Loyola Elementary School is a CHPS major modernization of a 1948 campus that was considered for demolition. Existing north facing window walls provided excellent daylighting but no lateral system for resisting earthquakes. The modernization created shear panels and balanced the daylight with new roof monitors. With these elements and the removal of asphalt between the classroom wings the spaces between the wings became usable space for outdoor activities.

▶ The new light monitors also have operable windows that provide natural stack ventilation in the classrooms. The energy management system signals a motor to open the windows when appropriate in lieu of running an exhaust fan or economizer cycle.

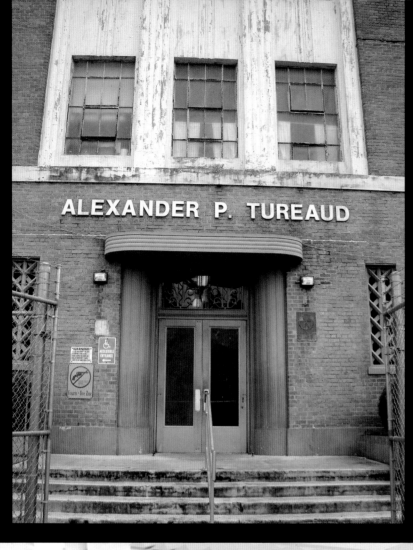

◀ A.P Tureaud Elementary School, New Orleans, Global Green.

▼ Andrew H. Wilson Elementary School, New Orleans, Global Green.

11

OPERATIONS

Sustainable Schools: Maintenance and Operation

Guest Essay by Virginia Waik and Rosanna Lerma of San Francisco–based EDesignC Incorporated, a community-based engineering design collaborative focused on sustainable educational facilities

The core mission of campus maintenance and operations (M&O) is stewardship of existing facilities. Vibrant M&O programs integrate cost-effective resource conservation while also addressing a wide range of other issues, such as occupant health, safety, and comfort. M&O requires management support and recognition for dedicated funding, at adequate levels, to support a well-trained, tooled, and informed workforce.

The M&O workforce can provide valuable and unique input to the organization as it sets priorities for campus stewardship. For existing buildings, this can come in the form of benchmarking, energy use profiles, and building systems manuals. M&O staff input can also save significant costs for the organization if the input is integrated into new building design decisions.

But the primary focus is to have adequate and regular funding for M&O. This funding baseline should be set and protected throughout the life of the building. We have seen many cases where budgets "borrow" resources from operations to support new programs or projects. The core mission is further compromised when inadequate allocation is made within the new program or project for M&O. Like a stock portfolio, if you do not consider all the costs of an investment and do not monitor and watch the performance, you can end up losing a lot of money. But if you benchmark and monitor regularly, you can make the necessary adjustments to grow your asset and keep it healthy.

Second, it is critical to recognize the value of M&O both for new buildings and existing sites. Research indicates that the cost for M&O over the life of the building is three times the price paid for design and construction. It is a fiduciary responsibility to include M&O staff within the design process. For instance, if you are building a two-story building, plan for custodial spaces on each floor. Ask for input on building systems monitoring, control, and how materials selection might impact long-term maintenance and inventory management.

From an M&O perspective, stewardship for existing buildings starts with the building roof, followed by windows and walls. A good building shell goes a long way in supporting thermal, visual, and acoustic occupant comfort. The next priorities are space conditioning and lighting systems, followed by finishes, furniture, and equipment. M&O staff can balance the resources given to them to address, equitably, the service given to occupants and users. They are in the position of knowing not only specific but also campus-wide needs and trends. They can provide unique input—beyond just one space, one building, or one user.

Maintenance and operations is integral to a truly sustainable school. We must not only ensure that the systems work but that they are reliable, safe, healthy, and resource and cost efficient, with adequate control, benchmarking, and monitoring. It is imperative that the key stakeholders and decision makers not lose sight of the core mission: to maintain and operate *existing* facilities. Given adequate resources, they can provide the community with information and achievements that everyone can celebrate. Their work is truly worthy of a community ribbon-cutting ceremony.

SCHOOL CULTURE

Schools are microcosms of the world outside. To fulfill their twofold function—to pass on the skills and knowledge children need to thrive in the adult world and to foster the healthy development of children and young adults—schools teach in a variety of ways, not all of which are based in the classroom. Each school seeks to create a culture that will nurture the values that are most important to it. In addition to teaching subject matter, a school often identifies itself by its dedication to a mission, such as supporting respect and cooperation, for example, or by prioritizing excellence and critical thinking.

While these kinds of words and goals often seem abstract, they nevertheless help distinguish school cultures from each other and are the kinds of things parents seek to understand when they are looking for a school for their child, and students themselves seek to understand as they make decisions about secondary or higher education. School cultures influence everything from relations among the students, to the way lessons are managed, to trash collection. The impression that the campus makes is one of the ways the school identifies itself both to the students and to the community at large.

Management of the facility of the school can be constructive or toxic to the culture of the school. A lawsuit in California was successful in linking student body socioeconomics, poor academic performance, and the lack of basic maintenance in schools. The settlement forced the state to create an emer-

gency repair program to immediately address complaints and fix facility items such as leaking roofs, deteriorated finishes, and heaved and cracking pavement in poor-performing schools. The decision was based on the argument that the material conditions contribute to an inherently discriminatory environment.

Just as an archaeologist examines Mayan artifacts to help understand Mayan culture, the artifacts of a school—from buildings to notice boards—communicate important information to the school community. A campus that is attractive, clean, and efficient and provides the necessary support to curriculum does more than make the teachers' jobs easier. It speaks to the value the rest of society places on the activity that goes on there and ultimately to the value that the society places on its young people. Virtues often spoken of as goals of school culture—respect, support of one another, diligence, and honesty—are also visible in the campus atmosphere.

▲ Emergency Repair Program money will allow new roofs, window repair, a new heating system, and repairs to deteriorated finishes at this high school. *Source: Gelfand Partners Architects*

▶ The values of the Almond School are embedded in the pavement. *Source: Gelfand Partners Architects*

SCHOOL FACILITIES AS VEHICLES FOR LEARNING

Foundations of Democracy

Education freely available to all children is the primary strategy for social mobility all over the world. It is a basic part of the function of political systems that involve all citizens in their own governance. Education also helps workers improve their skills and helps nations compete economically. Making high-quality education available to all is not a luxury for any nation. But all nations operate with limited resources.

The benefits of a child's education may not pay society back until adulthood. At any given time, there is pressure to keep the costs of education within the means of the society at that time. Sustainability can be seen as a frill by an already underresourced system. But sustainability helps create better schools. Just as the Williams Act in California mandated that the state must immediately remedy the discrimination embodied by substandard schools, the benefits of sustainability in terms of the learning environment, the long-term affordability, and the health of students and teachers must be broadly applicable to uphold the promise and opportunity offered by education to all of a society's youth. If this is not done, the disparity in school environments will be evident and will impart its own lesson.

The desire of school systems to achieve equity in terms of facilities helps put pressure on cost. Every decision made on an individual campus could be multiplied through all the rest of the campuses. Throughout the process of design and construction, this pressure will have been balanced with the priorities of the individual building program. But the fortunate thing about sustainability in long-term operations is that major characteristics, such as energy and water saving, reduce cost and enable the transfer of resources from running the facility to instructional needs. A truly sustainable campus will be a step on the path to providing greater opportunity for students to realize their potential.

Tuning Sustainability for Teaching

Sustainability is a way of thinking and acting. The design and construction of the school facility should make sustainability easier to pursue and may even automate some of it. Energy management systems regulate climate control depending on weather conditions, school schedules, and predetermined comfort ranges. This both saves energy and allows students and teachers to concentrate on other things. But there are advantages in making the system visible.

Various Web sites make it possible to track the operation of the systems at the same time that local weather conditions are recorded. Teachers can coordinate science lessons with the performance of the classrooms they occupy. Using the Web site students track the decrease in lighting load on sunny days when a daylight compensation system is operating or the increase in energy used for heating when it is cold outside. Monitoring systems clearly help maintenance and operations staff members keep an eye on systems. Making it possible for students to tune in does something else: it helps them understand the forces at work and helps them see the benefits of energy-savings strategies they may be trying out.

Students hear interlocks turn off air conditioning when doors are open. Elementary students at Santa Rita School remarked that their school was "smart" – it knew when to turn off the air conditioning to save energy.[1] Helping students gain the sense that buildings are responsive to the environment helps them become alert to the world around them.

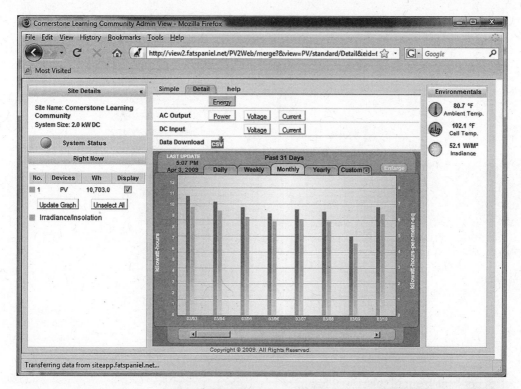

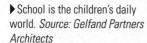 Web site readout. *Source: Cornerstone Learning Community*

▶ School is the children's daily world. *Source: Gelfand Partners Architects*

◀ Blach School students check out pavement markings under the sundial. *Source: Mark Luthringer*

▼ Light from overhead skylights makes changing patterns on the Blach walkway. *Source: Mark Luthringer*

At Blach School, the front of the school has a covered waiting area that is a sundial. At the other end of the walkway is a clock tower with another sky window, linking the analog understanding of the passage of time with the passage of the sun. The skylights in the walkway were installed in a pattern that would draw attention to the light they cast on the pavement. This is not intended to be a curriculum item that will be tested later but a piece of a strategy that invests meaning in the world outside the self and the classroom. When students actually do study the solar system in the classroom and learn about the seasonal changes in sunshine and their effect on climate, they will have a visible sign on their campus of the changing effects of the sun.

In most schools, value is placed on the children's participation in maintaining the campus in an attractive condition. Rules such as cleaning up after yourself after lunch, wiping your feet before entering a class-

Japanese kids clean up their school. *Source: Chikako Yano*

room, or replacing school equipment in an orderly way are part of teaching students responsibility for their actions. In public restrooms in locations such as airports, there is little debate about the advantages of automatic flush valves, but in schools, there is often a discussion not only about maintenance, changing batteries, and the like but about whether the school should reinforce children in remembering to flush.

A more overt didactic connection with caring for the environment has been part of the approach of some schools. In Friends schools, traditionally children were required to participate in maintaining the whole school as well as cleaning up after their own individual actions. This is also an expectation in Japan.

At Stewart Middle School at Sidwell Friends School, the highly sustainable building is part of the culture of the school in many ways.

Guided by its Quaker values, Sidwell Friends is committed to practicing responsible environmental stewardship. Our curriculum is grounded in teaching students about the natural world and their relationship to it. With the decision to construct a new green Middle School, Sidwell Friends chose sustainable design as a logical expression of its values. This commitment continued with the renovation of our Lower School campus. We believe that green design provides an opportunity to achieve an outstanding level of integration between the curriculum, values, and mission of the School.

Explicit sustainable actions—recycling, walking/biking to school, maintaining a school garden, reducing waste—become a conscious part of a culture of sustainability. Recycling receptacles should be readily available in offices and classrooms where paper waste

At Stewart Middle School at Sidwell Friends School, surface water filters through a pond area. *Source: © KieranTimberlake*

is generated and in food areas where cans and bottles need to be disposed. Tracking the energy, waste, and carbon reduction effects of such actions can be done with the help of monitoring Web sites or individually. Adult behaviors—recycling, walking/biking to work, maintaining yards and gardens but also parks and wilderness areas—are clearly linked. It is also clear that if the children see only that they are expected to do this kind of thing at school while their families continue in a different lifestyle, the culture of the school will be undermined.

Linking self-respect, respect for one another, and respect for material property is traditional. In large high schools, there is often an assistant principal whose job includes both discipline of the students and management of the facility and the noninstructional staff who are vital to its operation. This frequent association of responsibilities speaks to the psychological association of behavior and the environment. Malcolm Gladwell's book *The Tipping Point* provides a convincing analysis of the beneficial effect of taking control of graffiti in New York subways on the incidence of much more serious crimes.

Sustainability is about caring for our nest in a larger sense. Children are much more sensitive to what we do than what we say. For a school to continue as a sustainable facility for its entire life, it must be maintained and operated in a sustainable way. Sustainability must become as much a part of the school culture as the traditional values of order and cleanliness. Visible demonstration of sustainable behavior is part of teaching sustainability as a value children will respect.

Many sustainability projects can be independent of facilities. Such initiatives as Safe Routes to School seek to get students back on their feet and their bikes. Turning off lights when not in use, setting back thermostats, replacing lamps with more energy-efficient ones, and retro-commissioning existing building systems to work as they were intended give immediate results.

The Palo Alto Unified School District has a volunteer sustainable schools committee that has brought many aspects of sustainability to the attention of the district. The committee also has worked with school sites on a variety of projects undertaken by school-based green teams that receive additional facilitation assistance from the City of Palo Alto. Their projects have included getting rid of plastic bags in children's lunch boxes and incorporating recycling in the waste management of the schools.

Green teams have focused on reducing waste operation, facilitating recycling, expanding gardens and tree planting, and organizing carpools, walking, and biking. Brainstorming the resource and energy use of schools gets kids involved and spreads into their homes and parents' businesses.

Sustainability and Curriculum

In addition to the "soft" teaching of sustainable operations, there are many areas where sustainable features

---

Energy-Saving Measures

Methods that could be implemented by school districts immediately in classrooms and in administrative offices with no additional costs to school districts, thereby reducing demand and cutting energy costs:

- Turn off all unnecessary lights, especially in unused offices, classrooms, and conference rooms, and turn down remaining lighting levels where possible.
- Set computers, monitors, printers, copiers, and other business equipment to energy-saving feature, and turn them off at the end of the day.
- Minimize energy usage during peak demand hours from 5:00 A.M. to 9:00 A.M. and 4:00 P.M. to 7:00 P.M. The major peaks occur from 12 noon to 6 P.M. during normal school hours. The energy use during this period can be reduced by "load shedding," thereby reducing the demand at the time the state needs it the most.
- Use laptop computers when possible—they consume 90 percent less energy than standard computers.
- Use inkjet printers (on print jobs not requiring highest quality)—they consume 90 percent less energy than laser printers.
- Use e-mail instead of sending memorandums and faxing documents.
- During the heating season, turn thermostats down to 68 degrees or below. Reduce settings to 55 degrees at the end of the day. (Each 1 degree saves up to 5 percent on your heating costs.) Turn thermostats up to 76 degrees during the cooling season.
- Clean or replace your furnace and air-conditioner filters.

Source: California Office of Public School Construction (OPSC) and California Energy Commission (CEC)

Seeing a starry sky can be the gateway to a child's awe of the universe.

are tied directly to the curriculum at various grade levels. School gardens decrease impervious paving, provide habitat, and absorb carbon, and those are all sustainable features. But they also provide a wonderful resource for a wide variety of classes.

School gardens can include plants from the era of the dinosaurs; plants used by indigenous people of the area; medicinal plants; opportunities to repeat Mendel's experiments; plants that will attract interesting birds, butterflies, and insects; plants that are beautiful to draw or paint; or plants that produce wonderful aromas.

A school that has contributed to a decrease in light pollution of the night sky is a good place to have star parties or to observe what creatures are active once the sun goes down. Observing the constellations is both a way to teach about astronomy and a way to teach about the Greeks and the Arabs, who named so many of the stars and created so many of their stories. For many urban children, a visit to a planetarium shows them more stars than they have ever seen in the sky.

Changing the outdoor lighting at schools may not eliminate that problem, but it is a first step, and it is a step that can be linked immediately to education.

OPERATIONS

Many of the operations of schools involve the children and their education. But some concern activities that children interact with in a much more dependent way. These operations include food programs, transportation, cleaning, and repairs. Although it is possible to involve children in them (school gardens, bike to school, picking up trash, learning shop skills), the final responsibility belongs to the adults.

Material Durability and Maintenance

Two aspects determine material durability and maintenance. The first is serviceability, and the second is appearance. *Serviceability* means that the material is performing its intended function without degradation. For example, exterior wall finishes are part of a system that provides waterproofing, appropriate thermal transfer, breathability, security, and sometimes structural performance. They are also what is seen on the face of the building. Although a material may be performing all the service requirements it is meant to provide, if, for example, it is heavily tagged with graffiti, its appearance may still be a burden on maintenance staff.

Life cycle cost analyses of materials include the initial cost at installation, the ongoing costs of maintenance, and the ultimate disposition of the material. A comparison of linoleum and vinyl tile, for example, will compare the much lower initial cost of vinyl with its life cycle cost including the ongoing

waxing that the floor will receive, in contrast with the much-reduced routine maintenance required by linoleum.

Maintenance estimates are based on manufacturers' recommendations. For meaningful comparisons, the maintenance practices of the school should be considered in addition to the recommendations of the manufacturer. A maintenance department may not wax vinyl tiles as often as suggested by the manufacturer for best appearance because the floor is still serviceable. Such a judgment may miscalculate the importance of appearance, but the sustainable team must be able to discuss real maintenance practices in any life cycle comparison of materials.

Overstretched maintenance departments may also make judgments in favor of appearance. Carpets

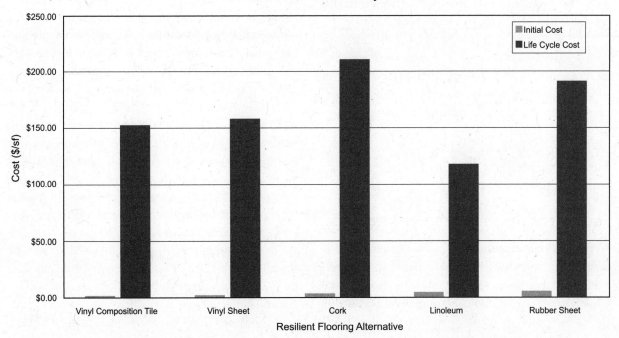

These resilient floor products are shown in ascending order of initial cost. *Source: Helena Moussatche and Jennifer Languell.*

hide dirt better than resilient floors. Custodians may love them for that while hating them for problems in cleaning up wet spills. The appearance of acoustic tile ceilings can be compromised by everything from roof leaks, to messy repair jobs, to student pea shooters. But besides hiding what is above them, acoustic tiles also provide the important service of reducing the reverberation time in classrooms and making speech intelligible. All too often, a maintenance department that is pressured to fix a cosmetic problem will roll a coat of paint over the tiles, bridging the fissures and gaps that provide the acoustic performance and severely reducing its serviceability.

Some materials fall apart quickly in both serviceability and appearance. An example is particle board surfaced with plastic laminate. If the surface is compromised, such as at a joint or seam of the plastic laminate, and water can intrude, the resulting swelling of the particle board core will interfere both with the working of the item and with its appearance.

Two examples of durable products for restroom flooring are ceramic tile and resin-based terrazzo. The tile can be cleaned with a mop and the terrazzo, with a stiff brush. In the sustainable school, materials have been selected in consultation with maintenance personnel. The problems will be reduced to fine-tuning the products, schedules, and methods of operating and maintaining the materials to ensure longevity both in service and appearance.

Equipment Durability and Maintenance

A tremendous challenge for school operations is maintaining increasingly complex equipment. As such equipment becomes "smarter," it may also become less fail-safe. A very reliable motor may fail because its electronic switch or sensor is malfunctioning. Troubleshooting the device involves understanding all its controls. In the first year of occupancy, the sustainable school will be fully commissioned. At the end of commissioning, all systems are working as designed. The specialist commissioning agent will have instituted details like burning in new fluorescent lamps installed in fixtures where the lamps will be subject to dimming at full output. This helps lamps achieve greater longevity. But operations staff must learn a hundred such details and pass on the knowledge over the life of the facility.

The same integrated systems approach that commissioning agents bring to the initial start-up of building systems is required throughout the life of the facility to keep the systems running as designed. This is not to suggest that commissioning is needed annually but that the staff must be trained in the interconnections of the systems and be able to apply the same kind of reasoning to operational issues. A regular schedule of more comprehensive commissioning is also a good idea.

Whether or not commissioning all systems occurs on an annual or biannual basis, scheduled maintenance and replacement of things that get dirty or wear out—lubrication, filters, and the like, must be completed in a timely manner. Before the school is fully turned over to its own staff, the staff must get full training in the needs of the systems. No one expects to weld shut the hood of a car for 100,000 miles, but they do expect the car to run for 100,000 miles with regular oil and filter and tire and battery changes. In the same way, an expectation of durability of school equipment must be accompanied by an expectation of the need for regular skilled maintenance.

In addition to the equipment installed at the time a school is built, other equipment accumulates over time. Staff members equip their lounges with refrigerators, coffeemakers, and microwave ovens. While the school may have been equipped with ENERGY STAR appliances when designed, much of the after-construction equipment comes from donations. If teachers are remodeling their homes, they may donate the old refrigerator—and it may cost the school the price of a new ENERGY STAR one to run it for just one year.

Keeping an eye on the accumulation of things that get plugged in is an important part of keeping a sustainable school operating at its intended level.

Postoccupancy Evaluations

Postoccupancy evaluations, particularly by third parties, are extremely valuable. It is difficult for the participants in a building process to be objective about the result of so much hard work and thought. But lessons can be learned both about the successful elements of a campus and about the things that could be better or are more or less important than the team expected.

In a project with commissioning, performance standards are set ahead of time. A target of 40 footcandles on the desktop through combined electric and daylighting might have been chosen by the team for design. Once the project is built, commissioning agents will have verified that the target was met. The postoccupancy evaluation does not repeat that work and does not deal with issues of contract performance. But it does ask users whether the light level is comfortable and appropriate to the tasks performed in the room.

Some systems will be able to be adjusted based on user responses. Some will not, or will be accepted because of other benefits. It is important that everyone understands the parameters of the evaluation. Asking a question does not promise an action in response. Trying to learn from a completed project does help everyone improve their practices and is usually appreciated by people in that spirit. Particularly if a district is embarking on a multicampus building program, formal scrutiny of the first few projects can be an important step in improving all future projects.

Staff Training

Part of turning over the school to the staff is training the staff in the use of the building systems. Contract documents should specify that the manufacturer and/or contractor installing the system meet with a specific person or people from the owner's team to explain the system, run through the manuals, and discuss the warranty and customer service available in future years.

But while this may have been done, in considering the operations of a school, the first year is not really the issue. The next 30 years are. Training augments the qualifications staff members bring with them to the job. But whatever their qualifications, they will need to know what has been installed, when or if it has been modified, who the manufacturer was, what the warranty is, and the best practices for maintaining and running it. All too often staff "training" amounts to trial-and-error discovery by looking for identifying plates and logos on equipment and talking to people who have been around longer and know that somebody did something at some point.

This kind of information should be in a building systems manual, which should be updated as equipment is updated, and the manual should be in a place where people can find it. An appropriate building systems manual summarizes the proper operation of all systems so that new staff can come up to speed quickly. The manual does not replace factory manuals for each piece of equipment but can help M&O staff keep the overall logic intact. The promise of computerized systems is that the plans, specifications, manuals, warranties, monitoring, and troubleshooting are all there on the maintenance supervisor's desktop and always kept up to date. That may yet occur. Considerable excitement is being generated about building information management (BIM) systems, which are integrated models of buildings including all the in-

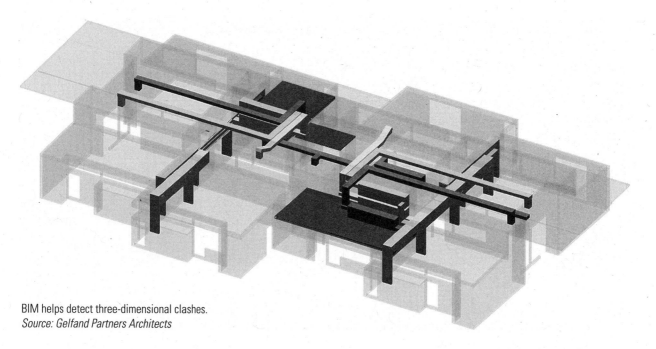

BIM helps detect three-dimensional clashes.
Source: Gelfand Partners Architects

formation traditionally found in plans, specifications, and manuals.

When BIM becomes general practice, it promises to streamline design, construction, and operations by providing a tool that can be used by the entire integrated team. Because the building and its systems are modeled three-dimensionally in BIM, it is much more powerful in locating all the components relative to each other and to space. The database function of the program can also be tied to quantity take-offs, energy modeling, warranty records, and endless other details.

Today, even the conversion from two-dimensional hand-drawn plans to two-dimensional digital plans is not complete. Modernization of an existing building typically begins with a process of discovery of the conditions of the building and its systems. To fully document an existing building using BIM, all the conditions inside the walls would have to be known. It is likely that a combination of methods will be needed to keep track of building systems and operations for the foreseeable future.

At this point, good practices include permanent labeling of all circuiting; posting of permanent, laminated single-line diagrams of heating and plumbing systems in mechanical equipment rooms; updated paper plans of as built conditions as well as electronic files; and a central paper file of warranties and product information. If the information is consolidated and up to date, it is a relatively simple matter to help new staff get familiar and to seek out the resources that most manufacturers have in supporting the maintenance of their products.

In schools, operations staff members are not the only ones who operate equipment. Another challenge is teaching academic staff to regulate heating, ventilating, and air-conditioning (HVAC) systems, lighting, and other equipment. Many systems restrict the range within which a teacher can reset mechanical equipment or include timers that reset to the original program if the equipment is manually adjusted. As people become accustomed to the interface with smart equipment such as cell phones, some of the problems with controls may ease. But it should be assumed that a new teacher will need training if there is anything more sophisticated than a switch and a thermostat in the classroom. It may be appropriate to limit adjustments to some equipment to people who have been trained on it.

The sustainable school should have a quiet HVAC system. Many teachers will have long experience with systems that were very noisy. A high percentage of portable classrooms had units that were so loud that quiet students could not be heard over them. Many teachers solved the problem by turning off the units and leaving the doors and windows open all the time. The new system may not have that problem, yet teachers may still leave the doors open. An interlock on the doors will stop the air conditioning from running when they are open.

Monitoring

As noted, monitoring systems have a wide range of benefits, including educational ones if students can access the results. During commissioning, many agents use a variety of instruments to test the systems operations. For example, the temperature of a room may be monitored at the thermostat and at a variety of other locations. Sensors can measure the temperature and velocity of air leaving an air handler and at diffusers. A data log of the instruments, of the ma-

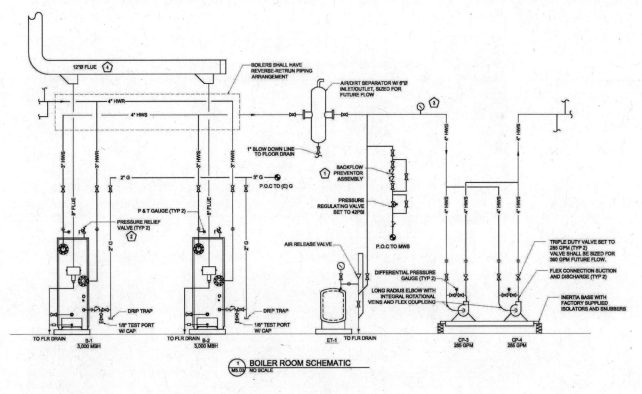

Diagrams need to be posted in boiler rooms. Source: EDesignC Inc.

chines cycling on and off, and of the weather outside can help pinpoint problems in the operations of the systems. The instruments are on site but the readout can be anywhere.

The same data gathering and analysis that a commissioning agent can do could be done at a central location in a school district. While the analysis is specialized work, and it is unrealistic to suppose that every school has someone on site who can do it, if the monitoring instruments are included in the design, either a single district employee or a consultant will be able to help identify operational problems and potential solutions throughout the life of even a highly sophisticated system. In the old days, a "building engineer" kept a complicated steam boiler running through the years. Today it is more realistic to

suppose that a single district engineer will supervise the operations of hundreds of pieces of equipment at dozens of schools. In the near future, computerized monitoring systems will help make this task more efficient.

Supplies

Schools consume. With 2,000 students in a high school, nobody is running to the store when the toilet paper runs out. Organized purchasing programs are required. The original 3 Rs of sustainability—reduce, reuse, recycle—need to be part of purchasing programs. Due to schools' tight budgets, "reduce" is likely to be part of the picture already. But sustainability can become one of the requirements for a vendor that wants to provide supplies to the school. Because of its

The Mission High School boiler room has a complex set of machines to operate. *Source: Gelfand Partners Architects*

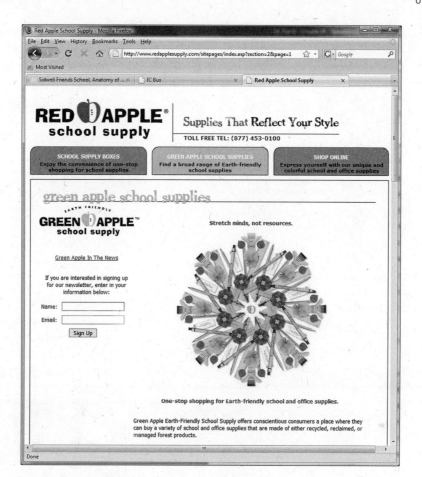

The Web has many resources for school supplies. *Red Apple School Supplies*

greater clout in the marketplace, a school may be more able than an individual to specify the kind of packaging its supplies come in or even to make disposal of waste a part of the deal. Maybe the paint contract comes with a requirement that the vendor remove and properly dispose of all old paint and empty paint cans when new paint is delivered.

Classrooms need to have a variety of materials on hand. Students often come to school prepared with some of it—notebook paper, binders, pens, pencils, and markers—but the school needs to provide other items. In response to tight budgets, some teachers find ways to run around middlemen; for

example, a seventh-grade science teacher found a way to buy owl pellets direct from a farmer instead of from a supply house and saved $2 per pellet, which was significant when multiplied over 200 children needing their own pellet to dissect. The significance for sustainability is that while supplies may have a central purchasing source, additional materials always will be required, and it is important for staff members to understand what they are looking for in terms of sustainability. For example, nontoxic whiteboard markers are available and no longer need special ventilation. It is important that staff use them.

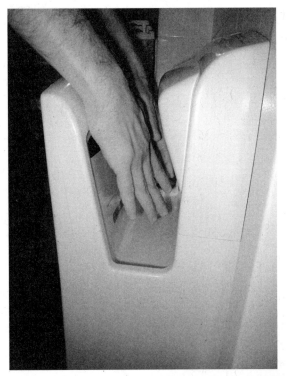

In addition to materials supporting educational activities, the school stocks office supplies, food, restroom paper goods, cleaning supplies, landscape maintenance materials, bandages, light bulbs, and computer paraphernalia, among other things. All these items come in shades of green and not so green. Similar to businesses, schools can cut down their use of paper by using two-sided printing and copying, creating scratch pads out of paper that has been used on one side, and refraining from printing everything.

The paper towel versus hand dryer choice pits wasting paper against using energy. Paper towels often are eliminated in restrooms both for their potential in clogging toilets and for the waste of resources they represent. Hand dryers can be more energy efficient, particularly if the drying area is confined. If paper towels are used, their dispensers should make it convenient to use less. Product vendors often provide dispensers for the product. The school's purchasing contracts need to be considered during design.

▲ This hand dryer concentrates energy in a confined space. *Source: Gelfand Partners Architects*

▶ With an overnight charge, this bus increases fuel efficiency by 70%. *Source: Napa Unified School District*

Energy-saving light bulbs, glazing, or water-saving plumbing or irrigation devices should be replaced with like products. For operations people, the issues include budget, information, and ordering times. Windows at schools get broken often. It is important that glazing replacement can be immediate.

Transportation

Vehicular transportation can be a major contributor to a school's carbon footprint. Many children are dropped off and picked up individually in the family car. Up to a quarter of the morning rush-hour traffic in Marin County, California, is due to parents taking their kids to school.

School buses are the traditional way to reduce trips to school when schools are too far apart for walking or bicycling. Taking the already sustainable choice of transit to the next level would be using renewable sources for running the buses. Diesel buses could be retrofit for biodiesel. The relative short hours of operation and slow speeds are also an excellent fit for electric vehicles. Plug-in hybrid buses are already in operation. Creating a photovoltaic shade structure for the bus yard could provide the buses power from the sun.

Food Service

The commercial kitchen that serves a school breakfast and/or lunch program can be a big energy hog. Simple operational measures such as timing oven preheating close to when ovens are needed can be instituted at any time. But during the planning phase, the food program should compare the efficiency of central kitchens with their attendant heated/refrigerated transportation costs to satellite serveries at school sites with site-based cooking. PG&E, a Northern California utility, has a food service technology center (www.pge.com/mybusiness/edusafety/training/fstc) to help with more specific ideas for saving energy in the kitchen.

Some schools, assisted by Alice Waters's Chez Panisse Foundation, approach food in an entirely new way, integrating the garden, cooking, and eating healthy food. The first Edible Schoolyard, at Martin Luther King Middle School, in Berkeley, California, has influenced schools across the country. The foundation also helped create a garden in New Orleans in a green charter school built after Hurricane Katrina.

Children enjoy preparing healthy food from ingredients grown in the school garden. *Source: Edible Schoolyard New Orleans*

COMMUNITY CONNECTIONS

A school is a big investment. The more hours it can serve the community, the more that investment returns. Before- and after-school child care or recreation is vital in communities where both parents work. But facilities can also serve the broader community. In many suburban areas, schools may be the only community centers, providing athletic fields, libraries, gyms, and meeting spaces that the whole community can use. Classrooms can serve adult education after hours. Alice Waters's school garden also serves as a site for community members to learn organic gardening techniques. It is more sustainable to use fewer facilities more of the time.

But such community uses put pressure on school operations. It is likely that only part of the facility is needed outside of normal school hours. Clearly heating and cooling only necessary spaces is a good way to save energy. But beyond simple switching, the needs of 6 people in a school library are different in terms of heating, cooling, and ventilating from the needs of 60 people in a school library. Occupancy sensors—a good way of making sure that selected systems, such as lighting and cooling, do not run needlessly in empty rooms—do not make distinctions about the

Community meetings use the school multipurpose space. *Source: Gelfand Partners Architects*

size of the group in the room. Using carbon dioxide sensors in large rooms can help turn on ventilation only when needed.

Assuming such sensors were built into the controls of the energy systems, operations people need only maintain them and monitor their proper functioning. But if the system is less automatic, then people either need to know when and how to operate lights, heat, and power, or they need to use lower-tech devices, such as timers, to limit waste.

Another factor in making school facilities flexible enough to be used efficiently after hours is zoning energy systems at a fine enough level to allow appropriate areas of the school to be turned on. Obviously, the more detailed this zoning is, the more complex it is to manage unless it is decentralized. While central systems can be more efficient, individual HVAC units in each space give straightforward individual controls and also have less catastrophic consequences if a unit is down. But each unit then has its own separate maintenance needs. The balancing act of sustainability continues through the life of the school.

Sustainable school operations:

- Influence the culture of the campus.

- Make possible efficient use by the community.

- Depend on good data and training for staff.

- Extend into every activity of the school.

LEED for Schools

Operations contributes to the following points on the LEED for Schools 2007 checklist:

Category: Sustainable Sites

- SS Credit 4.1: Alternative Transportation, Public Transportation

- SS Credit 4.2: Alternative Transportation, Bicycle Use

- SS Credit 4.32: Alternative Transportation, Low-Emitting & Fuel Efficient Vehicles

- SS Credit 10: Joint Use of Facilities

Category: Energy & Atmosphere

- EA Credit 3: Enhanced Commissioning

- EA Credit 5: Measurement & Verification

- EA Credit 6: Green Power

Category: Innovation & Design Process

- ID Credit 3: School as a Teaching Tool

NOTES

1. Joann Gonchar, "More than a Makeover," California Schools: A Special Publication of Engineering News-Record (December 2004): 16–21.

2. Helena Moussatche and Jennifer Languell, "Flooring Materials—Life-Cycle Costing for Educational Facilities," Facilities 19, No. 10 (2001): 341.

chapter 12
MAINTENANCE

Lighting Strategies
- Schools can save anywhere from 8% to 20% of lighting energy simply by turning off lights in unoccupied rooms.
- Periodic cleaning of lamps and light fixtures can save up to 15% of lighting energy.

Computers and Office Equipment
- ENERGY STAR monitors have a low-power sleep mode that uses only between 2 to 10 watts.
- ENERGY STAR printers can save a school $25 per year.
- ENERGY STAR copiers can achieve savings of 40% compared to standard models.

Building Envelope
- All doors and windows should be inspected periodically for air leaks.
- The building should be inspected periodically for water leaks.

Heating, Ventilation, and Air Conditioning
- Proper boiler maintenance can lead to energy savings of 10% to 20%.
- Regular maintenance of the air-conditioning system maintains optimal cooling performance and saves money and energy.

Water Heating
- Periodic maintenance on the hot water system can keep it operating efficiently and extend its life.
- Timers can be installed to shut off electric hot water tanks during periods when the building is unoccupied.

Kitchen
- Schools can reduce energy consumption by preheating ovens for no more than 15 minutes before use.

Swimming Pools
- Pool covers can save as much as 50% to 70% in energy, 30% to 50% in makeup water, and 35% to 60% in chemicals.

Vending Machines
- An energy control device for vending machines can save as much as 47% with a payback of less than two years.[1]

PREVENTIVE MAINTENANCE

Another word for *sustain* is *maintain*. The unsung heroes of sustainable schools are the maintenance staff. Their work keeps the environment of the school clean, attractive, and efficient. Without their thorough understanding and support, new systems and methods of operation can go awry quickly. Maintenance staff members have deep knowledge of existing schools and what it takes to keep them going. They should be involved in planning and design from the beginning of the project.

Most of the claimed economic return on green design is calculated based on energy efficiency continuing through decades of operation. But returning to showcase energy-saving schools built decades ago only serves to reinforce the need to involve maintenance in the planning and design. As reported in the Alliance to Save Energy's (ASE) *School Operations and Maintenance,* one 1980s progressive suburban school with an automatic lighting system; energy management system; multiple heating, ventilation, and air conditioning (HVAC) zones; and an air-to-air heat exchanger was using more energy than the average elementary school in the district after only a few years. The maintenance manager had been given no training, no manuals, no spare parts, and no budget. When energy systems did not work, they were bypassed.[2]

Systems need routine maintenance to prevent failures rather than deferred or reactive maintenance that occurs only when a problem becomes critical. Examples from ASE of the impact of routine maintenance and repair on energy savings include:

- **Cleaning centrifugal chiller water tubes.** This is necessary to prevent scale buildup on the inside of the tubes. If it is not done periodically, the buildup will lessen the chiller system's efficiency.

- **Cleaning air conditioning evaporator and condenser coil fins.** They can get clogged and lose efficiency due to reduced heat exchange.

- **Operation of air conditioning and heating controls.** If a relay goes bad and a system operates 24/7, the next electric bill could be $1,200 to $2,000 higher.

Basic to sustainable maintenance is tracking performance. The old way of doing performance tracking was to wait for the phone to ring with an irate teacher on the other end. But actually monitoring and recording system performance can be an early warning that systems need attention. One tracking strategy that is free from external charges is building a database of utility bills. Tracking changes period to period and year to previous year identifies whether systems are meeting expectations. Maintenance staff members know if school schedules have changed, extending hours of operation, or whether especially severe weather was involved, and can make the data useful.

In addition to monitoring energy performance, maintenance workers are responsible for water use, lawn and garden maintenance, repairs, painting, changing light bulbs, cleaning, and stocking supplies. A large district may have a single team of gardeners who mow all turf and take care of all planting areas. They will not be on site to see sprinklers watering in the wrong direction or at the wrong time. Here again remote monitoring through satellite-controlled systems can report on 50 schools to a single district office. But the more data coming in, the better trained the person monitoring it needs to be.

The additional cost of such monitoring, and potentially of contracting outside consultants to assist, needs to be included in school budgets. For example, the school board may need to know and to record that part of the water and energy bill savings that a school achieves needs to be allocated to the maintenance department to keep its preventive program going.

On top of the systems that manage energy and water use are all the traditional maintenance tasks. Preventive maintenance keeps building envelopes sound through repairing leaks immediately, painting when needed, cleaning out gutters and downspouts, and caulking windows and doors. While deficiencies in these areas might be expected to be noticed and dealt with immediately, often that is not the case, and consequences can be much more expensive than routine maintenance. But it is important to realize that maintaining the systems included in high-performance schools does not replace the maintenance the facility has always required, although some product and design choices may contribute to its reduction. The overall maintenance burden needs to be realistically identified and budgeted.

Finally, it should not be assumed that what was state of the art 20 years ago is state of the art today or that today's state-of-the-art product will remain state of the art 20 years from now. Fluorescent lamps and ballasts have been improving rapidly, and even an energy-saving upgrade done 10 years ago can be significantly improved today. In the near future light-emitting diode (LED) light fixtures will be even more cost effective and will have important maintenance implications because of their extended lamp life. Staying informed about these opportunities is part of sustainable maintenance.

Water damage has affected the ceiling, walls, floor, and lockers.
Source: Gelfand Partners Architects

Mold and Microbial Control Techniques

Mold and microbes are alive. Mold spores are present in the environment all around us. The best approach to mold growth is prevention. Disinfecting with nonpolluting cleaning and antimicrobial agents can provide some protection against mold growth. But controlling moisture indoors is the key strategy. Part of the pre-vention strategy must be undertaken during design of the HVAC system and envelope. Condensation from water vapor inside rooms or wall or ceiling cavities is one source of moisture in a building that is not leaking. Particularly if setting back the thermostat at night is part of the energy strategy, careful design of ventilation and humidity is needed to keep air flowing and prevent condensation.

The U.S. Environmental Protection Agency (EPA) has a useful Web site with detailed information on mold. Some of the recommendations will be challenging for schools to follow. For example, EPA recommends replacement of both ceiling tiles and insulation if they get wet, because they cannot be cleaned effectively.[3] This means a maintenance department needs a stock of tiles to be used for replacement or they will not match. And they need to be stored someplace dry.

One of the challenges for schools, particularly elementary schools, is the likelihood of spills of all kinds wherever the kids are. As user friendly as carpet is for sitting on the floor, absorbing sound, and looking acceptable after a quick vacuum, it can be a real challenge if it gets wet. To avoid mold, EPA recommends using a water-extraction vacuum to remove spills on carpet within 48 hours and then cleaning the vacuum. If water cannot be kept away from carpets, it is questionable whether any maintenance department can keep them healthy.

The Carpet and Rug Institute states that improperly maintained HVAC systems are the leading source of mold spores and that "shutting off the HVAC system at night or otherwise extending periods of system downtime increases relative humidity, encouraging mold spore growth. Reactivating the system thrusts spores into the air."[5] Although this does not address carpet's own issues, it is true about HVAC, and it does raise one issue that the design needs to take into account if shutting off the HVAC is one of the energy-saving strategies.

HVAC systems harbor their own problems. Cooling coils for air conditioning drip condensate onto pans, where the water should then be directed somewhere else: onto the roof and toward a drain, into the landscape, into a drain, or into a cistern for reuse in irrigation or toilet flushing. Humidification and dehumidification equipment needs to be maintained so that water does not gather on surfaces or contact duct linings. Air filters should be replaced or cleaned either on a scheduled basis or on the basis of pressure drop across the filter. Filters come in many grades and need to fit both the filtration efficiency and the expected air flows to the equipment.[6] One of the consequences of

---

Mold Prevention EPA

- Fix leaky plumbing and leaks in the building envelope as soon as possible.
- Watch for condensation and wet spots. Fix source(s) of moisture problem(s) as soon as possible.
- Prevent moisture due to condensation by increasing surface temperature or reducing the moisture level in the air (humidity). To increase surface temperature, insulate or increase air circulation. To reduce the moisture level in the air, repair leaks, increase ventilation (if outside air is cold and dry), or dehumidify (if outdoor air is warm and humid).
- Keep HVAC drip pans clean, flowing properly, and unobstructed.
- Vent moisture-generating appliances, such as dryers, to the outside where possible.
- Maintain low indoor humidity, below 60% relative humidity (RH), ideally 30% to 50%, if possible.
- Perform regular building/HVAC inspections and maintenance as scheduled.
- Clean and dry wet or damp spots within 48 hours.
- Do not let foundations stay wet. Provide drainage and slope the ground away from the foundation.[4]

systems with HVAC units in every classroom is that there are filters and condensate issues for each unit.

HVAC units on flat roofs can cause many maintenance issues. If the condensate water ponds near the units and microbes start growing there, they will also be near the intake for the outside air. The units usually are out of sight and out of mind. Their filters may be relatively difficult to access. Will they be replaced often enough? In addition, the ducts penetrate the roof, and although the unit usually sits above the duct penetration, there also may be holes for pipes and conduit that can breach the membrane of the roof.

The rise in asthma and allergies has prompted research into possible environmental culprits. The sustainable school is designed to deal with contributions to air quality issues from materials, construction techniques, ventilation, and envelope design. In theory, the maintenance department should have an easier time keeping the school healthy. But the maintenance

When HVAC units are installed on the roof, special care must be taken to provide access for maintenance and to seal all roof penetrations properly. *Source: Gelfand Partners Architects*

department still will be the front line in dealing with moisture and the mold growth it facilitates.

Pest Control

Pests are another problem where the maintenance philosophy is very different from what it once was. Poisons are no longer the first line of defense because

---

EPA Pest Management

- Keep vegetation, shrubs, and wood mulch at least one foot away from structures.
- Fill cracks and crevices in walls, floors, and pavement.
- Empty and clean lockers and desks at least twice a year.
- Clean food-contaminated dishes, utensils, and surfaces right away.
- Clean garbage cans and Dumpsters at least bimonthly.
- Collect and properly dispose of litter or garbage at least once a week.
- Identify the problem or pest before taking action.
- Apply smaller amounts of fertilizers several times during the year (e.g., spring, summer, and fall) rather than one heavy application.
- Use spot applications of pesticides (if necessary) rather than area-wide applications.
- Store pesticides in well-ventilated buildings that are inaccessible to undesignated personnel or located offsite.
- Lock lids of bait boxes and place bait away from the runway of the box.[7]

The local water quality board requires all Dumpsters at the school to be roofed to prevent the trash from contaminating storm water. *Source: Gelfand Partners Architects*

their actions in the environment proved to be indiscriminate and dangerous to many living things that are not pests. Children have higher sensitivity to many toxins than adults and should have as little exposure to these chemicals as possible.

Like molds, the first strategy against pests is prevention. Pests should not find hospitable habitats, and they should be blocked from access to buildings. Where pests are present, an integrated pest management (IPM) program is the way to deal with them. IPM depends on knowledge about the pests and their biology. The recommended EPA IPM program includes:

- A commitment to using IPM
- Training for everyone in the school community, including the children
- Different goals for different areas of the campus
- Site inspection and physical improvements
- Thresholds for taking action
- Using IPM methods when action is required
- Written record of pest control actions and results[8]

A potential attraction for pests is food garbage. Garbage Dumpster enclosures should be located far away from children's play areas. Of course, they should also be close enough to the school that bringing individual cans to the Dumpster is not onerous for maintenance. A hose bib and area drain helps maintenance keep the area clean. But some water districts protect water quality by requiring a roof over the enclosure so that storm water does not wash contaminants from the garbage down the drain. Design of the enclosure must be coordinated with the local scavenger service so that the equipment it uses to empty Dumpsters will not conflict.

Children usually go directly from lunch to recess, and the food in trash cans from lunch can attract pests close to where the children are playing. Tidiness pays, and can be part of the expectation for the children. But maintenance should also be on the lookout for nests and hives that are close to lunch and play areas so that they can be removed.

The University of Seattle integrated pest management in its landscape management plan as well as its waste management plan. The use of compost tea made from their food waste also turned that potential nuisance into a resource for the site. A truly integrated strategy that turns garbage into compost that goes into the school garden and removes attractions to pests is real sustainability.

MAINTENANCE TECHNIQUES

Matching maintenance techniques to materials and systems is a key part of keeping them serviceable and attractive. Maintenance techniques must meet a number of criteria:

- Practicality
- Cost effectiveness
- Low impact

Sustainable practices differ from typical practices only in that they are mindful of impacts on the environment. Some examples include using a broom to clear sidewalk areas instead of routinely hosing them down, developing a mowing regimen that allows clippings to stay in the turf where possible, and being careful about what goes down the drain.

Prevention is a maintenance technique. When walks are swept and exterior doors have walk-off mats, it is easier to keep floors clean. Confining food to areas where there are washable surfaces and convenient trash disposal makes it possible to keep up with food waste and its attraction to pests.

Resources for raising consciousness about the possible impacts of maintenance activities include the EPA and local water quality districts. Activities like burning leaves have obvious issues. But less obvious are the effects of the small engines maintenance workers use, such as leaf blowers and lawn mowers. Pollution controls on these machines have lagged behind those on cars; for example, a tractor may produce 40 times the pollutants of an automobile.

The maintenance department at Woodland Community College has a golf cart to get around the campus. It is powered by its own photovoltaic panels that also shade the maintenance worker. Could lawn mowers be next?

Maintenance staff at Woodland Community College retrofitted this golf cart for errands around the campus. *Source: EDesignC Inc.*

Protect Human Health

healthyschools.org

Choose products that:

- Contain no known, probable, or possible carcinogens.
- Have neutral pH.
  - High pH= caustics; low pH=acids. Choose products with moderate pH (7).
- Are nonirritating to eyes and skin.
  - If irritation information is not available, go back to neutral pH.
- Have no short-term (acute) or long-term (chronic) health hazards.
  - Check the MSDS and product label.
- Are free of, or are low in, volatile organic compounds (VOCs).
  - VOCs are organic chemicals that evaporate easily. They contribute to indoor air pollution and may cause headaches, nausea, and respiratory problems and may cause the formation of ground-level ozone/smog.
- Use disinfectants only as required by state health laws.
  - Disinfectants are designed to kill living organisms. They are rarely required.
- Avoid fragrances (odors) and dyes.
- Are nonflammable.
- Are nonreactive.
  - Mixing should not create toxic gases, fire, or other violent reactions.

- Are not packaged in aerosol/spray cans.
  - Instead of pressurized propellants, they use pump-action dispensers.
- Provide dispensing systems that minimize exposure to concentrated solutions.
  - Dispensing method should be designed to eliminate exposure to the concentrated solution and reduce waste.
- Protect the environment.

Choose Products that:

- Are biodegradable.
- **Contain no ozone-depleting chemicals** such as chlorofluorocarbons (CFCs) and chlorinated solvents.
- Are not disposed of as a hazardous waste.
- Can be used for more than one task (multipurpose cleaners) to reduce waste containers and the need for use and storage of several products.
- Are made from or contain **ingredients from renewable resources,** such as corn (corn starch), coconut oils, and orange peels.
- **Are sold with reduced packaging** for both the product and shipping container.
- **Are packaged in a refillable or recyclable HPDE or PET container.** (Make sure the product meets school or local recycling system requirements.)[9]

Cleaning Products

Cleaning products can have adverse impacts on the environment and on users of facilities. But the biggest dangers are to the people with the most exposure to them: janitors. According to the Janitorial Products Pollution Prevention Project, each year in the United States, 6 out of every 100 professional janitors are injured by the chemicals they use.[10] The first line of defense is reading the label. But schools have organized procurement programs and can go beyond reading the label. Each product must have a material safety data sheet (MSDS) for the product. The MSDS is an important resource in choosing the chemicals that will be part of the cleaning program. Cleaning programs do not need to include chemicals that will blind or maim janitors.

It is also important to control potentially harmful chemicals such as toilet and oven cleaners that individuals may have brought in from home or picked up at the hardware store. Some of these readily available products can blind. Readily available carpet spot removers contain a solvent called butoxyethanol that

can be absorbed through the skin and poisons blood, liver, and kidneys. New York law bans the use of cake toilet deodorizers that contain paradichlorobenzene in schools.

Snow Removal

Like getting to school, snow removal used to be a human-powered activity. With dangers from slips and falls and lower back injuries due to shoveling, increasing numbers of powered ways to remove snow have come about. In addition to plows and snow blowers, treatments are put on the ground to provide traction. Salt is bad for receiving waterways when it is washed down drains. It is also corrosive to both metal and concrete. Sand is a lower-impact solution.

As with lawn mowing, finding better tractor fuels or engines for plows could be a long-range solution. If a school has a geoexchange heat pump or other highly efficient heating system, it could be feasible to run heating coils under pavement in highly trafficked locations on the campus. And then there are things that ingenious people come up with like the "Wovel."

Mounting the shovel on the wheel helps move the snow and provides a fulcrum for lifting. *Source: SnoWovel*

THE LAST WORD

The most important thing to remember about maintenance workers is that they are the ones who have the last word when it comes to whether a school and its systems, materials, equipment, and practices are truly sustainable. Maintenance workers should have a say throughout the process of design and in creating a program for the life of the school. Such a program should:

- Emphasize prevention
- Control pests and pathogens in healthy ways
- Stay up to date with healthy products and practices
- Be part of the culture of the school

LEED (Leadership in Energy and Environmental Design) for Schools

Maintenance contributes to the following points on the proposed (2009) LEED for Schools checklist:

Category: Energy & Atmosphere
- EA Credit 5: Measurement and Verification

Category: Indoor Environmental Quality
- EQ Credit 5: Indoor Chemical and Pollutant Source Control
- EQ Credit 10: Mold Prevention

Category: Innovation and Design Process
- ID Credit 1: Cradle to Cradle certification
- ID Credit 3: School as a Teaching Tool

A.P. Tureaud Elementary School, New Orleans, Louisiana

Global Green

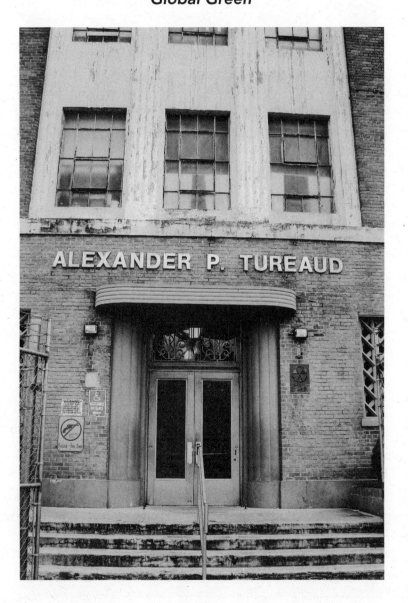

PLANNING: KATRINA FOCUSES A NEW LOOK ON GREEN REBUILDING IN NEW ORLEANS

A.P. Tureaud Elementary School was designed by E.A. Christy and was constructed in 1939 in the Seventh Ward in New Orleans. In 2007, an energy audit was conducted and ranked the school in the bottom 29th percentile for energy performance with 530,331 kilowatts of electricity and 9,271 ccf of natural gas used annually. The carbon dioxide emissions were 15.8% higher than an average industry facility. Therefore, Global Green selected it as the first Green Seed School. With limited modernizations and changes in building maintenance, it achieved savings of $26,588 annually in utility costs. The changes have reduced the school's carbon dioxide emissions by 220,216 pounds each year.

A.P. Tureaud still requires work, but a first pass yields impressive energy savings. *Source: Global Green*

Global Green achieved these results in many ways. First, it installed solar shades in the classrooms, which improved natural lighting in the rooms, controlled solar heat gain, and reduced glare. In addition, occupancy sensors were installed so that the lights would turn off when nobody was occupying the classroom, especially at night. Light bulbs were changed from incandescent to compact fluorescent light bulbs. All windows and doors were replaced if they were missing and were caulked in order to reduce the amount of air leakage. Finally, Global Green worked with the building automation company to adjust the thermostat temperatures to take into account the season and the amount of people. Along with all of these changes, Global Green made sure that equipment was inspected and repaired where necessary and that all equipment could be turned off or in its energy-saving modes so that the building could operate as efficiently as possible.

Andrew H. Wilson Elementary School, New Orleans, Louisiana

Global Green

PLANNING: A HISTORIC SCHOOL GETS A NEW SUSTAINABLE LIFE

Andrew H. Wilson Elementary School is located in the Broadmoor neighborhood in New Orleans, was designed by E.A. Christy, and was constructed in 1928. Hurricane Katrina left it damaged due to winds and flood waters. Global Green, with the help of the Recovery School District, has put $300,000 toward the green renovation of the school, which includes the restoration of the existing 37,000-square-foot building and two additions that will increase the school to 43,000 square feet. It will preserve the historical features of the original building but will be renovated to modern standards to become LEED Silver status. The school will seek the highest levels of efficiency and sustainability when redesigned.

The new addition is sympathetic to the existing school. *Source: Global Green*

Sunscreens and a sundial proclaim the new priorities of the reoriented school. *Source: Global Green*

DESIGN: LEED SILVER AND HISTORIC PRESERVATION

In order to raise efficiency standards, Global Green will include many features. First, it will install 12 to 15 solar domestic hot water panels to be placed above the kitchen. These panels will help provide enough energy to account for 90% of the hot water the kitchen needs. Global Green also will include photovoltaic panels to provide the rest of the school with renewable energy. In addition, a 12,000-gallon cistern will be installed aboveground to collect and store rainwater for irrigation to save and recycle water. It also will install technology that will display the energy and water usage so the school can learn from the data shown.

A wetland habitat with 90% native species will be planted. The school will be able to use it as an outdoor classroom, and it will reduce the amount of stormwater leaving the area. It will also improve the quality of that water. Finally, Global Green will place signs throughout the school to display the school's sustainability and green technologies.

NOTES

1. U.S. Department of Energy, "Guide to Operating and Maintaining Energy Smart Schools," http://apps1.eere.energy.gov/buildings/publications/pdfs/energysmartschools/ess_o-and-m-guide.pdf, accessed June 12, 2009.

2. Alliance to Save Energy, "School Operations and Maintenance, Best Practices for Controlling Energy Costs, http://ase.org/uploaded_files/greenschools/School%20Energy%20Guidebook_9-04.pdf, August 2004, accessed June 12, 2009.

3. U.S. Environmental Protection Agency, "Mold Remediation in Schools and Commercial Buildings," March 2001, www.epa.gov/mold/mold_remediation.html, accessed June 12, 2009.

4. U.S. Environmental Protection Agency, "Mold Remediation in Schools and Commercial Buildings," September 18th, 2008, www.epa.gov/mold/prevention.html, accessed June 12, 2009.

5. The Carpet and Rug Institute, "Carpet and Health," www.carpet-rug.org/commercial-customers/carpet-and-health/index.cfm, accessed June 12, 2009.

6. Camplin, Jeffrey C. "HVAC Systems and Mold," www.facilitiesnet.com/iaq/article/HVAC-Systems-and-Mold--2998, accessed June 12th, 2009.

7. U.S. Environmental Protection Agency, "IAQ TfS Action Kit: IAQ Reference Guide: Appendix K—Integrated Pest Management," accessed June 12th, 2009.

8. Ibid.

9. Healthy School Networks, Inc., "Guide to Green Cleaning: Healthier Cleaning & Maintenance Practices and Products for School," www.healthyschools.org/documents/green_cleaning_guide.pdf, accessed June 12th, 2009.

10. Western Stability and Pollution Prevention Network, "Janitorial Products: Pollution Prevention Project," January 2002, www.wrppn.org/janitorial/jp4.cfm, accessed June 12th, 2009.

chapter 13

A LOOK INTO A FUTURE FOR EDUCATION

INTRODUCTION

Looking forward along a timeline as long as the look backward to the 1962 publication of *Silent Spring* takes us into a future where sea levels are predicted to rise at least ten feet and all easily accessed reserves of oil have been exhausted. But predictions at the time of *Silent Spring* failed to foresee the flattening of population growth in China, the increases in agricultural productivity, and the successes we have had in air and water pollution cleanup efforts in industrialized nations. Certainly it was inconceivable that in 50 years world manufacturing would be concentrated on the South China coast.

If the future holds any promise for the planet, then it holds solutions to the environmental crisis. These solutions are the responsibility of adults today and of children in schools today and in schools tomorrow. Education is changing to meet that responsibility, and education is changing because the world of knowledge is changing. School facilities built today must support tomorrow's changes

INFORMATION TECHNOLOGY

Ideas about education have undergone great changes in the last decade. Access to knowledge that the Internet provides around the world puts a massive research library in the hands of every student who has access to a computer. In addition to the recorded knowledge of the past, the Internet connects people around the world who may be working on the same problem. If a student wants to learn how to play the blues, there is a guitar lesson on YouTube the student can access and a community of guitar players who will enter into conversation with aspiring guitar players. This wealth of information, which might once have been in a book, is now visual, aural, and collaborative.

Knowledge on the Internet is a living, breathing thing—for example, Wikipedia is an encyclopedia made entirely of voluntary contributions, and blogs detour around the gatekeepers of traditional publishing, reporting, and reviewing. Some of this information is opinion, but accuracy, eyewitness video, and the latest science are also to be found. Wikipedia in

Soboto tribe members gather to dedicate this wind-powered cell phone tower in Africa, where cell phone growth is outpacing the electric grid. *Source: Mike Bergey, Bergey Windpower Co*

magnitude of the printing press, or beyond. Many countries have already skipped the technological stage of hard-wired telephones. And where there are cell phones, there is access to the Internet and its vast connectivity.

Schools are set up to teach skills such as reading, writing, and arithmetic, to pass on knowledge such as history, science, and world languages, and to nurture the cultural and personal qualities expected of children as they mature. In the traditional intensely controlled environment of a contemporary school or classroom, children read what they are assigned, complete skill-building exercises, and pursue activities that are organized for them. They learn to participate in discussions, to do projects together, and to take in information. That information may be presented to them visually on a screen or board, aurally, by an instructor, or in haptic ways through movement and practice of writing, sport, art, and music.

Working and playing together, learning the cultural expectations of their community, and receiving the coaching and guidance of skilled adults as they physically do tasks or interact with their peers are parts of education that are likely to endure. As school facilities support these experiences individually and in groups small, medium size, and large, the school facilities themselves are likely to endure. But the interface with information has changed permanently. People need to learn new skills and knowledge throughout adulthood. And schools are only beginning to accommodate this change.

From a sustainability viewpoint, looking into the future is more than trying to predict utility bills; it is about creating campuses whose embodied energy remains useful for generations. For all the attention to deconstruction and flexibility, the best framework is the one that does not have to be entirely reconfigured to adapt to changing needs. An infrastructure that sup-

particular rivals traditional encyclopedias in accuracy. Using the Internet requires literacy and basic skills to interact with the technological gate that opens this virtual world. Using the Internet also requires a critical mind and an ability to judge the content and context of a given source of information.

Learning and knowledge are no longer controlled by any state or religion. The efforts of authoritarian regimes to clamp down on the Internet illustrate the perceived threat of open access to international ideas. The creation of the Internet is a change on the

ports change in education is one that is built around the ontological needs of human beings as they mature rather than a specific skill set related to a temporary technological tool.

ADAPTATION

Adaptation to the environment is beginning to bypass centralized grids and controls. With half of all generated power lost in transmission, decentralized systems offer the potential not only to replace gas- or coal-fired power plants by producing local energy but to replace it twofold by also limiting losses. California has legislated a greenhouse gas reduction goal for itself that resets its production to 1990 levels by the year 2020 and to 80% below by 2050. One of the steps the California Division of the State Architect has taken is to set a goal that, by 2010, all new public school projects should be grid neutral by producing renewable energy on site.

Decentralization on this scale is a paradigm shift. At the level of the grid, it requires smart meters and an ability to transfer power seamlessly from surplus sites to sites that need additional power. At the level of the site, it requires broad training of the operators of all these micro-power sources so that they remain operational. Even if the initial power-generating system is operated by an outside vendor, as in a power purchase agreement (PPA), each local site still is maintained individually in response to the specifics of its individual circumstances.

But in this model, the electric grid still is the context for considering renewable energy. With solar power and wind power subject to the hours when the sun is shining and the wind is blowing, feeding power back into the grid seems a natural way to insure the constant availability of power and limit dependence on imperfect storage devices such as batteries. However, there are alternatives.

In the remote Chalanbeel region of Bangladesh, there is no electric grid. The nongovernmental organization Shidhulai Swanirvar Sangstha has created a fleet of locally constructed boats with photovoltaic (PV) panels on their roofs. Each boat is a single classroom size, flat bottomed, and typical of local boat-building technology. The boats bring education, libraries, health services, and training in sustainable agriculture to the villages. The PV panels run computers and other electronics for boat activities and also charge batteries for solar lanterns that can be brought back to the villages at night, reducing use of kerosene lamps.

Shidhulai also distributes bicycle pumps for irrigation of fields during the dry season, expanding the number of crops a farmer can produce. Shidhulai is able to support sustainable livelihoods, provide health services, and bring education to the children even when the monsoon rains have drowned all the roads. By making education easily accessible, Shidhulai is able to make particularly large differences in the number of girls who can attend classes.

Starting from an attitude of adaptation yields a very different result from waiting for the extension of uniform centralized power systems or massive flood control works that might extend the season during which roads are passable. With many more coastal areas facing rising water levels, revisiting the truly portable boat is a compelling idea. But more than that, new methods of decentralization could make the grid itself obsolete while creating structures that adapt to their situation efficiently and comfortably.

The Bangladesh boat schools do not have playing fields or gardens. They do not have specialized gyms or science labs. They do, however, fit into the lives of the villagers and bring educational opportunity without reducing farmland or other enterprises. These schools are not grid neutral but are off the grid entirely, giving them tremendous flexibility. As industrialized nations

▲ The Shidhulai boat school is a leap into a sustainable future ahead of many developed countries. *Source: Shidhulai Swanirvar Sangstha*

▶ The boats bring school to the children in areas where ground transportation is seasonally impractical. *Source: Shidhulai Swanirvar Sangstha*

plan for the future, this model challenges the ideas that a revamped grid is what we need or that the only way to achieve sustainability is through permanence.

The boat schools solve problems beyond power generation. Their adaptation to the social and geographical demands of Bangladesh is different from the adaptations that would be made to a high mountain town or the middle of a large city. What is applicable to any sustainable school is adaptation itself.

Sustainable schools must take into account local hydrology, transportation, habitats, and light. This paradigm extends beyond schools and depends on many other facilities similarly taking control of their own power, waste, and water budgets, so that the grid assumes less and less importance in the creation of energy. Africa and Bangladesh have missed the first wave of industrial infrastructure; it is fascinating to wonder whether they will pioneer a new connectivity and independence and completely skip the centralized power system just as they are skipping wired phones.

Part of the role of education will be to spread the knowledge and skill to adapt among the broad population of students. Adaptation will not be the job of experts but the job of everyone, just as Wikipedia is not the creation of experts but of many interested people. The kind of educational advantages to be gained from understanding the sustainable elements employed in today's leading sustainable schools may very well be core curriculum for a future population that will have to manage its own building metabolism.

Adaptation is the way living beings thrive in relation to each other and to their environment. Plants and animals that cannot adapt die. Human society and invention have sought both to adapt to the environment and to modify the environment so that adaptation will be less onerous. The advent of increased data-processing capabilities has enabled building sensors, logic, and controls to advance to the point where adaptation can be much more automatic, more efficient, and may even lead to a higher level of comfort than the outmoded strategy of modifying the environment.

TRAILBLAZING PROJECTS

Solar power generation, geothermal exchange heat pumps, cogeneration, displacement ventilation, and small wind have all found their place in reducing school energy use via generation and improved heating, ventilating, and air-conditioning. Improved daylighting and daylight compensation lighting controls reduce electrical load and improve learning environments. Edible schoolyards, adventure playgrounds, and alternative pavings are reshaping school play areas. Schools around the world are utilizing local materials, local building techniques, solar heating, and optimized natural ventilation to adapt to their local environments. Electric school buses and green relocatable and modular classrooms are appearing.

As the market changes, manufactured solutions such as these will be more readily available to individual schools. But it will always be a matter of local adaptation to put together the right mixture of sustainable solutions for a given site. The ongoing health of the community depends on it.

School and Community Interface

One of the notions about sustainable communities of the future is that they will be more compact than the suburban sprawl so ubiquitous in new-world countries such as the United States, Australia, and New Zealand. A more compact (denser) community makes walking, biking, and public transit more feasible. It leaves more space for wilderness, farming, and forestry. It reduces paving. But it also puts more pressure on the open space that exists within the community.

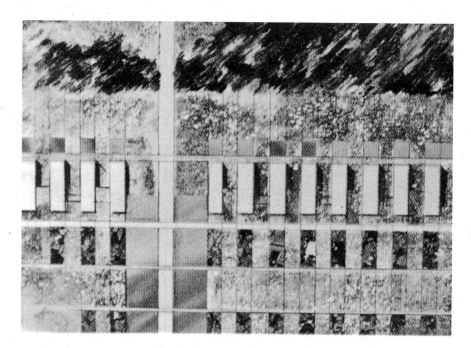

In the international 13-acres competition, the first-place project, Les Jardins D'East Clayton, by Nicholas Gilsoul, applied an organizational grid to the site that reflects the prevailing land use organization in East Clayton, provides for a straightforward building grid, and is then able to be subverted by the natural processes. *Source: Susan Herrington, Nicholas Gilsoul*

In dense areas, the open space of a school's campus is also a community resource.

The 13-acres Competition was an international ideas competition for a 13-acre school site in British Columbia. Plans for prototype buildings were provided to competitors to configure as they wished. The resulting emphasis on the campus yielded a notion of schoolyard park that transcended school uses by opening the campus to community members after school hours. The result was more sports on the sport fields, more play in the playground, gardens, art uses, and habitat restoration.

In addition to getting more intensity of use on the campus, schools are reaching to unconventional places within the community, such as storefronts, zoos, old warehouses, and commercial establishments. The Gates Foundation helped support the start-up of 47 small public high schools in New York City to address the crisis in high school education there. These schools varied from small schools on larger school campuses to a museum school with classes in some of New York's most famous museums. A new high school focused on law used facilities in the Bronx Supreme Court complex. A new middle and high school provides pre-professional ballet apprenticeships; a school in Brooklyn includes work internships. The community partnerships that characterize the Gates program use facilities beyond school campuses and foster connectivity throughout the city.

826 Valencia is a storefront that houses a pirate store and a writing program started by author Dave Eggers that reaches out to students ages 6 to 18 both on site and through volunteers in their schools in the San Francisco Bay area. The program now has chapters in other U.S. cities and works with classroom teachers to excite children about reading and writing. Directly focusing on writing, a traditional core subject of schools, 826 Valencia takes education out of the classroom and into the neighborhood. The outlaw nature of the storefront facility appeals to students looking for a way into independent thought.

◀School of Environmental Studies in Minnesota takes advantage of the adjacent zoo as part of the educational environment. *Source: School of Environmental Studies, B. Johnson*

▼ 826 Valencia makes after-school reading and writing an adventure. *Source: Gelfand Partners Architects*

Schools do provide a safe place for kids to grow, but they do not create an alternative universe. These innovative programs are reconnecting children with a community larger than their immediate family. Even in urban areas, where villages disappeared long ago, it takes the organized efforts of cohesive collectives of families, neighbors, local businesses, local institutions, and interested adults to create schools that truly reflect the ethos of the place.

NEW MODELS OF SUSTAINABILITY

Beyond green, beyond the Collaborative for High Performance Schools, and beyond Leadership in Energy and Environmental Design is the integration of community identity, local environmental needs, and adaptive solutions. The sustainable school is based on a deep understanding of biology, on the creation of a habitat for learning instead of a *machine* for learning. We can look to the natural world and learn from animal homeostasis and from the way skin and fur and feathers work to develop better sensors and controls for building comfort, building skins that keep rain outside and also allow water vapor from inside to filter out, and building skins that can insulate when it is important to maintain temperature differences and allow buildings to come to equilibrium with temperate conditions.

We can look to the plant and animal communities that must thrive with and around us to design campuses where the water cycle is restored and open space serves ecological needs as well as human convenience. Learning to be stewards of the biosphere can start in the fresh air and daylight of a sustainable kindergarten.

This child takes the A Train into the future. *Source: Gelfand Partners Architects*

The sustainable school will graduate students who are experts on being in the world. These students will join the adult society in the restoration of a global balance that must occur if we are to sustain civilized life. The school of the future will accommodate the sensory explorations of early childhood, the social investigations of grade-school years, and the research and experimentation of the voracious adolescent challenging all prior ideas. The solutions that the imaginative and adaptive mind invents will change. But our children will need all the wisdom and empathy and maturity they can develop to meet the challenge of sustaining life on our glorious and limited planet.

APPENDIX

LEED 2009 for Schools New Construction and Major Renovation

Project Checklist

Project Name

Date

Sustainable Sites — Possible Points: 24

Y	N	?			
Y			Prereq 1	Construction Activity Pollution Prevention	
			Prereq 1	Environmental Site Assessment	
			Credit 1	Site Selection	1
			Credit 2	Development Density and Community Connectivity	4
			Credit 3	Brownfield Redevelopment	1
			Credit 4.1	Alternative Transportation—Public Transportation Access	4
			Credit 4.2	Alternative Transportation—Bicycle Storage and Changing Rooms	1
			Credit 4.3	Alternative Transportation—Low-Emitting and Fuel-Efficient Vehicles	2
			Credit 4.4	Alternative Transportation—Parking Capacity	2
			Credit 5.1	Site Development—Protect or Restore Habitat	1
			Credit 5.2	Site Development—Maximize Open Space	1
			Credit 6.1	Stormwater Design—Quantity Control	1
			Credit 6.2	Stormwater Design—Quality Control	1
			Credit 7.1	Heat Island Effect—Non-roof	1
			Credit 7.2	Heat Island Effect—Roof	1
			Credit 8	Light Pollution Reduction	1
			Credit 9	Site Master Plan	1
			Credit 10	Joint Use of Facilities	1

Water Efficiency — Possible Points: 11

Y	N	?			
Y			Prereq 1	Water Use Reduction—20% Reduction	
			Credit 1	Water Efficient Landscaping	2 to 4
			Credit 2	Innovative Wastewater Technologies	2
			Credit 3	Water Use Reduction	2 to 4
			Credit 3	Process Water Use Reduction	1

Energy and Atmosphere — Possible Points: 33

Y	N	?			
Y			Prereq 1	Fundamental Commissioning of Building Energy Systems	
Y			Prereq 2	Minimum Energy Performance	
Y			Prereq 3	Fundamental Refrigerant Management	
			Credit 1	Optimize Energy Performance	1 to 19
			Credit 2	On-Site Renewable Energy	1 to 7
			Credit 3	Enhanced Commissioning	2
			Credit 4	Enhanced Refrigerant Management	1
			Credit 5	Measurement and Verification	2
			Credit 6	Green Power	2

Materials and Resources — Possible Points: 13

Y	N	?			
Y			Prereq 1	Storage and Collection of Recyclables	
			Credit 1.1	Building Reuse—Maintain Existing Walls, Floors, and Roof	1 to 2
			Credit 1.2	Building Reuse—Maintain 50% of Interior Non-Structural Elements	1
			Credit 2	Construction Waste Management	1 to 2

Materials and Resources, Continued

Y	N	?			
			Credit 3	Materials Reuse	1 to 2
			Credit 4	Recycled Content	1 to 2
			Credit 5	Regional Materials	1 to 2
			Credit 6	Rapidly Renewable Materials	1
			Credit 7	Certified Wood	1

Indoor Environmental Quality — Possible Points: 19

Y	N	?			
Y			Prereq 1	Minimum Indoor Air Quality Performance	
Y			Prereq 2	Environmental Tobacco Smoke (ETS) Control	
Y			Prereq 3	Minimum Acoustical Performance	
			Credit 1	Outdoor Air Delivery Monitoring	1
			Credit 2	Increased Ventilation	1
			Credit 3.1	Construction IAQ Management Plan—During Construction	1
			Credit 3.2	Construction IAQ Management Plan—Before Occupancy	1
			Credit 4	Low-Emitting Materials	1 to 4
			Credit 5	Indoor Chemical and Pollutant Source Control	1
			Credit 6.1	Controllability of Systems—Lighting	1
			Credit 6.2	Controllability of Systems—Thermal Comfort	1
			Credit 7.1	Thermal Comfort—Design	1
			Credit 7.2	Thermal Comfort—Verification	1
			Credit 8.1	Daylight and Views—Daylight	1 to 3
			Credit 8.2	Daylight and Views—Views	1
			Credit 9	Enhanced Acoustical Performance	1
			Credit 10	Mold Prevention	1

Innovation and Design Process — Possible Points: 6

Y	N	?			
			Credit 1.1	Innovation in Design: Specific Title	1
			Credit 1.2	Innovation in Design: Specific Title	1
			Credit 1.3	Innovation in Design: Specific Title	1
			Credit 1.4	Innovation in Design: Specific Title	1
			Credit 2	LEED Accredited Professional	1
			Credit 3	The School as a Teaching Tool	1

Regional Priority Credits — Possible Points: 4

Y	N	?			
			Credit 1.1	Regional Priority: Specific Credit	1
			Credit 1.2	Regional Priority: Specific Credit	1
			Credit 1.3	Regional Priority: Specific Credit	1
			Credit 1.4	Regional Priority: Specific Credit	1

Total — Possible Points: 110

Certified 40 to 49 points   Silver 50 to 59 points   Gold 60 to 79 points   Platinum 80 to 110

Collaborative for High Performance Schools (CHPS) Designed Scorecard
Based on the 2009 Edition For Major Modernizations or a New Building on an Existing Campus

COLLABORATIVE FOR HIGH PERFORMANCE SCHOOLS
Better buildings. Better students.

School Name:

Expected Completion:

School District:

School Address: State: Zip:

School Contact/Principal:

Student Capacity:

Approximate Square Feet:

Verification

Is this the final CHPS scorecard?   YES or NO (Please circle)

Registered Principal Architect (Signature)

Name, Title, Date (Please print)   Name, Title, Date (Please print)

CHPS SECTION	CREDIT NUMBER	TITLE	POSSIBLE POINTS	SUMMARY**	TARGET	POINTS EARNED	FOR SELF CERTIFICATION, PROVIDE NARRATIVE, CALCULATIONS, DOCUMENT/ PLAN REFERENCE HERE. (Use Separate Sheet as Necessary) .
LEADERSHIP, EDUCATION AND INNOVATION (1 prerequisite; 13 possible points)							
1. Leadership (4)	LEI1.1	District Level Commitment	1-2	District must maintain CHPS membership and pass a board-level resolution that mandates compliance with CHPS. Two point if resolution incorporates CHPS Maintenance and Operations program.			Add Narrative
	LEI1.2	Integrated Design	1-2	Implement at least two integrated design team workshops to discuss high performance goals. Workshops must be conducted at SD and CD phases of project.			
2. Schools as Learning Tools (1)	LEI2.0	Educational Display	Req	Provide a permanent educational display in prominent school location.	X	X	
	LEI2.1	Demonstration Areas	1	Provide at least three education demonstration			
3. Innovation (8)	LEI3.1	Innovation	1-4	Implement new technologies or strategies that further high performance goals.			
	LEI3.2	Design for Adaptability, Durability and	2-4	Provide a plan and implement strategies that promote material conservation and ease of			
SUSTAINABLE SITES (2 prerequisites; 14 possible points)							
1. Site Selection (5)	SS1.0	Code Compliance	Req	Comply with all requirements of Title 5 and CA Education Code and Public Resource Code sections specified.	X	X	
	SS1.1	Environmentally Sensitive Land	1	No development on sites that are: prime agricultural land, in flood zone, habitat for endangered species, greenfield, near a wetland or considered parkland.			
	SS1.2	Central Location	1	Create centrally located sites within which 50% of students are located within minimum distances of the school.			
	SS1.3	Joint-Use of Facilities	1	Design at least one space for "joint-use" and provide specified security measures.			
	SS1.4	Joint-Use of Parks	1	Share park or recreation space.			
	SS1.5	Reduced Footprint	1	Reduce the building footprint.			
2. Transportation (3)	SS2.1	Public Transportation	1	Locate near public transportation.			
	SS2.2	Human Powered Transportation	1	Provide bike, scooter or skateboard racks & bike lanes for a percentage of the school population.			
	SS2.3	Minimize Parking	1	Minimize parking lot & create preferred parking for carpools.			
3. Stormwater Management (2)	SS3.0	Construction Site Runoff Control	Req	Control erosion & sedimentation to reduce negative impacts on water & air quality.	X	X	
	SS3.1	Limit Stormwater Runoff	1	Minimize runoff.			
	SS3.2	Treat Stormwater Runoff	1	Treat runoff.			
4. Outdoor Surfaces & Spaces (3)	SS4.1	Reduce Heat Islands - Landscaping Issues	1	Shade or lighten impervious areas, or reduce impervious parking.			
	SS4.2	Reduce Heat Islands - Cool Roofs	1	Install cool or green roof.			
	SS4.3	School Garden	1	Provide infrastructure for a school garden with size dependent on student capacity.			
5 Outdoor Lighting (1)	SS5.1	Light Pollution Reduction	1	Minimize outdoor illumination.			

WATER (1 prerequisite; 9 possible points)

1. Outdoor Systems (4)	WE1.0	Create Water Use Budget	Req	Establish water use budget & conform to the local water efficient landscape ordinance.	X	X	
	WE1.1	Reduce Potable Water for Use for Non-Recreational Landscaping Areas	1-2	Reduce potable water by 50% or 100%, or do not install permanent irrigation systems for landscaping areas.			
	WE1.2	Reduce Potable Water for Recreational Area Landscaping	1	Reduce potable water by 50% and install soil moisture meters or ET Controllers on recreation fields.			
	WE1.3	Irrigation System Testing and Training	1	Create irrigation commissioning plan, test irrigation systems and train staff.			
2. Indoor Systems (4)	WE2.1	Reduce Sewage Conveyance from Toilets and Urinals	2	35% reduction in potable water use for sewage conveyance and provide shut-off capabilities for water supply to all urinals and water closets.			
	WE2.2	Reduce Indoor Potable Water Use	1-2	Decrease water use by and additional 20% or 40% after meeting Energy Policy Act of 1992.			
3. Water Efficiency (1)	WE3.1	Water Management System	1	Install a water management system to monitor usage and reduce consumption.			

ENERGY (2 prerequisites; 29 possible points; minimum 2 points required)

1. Energy Efficiency (22)	EE1.0	Minimum Energy Performance	Req	Design building to exceed Title 24-2008 by 15%.	X	X	
	EE1.1	Superior Energy Performance	1-15	16% to 44% reduction in total net energy use from Title 24-2008 baseline.			
	EE1.2	Energy Conservation Interlocks	1	Install interlocks to turn off heating and cooling equipment if doors and windows are open.			
	EE1.3	Natural Ventilation	1-4	Comply with Title 24, Part 6, 121b for assembly spaces and/or 90% of typical classrooms.			
	EE1.4	Energy Management Systems	1-2	Install Energy Management System and provide training and manuals for maintenance personnel. Additional point for plug load.			
2. Alternate Energy Sources (5)	EE2.1	On-Site Renewable Energy	1-5	Install web-based performance monitoring system and provide 1-90% of the building's TDV energy use through on-site renewable systems.			
3. Commissioning & Training (2)	EE3.0	Fundamental Commissioning	Req	Third party or district verification of building systems & training.	X	X	
	EE3.1	Enhanced Commissioning	1-2	Additional third party or district verification of building systems, training and best practices.			

CLIMATE (8 possible points)

1. Greenhouse Gas Emission Reduction (3)	CL1.1	Climate Change Action	1-3	Choose strategies that reduce greenhouse gas emissions and/or measure and report emissions annually.			
2. Greenhouse Gas Emission Reduction (5)	CL2.1	Grid Neutral	2	Create a school that produces at least as much electricity as it uses in a year and uses renewable energy strategies.			
	CL2.2	Zero Net Energy	5	Create a school that produces at least as much electricity as it uses in a year (without using fossil fuel based energy sources produced off-site) and uses renewable energy strategies.			

MATERIALS AND WASTE MANAGEMENT (2 prerequisite; 18 possible points)

1. Recycling (0)	ME1.0	Storage and Collection of Recyclables	Req	Meet local standards for recycling space & facilitate the separation and collection of materials for	X	X	
2. Construction Waste Management (2)	ME2.0	Minimum Construction Site Waste Management	Req	Recycle, compost and/or salvage at least 50% of non-hazardous construction and demolition debris.	X	X	
	ME2.1	Construction Site Waste Management	1-2	Recycle, compost and/or salvage at least 75% or 90% of non-hazardous construction and demolition			
3. Building Reuse (3)	ME3.1	Building Reuse - Structure and Shell	1-2	Reuse 75% or 95% of existing structure and shell.			
	ME3.2	Building Reuse - Interior Non-structural Elements	1	Use existing on-site non-shell elements in at least 50% of completed building.			
4. Sustainable Materials (7)	ME4.1	Recycled Content	1-2	Follow prescriptive or performance approach.			
	ME4.2	Rapidly Renewable and Organically Grown Materials	1-2	2.5% of materials are rapidly renewable or specify rapidly renewables for 50% of one of the listed major interior finishes or structural materials. Extra point for using organic materials.			
	ME4.3	Certified Wood	1	50% of wood must be certified			
	ME4.4	Salvaged Materials	1-2	Follow prescriptive or performance approach.			
5. Sustainable Materials - Multi Attribute (2)	ME5.1	Environmentally Preferable Products	1-2	Use this credit instead of 4.1-4.4. Interior finishes must meet EQ2.2. Earn a one-half point for each certified EPP Product.			
6. Sustainable Materials - LCIA (4)	ME6.1	Environmental Performance Reporting	1-4	Choose products that have undergone a life cycle impact assessment by national standards.			

INDOOR ENVIRONMENTAL QUALITY (4 prerequisites; 25 possible points)							
1. Lighting and Daylighting (6)	EQ1.1	Daylighting	1-4	Meet minimum requirements and choose one of three options.			
	EQ1.2	View Windows	1	Direct line of site glazing for 90% of classrooms, libraries and administration areas and provide view glazing equal to or greater than 7% of the floor area			
	EQ1.3	Electric Lighting	1	Provide high quality and flexible classroom lighting.			
2. Indoor Air Quality and Thermal Comfort (16)	EQ2.0A	Minimum HVAC and Construction IEQ Requirements	Req	Establish minimum standards for indoor air quality that includes construction ventilation, building flush-out, outside air ventilation and HVAC basic requirements among other things.	X	X	
	EQ2.0B	ASHRAE 55 Thermal Comfort Code Compliance and Moisture Control	Req	Comply with ASHRAE 55-2007 thermal comfort standard and employ moisture control measures to prevent mold growth.	X	X	
	EQ2.0C	Minimum Filtration	Req	Use HVAC with MERV 8 or greater rated filters through the HVAC system.	X	X	
	EQ2.1	Enhanced Filtration	1-2	Use HVAC with minimum MERV 11 or 13 rated filters through the HVAC system.			
	EQ2.2	Low-Emitting Materials	1-4	Earn one-half point for each category of low-emitting products used in all classrooms and staff work			
	EQ2.3	Ducted Returns	1	Install ducted HVAC returns.			
	EQ2.4	Thermal Displacement Ventilation	2	Use thermal displacement ventilation in at least 90% of the classrooms.			
	EQ2.5	Controllability of Systems	1-4	Provide operable windows, dedicated outside air ventilation system and/or separate controls for each classroom.			
	EQ2.6	Chemical and Pollutant Source Control	1-2	Control dust, segregate pollutant sources and local exhaust in kitchens. Install walk-off mats.			
	EQ2.7	Mercury Reduction	1	Create inventory of all devices containing mercury and purchase or replace lamps with low mercury			
3. Acoustics (3)	EQ3.0	Minimum Acoustical Performance	Req	Classrooms must have a maximum (unoccupied) noise level of 45 dBA LAeq, with maximum (unoccupied) reverberation times of 0.6 sec.	X	X	
	EQ3.1	Improved Acoustical Performance	1 or 3	Classrooms must have a maximum (unoccupied) noise level of 40 or 35 dBA LAeq, with maximum (unoccupied) reverberation times of 0.6 sec.			
TOTAL (Minimum points required for CHPS school is 25 of possible 116)					0	0	

** The summary should not be used to determine requirements for a specific credit or prerequisite. Refer to the CHPS Best Practices Manual, Volume III, Criteria available at www.CHPS.net for credit and prerequisite specific requirements.

SECTION 01350: SPECIAL ENVIRONMENTAL REQUIREMENTS

The tools for conveying project requirements to contractors are the drawings and specifications, which must describe precisely what the contractor is expected to provide. The document following was prepared by the Collaborative for High Performance Schools as a model specification for sustainable school projects. It is a succinct summary of the goals of a high performance school design and it also gives detailed descriptions of products, chemicals, and processes that may be involved in construction, furnishing, and cleaning. It is a particularly valuable tool in focusing on indoor environmental quality. The document was prepared in 2002, but CHPS posts a database of environmentally preferable products on their website, www.chpsregistry.com/live.

PART 1—GENERAL

1.1 SUMMARY

A. Section Includes Special Environmental Requirements: Work includes special environmental, sustainable, and "green" building practices related to energy conservation and efficiency, indoor air quality, and resource efficiency, including the following:

1. Special Requirements:
   a. Require practices to ensure healthy indoor air quality in final Project.
   b. Maximize use of durable products.
   c. Maximize use of products easy to maintain, repair, and that can be cleaned using non-toxic substances.
   d. Maximize recycled content in materials, products, and systems.
   e. Require use of wood that is certified sustainably harvested by the Forest Stewardship Council (FSC).
   f. Maximize use of reusable and recyclable packaging.
   g. Maximize use of products with low embodied energy (production, manufacturing, and transportation).

2. Construction team is required to comply with sustainable building practices during construction and when considering materials for substitutions. Refer to Article 1.2—Design Requirements.

B. Related Requirements:

Refer to Specification sections for special environmental requirements for specific products.

1. Section 01565: Site Waste Management Program.
2. Section 01600: Product Requirements.
3. Section 01810: Building Commissioning.
4. Section 01820: System Demonstration.

1.2 DESIGN REQUIREMENTS (Note 2)

A. General: Owner has established with design team general environmental goals for design and for construction of Project; Contractor, subcontractors, suppliers, and manufacturers (construction team) are encouraged to participate where possible to realize Owner's environmental goals.

1. Intent is for environmental goals to be achieved in manner that ultimately provides safe and healthy

environment for building occupants with minimal impact on local, regional, and global environment.

2. Contract Documents are not intended to limit alternative means of achieving environmental goals.

   a. Suggestions from construction team for implementing goals are encouraged.

   b. Team approach is encouraged.

B. Environmental Goals:

   1. Refer to specific Specifications sections for more detailed construction requirements related to specific materials and systems.

      a. Energy Efficiency (Operations Throughout Project Life): Materials and systems are intended to maximize energy efficiency for operation of Project throughout service life (substantial completion to ultimate disposition—reuse, recycling, or demolition).

      b. Indoor Environmental and Air Quality: Materials are selected and processes specified, such as preconditioning and temporary ventilation, to maximize healthy indoor air quality. Cleaning, surface coating, and renewal or replacement of interior materials should be feasible with lowest practical use of toxic, irritating, or odorous compounds. Ventilation system design, construction, and commissioning ensure adequate outside air supply under all anticipated conditions of use. Documentation of system design assumptions is included in Project Manuals to enable building operators and management to use and modify the system as required to provide continued assurance of indoor air quality.

Additionally, materials are selected to provide appropriate indoor environmental qualities such as good acoustics and lighting.

      c. Resource Efficiency (Project Construction): Materials and systems are to maximize environmentally-benign construction techniques, including construction waste recycling, reusable delivery packaging, and reusability of selected materials.

C. Energy Conservation: Maximize energy conservation strategies in order to reduce life-cycle energy requirements.

   1. Reduce undesirable heat gain and heat loss through exterior envelope.

   2. Use daylight as the primary lighting source in classrooms and supplement with integrated and energy-efficient electrical lighting systems.

   3. Choose equipment with high-end energy performance characteristics, including lighting, HVAC systems, appliances, and office equipment.

   4. Where appropriate, use thermal storage strategies such as thermal mass of building or ground to minimize total energy consumption.

   5. Design mechanical systems for efficient operation throughout the typical operating range, from minimum to peak load.

D. Sustainable Site Planning and Landscape:

   1. Maximize erosion and sedimentation control.

   2. Minimize site disturbance.

   3. Maximize planted areas.

   4. Reduce heat islands.

   5. Where possible, reduce or eliminate light pollution from site lighting. (Note 3)

6. Reduce or eliminate use of pesticides.

7. Rely on indigenous, dry or xeriscape planting. Maintain existing planting on site to reduce costs.

8. Implement seasonal plant and soil maintenance schedule to maintain healthy soil and landscaping.

9. Maximize stormwater runoff.

10. Reduce water use with water efficient irrigation systems and local vegetation.

E. Durable Materials:

1. Select materials with longest useful service life.

2. Select materials that deteriorate minimally under installed conditions, exposures, and uses.

3. Select materials with surfaces that require minimal or no refinishing or resurfacing.

4. Select materials with protective coating requirements that do not involve frequent application of toxic or odorous components for materials that require surface renewal or protection

5. Select materials that can be re-used after their service life in this building.

6. Select materials that can be recycled at the end of their useful lives for materials that cannot be re-used.

F. Resource Efficient Materials: Use resource efficient materials; consider energy use over life cycle of material including harvesting, mining, manufacturing, transport, installation, use, operations, recycling and disposal.

1. Where possible and allowable by the Agency and Code with jurisdiction over the project, re-use existing building materials to extent feasible within design concept expressed in Contract Documents.

2. Select materials that efficiently use resources such as energy, water, and component materials.

3. Use construction practices such as material reduction and dimensional planning that maximize efficient use of resources and materials.

4. Provide materials that utilize recycled content to maximum degree possible without being detrimental to product performance or indoor air quality.

5. Where possible and feasible, provide for non-destructive removal and re-use of materials after their service life in this building.

6. Select materials that use less embodied energy to manufacture.
   a. Exceptions might include materials that result in net energy conservation during their useful life in building and building's life cycle.

7. Select materials that conserve energy during building operations.

8. Where possible, select materials harvested and manufactured regionally, within a 500-mile radius of the project site.

G. Scarce, Irreplaceable, and Endangered Resources:

1. Select materials from abundant resources.
   a. For natural resources, determine abundance based on ratio of removal rate from existing stocks to natural replacement/renewal rate, where this information is available.
   b. For mineral resources, determine abundance based on ratio of removal rate from terrestrial storage minus amount re-entering commerce through recycling or resource recovery compared to total in terrestrial storage, where this information is available.

2. Select renewable materials, and materials which can be replenished.

3. Select materials that create minimal or no damage to natural habitats and natural environment.

4. Select materials that can be easily refinished, repaired, or refurbished to extend their useful life.

H. Pollution: Select materials that generate least amount of pollution during mining, manufacturing, transport, installation, use, and disposal.

1. Avoid materials that emit greenhouse gases

2. Avoid materials that require energy intensive extraction, manufacturing, processing, transport, installation, maintenance, or removal.

3. Avoid materials that contain ozone-depleting chemicals (e.g. CFCs or HCFCs).

4. Avoid materials that emit potentially harmful volatile organic chemicals (VOCs), as described in Article 2.2.

5. Employ construction practices that minimize dust production and combustion by-products.

6. Avoid materials that can leach harmful chemicals into ground water; do not allow potentially harmful chemicals to enter sewers or storm drains.

7. Protect soil against erosion and topsoil depletion.

8. Minimize noise generation during construction; screen mechanical equipment to block noise.

9. Select materials that can be reused or recycled and materials with significant percentage of recycled content; conform with or exceed specified Project recycled content percentages for individual materials; avoid materials difficult to recycle.

10. Protect natural habitats; restore natural habitats where feasible within scope of Project.

I. Wood Products:

1. Use woods from Forest Stewardship Council (FSC) accredited certified sustainably harvested sources, and verify that the material itself is FSC-certified.

2. Composite wood products with high-recycled content, which meet the indoor air quality data requirements, are acceptable. (Note 4)

J. Water Efficiency:

1. Reduce the use of municipally supplied potable water.

2. Reduce dependence on municipal storm water system for plumbing fixtures and irrigation. Eliminate irrigation or use micro-irrigation. Use no moisture sensors or clock timers on irrigation systems.

3. Maintain natural aquifer conditions.

4. Consider roofwater or groundwater collection system.

5. Consider graywater collection system for irrigation systems.

6. Commission irrigation, graywater, roofwater collection systems. Provide measurement and verification for these systems. Train maintenance staff on performance of all water collection and distribution systems.

1.3 SUBMITTALS

A. Resource Efficient Product Data:

1. Environmental Issues Data: Submit following information, including manufacturer's certifications, verifying information, and test data, where Specifications sections require data relat-

ing to environmental issues including but not limited to:

a. Project Recyclability: Submit information to assist Owner and Contractor in recycling materials involved in shipping, handling, and delivery, and for temporary materials necessary for installation of products.

b. Recycled Content: Submit information regarding product post industrial recycled and post consumer recycled content.

　1) Use the "Recycled Content Certification Form," attached as Appendix A to this Section, signed by a corporate office holder (i.e. Chairman of the Board, President, Vice President, Secretary, or similar position of authority). (Note 5)

c. Product Recyclability: Submit information regarding product and product's component's recyclability including potential sources accepting recyclable materials.

d. Provide certification for all wood products provided by a Forest Stewardship Council (FSC) accredited certifier.

e. Provide final certification of well-managed* forest of origin to provide final documentation of FSC-certified sustainably harvested status: Acceptable wood "certified sustainably harvested" certifications shall include:

　1) Wood suppliers' certificate issued by one of the Forest Stewardship Council-accredited certifying agencies, such as Smart wood (800-434-5491) or Forest Conservation Program (510-832-1415);

　2) Suppliers' invoice detailing the quantities of certified wood products for project;

　3) Letter from one of a certifying agency corroborating that the products on the wood supplier's invoice originate from FSC-certified well-managed forests. (Note 6)

B. Indoor Air Quality (IAQ) Data: (Note 7)

1. Environmental Issues: Submit emission test data produced by acceptable testing laboratory listed in Quality Assurance Article for materials as required in each specific Specification section.

a. Laboratory reports shall contain emissions test data on VOCs including total VOCs (TVOC), specific individual VOCs, formaldehyde and other aldehydes as described in this Specification Section.

b. In special cases it may be necessary to identify other specific chemicals for listing based on known quantity present or on known odor, irritation or toxicity.

c. Identify all VOCs emitted by each material as required in these Specifications.

d. Specific test conditions and requirements are set forth in this Section. For required tests, submit documentation of sample acquisition, handling, and test specimen preparation, as well as test conditions, methods, and procedures. The tests consist of a ten-day conditioning period followed by a 96-h test period.

　1) Samples collected during the test period at 24, 48, and 96 hours shall be analyzed for TVOC and formaldehyde. (Note 8)

　2) VOC samples collected at 96 hours shall be identified and quantified for all compounds that are Chemicals of Concern on lists in Article 2.

2. Cleaning and Maintenance Products: Provide data on manufacturers' recommended maintenance, cleaning, refinishing and disposal procedures for materials and products. These procedures are for final Contractor cleaning of the project prior to substantial completion and for provided materials and products as required by the specific specification sections.

a. Where chemical products are recommended for these procedures, provide documentation to indicate that no component present in the cleaning product at more than 1% of the total mass of the cleaning product is a carcinogen or reproductive toxicant as defined in the lists in this specification section.

b. For purposes of reporting, identification of product VOC contents shall not be limited to those regulated under Clean Air Act (CAA) but shall also include compounds exempted from the CAA definition and listing of VOCs.

c. California EPA and local air district definitions of VOCs based on CAA are not sufficient as they exempt compounds based on non-reactivity for outdoor air pollution control but still important for indoor air quality.

d. Avoid cleaning products containing alpha-pinene, d-limonene or other unsaturated carbon double bond alkenes due to chemical reactions with ozone to form aldehydes, acidic aerosols, and ultra fine particulate matter in indoor air. For State buildings, DGS has published specifications for Environmentally Preferable Janitorial Chemicals and a list of cleaning/maintenance products meeting these specifications. Both are available on the internet at: http://www.ciwmb.ca.gov/greenbuilding/Specs/Janitorial.doc and http://www.resd.dgs.ca.gov/BPM/lists.htm.

C. Certificates:

1. Environmental Issues Certifications:

a. Submit documentation certifying accuracy of post-industrial and post-consumer recycled content, and recyclability.

b. Prior to Final Completion, submit certificate signed by corporate office holder (i.e. Chairman of the Board, President, Vice President, Secretary, or similar position of authority) of contractor, subcontractor, supplier, vendor, installer or manufacturer, provided they are primarily responsible for manufacture of product, indicating:

1) Post-industrial and post-consumer recycled content of materials installed are same as those required by Project requirements.

2) Product recyclability of materials installed is same as those required by Project requirements.

3) Indoor air quality requirements. Certification shall state products and materials provided are essentially same, and contain essentially same components as products and materials tested.

c. Comply with requirements specified in Section 01770 – Closeout Procedures.

D. Closeout Submittals: Submit data relating to environmental issues.

1. Submit environmental product certifications, in two forms:

a. Two CD-ROMs organized by CSI 16 Division Format.

b. Four three-ring binders organized by CSI 16 Division Format with Table of Contents and with dividers for each division.

1.4 QUALITY ASSURANCE

A. Environmental Project Management and Coordination: Contractor to identify one person on Contractor's staff to be responsible for environmental issues compliance and coordination.

1. Experience: Environmental project manager to have experience relating to sustainable building construction.

2. Responsibilities: Carefully review Contract Documents for environmental issues, coordinate work of trades, subcontractors, and suppliers; instruct workers relating to environmental issues; and oversee Project Environmental Goals.

3. Meetings: Discuss Environmental Goals at following meetings.
   a. Pre-construction meeting.
   b. Pre-installation meetings.
   c. Regularly scheduled job-site meetings.
   d. Special sustainability issues meetings.

B. Environmental Issues Criteria: Comply with requirements listed in various Specification sections.

C. Acceptable Indoor Air Emissions Testing Laboratories: (Note 10)

1. Berkeley Analytical Associates; 815 Harbour Way South, Suite 6, Richmond, California 94804; telephone 510.236.2325; fax 510.236.2335; e-mail berkeleyanalytical@ att.net .

2. Air Quality Sciences, Inc.; 1337 Capital Circle, Atlanta, Georgia 30067; telephone 770.933.0638; fax 770.933.0641; e-mail info@aqs.com.

3. Other Laboratories:
   a. Selection of testing laboratories shall include assessment of prior experience in conducting indoor source emissions tests.
   b. Many laboratories participate in and are certified by American Industrial Hygiene Association laboratory accreditation program. http://www.aiha.org/lists.html.
      1) These laboratories are accredited to do analysis for hazards at levels of concern for industrial workplaces and not necessarily accredited, organized, or able to perform analysis for chemicals and particulate matter at concentrations of concern for indoor air.
   c. The proposed laboratory shall be an independent company or organization not related to manufacturer of product to be tested.
   d. Submit documentation on proposed laboratory for review and approval by Owner.

D. Indoor Air Emissions Tests: (Note 11)

1. Provide environmental chamber test data from tests based on ASTM Standard D5116-97, Guide for Small Scale Environmental Chamber Determination of Organic Emissions from Indoor Materials/Products. (Refer to ASTM, Annual Book of Standards, Volume 11.03. West Conshohocken, PA: American Society for Testing and Materials. http://www.astm.org.)

2. Tests shall be conducted according to guidance contained in ASTM Standard D5116-97 on material test specimens pre-conditioned in clean air prior to testing.
   a. Review test specimen collection, documentation, collection, preparation, and shipping procedures with testing laboratory prior to preparing and shipping sample.

b. Test specimens shall be packaged in the normal manner at the factory and shipped directly to testing laboratory by the manufacturer. For materials that are not packaged in convenient consumer units, alternate procedures to preserve the chemical integrity of the specimen are required. Obtain test laboratory procedure sheet covering the handling and shipping of materials. If such information is not provided by the laboratory, then wrap the specimen in a manner that will eliminate direct contact with air or packaging materials other than an inert air barrier such as foil or laboratory grade plastic sheet wrapping material.

c. Conditioning: Condition all test specimens for ten days in clean air. Clean air should be free from the Chemicals of Concern listed in Article 2. Hold in clean vessels approximately the size of the test chambers and ventilated at the same air flow rate to be used in the test period. Suspend or place specimens on wire racks so that air freely circulates around all sides during the conditioning period. The air temperature and relative humidity during the conditioning period shall be 23±2ºC and 50±10% RH. Otherwise, the material must be held in an environmental chamber for the entire period.

d. For wet-applied products and material assemblies, a realistic test specimen shall be prepared using the substrate material on which it will be applied in the building. Alternately, it may be necessary to use a substrate material that closely simulates the actual building substrate.

e. For material assemblies (e.g., floor and wall systems where the finish material is placed over a substrate, either with or without the use of adhesives), individual components of the assembly system shall be tested separately. If all components meet the emissions criteria established herein, no further testing shall be required. For assemblies where one component, such as a floor or wall covering adhesive, does not meet the criteria, the assembled system may be tested with specimen preparation following the manufacturer's recommended procedures for application of wet components and assembly of the system. If there is a difference between the manufacturers' recommended procedures and procedures required by the project specifications, the project specifications shall be followed.

f. Wall and other types of paints shall be tested according to the specifications for the particular material. For example, if two coats are to be applied over a primer coat, then the test specimen shall be prepared accordingly, dried between coats per manufacturer's label instructions, and tested as a complete assembly after required conditioning. The total quantity of paint applied shall be reported based on the weight of the assembly immediately before and after the application of each coat.

3. The maximum concentration for any chemical emitted at 96 hours in emissions tests shall not result in a modeled indoor air concentration greater than ½ the chronic inhalation REL concentration of California Office of Environmental Health Hazard Assessment (OEHHA)

Chronic Reference Exposure Limit (REL), with the exception of formaldehyde, which is discussed separately below.

4. Formaldehyde: No single product shall contribute more than one half (½) the OEHHA staff recommended indoor air limit of 33 µg/m3 (27 ppb) for formaldehyde. The calculated concentration of formaldehyde shall not exceed 16.5 µg/m3. Same modeling procedure as described above shall be used for formaldehyde. This concentration limit shall apply to all building and occupancy types. (Note 12)

5. Construction adhesives used in Work shall comply with following requirement: no component present in adhesive at more than 1% of total mass of adhesive shall be a carcinogen or reproductive toxicant as defined in the lists in this specification section.

6. Provide calculations of modeled concentrations based on emissions test results.

   a. Calculations shall be submitted with all other documentation. This requires the calculation of emission factors based on emissions tests, then application of the emission factors, product loading factors in the building, and building parameters in a steady state mass-balance model. The model assumes zero outdoor concentrations, perfect mixing and no sink effects. Alternatively, follow procedures in ASTM D5116-97 and submit assumptions and calculations.

   b. The concentration of a compound in the building shall be calculated using the following Equation;

$$\text{Concentration} = \frac{(\text{Emission factor}) * (\text{Loading factor})}{(\text{Air change rate})}$$

For this equation, the units are: $\mu g/m^3 = (\mu g/m^2\ hr) * (m^2/m^3)\ (h^{-1})$

This can be simplified as follows:

$$\text{Concentration} = \frac{\text{Emission rate}}{\text{Air change rate}}$$

Note that the weekly average air change rate must be used in the calculations of concentrations of contaminants.

   c. Calculation of emission rate. Determine the emission rate by multiplying the emission factor by the amount of the material to be used in the building or air handler zone being evaluated. Multiply the emission factor by the area of the material in the building zone being assessed. Note that in some cases a length or mass may be the appropriate unit for emission factor that must then be multiplied by the length or mass of the emission source.

   d. Provide to the laboratory the total area of the zone being assessed by consulting the Contract Documents or the design engineer, to identify the total area served by the air handler that serves the area(s) within it where the material will be applied. If the material is used in multiple zones, then calculations shall be made to determine the concentration in the zone with the highest loading ratio of material to volume or material to weekly average minimum air change rate, whichever is greater.

   e. Provide to the laboratory the volume of the space served by the air handler by multiplying the floor area by the floor-to-floor clear height (top of finish floor to bottom of structure of floor above) and multiply by 0.9 (to take account of the portion of the volume that is occupied by solid objects). This value represents the ventilated volume for purposes of the calculations required here.

f. Determine the air change rate by dividing the volume of outside air introduced into the space per hour by the ventilated volume of the space.

g. Determine the weekly average air change rate by adding the minimum design air change rate during ventilation system operating hours times the number of hours the system is operated to an assumed air change rate from infiltration during ventilation system non-operational hours times the number of hours the system is off; then divide the total by the number of hours in a week, (168). Where no values are available from the design documents, use default values as follows:

1) Offices:

   a) Where design data are not available to calculate the weekly average air change rate, the modeling shall assume a weekly average air change rate for office buildings of 0.75 air changes per hour (ach). This "default" office air exchange rate is based on a typical weekly State office building 55 hour operating schedule and an assumed off-hours air change rate of 0.3 ach (assumed air change rate during normal operating hours is in excess of 1.0 per hour).

   b) Where specific information is available, the project specific data should be used to calculate the weekly average air change rate. A default building air change rate of 0.2 per hour during non-HVAC operations should be used.

2) Schools:

   a) Modeling shall assume weekly average air change rate for school buildings of 0.9 per hour. This air change rate is based on an assumed 40 hours per week of ventilation system operation at 3.0 ach and 128 hours per week of 0.2 ach through infiltration.

   b) Where specific information is available, the project specific data should be used to calculate the weekly average air change rate. A default building air exchange rate of 0.2 per hour during non-HVAC operations should be used.

3) Other building types or occupancy types: Use ASHRAE Standard 62.1999 default occupant densities and ventilation rates for hours of operation and 0.2 ach for non operating hours unless actual rates are known in which case the actual rates and hours of operation are to be used.

7. Environmental Chamber Testing: Indoor Air Emissions Testing Laboratories may use a range of acceptable loading ratios in order to make use of various size chambers, since these are not standardized across laboratories. Loading ratios ranging from 0.25 m2/m3 to 0.45 m2/m3 will be acceptable.

a. For dry products, loading ratios within reasonable limits are not critical for determining emission factors; conditioning of test specimens prior to testing will reduce or eliminate differences that may occur in unconditioned samples due to evaporation-limited emissions and sink effects from adsorption of VOCs during final stages of manufacturing or while in packaging during transport to and storage at the laboratory.

b. Higher loading ratios lower expected emission factor; however, the relationship is not linear, especially at higher concentrations. Therefore, where strong formaldehyde (or other chemical) sources are known or expected to be present, loading ratios should be selected to represent a median value for the plausible range of actual building loading ratios.

c. Loading ratios used shall be included in test report.

d. Contractors shall provide to product manufacturers information on actual quantity of material to be used in Project. The product manufacturers will then forward this information to Indoor Air Emissions Testing Laboratory so loading ratios can be adjusted toward actual loading ratio of Project. However, for most low-emitting materials used in construction, actual loading ratio will not significantly affect emission rates except for strong formaldehyde sources, primarily products using urea-formaldehyde resins. (Note 13)

8. Sample Preparation Requirements:

a. Substrates for environmental chamber emissions tests of individual products or materials (materials tested separately):

1) Dry solid sheet type products:

2) Sheet stainless steel or aluminum tray to provide tight fit at edges and reduce emissions from edge of material specimen. If material does not fit very snugly, then use aluminized, low-emitting, clean room tape to seal edges.

Dry fabric type products:

a) No substrate necessary.

3) Wet products such as adhesives and sealers:

a) Sheet stainless steel, aluminum, or glass unless product is to be applied to gypsum board or other highly absorbent material. If substrate is a highly absorbent material, use a sample the substrate pre-conditioned for 24 hours to the temperature and humidity of the test chamber.

4) Substrates for specific products:

a) Composite wood products (Section 06400): sample to be suspended or supported in chamber with all edges exposed and no edge masking.

b) Gypsum Board (Section 09260): no substrate (testing required ONLY if recycled content gypsum board or if water resistant types are used).

c) Acoustical Ceiling Panels (Section 09510): no substrate, sample to be suspended or supported in chamber with no edge masking.

d) Resilient flooring (Section 09650): stainless steel tray, fitted tightly so that only the upper surface is exposed. Alternately, cover back of flooring with sheet stainless steel and seal edges with low-VOC emitting aluminized clean room tape so only wear surface of flooring is exposed.

e) Carpet Tile and Broadloom Carpet (Section 09680): stainless steel tray, fitted tightly so that only the upper surface is exposed.

f) Flat and eggshell Paints (Section 09900): ⅝" gypsum board.

g) Semi-gloss paints (Section 09900): Where applied to metal, use sheet stainless steel. Where applied to gypsum board, use gypsum board conditioned as described in subsection c below.

h) Joint Sealers (Section 07900): Steel channel 0.64 cm by 0.64 cm by 25.4 cm Channel shall be filled with sealant.

b. Substrates for environmental chamber emissions tests of assemblies of products or materials (materials tested in an assembly):

1) Laminates or wood veneers applied with adhesives (Section 06400): Medium density fiberboard (MDF).

2) Resilient flooring applied with adhesives (Section 09650): Sheet stainless steel or glass plate.

3) Carpet Tile/Broadloom Carpet applied with adhesives and adhesives (Section 09685/Section 09680): Sheet stainless steel or glass plate.

4) Wall Coverings applied with adhesives (Section 09700 Series): ⅝" gypsum board. Prior to preparation of the test specimen, Gypsum board substrate shall be preconditioned for at least 24 hours at 23 ± 2°C and 50 ± 10% RH while ventilated with clean air. [Ventilation rate is not important.]

c. Protocol for Paint Testing: Preparation and handling of paint test specimen.

1) Flat and Eggshell Paints:

a) Apply paints to ⅝" thick gypsum board. Hold Gypsum board substrate for at least 24 hours at 23 ± 2°C and 50 ± 10% RH while ventilated with clean air. Accurately weigh substrate just prior to painting, mask borders to avoid paint dripping on edges and leave center area for paint. Alternative approaches to protecting the edges are acceptable and shall be reported if used.

b) Apply paint using standardized roller procedure that simulates application of paint in building. For most wall paint applications use a 4" wide ⅜" nap roller intended for smooth surfaces.

c) Stir paint in container and transfer 100 mL of paint to heavy-duty aluminum foil disposable tray.

d) Saturate roller cover with paint by running back and forth in tray.

e) Apply paint to substrate using four strokes, two in vertical direction and two in horizontal direction, so entire area is uniformly covered.

f) Remove tape from substrate and re-weigh substrate.

g) Difference in weight determines amount of applied paint and coverage in grams of wet paint per square meter of substrate surface.

h) Place substrate on 6" by 6" piece of sheet stainless steel to cover entirely the back surface. Attach substrate to stainless steel with strips of low VOC aluminized clean room tape so only painted surface is exposed. For a blank specimen, similarly prepare an unpainted piece of gypsum. Alternate procedures to cover unpainted surfaces of gypsum board may be used and must be adequately described in the laboratory report if used.

i) Place sample in conditioning environment immediately and hold for ten days.

j) Where multiple coats, which may include primer, are being tested, apply paints and follow manufacturers' instructions for drying time between coats. Report weight of test specimen prior to and after each coat of paint is applied. Hold specimen in conditioning environment between coats. The ten-day conditioning period begins after application of final coat. Apply semi-gloss paint to clean steel sheet following same procedure as above for "flat and eggshell paints." No tape should be used. Sheet should be weighed immediately before and after painting.

9. Chemical Analyses:

   a. VOC Analysis: Make multi-point calibrations using pure compounds whenever such compounds are available from commercial suppliers (such as Aldrich Chemical Company, Sigma Aldrich). Quantitative analyses performed using surrogate compounds shall be indicated in reported test results. Identify EPA and ASTM standard methods and practices, and testing laboratory calibration procedures, which should include a calibration at least once every three (3) months.

   b. Formaldehyde and Acetaldehyde Analysis: Formaldehyde and Acetaldehyde analysis shall be performed following ASTM Standard D 5197 "Standard Test Method for Formaldehyde and other Carbonyl Compounds in Air (Active Sampler Methodology)"

10. Reporting Requirements: In addition to reporting requirement stated elsewhere in Specifications, reports shall include: (a) all compounds emitted from sample that are on the most recent Chronic Reference Exposure Level list as published by the California Office of Environmental Health Hazard Assessment and listed in their website at http://www.oehha.org/air/chronic_rels/allChrels.html, (b) all compounds on the California Proposition 65 list, and (c) all compounds on the California Toxic Air Contaminant list. In addition, the ten most abundant compounds shall be reported separately if not listed on any of these lists. For these compounds, report following:

   a. measured chamber concentrations at each required time point.

   b. calculated emission factors.

   c. calculated building concentrations and assumptions used to make calculation. (Note 14)

E. State Agency Buy Recycled Campaign (SABRC) Recycled Content: Implement the SABRC recycled-content goals for specific building products, including but not limited to: (Note 15)

1. Paper products;

2. Glass products (windows, glazing, fiberglass, tile, construction blocks, loose-grain abrasives);

3. Plastic products (carpet, plastic lumber, furniture made from plastic, fencing, parking bumpers, toilet partitions, entry mats, signage, sheet plastic and other plastic-containing building products);

4. Solvents;

5. Tire-derived products (entry-mats, resilient flooring, wheelchair and other ramps, playground

surfacing, parking bumpers, speed bumps, tree ties, road surfacing);

6. Steel products (structural steel, steel framing, architectural metal, reinforcing bars, sheet metal, metal siding, metal roofing, lockers, toilet partitions, office furniture for filing and storage);

7. Paint (allowed only in exterior installations).

8. Compost

1.5 DELIVERY, STORAGE, AND HANDLING

A. Packaging: Deliver materials in recyclable or in reusable packaging such as cardboard, wood, paper, or reusable blankets, which will be reclaimed by supplier or manufacturer for recycling.

1. General: Minimize packaging materials to maximum extent possible while still ensuring protection of materials during delivery, storage, and handling.

   a. Unacceptable Packaging Materials: Polyurethane, polyisocyanate, polystyrene, polyethylene, and similar plastic materials such as "foam" plastics and "shrink-fit" plastics.

2. Reusable Blankets: Deliver and store materials in reusable blankets and mats reclaimed by manufacturers or suppliers for reuse where program exists or where program can be developed for such reuse.

3. Pallets: Where pallets are used, suppliers shall be responsible to ensure pallets are removed from site for reuse or for recycling.

4. Corrugated Cardboard and Paper: Where paper products are used, recycle as part of construction waste management recycling program, or return to material's manufacturer for use by manufacturer or supplier.

5. Sealants, Paint, Primers, Adhesives, and Coating Containers: Return to supplier or manufacturer for reuse where such program is available.

1.6 PROJECT CONDITIONS

A. No smoking will be permitted in indoor Project site locations, as per California Labor Code (Section 400-6413.5).

B. Certifications:

1. Environmental Product Certification:

   a. Include manufacturer certification indicating product contains maximum recycled content possible without being detrimental to product performance

   b. Include certification indicating cleaning materials comply with requirements of these Specifications.

C. Construction Ventilation and Preconditioning:

1. Temporary Construction Ventilation: Maintain sufficient temporary ventilation of areas where materials are being used that emit VOCs. Maintain ventilation continuously during installation, and until emissions dissipate after installation. If continuous ventilation is not possible via building's HVAC system(s) then ventilation shall be supplied via open windows and temporary fans, sufficient to provide no less than three air changes per hour.

   a. Period after installation shall be sufficient to dissipate odors and elevated concentrations of VOCs. Where no specific period is stated in these Specifications, a time period of 72 hours shall be used.

   b. Ventilate areas directly to outside; ventilation to other enclosed areas is not acceptable.

2. During dust producing activities (e.g. drywall installation and finishing) turn ventilation system off, and openings in supply and return HVAC system shall be protected from dust infiltration. Provide temporary ventilation as required.

3. Preconditioning: Prior to installation, allow products which have odors and significant VOC emissions to off-gas in dry, well-ventilated space for 14 calendar days to allow for reasonable dissipation of odors and emissions prior to delivery to Project site.

   a. Condition products without containers and packaging to maximize off-gassing of VOCs.

   b. Condition products in ventilated warehouse or other building. Comply with substitution requirements for consideration of other locations.

D. Protection:

1. Moisture Stains: Materials with evidence of moisture damage, including stains, are not acceptable, including both stored and installed materials; immediately remove from site and properly dispose. Take special care to prevent accumulation of moisture on installed materials and within packaging during delivery, storage, and handling to prevent development of molds and mildew on packaging and on products.

   a. Immediately remove from site and properly dispose of materials showing signs of mold and signs of mildew, including materials with moisture stains.

   b. Replace moldy materials with new, undamaged materials.

2. Ducts: Seal ducts during transportation, delivery, and construction to prevent accumulation of construction dust and construction debris inside ducts.

1.7 SEQUENCING

A. Environmental Issues:

1. On-Site Application: Where odorous and/or high VOC emitting products are applied on-site, apply prior to installation of porous and fibrous materials. Where this is not possible, protect porous materials with polyethylene vapor retarders.

2. Complete interior finish material installation no less than fourteen (14) days prior to Substantial Completion to allow for building flush out.

PART 2—PRODUCTS

2.1 CHEMICALS OF CONCERN

A. Chemicals of Concern are those chemicals listed below as toxic air contaminants, carcinogens, teratogens, reproductive toxins, and chemicals with established Chronic Reference Exposure Levels (REL):

B. Carcinogens: Chemicals listed as probable or known human carcinogens in the latest published edition of the following two lists:

1. California Environmental Protection Agency, Air Resources Board (ARB), list of Toxic Air Contaminants (California Air Toxics). http://www.arb.ca.gov/toxics/summary/summary.htm

2. California Environmental Protection Agency, Office of Environmental Health Hazard Assessment (OEHHA), Safe Drinking Water and Toxic Enforcement Act of 1986 (Proposition 65). http://www.oehha.ca.gov/prop65/prop65_list/Newlist.html.

C. Reproductive Toxicants: Chemicals known to cause reproductive toxicity including birth defects or other reproductive harm in the latest published edition of the following list: California Environmental Protection Agency, Office of Environmental Health Hazard Assessment (OEHHA), Safe Drinking Water and Toxic Enforcement Act of 1986 (Proposition 65). www.oehha.ca.gov/prop65/prop65_list/Newlist.htm.

D. Chemicals with established Chronic Reference Exposure Levels (REL): Chronic RELs have been developed for 65 hazardous airborne substances as of January 2001. A chronic REL is an airborne concentration level that would pose no significant health risk to individuals indefinitely exposed to that level. RELs are based solely on health considerations, and are developed from the best available data in the scientific literature. The California Environmental Protection Agency, Office of Environmental Health Hazard Assessment (OEHHA) establishes and publishes RELs. (Note 16)

Table 1. Chronic Reference Exposure Levels for organic chemicals with possible indoor sources, based on the California OEHHA list as of September 2002 (The most recent list shall be used for this specification as published at http://www.oehha.org/air/chronic_rels/allChrels.html)

	Substance (CAS #)	Listed in CAPCOA (1993)	Chronic Inhalation REL ($\mu g/m^3$)	Hazard Index Target(s)	Human Data
1	Acetaldehyde* (75-07-0)	☑	9	Respiratory system	
2	Acrolein (107-02-8)	☑	0.06	Respiratory system; eyes	
3	Acrylonitrile (107-13-1)	☑	5	Respiratory system	

4	Ammonia (7664-41-7)	☑	200	Respiratory system	☑
5	Arsenic (7440-38-2) & arsenic compounds	☑	0.03	Development; Cardiovascular system; Nervous system	
6	Benzene (71-43-2)	☑	60	Hematopoietic system; development; nervous system	☑
7	Beryllium (7440-41-7) and beryllium compounds	☑	0.007	Respiratory system; immune system	☑
8	Butadiene (106-99-0)		20	Reproductive system	
15	Chlorobenzene (108-90-7)	☑	1000	Alimentary system; kidney; reproductive system	
16	Chloroform (67-66-3)	☑	300	Alimentary system; kidney; development	
17	Chloropicrin (76-06-2)	☑	0.4	Respiratory system	
18	Chromium hexavalent: soluble except chromic trioxide	☑	0.2	Respiratory system	
19	Chromic trioxide (as chromic acid mist)	☑	0.002	Respiratory system	☑
20	Cresol mixtures (1319-77-3)	☑	600	Nervous system	
21	Dichlorobenzene (1,4-) (106-46-7)	☑	800	Nervous system; respiratory system; alimentary system; kidney	
22	Dichloroethylene (1,1) (75-35-4)	☑	70	Alimentary system	
23	Diesel Exhaust*		5	Respiratory system	
24	Diethanolamine (111-42-2)		3	Cardiovascular system; nervous system	
25	Dimethylformamide (N,N-) (68-12-2)		80	Alimentary system ; respiratory system	☑
26	Dioxane (1,4-) (123-91-1)	☑	3,000	Alimentary system; kidney; cardiovascular system	
27	Epichlorohydrin (106-89-8)	☑	3	Respiratory system; eyes	
28	Epoxybutane (1,2-) (106-88-7)		20	Respiratory system; cardiovascular system	
29	Ethylbenzene (100-41-4)		2,000	Development; alimentary system (liver); kidney; endocrine system	

30	Ethyl chloride (75-00-3)	☑	30,000	Development; alimentary system	
31	Ethylene dibromide (106-93-4)	☑	0.8	Reproductive system	☑
32	Ethylene dichloride (107-06-2)	☑	400	Alimentary system (liver)	
33	Ethylene glycol (107-21-1)		400	Respiratory system; kidney; development	
34	Ethylene glycol monoethyl ether (110-80-5)	☑	70	Reproductive system; hematopoietic system	
35	Ethylene glycol monoethyl ether acetate (111-15-9)	☑	300	Development	
36	Ethylene glycol monomethyl ether (109-86-4)	☑	60	Reproductive system	
37	Ethylene glycol monomethyl ether acetate (110-49-6)	☑	90	Reproductive system	
38	Ethylene oxide (75-21-8)	☑	30	Nervous system	
39	Formaldehyde (50-00-0)	☑	3	Respiratory system; eyes	
40	Glutaraldehyde (111-30-8)	☑	0.08	Respiratory system	
41	Hexane (n-) (110-54-3)		7000	Nervous system	
42	Hydrazine (302-01-2)	☑	0.2	Alimentary system; endocrine system	
43	Hydrogen chloride (7647-01-0)	☑	9	Respiratory system	
44	Hydrogen cyanide (74-90-8)	☑	9	Nervous system; endocrine system; cardiovascular system	
45	Hydrogen sulfide (7783-06-4)	☑	10	Respiratory system	
46	Isophorone (78-59-1)		2000	Development; liver	
47	Isopropanol (67-63-0)		7,000	Kidney; development	
48	Maleic anhydride (108-31-6)	☑	0.7	Respiratory system	
49	Manganese & manganese compounds	☑	0.2	Nervous system	☑

50	Mercury & mercury compounds (inorganic)	☑	0.09	Nervous system	☑
51	Methanol (67-56-1)	☑	4,000	Development	
52	Methyl bromide (74-83-9)	☑	5	Respiratory system; nervous system; development	
53	Methyl chloroform (71-55-6)	☑	1,000	Nervous system	
54	Methyl isocyanate (624-83-9)		1	Respiratory system; reproductive system	
55	Methyl t-butyl ether (1634-04-4)		8,000	Kidney; eyes; alimentary system (liver)	
56	Methylene chloride (75-09-2)	☑	400	Cardiovascular system; nervous system	☑
58	Methylene Diphenyl Isocyanate (101-68-8)		0.7	Respiratory system	
52	Methyl bromide (74-83-9)	☑	5	Respiratory system; nervous system; development	
53	Methyl chloroform (71-55-6)	☑	1,000	Nervous system	
54	Methyl isocyanate (624-83-9)		1	Respiratory system; reproductive system	
55	Methyl t-butyl ether (1634-04-4)		8,000	Kidney; eyes; alimentary system (liver)	
56	Methylene chloride (75-09-2)	☑	400	Cardiovascular system; nervous system	☑
58	Methylene Diphenyl Isocyanate (101-68-8)		0.7	Respiratory system	
59	Naphthalene (91-20-3)	☑	9	Respiratory system	
60	Nickel & compounds (except nickel oxide)	☑	0.05	Respiratory system; hematopoietic system	
61	Nickel oxide (1313-99-1)		0.1	Respiratory system; hematopoietic system	
62	Phenol (108-95-2)	☑	200	Alimentary system; cardiovascular system; kidney; nervous system	
63	Phosphine (7803-51-2)	☑	0.8	Respiratory system; alimentary system; nervous system; kidney; hematopoietic system	
64	Phosphoric acid (7664-38-2)		7	Respiratory system	
65	Phthalic anhydride (85-44-9)	☑	20	Respiratory system	☑

66	Propylene (115-07-1)		3,000	Respiratory system	
67	Propylene glycol monomethyl ether (107-98-2)		7,000	Alimentary system (liver)	
68	Propylene oxide (75-56-9)	☑	30	Respiratory system	
69	Selenium and selenium compounds (other than hydrogen selenide)	☑	20	Alimentary system; cardiovascular system; nervous system	☑
70	Styrene (100-42-5)	☑	900	Nervous system	☑
71	Sulfuric acid (7664-93-9)		1	Respiratory system	
72	Tetrachloroethylene* (perchloroethylene) (127-18-4)	☑	35	Kidney; alimentary system (liver)	
73	Toluene (108-88-3)	☑	300	Nervous system; respiratory system; development	
74	Toluene diisocyanates (2,4- &2,6-)	☑	0.07	Respiratory system	☑
75	Trichloroethylene (79-01-6)	☑	600	Nervous system; eyes	☑
76	Triethylamine (121-44-8)		200	Eyes	
77	Vinyl acetate (108-05-4)		200	Respiratory system	
78	Xylenes (m-, o-, p-)	☑	700	Nervous system; respiratory system	☑

2.2 SUBSTITUTIONS

A. Substitutions Environmental Issues: Requests for substitutions shall comply with requirements specified in Section 01630 – Product Substitution Procedures, with following additional information required where environmental issues are specified.

1. Indicate each proposed substitution complies with requirements for VOCs.

2. Owner, in consultation with Architect reserve right to reject proposed substitutions where data for VOCs is not provided or where emissions of individual VOCs are higher than for specified materials.

3. Comply with specified recycled content and other environmental requirements.

PART 3—EXECUTION

3.1 FIELD QUALITY CONTROL

A. Building Flush Out: Just prior to Substantial Completion, flush out building continuously (i.e. 24 hours per day, seven (7) days a week) using maximum tempered outside air (or maximum amount of outside air while achieving reasonable indoor temperature) for at least fourteen (14) calendar days. If interruptions of more than a few hours are required for testing and balancing purposes, extend flush out period accordingly.

1. When Contractor is required to perform touch-up work, provide temporary construction ventilation during installation and extend building flush-out by a minimum of four (4) days after touch-up installation with maximum tempered outside air for 24 hr per day.

2. If construction schedule permits, extend flush-out period beyond 15 days.

3. Return ventilation system to normal operation following flush-out period to minimize energy consumption.

3.2 CLEANING

A. Final Cleaning Environmental Issues:

1. Clean interior and exterior surfaces exposed to view; remove temporary labels, stains, and foreign substances; polish transparent and glossy surfaces using cleaning and maintenance products as described in Part 1 of this Section.

2. Clean equipment and fixtures to sanitary condition using cleaning and maintenance products as described in Part 1 of this Section.

3. Vacuum carpeted and soft surfaces with high efficiency particulate arrestor (HEPA) vacuum.

4. If ducts were not sealed during construction, and contain dust or dirt, clean ducts using HEPA vacuum immediately prior to Substantial Completion and prior to using ducts to circulate air. Oil film on sheet metal shall be removed before shipment to site. However, ducts shall be inspected to confirm that no oil film is present. Remove oil.

5. Replace all air filters (i.e., pre and final filters) just prior to Substantial Completion.

6. Remove and properly dispose of recyclable materials using construction waste management program described in Section 01565 – Site Waste Management Program.

3.3 PROTECTION

A. Environmental Issues:

1. Protect interior materials from water intrusion or penetration; where interior products not intended for wet applications are exposed to moisture, immediately remove from site and dispose of properly.

2. Protect installed products using methods that do not support growth of molds and mildews.
   a. Immediately remove from site materials with mold and materials with mildew.

INDEX

A

absenteeism, sustainable schools, 4–5, 143
acoustics, 3, 16–17, 62–70
    background noise, 62–63
    building structure and envelope, 124
    carpet tiles, 203
    ceiling finishes, 67, 204, 206, 256
    daylighting, 68–69
    guidelines, 66, 70
    HVAC systems, 17, 63, 138
    materials, 66–67
    mechanical systems, 67–68
    room reverberation, 64
    sound isolation, 64–66
    wall finishes, 202
adaptation, future prospects, 283–285
adaptive reuse
    case study, 108–109, 213–215
    funding, life cycle costing, 41–42
    resource efficiency, 12–13
Aga Khan Award, 55, 56, 57
age level. *See* developmental considerations
air conditioning, 16. *See also* heating, ventilating, and air-conditioning (HVAC) systems
air quality. *See* indoor air quality
air velocity, HVAC systems, 138
allergens, 73, 271
Alliance to Save Energy (ASE), 268
alternative energy generation, future prospects, 283–285
alternative project delivery methods, costs and bidding process, 224–227
aluminum windows, 120
American Academy of Pediatricians, 72
American Institute of Architects (AIA), 22
American National Standards Institute (ANSI), 63, 64, 66, 69, 70, 125, 199
American Society for Testing and Materials (ASTM), 69
American Society of Heating,

Refrigerating and Air Conditioning Engineers (ASHRAE), 125, 138
Andrew H. Wilson Elementary School (New Orleans, Louisiana), 279–280
A. P. Tureaud Elementary School (New Orleans, Louisiana), 277–278
architectural contracts, planning strategies, 24–26. *See also* cost and bidding process
architectural style, design strategies, 54–55. *See also* design process and strategies
architecture, sustainability concept, 2
Architecture Involution LLC, 129–131
artificial lighting systems. *See* daylighting; lighting systems
Arup Associates, 48–51
asbestos, ceiling finishes, 205
asbestos removal, 236–237
asphalt, heat islands, 171
asthma, 271
astronomy, school culture, 254
athletic fields
    landscaping, 172–174
    lighting, 180
    playgrounds, landscaping, 180–184
    stormwater/groundwater management, 170
Atkins, Doug, 79, 166
attendance, sustainable schools, 4–5, 143
attention deficit disorder, landscaping, 164
attitudes, community factors, sustainable schools, 6
auditorium
    acoustics, 64
    daylighting, 93, 95
automobile, site selection, 31

B

Bacich School (Kentfield, California), 7
background noise, acoustics, 62–63
balloon framing, wall design, 114–115

Bangladesh boat schools, 283–285
bathrooms. *See* restrooms
batteries, energy efficiency, 38
batt insulation, 118
bicycles, 29–31, 178
bidding process. *See* cost and bidding process
bioswale, stormwater/groundwater management, 169
bird's-eye view, design strategies, 53
Blach School (Los Altos, California), 86, 88, 105–107, 250
blinds, window treatments, 122–123
boat schools (Bangladesh), 283–285
body metaphor
    daylighting, 85
    design strategies, 53
bonds, capital funding, 39–41
brainstorming, integrated design planning, 28–29
Braungart, Michael, 197
Bronx Charter School for the Arts (Hunts Point, Bronx, New York), 108–109
Brown v. Board of Education, 31
Brundtland Commission Report, 1–2, 16
budgets. *See also* cost and bidding process; economic factors; funding; life cycle costing
    acoustic materials, 67
    design strategies, 61
    mechanical systems, 67–68
building codes. *See also* government policy
    building type, design strategies, 58
    cost and bidding process, 219–220
    natural ventilation, HVAC systems, 143
    plumbing systems, 151
    sustainable schools, 8–9
    verification, 238–239
    wall design, 112–114
building information management (BIM) systems, operations, 257–258
building materials. *See* materials

building paper, insulation, 118
building standards, cost and bidding process, 219–220
building structure and envelope, 111–135
    acoustics, 124
    case study, 129–135
    design strategies, 53, 61
    doors, 124
    insulation, 117–119
    LEED, 128, 153
    overview, 111–112
    roof design, 124–127
    wall design, 112–117. *See also* wall design
    water and moisture control, 120
    weatherizing, 119
    windows, 120–122
    window treatments, 122–123
building systems, design strategies, 53
built environment, economic impact of, 2
Burling Slip playground (New York, New York), 182–183
business groups, supplementary funding, 43–44
bus transportation, site selection, 29–31

C
C. K. Choi Institute of Asian Research (University of British Columbia), 164–165
cafeteria, acoustics, 64. *See also* food service
campus concept. *See also* landscaping; plantings; site planning and design; solar orientation; topography
    case study, 186–195
    integrated design, 33–36
    LEED, 167, 185
    sustainable schools, 10
capital funding, 39–41
carbon dioxide
    HVAC systems, 138
    sustainability concept, 2
Carpet and Rug Institute (CRI), 200–201, 270
carpeting
    acoustics, 67
    operations and maintenance, 255–256, 270
    product certification, 200–201
    reverberation, 64
Carson, Rachel, 19, 197
casework, product information, 207–208

caulking, weatherizing, 119
ceiling finishes
    acoustics, 67, 204, 206
    operations, 256
    recommendations for, 204–206
cement sidewalks, 172
Centennial PK-12 School (San Luis, Colorado), 116, 155–158
central HVAC systems, individual systems compared, 139–140
centrifugal chiller water tubes, 268
certification, product information, 198–200
Chartwell School (Seaside, California), 77–79
Chez Panisse Foundation, 263
chilled beam cooling, HVAC systems, 146, 147
Choi, C. K., 164–165
CHPS (Collaborative for High Performance Schools)
    acoustics, 66, 69–70
    campus design, 167
    case study, 79, 105–107, 162
    commissioning, 17, 239
    daylighting, 97
    future directions, 288
    planning strategies, 26, 27
    product information, 199–200, 201
    sustainable schools, 8–9, 21
    verification, 238–239
Christy, E. A., 277–280
Chum Creek Outdoor Education Centre, Chum Creek, Victoria, Australia, 192–95
cladding, wall design, 114–115
Claire Lilienthal School (San Francisco, California), 44
classroom design
    HVAC systems, 139–140
    lighting requirements, 91–92
    sustainable schools, 14
cleaning products, maintenance, 274–275
clerestory windows, daylighting, 96–101. *See also* daylighting
climate
    daylighting, 87–89
    design strategies, 56–57
    doors, 124
    HVAC systems, 143, 146, 195
    integrated design, 36
    roof design, 124–125

    spatial considerations, 60
    thermal comfort, 16, 17
    water and moisture control, 120
    windows, 121–122
climate change, sustainability concept, 1–2, 19
coatings, product information, 207
codes. *See* building codes
cogeneration, HVAC systems, 150
Collaborative for High Performance Schools (CHPS). *See* CHPS (Collaborative for High Performance Schools)
comfort, HVAC systems, 137–138
commissioning requirements
    construction process, 239–240
    costs and bidding process, 224
    monitoring, 259–260
    operations, 257
    sustainable schools, 17
community-based planning, sustainable schools, 7–8, 19, 22. *See also* planning strategies
community factors. *See also* neighborhoods
    case study, 45–47, 155–158, 213–215
    daylighting, 87
    future prospects, 285–288
    integrated design, 31–33
    operations, 264–265
    supplementary funding, 43–44
    sustainable schools, 6
community organizing, 22
compost, landscaping, 174, 177
computer equipment, environmental impact, 208
computer modeling
    BIM systems, 257–258
    daylighting, 188
concrete block, wall design, 114–115
concrete floor covering, product certification, 201–202
Conoco Phillips refinery, 43
construction costs, sustainable schools, 3, 6
construction management multiprime methods, project delivery methods, 226–227
construction manager at risk methods, project delivery methods, 226–227
construction process, 231–244. *See also* cost and bidding process; wall design
    commissioning, 239–240

construction process (cont'd)
  community organizing, 22
  deconstruction versus demolition,
    242–243
  indoor air quality, 237
  job-site operations, 232–235
  LEED, 244
  planning, contractor participation in,
    231–232
  prefabrication, 240–242
  sustainable schools, 3, 6, 218–219
  verification, 238–239
  wall design, 112–114
  waste output and waste management,
    218, 236–237
Construction Specification Institute, 137
contextual concerns, design strategies,
    54–55
contractors, project delivery methods,
    226–227
contracts. See architectural contracts; cost
    and bidding process
controls
  HVAC systems, 140, 143, 150–151
  lighting systems, 92, 102–103
  operations, 259–60, 264–265
cool roof, 124–125
Cool Roof Rating Council, 125
copying machines, indoor air quality, 208
cost and bidding process, 217–230. See also
    budgets; economic factors; fund-
    ing; life cycle costing
  alternative project delivery methods,
    224–227
  bidding, 227–230
  contracts, 227
  high cost perceptions, 219–224
  overview, 217–219
cost cutting, sustainability concept, 229–230
counters, casework and furnishings,
    207–208
Cradle-to-Cradle approach, 197–198
cross ventilation, HVAC systems, 144
culture
  case study, 74–76
  daylighting, 87
  school culture, 246–247

D

dark skies, 178–179, 254
daylighting, 83–110. See also lighting
    systems

acoustics, 68–69
artificial lighting systems and, 83, 92,
    102–103
benefits of, 83–86
building design, 93–96
case study, 80–81, 105–109, 187–188
ceiling finishes, 205
classroom design, 14–15, 50
costs and bidding process, 222
energy efficiency, 12, 76, 131
historical perspective, 55, 86–87
integrated design, 9
lighting requirements, 91–92
openings design, 96–101
overview, 83
resources for, 104
school operations, 250
site design, 87–90
sustainable schools, 3, 79, 80
Daylighting Collaborative, 104
decibels, 63, 70. See also acoustics
deconstruction, demolition versus, 242–243
democracy, school operations, 248
demography, sustainability concept, 1–2
demolition, deconstruction versus, 242–243
design build methods, project delivery
    methods, 226–227
design process and strategies, 53–82. See
    also integrated design; planning
    strategies
  acoustics, 62–70. See also acoustics
  budgets, 61
  building type, 58
  case study, 74–81
  context and function, 54–57
  cost estimates, 217
  daylighting, 93–96
  daylight openings, 96–101
  developmental considerations, 71–73
  historical perspective, 55–56
  HVAC systems, 139
  hygiene, 61
  integrated design, 9–10, 53–54
  overview, 53
  robust construction, 61
  spatial considerations, 60–61
  visual expression, 58–59
design team selection, topics for, 22–24
developmental considerations
  design strategies, 71–73
  landscaping, 164
dew point, HVAC systems, 146

dimmers, lighting systems, 102–103
direct digital control (DCC) systems,
    HVAC systems, 150–151
displacement ventilation, HVAC systems,
    143
documentation, cost and bidding process,
    217–219, 223–224
domestic hot water (DHW) systems, 153
doors
  building structure and envelope, 124
  weatherizing, 119
dormer window, daylighting, 96
Dow, James, 59
drafts, HVAC systems, 138
drainage
  athletic fields, 173–174
  stormwater/groundwater management,
    168–170
drawings, cost and bidding process,
    217–218
drip irrigation systems, 176, 177
Druk White Lotus School (Ladakh, India),
    48–51
ductwork, construction process, 237
Dunlop, Alan, 210–212
durability
  cost and bidding process, 220
  materials, school culture, 254–256

E

earthquake
  acoustic materials, 67
  wall design, 112–14, 116
economic factors. See also budgets; cost
    and bidding process; funding; life
    cycle costing
  built environment, 2
  cost cutting, 229–230
  daylighting, 85
  funding, 39–44. See also funding
  HVAC systems, 145–146
  mechanical systems, 68, 153–154
  paving, 171–172
  prefabrication, 240–242
  school construction, 3
  sustainable schools, 5
Eco-Store (Wal-Mart, Lawrence, Kansas),
    84
Eggers, Dave, 286
EHDD Architecture, 77–79
826 Valencia (San Francisco, California),
    286–287

electrical costs. *See* energy efficiency
electrical power generation, future prospects, 283–285
electrical systems, design strategies, 53. *See also* mechanical systems
electric lights. *See* lighting systems
emergency repair programs, 246–247
energy efficiency
    campus concept, 33
    case study, 79, 129–131, 187, 277–278, 279, 280
    climate considerations, 36
    daylighting, 85, 87, 131
    doors, 124
    en, 80
    future prospects, 283
    HVAC systems, 138, 145
    mechanical systems, 68, 76, 80
    preventive maintenance, 268–269
    purchasing programs, 262–263
    scale and size, 38
    school culture, 253
    solar panels, 180
    spatial considerations, 60–61
    supplementary funding, 42–44
    sustainable schools, 2, 3–4, 12, 50–51
    Whitman-Hanson Regional High School (Whitman, Massachusetts), 129–131
    windows, 120–122
ENERGY STAR, 208, 238–239, 256–257
envelope. *See* building structure and envelope
environmental curriculum, 10–11. *See also* operations; school culture
environmental impacts
    case study, 186–188
    site selection, 29, 35
    sustainable schools, 6
    wall design, 116
equipment. *See* finishes, equipment, and furnishings
estimates, bidding process, 228–229
evapotranspiration (ET), 176–177
existing buildings, maintenance costs, 6. *See also* adaptive reuse; recycling
extended services, planning strategies, 24

F
fans, natural ventilation, 143–145
fertilizers, athletic fields, 173–174
fiberboard, casework and furnishings, 208

fiber cement panels, wall finishes, 117
Field Act (California), 113
fields. *See* athletic fields; playgrounds
finger plan, daylighting, 86, 87, 93
finishes, equipment, and furnishings, 197–216
    acoustics, 67
    case study, 210–215
    casework and furnishings, 207–208
    ceilings, 204–206
    computers and office equipment, 208
    floor coverings, 200–202
    lighting requirements, 92
    lockers, 208–209
    operations, 254–257
    overview, 197–198
    paints and coatings, 207
    product information, 198–200
    recycled, 80
    toilet partitions, 209
    wall coverings, 202
    wall design, 117
fire protection. *See also* health; safety; toxins
    ceiling finishes, 205, 206
    cost and bidding process, 220
    wall design, 112–114
flexibility
    bidding process, 228–229
    future prospects, 283–285
    integrated design, 39
    sustainable schools, 11, 264–265
flooding, stormwater/groundwater management, 168–170
floor(s)
    acoustics, 67
    radiant HVAC systems, 140–141
    wall design, 114
floor coverings. *See also* carpeting
    carpets, 200–201
    operations, 255–256
    resilient flooring, 201–202
FMSA Architects, 192–195
food service
    cafeteria, 64
    pest control, 272–273
    sustainable schools, 263
forced air HVAC systems, 141–143
Forest Stewardship Council (FSC), 116, 202
formaldehyde, 116, 205
foundation work, job-site operations, 235

funding, 39–44. *See also* budgets; cost and bidding process; economic factors
    capital funding, 39–41
    life cycle costing, 41–42
    supplementary funding, 42–44
fundraising
    landscaping, 171–172
    supplementary funding, 43–44
furniture, product information, 207–208. *See also* finishes, equipment, and furnishings

G
games, developmental considerations, 71–73. *See also* athletic fields; playgrounds
garbage compactor, solar, 180
Garden City Park (space2space, Richmond, British Columbia, Canada), 181
gardens, 184, 263
Gelfand Partners Architects, 105–107, 159–162
geoexchange heat pumps, 146–149
geothermal wells, 80, 81
Gladwell, Malcolm, 252
glare, lighting requirements, 92
glass, types of, 122. *See also* windows
glazing. *See* windows
Global Green, 277–280
goal setting, planning strategies, 20–28
Gordon Murray & Alan Dunlop Architects, 210–212
Gothic style, 55
government policy. *See also* building codes
    community-based planning, sustainable schools, 7–8
    integrated design, 10
    public contracting, 221–224
    sustainability concept, 2
grading, job-site operations, 235
graffiti, 96, 209. *See also* vandalism
grasses, athletic fields, 173–174
gray water. *See also* rainwater; stormwater; water supply
    irrigation systems, 175–177
    sustainable schools, 11, 75, 79, 129–131, 151–152
Greek style, 55
GREENGUARD, 199
Green Label Plus (Carpet and Rug Institute, CRI), 200–201

green roof design
    case study, 132, 134
    described, 126–127
    mechanical systems, 68, 75, 79, 80
green schools. *See* sustainable schools
Green Seed School, 277–278
groundwater management, landscaping,
        168–170
Guilford (North Carolina) Living
        Machine, 175
gymnasium, spatial considerations, 60–61

H
Hagia Sophia dome, 85
Hall, Elizabeth Blodgett, 53
hand dryers, 262
Harris, Arthur, 6
Hazelwood School (Glasgow, Scotland),
        210–212
health. *See also* fire protection; safety; toxins
    daylighting, 86
    developmental considerations, 71–73
    HVAC systems, 138
    irrigation systems, 176
    maintenance products, 274–275
    playgrounds, 181–182
    sustainable schools, 4–5
    ventilation, 73
    wall design, 112–114
hearing, developmental considerations,
        72–73
heating, ventilating, and air-conditioning
        (HVAC) systems, 137–162. *See also*
        mechanical systems
    acoustics, 17, 63, 138
    case study, 155–162, 194–195
    climate considerations, 36
    comfort, 137–138
    commissioning requirements, 240
    construction process, 237
    design strategies, 53
    doors, 124
    energy efficiency, 12, 14
    high-performance strategies, 145–51
    historical perspective, 55
    natural ventilation, 143–145
    overview, 137
    preventive maintenance, 268–271
    scale and size, 38
    spatial considerations, 60–61
    staff training, 258–259
    sustainable schools, 5, 67–68, 79, 265

    thermal comfort, 16
    types of, 138–143
heating costs. *See* energy efficiency
heat islands, 170–171, 180
heat pumps, geoexchange, 146–149
heat transfer
    geoexchange heat pump HVAC systems,
        146–149
    insulation, 117–119
    roof design, 124–125
    window treatments, 122–123
heavy metals. *See* health; toxins; volatile
        organic compounds (VOCs)
Herman Miller company, 84
Herrington, Susan, 163–165
Heschong Mahone Group, 3, 84
high cost perceptions, cost and bidding
        process, 219–224
high-performance HVAC strategies, 145–151
historic preservation, case study, 186–188,
        277–280
hospitals, daylighting, 86
hot water, HVAC systems, 150, 153
humidity
    HVAC systems, 138, 146
    water and moisture control, 120
Hundertwasser, Friedrich, 59
Hurricane Katrina, 277–280
Hybrid Wetland Living Machine®
        (Guilford, North Carolina), 175
hydrology, 29, 168–170
hygiene, 61, 86

I
Illuminating Engineering Society of North
        America (IESNA), 91, 104, 125
Imperial Valley (California) earthquake
        (1940), 113
individual HVAC systems, individual sys-
        tems compared, 139–140
indoor air quality
    computers and office equipment, 208
    construction process, 237
    HVAC systems, 138
    insulation, 118–119
    LEED, 153
    maintenance, 271
    materials, 76, 79, 197
    pollution sources, 198
    sustainable schools, 16
    tree planting, 180
    ventilation, 73

    wall design, 116
information technology, future prospects,
        281–283
insects
    athletic fields, 173–174
    construction process, 237
    pest control, 271–173
    playgrounds, 183
    school culture, 254
insulation, 117–119
    heat transfer, 117–118
    types of, 118–119
    wall design, 130
    water and moisture control, 120
integrated design, 28–39. *See also* design
        process and strategies; planning
        strategies
    campus concept, 33–36
    case study, 45–47
    climate considerations, 36
    daylighting, 93–96
    design strategies, 53–54
    site selection, 28–31
    size and scale, 37–39
    social forces, 31–33
    solar orientation, 36–37
    sustainable schools, 9–10
International Code Council, 9
International Commission on
        Illumination, 104
International Organization for
        Standardization (ISO), 200
international perspective
    case study, 48–51, 186–195, 210–212
    future prospects, 285–288
    playgrounds, 181–182
International Plumbing Code, 151
Internet, 248–249, 281–283
irrigation systems, 11, 175–177, 263
Italianate style, 55, 58

J
James Ward Public School (Chicago,
        Illinois), 55
job-site operations, 232–235
joints, weatherizing, 119
joint-use flexibility, sustainable schools, 11
joists, wall design, 114

K
KaBOOM, 182
Kahn, Louis, 83, 95

Katrina, Hurricane, 277–280
Kats, Gregory, 5, 6
Kelly, Kevin, 111
Kere, Diebedo Francis, 56
KieranTimberlake Associates, LLP, 74–76
KSS Architects, 213–215

L
labor unions, 223
landscaping, 163–196. *See also* campus concept; plantings; site planning and design; solar orientation; topography
  athletic fields, 172–174
  campus concept, 166–168
  case study, 186–195
  green roof design, 126–127
  heat islands, 170–171
  integrated design, 9–10
  irrigation systems, 175–177
  LEED, 185
  lighting, 178–179
  miscellaneous uses, 178–180
  paving, 171–172
  playgrounds, 180–184
  school culture, 254
  stormwater/groundwater management, 168–170
  sustainable schools, 76, 79, 80, 163–165
lawns, 174. *See also* athletic fields
Lawrence Berkeley Laboratory (Berkeley, California), 90
Leadership in Energy and Environmental Design (LEED). *See* LEED (Leadership in Energy and Environmental Design)
lead paint, construction process, 236–237
learning disorders, landscaping, 164
LEED (Leadership in Energy and Environmental Design)
  acoustics, 66, 67, 69–70
  building structure and envelope, 128, 153
  campus concept, 167, 185
  case study, 75–76, 79, 80–81, 132–135, 189
  commissioning, 17, 239
  construction process, 244
  daylighting, 103
  durability, 220
  finishes, equipment, and furnishings, 209

future directions, 288
HVAC systems, 138, 149
job-site operations, 233
maintenance, 276
operations, 265
planning strategies, 26, 27
product information, 198, 200
roof design, 125
sustainable schools, 8–9, 21
verification, 238–239
Lerma, Rosanna, 245–246
Life Cycle Assessment (LCA) protocol, 200
life cycle costing. *See also* budgets; cost and bidding process; economic factors; funding
  funding, 41–42
  HVAC systems, 145–146, 150
  mechanical systems, 68, 153–154
  operations, 255–256
life cycle design, Cradle-to-Cradle approach, 197–198
light bulbs, 263, 269
light-emitting diode (LED) lamps, 102, 269
lighting requirements, daylighting, 91–92
Lighting Research Center (LRC), School of Architecture, Rensselaer Polytechnic Institute, 104
lighting systems. *See also* daylighting
  case study, 279
  daylighting and, 83, 92, 102–103
  developmental considerations, 73
  energy efficiency, 87, 180
  landscaping, 178–179
  preventive maintenance, 269
  resources for, 104
  spatial considerations, 60
  sustainable schools, 76
light pollution, 178–179, 254
light shelves, 76
linoleum floor covering, product certification, 201–202
local governments, public contracting, 221–224. *See also* building codes; government policy
lockers, product recommendations, 208–209
Long Beach (California) earthquake (1933), 112–113
loose-fill insulation, 118
Louv, Richard, 165

Loyola Elementary School (Los Altos, California), 159–162
lunch programs, school gardens, 184, 263

M
maintenance, 267–280. *See also* operations
  athletic fields, 173–174
  case study, 277–280
  casework and furnishings, 207–208
  costs and bidding process, 6, 221
  healthy product choice, 274–275
  HVAC systems, 150, 268–273
  hygiene, 61
  LEED, 276
  overview, 267
  pest control, 271–273
  school culture, 250–252, 254–257
  snow removal, 275
  staff, 276
  techniques, 273
  wall finishes, 117, 202
maintenance and operations (M&O) mission, 245–246
marketing, community factors, 6
Martin Luther King Middle School (Berkeley, California), 263
masonry, wall design, 114–115
materials. *See also* recycling; specific materials
  acoustics, 66–67
  casework and furnishings, 207
  cost and bidding process, 217, 224
  doors, 124
  durability, school operations, 254–256
  job-site operations, 232–235
  maintenance techniques, 273
  paving, 171–172
  purchasing programs, 260–263
  reverberation, 64
  roof design, 125
  sustainable schools, 76, 79
  wall design, 116
  wall finishes, 117
  weatherizing, 119
  windows, 120–122
material safety data sheet (MSDS), 275
Matsuzaki, Eva, 164
McDonough, William, 197
mechanical systems. *See also* heating, ventilating, and air-conditioning (HVAC) systems
  background noise, 63

mechanical systems *(cont'd)*
case study, 155–162
design strategies, 53
sustainable schools, 67–68
water supply, 151–153
metal stud framing, wall design, 114–115
microbes, preventive maintenance, 269–271
microspray irrigation systems, 176
middle school, developmental considerations, 72
mind sets, community factors, 6
mixed-use spaces, acoustics, 64
modular furniture, 242–243
moisture control
building structure and envelope, 120
casework and furnishings, 207
HVAC systems, 146
preventive maintenance, 269–271
mold
preventive maintenance, 269–271
water and moisture control, 120
monitoring, operations, 259–260, 264–265
Mt. Angel High Performance Classroom Daylight and Ventilation Diagram (Oregon), 100–101
multiple-use flexibility, sustainable schools, 11
Murray, Gordon, 210–212
music classrooms, 64, 93

N
National Asphalt Pavement Association (NAPA), 172
National Environmental Education and Training Foundation (NEETF), 164
natural ventilation, HVAC systems and, 143–145
nature preserve, case study, 189–191. *See also* campus concept; landscaping; site planning and design
neighborhoods. *See also* community factors
case study, 186
design strategies, 54–55, 58–59
site selection, 31
New Jersey City University Academy Charter High School (Jersey City, New Jersey), 213–215
Nightingale, Florence, 86
noise, 62–63, 68–69, 79. *See also* acoustics

O
Oberland, Cornelia Hahn, 164
obesity, 72
odor, HVAC systems, 138
office equipment, environmental impact, 208
Ohlone Elementary School (Palo Alto, California), 89
openings, 96–101, 119. *See also* doors; windows
open-office system, 242–243
operating costs, sustainable schools, 3–4. *See also* budgets; cost and bidding process; economic factors; funding; life cycle costing
operations, 245–265. *See also* maintenance
community connections, 264–265
democracy, 248
LEED, 265
maintenance and operations (M&O) mission, 245–246
materials, 254–257
monitoring, 259–260
postoccupancy evaluations, 257
school culture, 246–247
staff training, 257–259
supplies, 260–263
teaching strategies, 248–253
organic metaphors, design strategies, 59
OWP&P, 132–135

P
paints, product information, 207
particleboard, casework and furnishings, 207
partitions, sound isolation, 65
partnering, alternative project delivery methods, 224–227
passive solar energy, site planning, 89
patios, campus concept, 178–179
Patkau Architects, 35, 45–47, 59, 167, 186–188
paved areas
heat islands, 170–171
landscaping, 171–172
playgrounds, 180
stormwater/groundwater management, 169–170
pedagogy, operations, 248–253
pedestrian transportation, site selection, 29–31
perception, design strategies, 53

performance measures, daylighting, 84, 85. *See also* test scores
performance spaces, acoustics, 64. *See also* auditorium
pest control, maintenance, 271–273. *See also* insects
photovoltaic panels
energy efficiency, 38, 76
roof design, 131
supplementary funding, 42–43
physical activity, developmental considerations, 71–73. *See also* athletic fields; playgrounds
Pine Jog Elementary School (West Palm Beach, Florida), 189–191
planning strategies, 19–52. *See also* community-based planning; design process and strategies; integrated design
architectural contracts, 24–26
case study, 45–51
contractor participation in, 231–232
design team selection topics, 20–24
extended services, 24
funding, 39–44
goal setting, 20–28
integrated design, 28–39
overview, 19
school boards, districts, and schools, 26–27
working groups, 27–28
workshop participants, 25–26
plantings. *See also* campus concept; landscaping; site planning and design; solar orientation
athletic fields, 173–174
green roof design, 126–127
integrated design, 33–36
irrigation systems, 175, 177
landscaping, 166–168
miscellaneous uses, 178–180
playgrounds, 180–184
sustainable schools, 10
playgrounds. *See also* athletic fields
developmental considerations, 71–73
landscaping, 180–184
playing fields. *See* athletic fields; playgrounds
plumbing systems
acoustics, 68
design strategies, 60, 61
fixtures, sustainable, 152–153, 263

water supply, 151–153
politics, community-based planning, sustainable schools, 7–8. *See also* building codes; government policy
Portland cement sidewalks, 172
postoccupancy evaluations, 240, 257
potable water. *See* gray water; rainwater; water supply
power generation, future prospects, 283–285
Power Purchase Agreement, 42–43
Prairie style, 58
precast concrete, wall design, 114–115
prefabrication, costs, 240–242
preschool, developmental considerations, 71
preventive maintenance, 268–273
printing and printing machines, indoor air quality, 208
privacy, design strategies, 58–59
private schools, 40–41, 222, 226
product information, sustainability concept, 198–200
project delivery methods, alternative, costs and bidding process, 224–227
public contracting, cost and bidding process, 221–224
public-private cooperation, case study, 77–79
public realm, design strategies, 58–59
purchasing programs, operations, 260–263

R
race, integrated design, 31
radiant HVAC systems, individual systems compared, 140–141
rain-screen systems, wall design, 114–115
rainwater, 75, 79, 129–131, 151–152, 187, 280. *See also* gray water; stormwater; water supply
rating systems, Cradle-to-Cradle approach, 197–198
reclaimed water. *See* gray water; rainwater; water supply
recycling. *See also* adaptive reuse; materials
    construction process, 236–237
    deconstruction versus demolition, 242–243
    landscaping, 164
    resource efficiency, 14, 80
    school culture, 251–252
    wall finishes, 117

relative humidity, HVAC systems, 138, 146
religion, daylighting, 85
Renaissance style, 55
resilient flooring, product certification, 201–202
resource efficiency, sustainable schools, 12–14
restrooms
    daylighting, 96
    design strategies, 60, 61
    operations, 256
    plumbing fixtures, 152–153
retrofitting
    case study, 159–161
    daylighting, 87
reuse. *See* adaptive reuse; recycling
reverberation, 64, 124, 203. *See also* acoustics
rigid-foam insulation, 119
risk management, playgrounds, 181–182
robust construction, design strategies, 61
Rockwell Group, 182
Roman style, 55
roof design, 124–127
    campus concept, 33
    generally, 124–125
    green roof, 126–127, 132, 134
    heat islands, 171
    HVAC systems, 142, 271
    materials, 125
    mechanical systems, 68
    photovoltaic power systems, 131
    stormwater/groundwater management, 170
    wall design, 114
roof water, sustainable schools, 11. *See also* gray water; rainwater; water supply
room finishes, acoustics, 67
room reverberation, acoustics, 64. *See also* acoustics; reverberation
rugs. *See* carpeting
R-value, insulation, 118–119

S
Safe Routes to School, 30, 253
safety. *See also* fire protection; health; toxins
    cost and bidding process, 219–220
    daylighting, 87
    developmental considerations, 71–73
    job-site operations, 235
    lighting, 178–179
    playgrounds, 181–182

prefabrication, 241
    wall design, 112–114
Salter, Charles M., 62–70
Salter, Ethan C., 62–70
San Francisco General Hospital, 86
Sangstha, Shidhulai Swanirvar, 283
scale and size, integrated design, 37–39
school boards, planning strategies, 26–27
school construction. *See* construction process
school culture, 246–254
school districts, planning strategies, 26–27
school gardens, 184, 263
Scientific Certification Systems (SCS), 199
Seabird Island School, Agassiz, British Columbia, Canada, 35, 45–47, 59
seasonal affective disorder (SAD), 84
Seattle University, 173–174, 177
security, lighting, 178–179
seismic activity
    acoustic materials, 67
    wall design, 112–114, 116
sewage systems, irrigation systems, 175. *See also* irrigation systems; waste output and waste management
shade, heat islands, 170–171
shading devices, window treatments, 122–123
sheathing, wall design, 116
sick days, sustainable schools, 4–5, 143
sidewalks, landscaping, 172
Sidi El-Aloui Primary School (Tunisia), 55, 56
Sidwell Friends School (Stewart Middle School, Washington, D. C., Bethesda, Maryland), 56, 74–76, 145, 152, 251–252
site planning and design. *See also* campus concept; landscaping; plantings; solar orientation; topography
    acoustics, 68–69
    athletic fields, 172–174
    campus concept, 10, 33–35, 166–168
    case study, 186–195
    community organizing, 22
    daylighting, 86, 87–90, 93–95
    design strategies, 53, 56–57, 58–59
    integrated design planning, 28–31
    job-site operations, 232–235
    LEED, 185
    miscellaneous uses, 178–180

size and scale, integrated design, 37–39
skylights, 76. *See also* daylighting; lighting systems
  daylighting, 84, 96–101
  school operations, 250
Slater Paull Architects, 155–158
small schools, integrated design, 37–39
snow removal, maintenance, 275
social forces, 31–33, 87. *See also* community factors
soils, job-site operations, 235
solar chimney, 144–145, 194
solar garbage compactor, 180
Solar Heat Gain Coefficient (SHGC), 121–122, 277–278
solar orientation. *See also* campus concept; landscaping; site planning and design; topography
  case study, 277–278
  daylighting, 86, 87–89, 93–95
  design strategies, 56–57, 75, 76, 80–81
  integrated design, 36–37
  roof design, 125
solar panels, 7, 180, 285
solar thermal energy, HVAC systems, 149–150
Solomon, Susan, 181–182
sound isolation, 64–66, 69. *See also* acoustics
Spanish style, 55
spatial considerations, design strategies, 60–61
special needs schools, case study, 210–212
specifications, cost and bidding process, 217–218, 224, 228–229
spectrum, daylighting, 84
speech intelligibility, acoustics, 63
sports events. *See* athletic fields; playgrounds
spray foam insulation, 118–119
spray irrigation systems, 176
sprinkler irrigation systems, 176–177
SRG Partnership, *100*
staff and staff offices
  daylighting, 93
  maintenance staff, 276
  operations, 256–257
  resource efficiency, sustainable schools, 13–14
  training, operations, 257–259
staging areas, job-site operations, 233–235
standards. *See* building codes; building standards

Stewart Middle School (Sidwell Friends School, Washington, D. C., Bethesda, Maryland), 56, 74–76, 251–252
stormwater, 75, 80, 132, 168–170. *See also* gray water; rainwater; water supply
Strawberry Vale School (Victoria, British Columbia, Canada), 167, 186–188
structure. *See* building structure and envelope
stucco wall finishes, 117
student attendance, sustainable schools, 4–5, 143
studs, wall design, 114–115
sunscreens, 76, 78, 188
supplementary funding, 42–44
supplies, operations, 260–263
Sustainable Building Industry Council, 10
sustainable development concept
  building structure and envelope, 111–112
  climate change, 19
  cost cutting, 229–230
  defined, 1–2
  historical timeline, 20–21
  job-site operations, 232–235
  need for, 2
  prefabrication, 241–242
  product information, 198–200
  school culture, 246–254
sustainable schools, 1–18
  acoustics, 16–17, 62–70
  air quality, 16
  benefits of, 3–6
  campus concept, 10
  classroom design, 14
  commissioning, 17
  community-based planning, 7–8
  construction process, 218–219
  costs and bidding process, 218–224
  daylighting, 14–15
  energy efficiency, 12
  environmental curriculum, 10–11
  flexibility, 11
  food service, 263
  future prospects, 281–288
  integrated design, 9–10
  landscaping, 163–165
  LEED and CHPS, 8–9
  need for, 2
  resource efficiency, 12–14
  sustainability concept, 1–2, 18

thermal comfort, 16
transportation, 263
water supply, 11
Sweden, 181

T
Tarkington Elementary School (Chicago, Illinois), 132–135
taxes, capital funding, 39–41
teacher performance, 5
teaching strategies, operations, 248–253
temperature, HVAC systems, 138
test scores, sustainable schools, 3. *See also* performance measures
thermal comfort, 16, 73
thermostats, HVAC systems, 140
third-party certification, product information, 198–200
three-dimensional models, design strategies, 53
tile floor covering, product certification, 201–202
tiles, acoustics, 67
toilet partitions, product recommendations, 209. *See also* restrooms
topography. *See also* campus concept; landscaping; plantings; site planning and design; solar orientation
  athletic fields, 173–174
  design strategies, 58–59
topsoil, job-site operations, 235
toxins. *See also* fire protection; health; safety
  athletic fields, 173–174
  ceiling finishes, 205
  cleaning products, 274–275
  construction process, 218, 236–237
  developmental considerations, 72–73
  insulation, 118–119
  materials, 197
  paints and coatings, 207
  pest control, 271–273
  wall design, 116
transportation
  school culture, 253
  site selection, 29–31
  sustainable schools, 263
trees
  heat islands, 170
  job-site operations, 235
  playgrounds, 180
Tunisia, 87

turbulence, forced air HVAC systems, 141–143
turf. *See* athletic fields; playgrounds

U
Uniform Plumbing Code, 151
United Nations Brundtland Commission Report, 1–2, 16
U. S. Department of Energy, 253
U. S. Environmental Protection Agency (USEPA), 16, 79, 201, 208, 270, 271, 273
U. S. Green Building Council (USGBC), 8, 9, 132, 151, 199
U. S. Safe Routes to School program, 30, 253
United States Supreme Court, 31
usage zoning, spatial considerations, 60–61
utility companies, supplementary funding, 42–43
U-value, windows, 121–122

V
values, school culture, 74–76, 246–247
vandalism. *See also* graffiti
    design strategies, 61
    lighting, 178–179
    toilet partitions, 209
vapor barrier, 118, 120
variable refrigerant volume (VRV), 142–143
vegetable gardens, landscaping, 184, 263
Venetian blinds, 122
ventilation. *See also* heating, ventilating, and air-conditioning (HVAC) systems
    acoustics, 68
    ceiling finishes, 205
    classroom design, 14–15
    computers and office equipment, 208
    design strategies, 56–57, 79
    health concerns, 73, 86
    historical perspective, 55

HVAC systems, 143–145
indoor air quality, 16
water and moisture control, 120
verification, construction process, 238–239
vinyl tile floor covering, 201–2, 255–256
visual expression, design strategies, 58–59
volatile organic compounds (VOCs), 76, 197, 201, 207. *See also* fire protection; health; safety; toxins

W
wages, costs and bidding process, 223
Waik, Virginia, 245–246
wall design, 112–117
    construction methods, 114–115
    finishes, 117
    initial considerations, 112–114
    insulation, 117–119
    sheathing, 116
    strategies, 116
wall finishes, 67, 202
Wal-Mart (Eco-Store, Lawrence, Kansas), 84
waste output and waste management
    construction process, 218, 236–237
    Cradle-to-Cradle approach, 197–198
    fertilizers, 174
    pest control, 272–273
    school culture, 251–252
    sewage systems, irrigation systems, 175
    sustainability, 2, 5, 6
water closets, 152–153. *See also* restrooms
water control, building structure and envelope, 120
water damage, preventive maintenance, 269–271
waterproofing, 114–115, 120
Waters, Alice, 263, 264
water supply. *See also* gray water; rainwater; stormwater
    case study, 129–131, 132–135, 187, 280–281
    irrigation systems, 175–177

job-site operations, 234, 235
mechanical systems, 151–153
stormwater/groundwater management, 168–170
sustainable schools, 6, 11, 75, 79, 80
weather, natural ventilation, HVAC systems, 143
weatherizing, 2, 119
weather proofing, wall design, 114–115
Web sites, school operations, 248–249
Weisz + Yoes, 108–109
wetland habitat, 280
Whitman-Hanson Regional High School (Whitman, Massachusetts), 129–131
wildlife, 173–174, 183. *See also* insects
Williams Act (California), 248
windows
    building structure and envelope, 120–122
    daylighting, 68–69, 78, 86, 96–101
    design strategies, 61
    weatherizing, 119
window treatments, 122–123
wood, wall finishes, 117
wood floor covering, product certification, 201–202
wood products, Forest Stewardship Council (FSC), 116
wood stud framing, wall design, 114–115
Woodward Academy Middle School (College Park, Georgia), 80–81
working groups, planning strategies, 27–28
workshop participants, planning strategies, 25–26
worm's-eye view, design strategies, 53
Wright, Frank Lloyd, 58

Z
zero net energy concept, case study, 79, 157–158
zoning, spatial considerations, 60–61
Zyscovich Architects, 189–191

WILEY BOOKS ON
Sustainable Design

Alternative Construction: Contemporary Natural Building Methods
by Lynne Elizabeth and Cassandra Adams

Biophilic Design: The Theory, Science, and Practice of Bringing Buildings to Life
by Stephen Kellert, Judith Heerwagen, and Martin Mador

Contractor's Guide to Green Building Construction: Management, Project Delivery, Documentation, and Risk Reduction
by Thomas E. Glavinich and Associated General Contractors

Design with Nature
by Ian L. McHarg

Ecodesign: A Manual for Ecological Design
by Ken Yeang

Environmentally Responsible Design: Green and Sustainable Design for Interior Designers
by Louise Jones

Green BIM: Successful Sustainable Design with Building Information Modeling
by Eddy Krygiel and Brad Nies

Green Building Materials: A Guide to Product Selection and Specification, Second Edition
by Ross Spiegel and Dru Meadows

Green Development: Integrating Ecology and Real Estate
by Rocky Mountain Institute

Green Roof Systems: A Guide to the Planning, Design and Construction of Landscapes Over Structure
By Susan Weiler and Katrin Scholz-Barth

The HOK Guidebook to Sustainable Design, Second Edition
by Sandra Mendler, William O'Dell, and Mary Ann Lazarus

The Integrative Design Guide to Green Building: Redefining the practice of Sustainability
by 7group and Bill Reed

Land and Natural Development (Land) Code
by Diana Balmori and Gaboury Benoit

A Legal Guide to Urban and Sustainable Development for Planners, Developers and Architects
by Daniel Slone, Doris S. Goldstein, and W. Andrew Gowder

Materials for Sustainable Sites: A Complete Guide to the Evaluation, Selection, and Use of Sustainable Construction Materials
by Meg Calkins

Modern Sustainable Residential Design: A Guide for Design Professionals
by William J. Carpenter

Packaging Sustainability: Tools, Systems, and Strategies for Innovative Package Design
by Wendy Jedlicka

Sustainable Commercial Interiors
by Penny Bonda and Katie Sosnowchik

Sustainable Construction: Green Building Design and Delivery
by Charles J. Kibert

Sustainable Design: Ecology, Architecture, and Planning
by Daniel Williams

Sustainable Healthcare Architecture
by Robin Guenther and Gail Vittori

Sustainable Residential Interiors
by Associates III

Sustainable Site Design : Criteria, Process, and Case Studies for Integrating Site and Region in Landscape Design
by Claudia Dinep, Kristin Schwab

Sustainable Urbanism
by Douglas Farr

 Environmental Benefits Statement

This book is printed with soy-based inks on presses with VOC levels that are lower than the standard for the printing industry. The paper, Rolland Enviro 100, is manufactured by Cascades Fine Papers Group and is made from 100 percent post-consumer, de-inked fiber, without chlorine. According to the manufacturer, the use of every ton of Rolland Enviro100 Book paper, switched from virgin paper, helps the environment in the following ways:

Mature trees	Waterborne waste not created	Water flow saved	Atmospheric emissions eliminated	Soiled Wastes reduced	Natural gas saved by using biogas
17	6.9 lbs.	10,196 gals.	2,098 lbs.	1,081 lbs.	2,478 cubic feet